STAR WARS

GUARDIANS OF THE WHILLS

THE MANGA

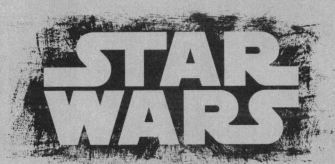

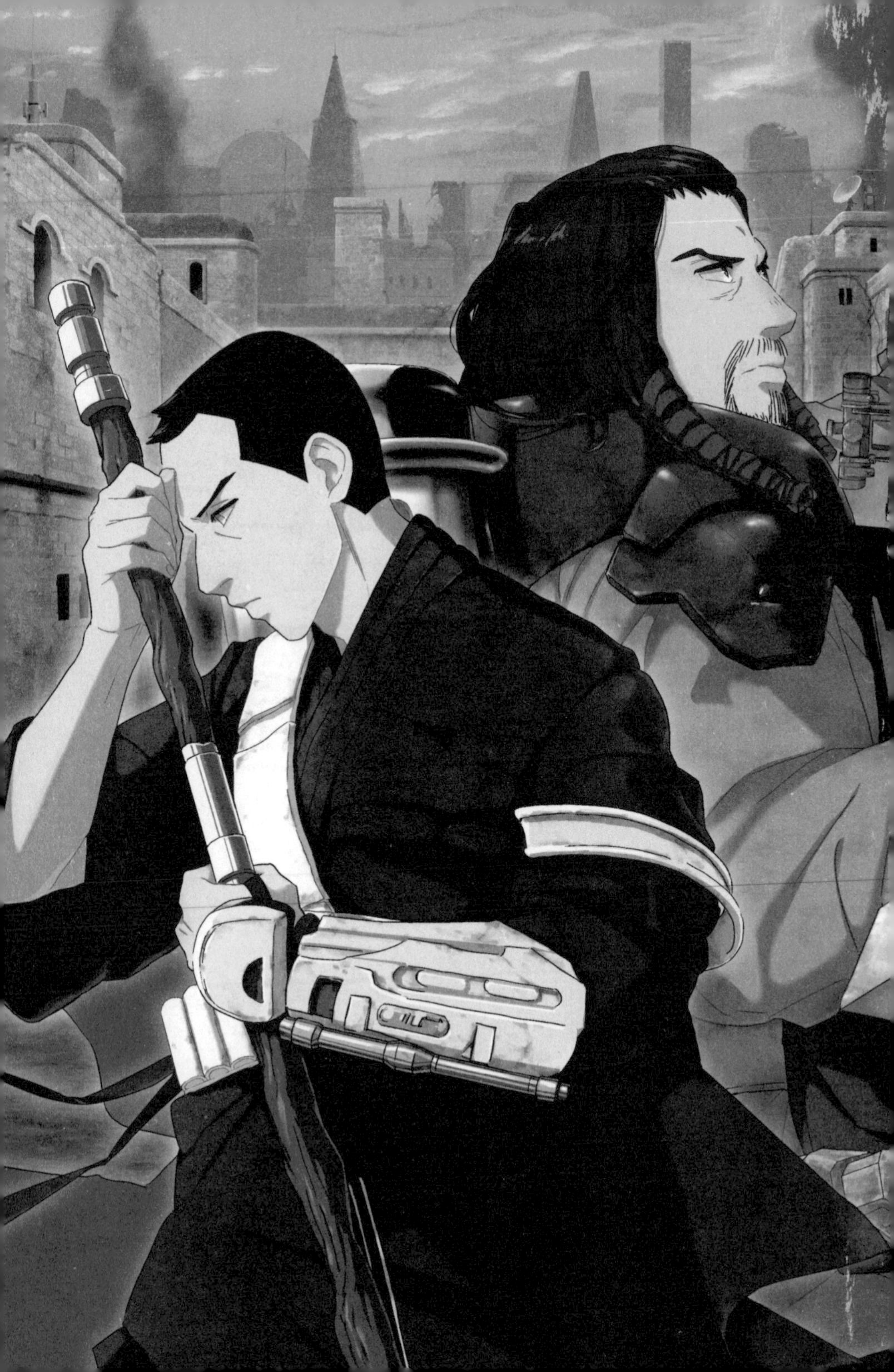

STAR WARS

GUARDIANS OF THE WHILLS
THE MANGA

ADAPTED BY **JON TSUEI**

ILLUSTRATED BY **SUBARU**

BASED ON THE NOVEL BY GREG RUCKA

VIZ MEDIA

Disney · LUCASFILM

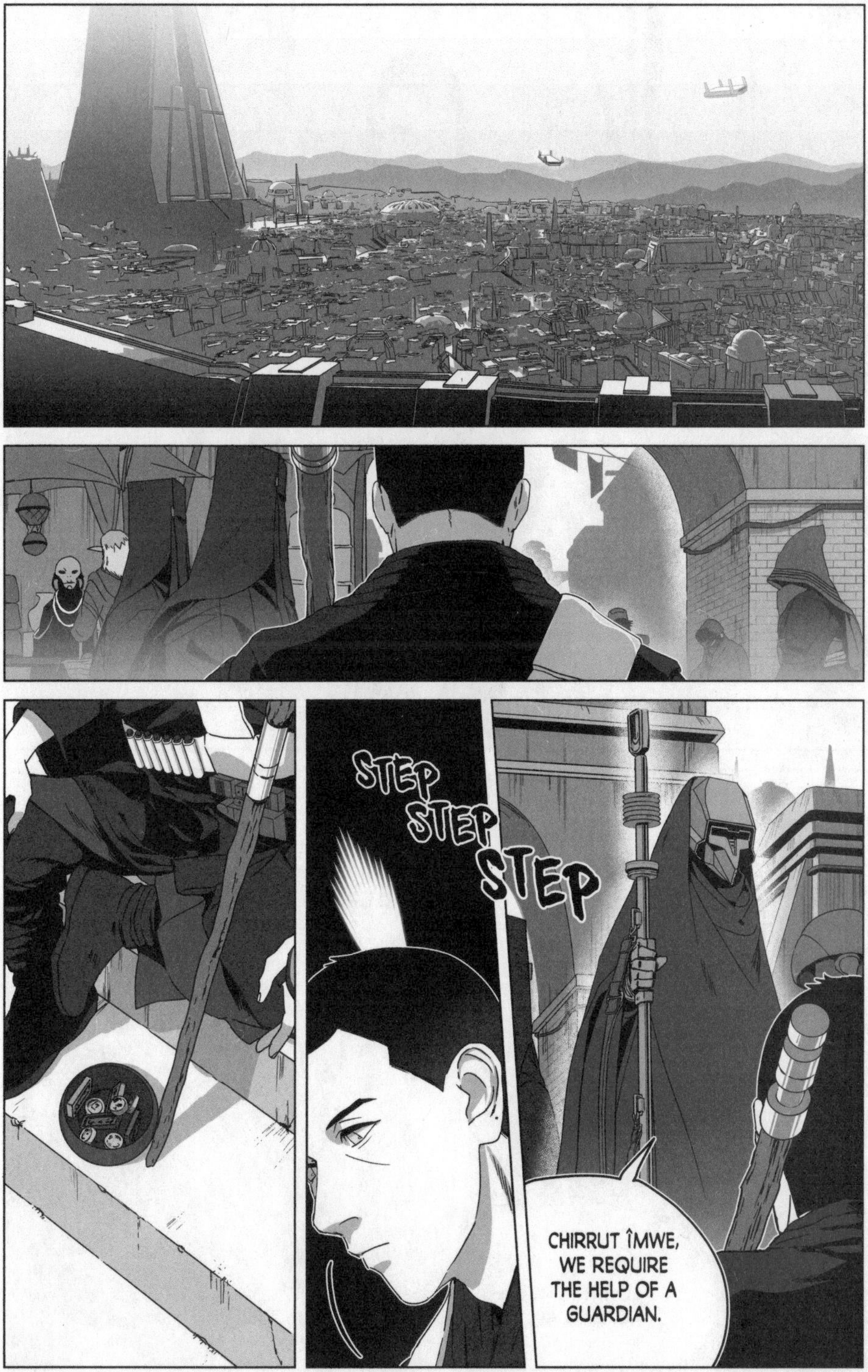
STEP
STEP
STEP
CHIRRUT ÎMWE, WE REQUIRE THE HELP OF A GUARDIAN.

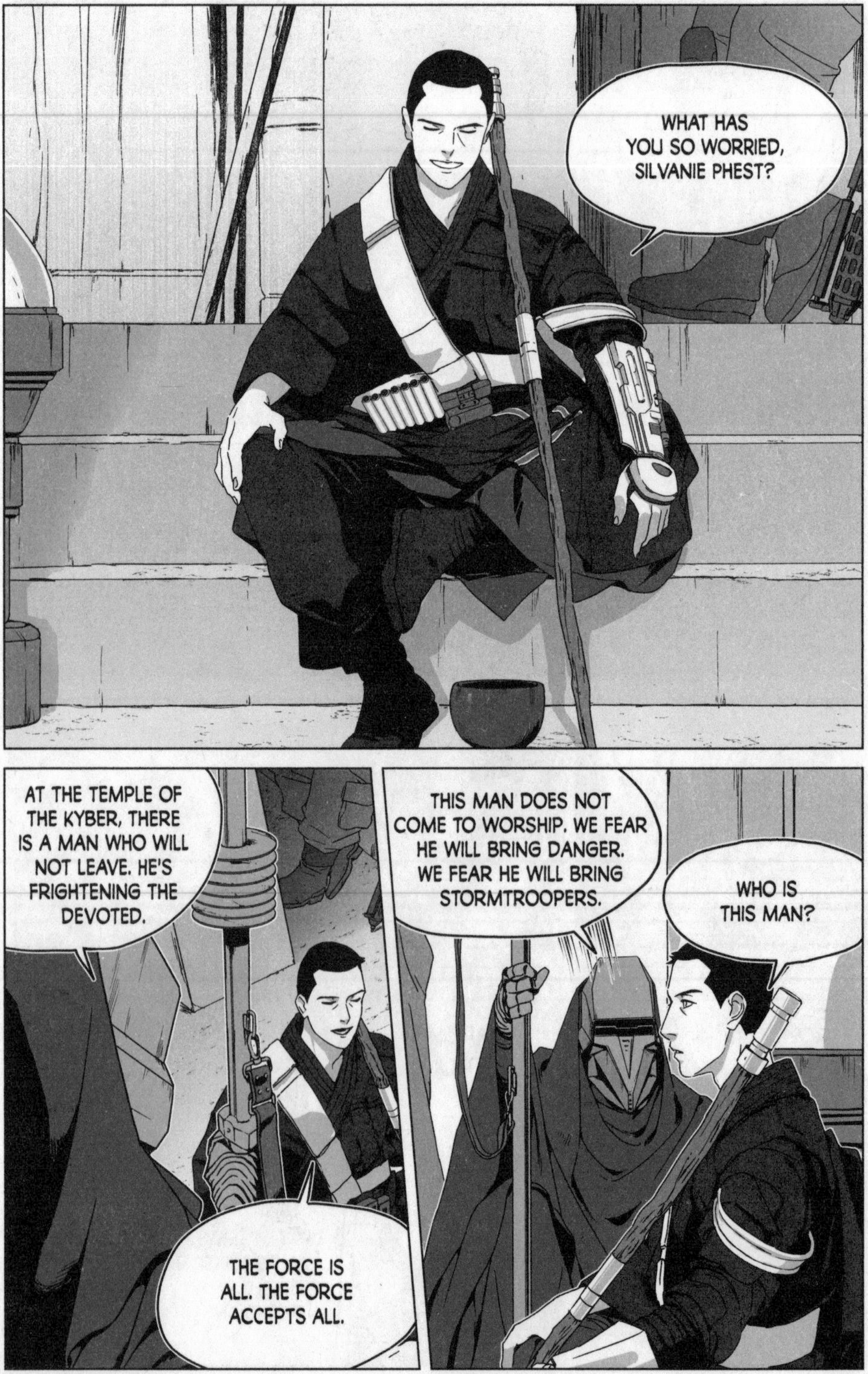
WHAT HAS YOU SO WORRIED, SILVANIE PHEST?
AT THE TEMPLE OF THE KYBER, THERE IS A MAN WHO WILL NOT LEAVE. HE'S FRIGHTENING THE DEVOTED.
THE FORCE IS ALL. THE FORCE ACCEPTS ALL.
THIS MAN DOES NOT COME TO WORSHIP. WE FEAR HE WILL BRING DANGER. WE FEAR HE WILL BRING STORMTROOPERS.
WHO IS THIS MAN?

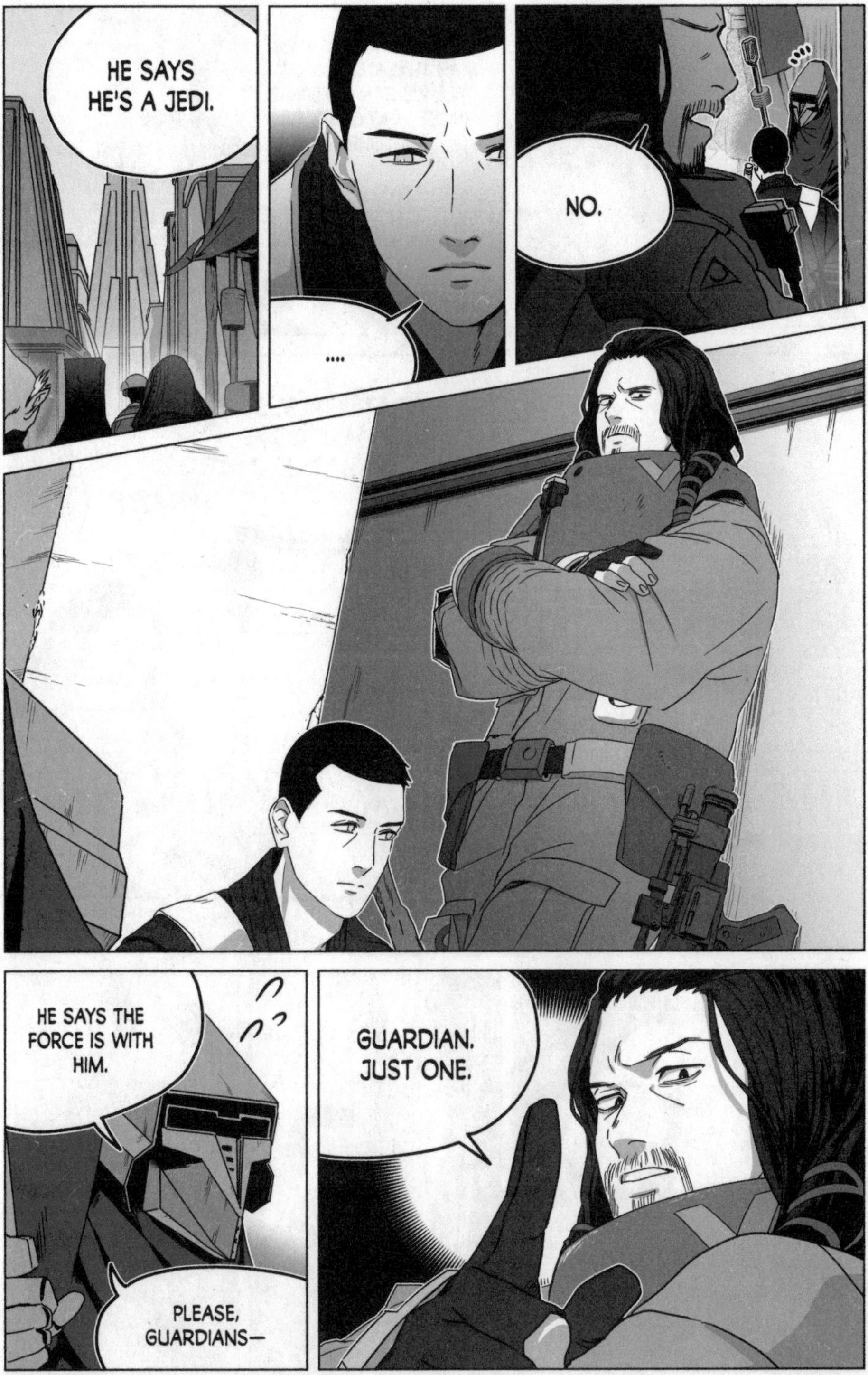
HE SAYS
HE'S A JEDI.
....
NO.
HE SAYS THE FORCE IS WITH HIM.
PLEASE, GUARDIANS—
GUARDIAN. JUST ONE.

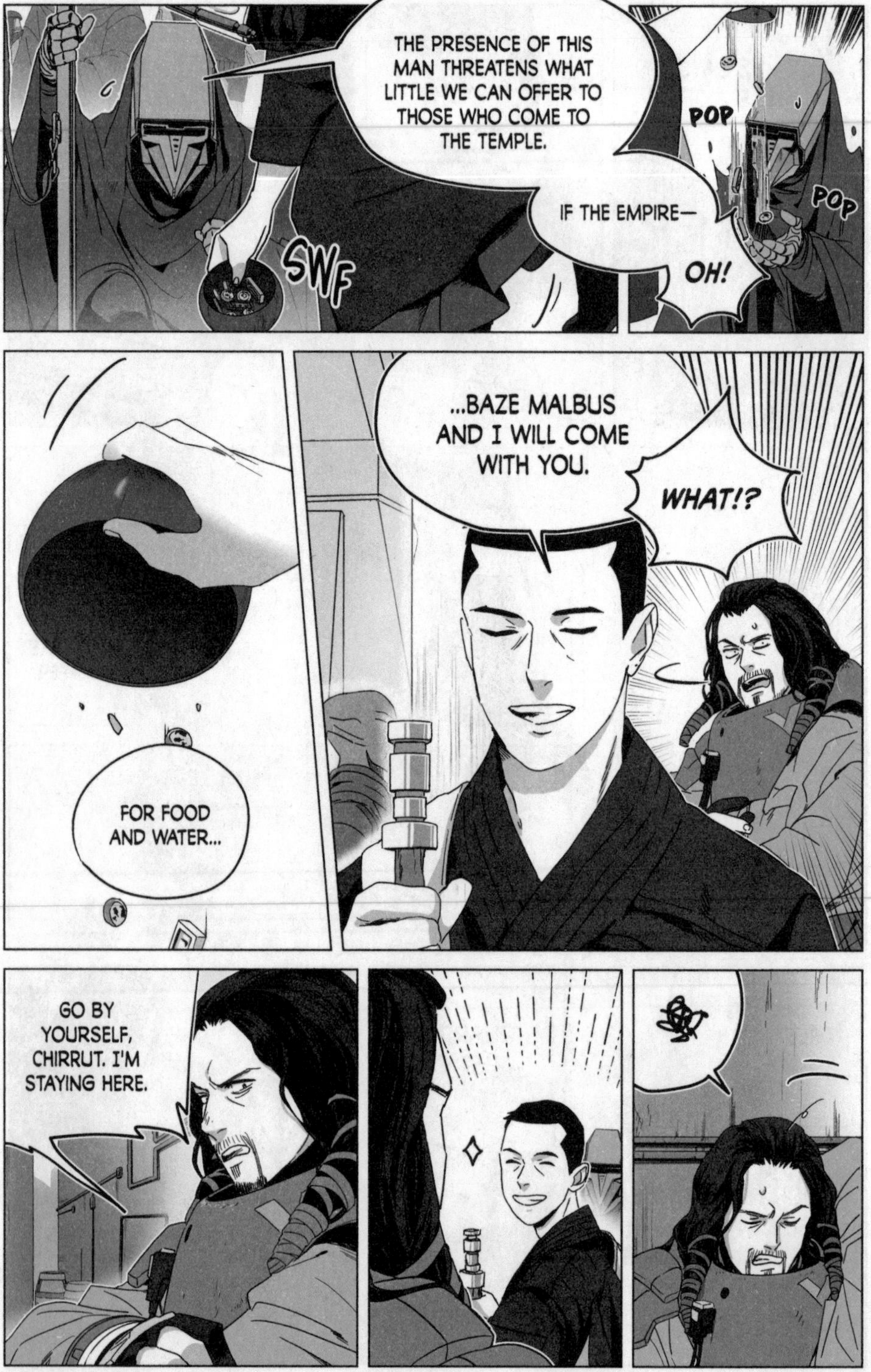
THE PRESENCE OF THIS MAN THREATENS WHAT LITTLE WE CAN OFFER TO THOSE WHO COME TO THE TEMPLE.
IF THE EMPIRE—
SWF
POP
POP
OH!
FOR FOOD AND WATER...
...BAZE MALBUS AND I WILL COME WITH YOU.
WHAT!?
GO BY YOURSELF, CHIRRUT. I'M STAYING HERE.

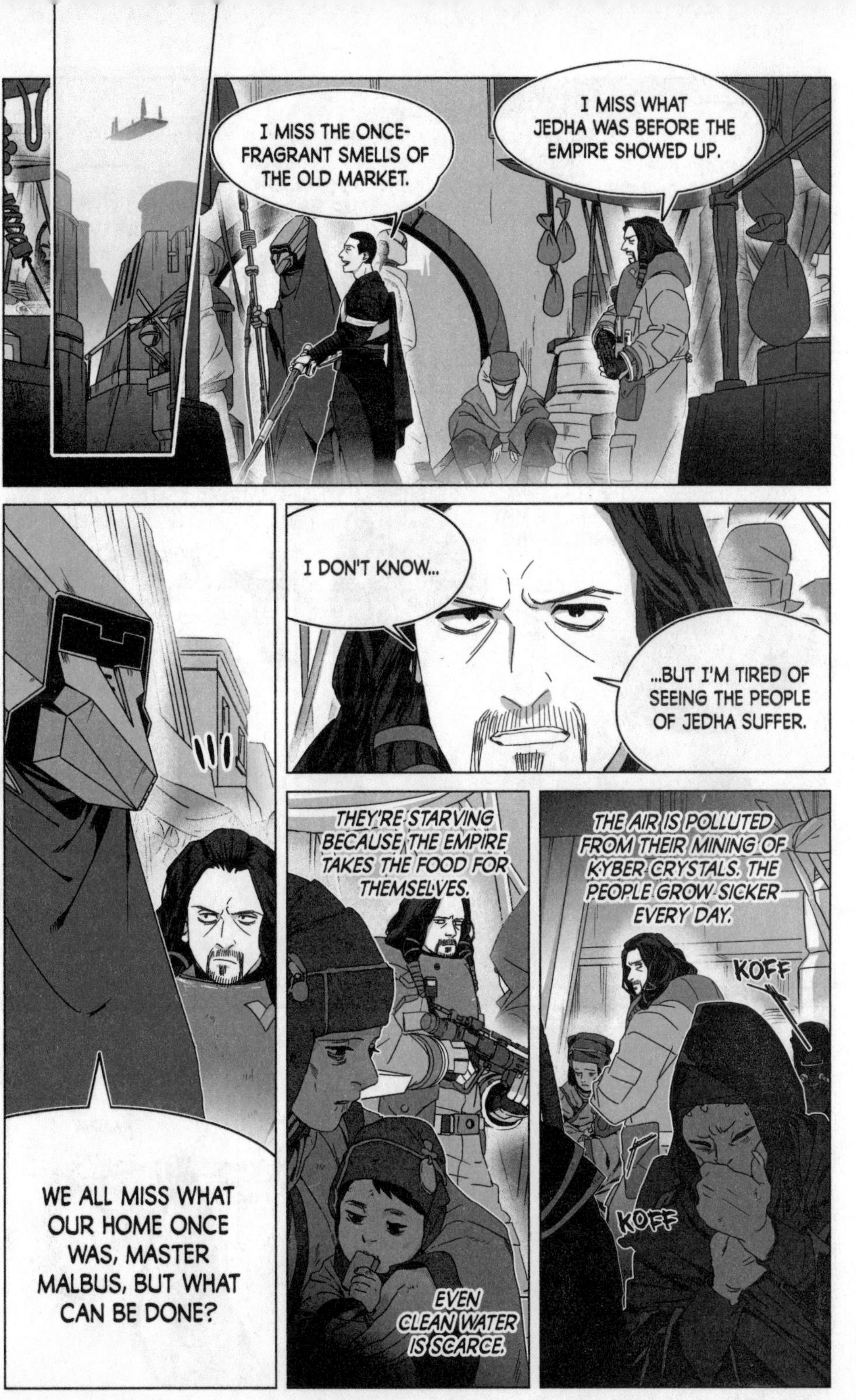
I MISS THE ONCE-FRAGRANT SMELLS OF THE OLD MARKET.
I MISS WHAT JEDHA WAS BEFORE THE EMPIRE SHOWED UP.
!!
WE ALL MISS WHAT OUR HOME ONCE WAS, MASTER MALBUS, BUT WHAT CAN BE DONE?
I DON'T KNOW...
...BUT I'M TIRED OF SEEING THE PEOPLE OF JEDHA SUFFER.
THEY'RE STARVING BECAUSE THE EMPIRE TAKES THE FOOD FOR THEMSELVES.
EVEN CLEAN WATER IS SCARCE.
THE AIR IS POLLUTED FROM THEIR MINING OF KYBER CRYSTALS. THE PEOPLE GROW SICKER EVERY DAY.
KOFF
KOFF

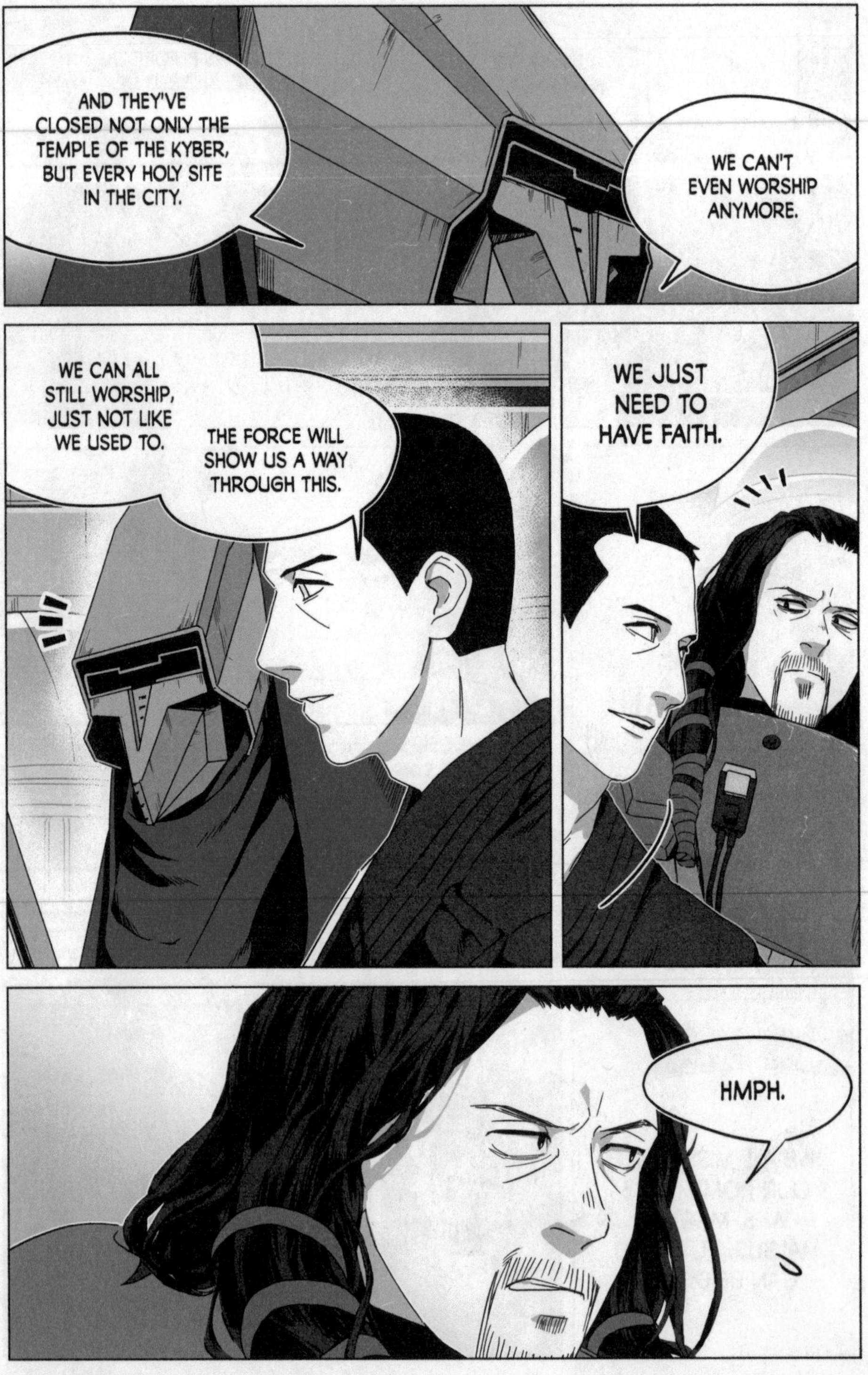
AND THEY'VE CLOSED NOT ONLY THE TEMPLE OF THE KYBER, BUT EVERY HOLY SITE IN THE CITY.
WE CAN'T EVEN WORSHIP ANYMORE.
WE CAN ALL STILL WORSHIP, JUST NOT LIKE WE USED TO.
THE FORCE WILL SHOW US A WAY THROUGH THIS.
WE JUST NEED TO HAVE FAITH.
HMPH.

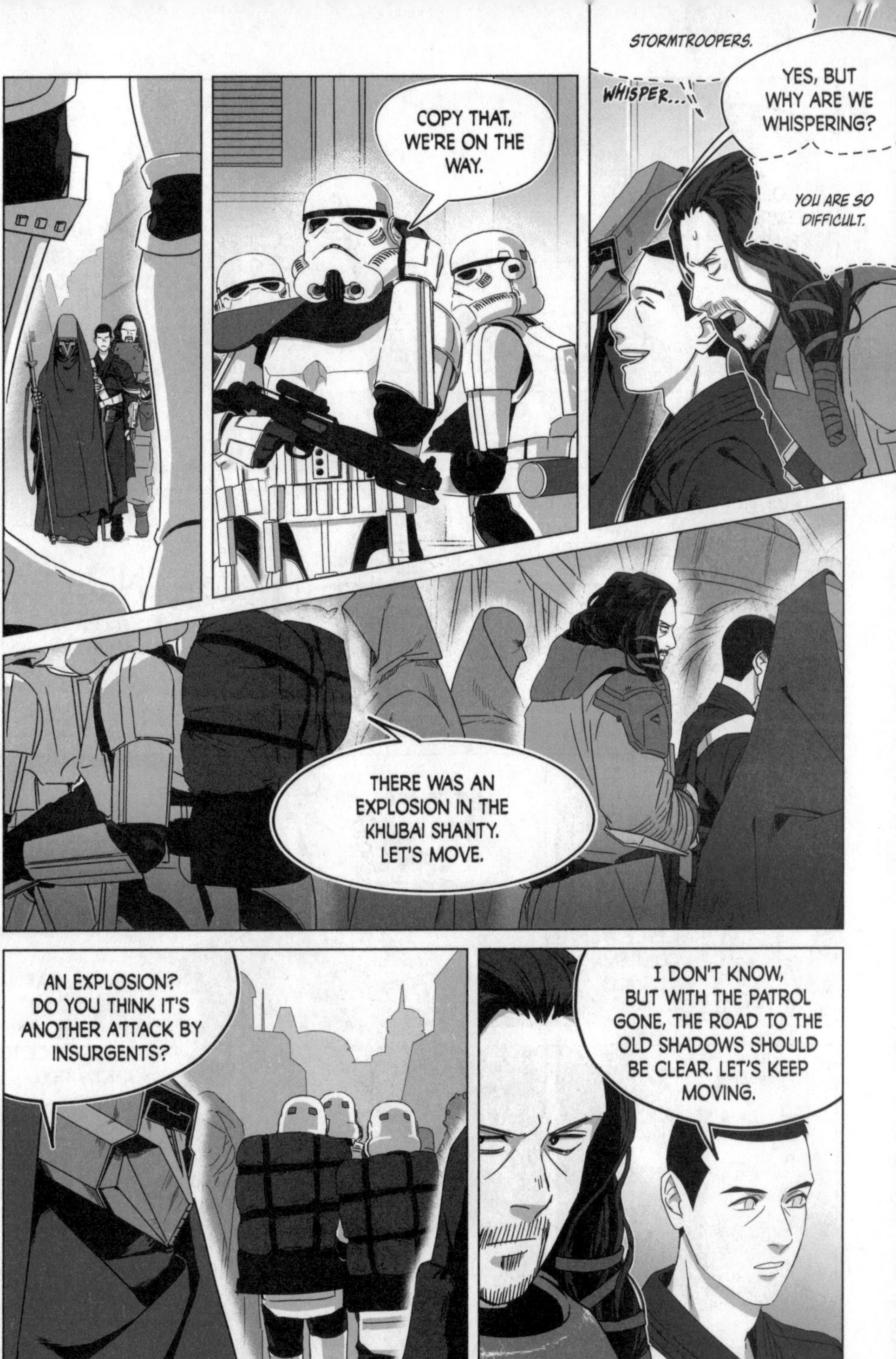
COPY THAT, WE'RE ON THE WAY.
STORMTROOPERS.
WHISPER...
YES, BUT WHY ARE WE WHISPERING?
YOU ARE SO DIFFICULT.
THERE WAS AN EXPLOSION IN THE KHUBAI SHANTY. LET'S MOVE.
AN EXPLOSION? DO YOU THINK IT'S ANOTHER ATTACK BY INSURGENTS?
I DON'T KNOW, BUT WITH THE PATROL GONE, THE ROAD TO THE OLD SHADOWS SHOULD BE CLEAR. LET'S KEEP MOVING.

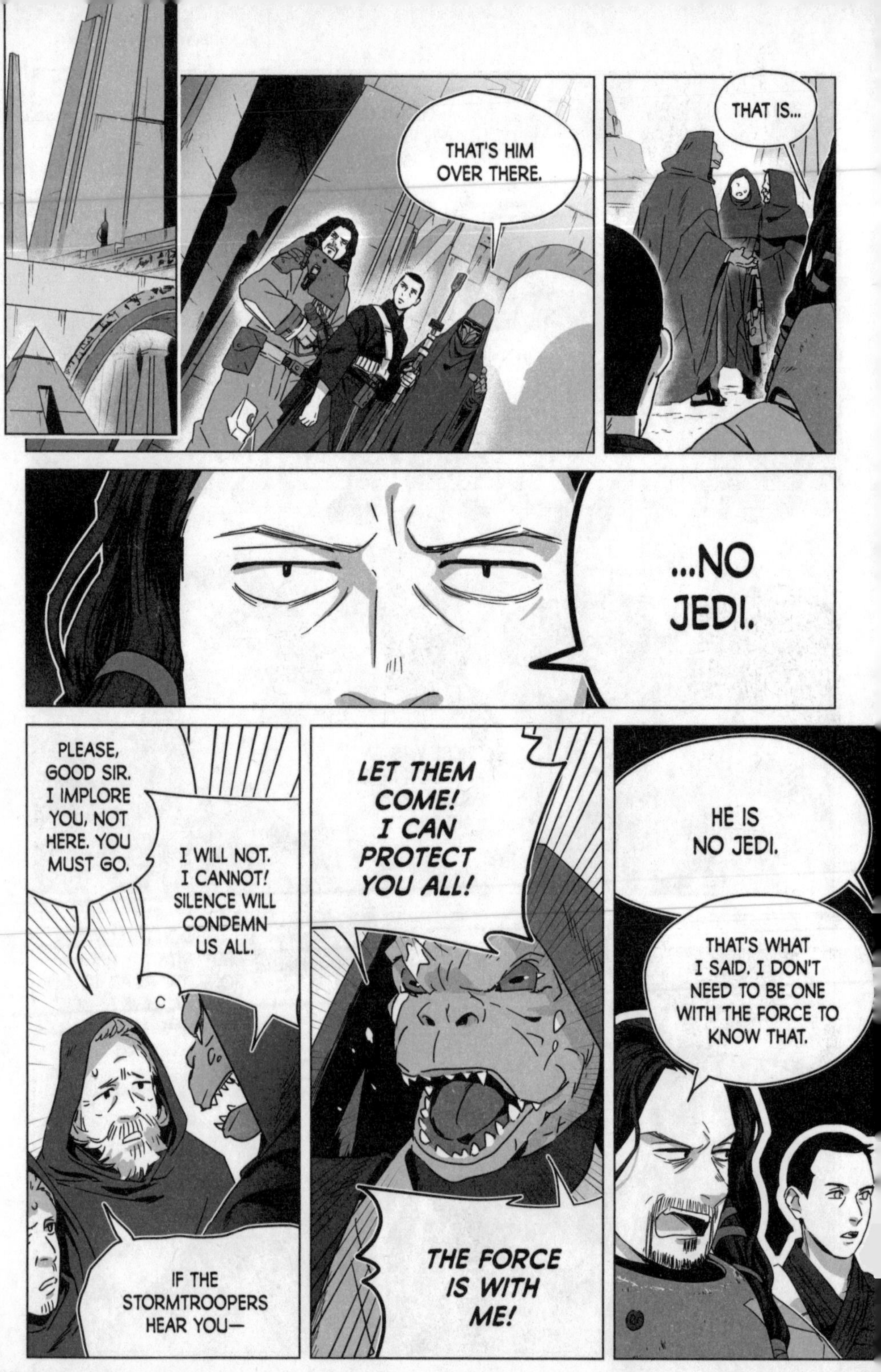
THAT'S HIM OVER THERE.
THAT IS...
...NO JEDI.
PLEASE, GOOD SIR. I IMPLORE YOU, NOT HERE. YOU MUST GO.
I WILL NOT. I CANNOT! SILENCE WILL CONDEMN US ALL.
IF THE STORMTROOPERS HEAR YOU—
LET THEM COME! I CAN PROTECT YOU ALL!
THE FORCE IS WITH ME!
HE IS NO JEDI.
THAT'S WHAT I SAID. I DON'T NEED TO BE ONE WITH THE FORCE TO KNOW THAT.

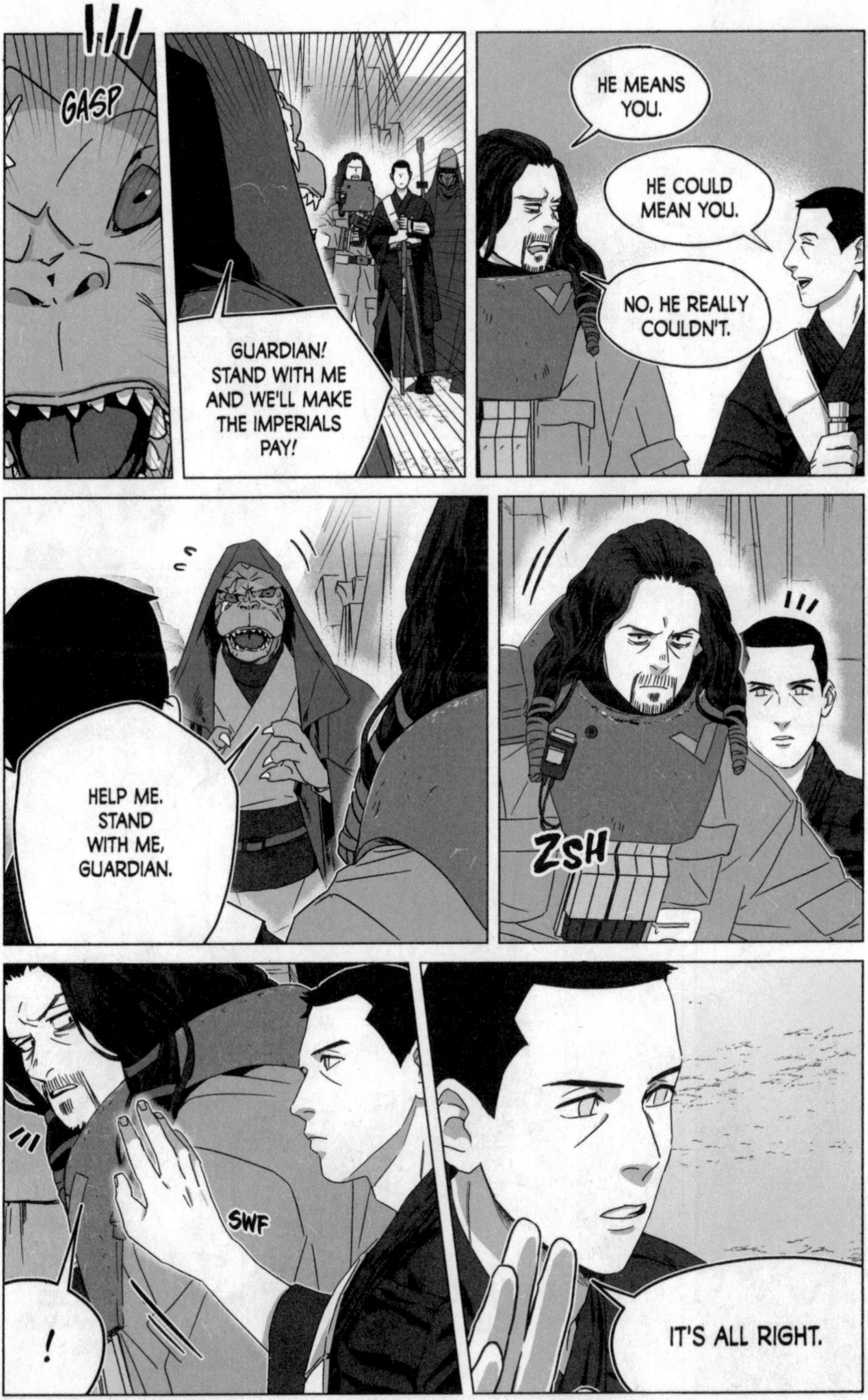
GASP
GUARDIAN! STAND WITH ME AND WE'LL MAKE THE IMPERIALS PAY!
HE MEANS YOU.
HE COULD MEAN YOU.
NO, HE REALLY COULDN'T.
HELP ME. STAND WITH ME, GUARDIAN.
ZSH
SWF
!
IT'S ALL RIGHT.

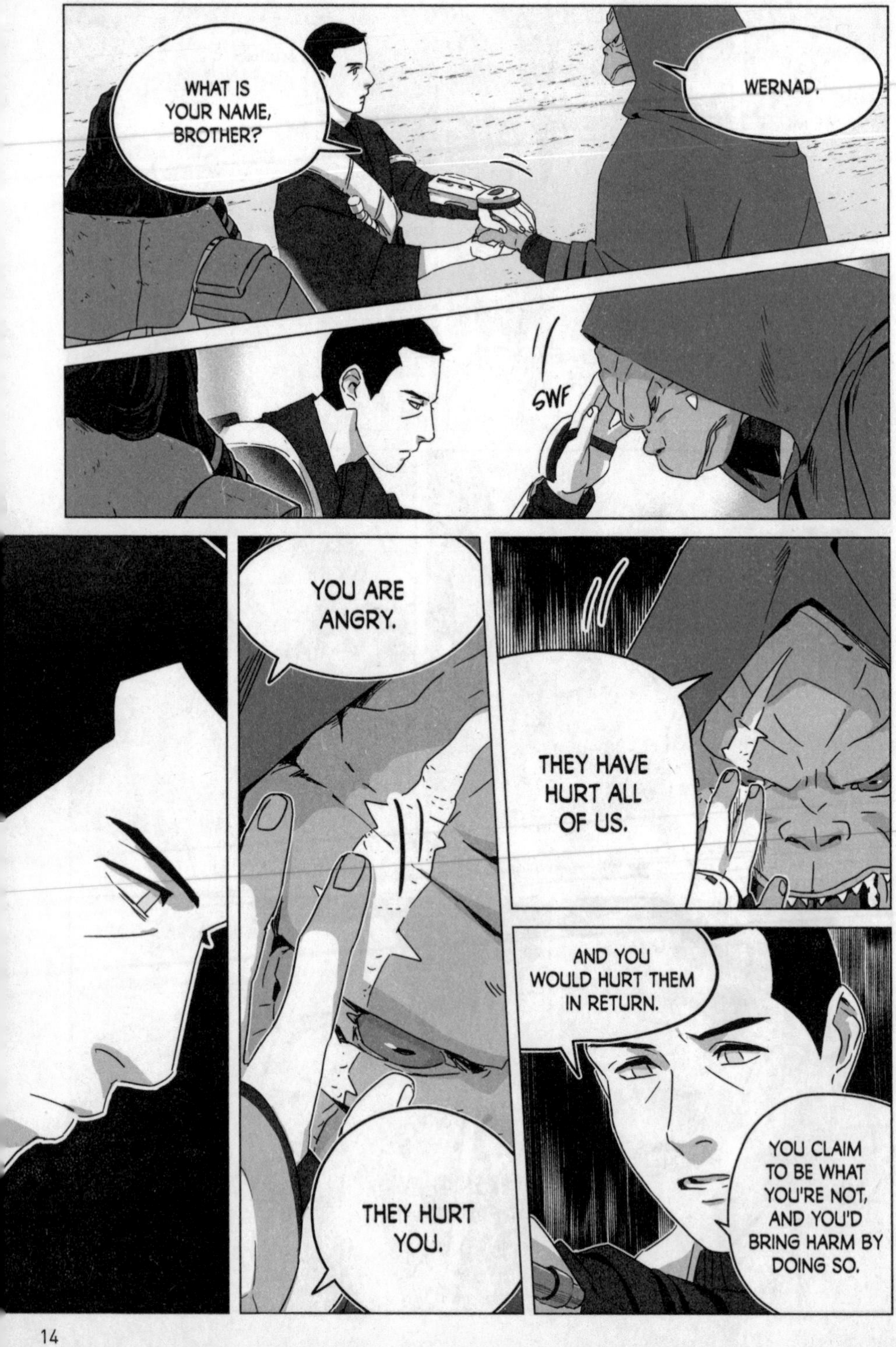
WHAT IS YOUR NAME, BROTHER?
WERNAD.
SWF
YOU ARE ANGRY.
THEY HURT YOU.
THEY HAVE HURT ALL OF US.
AND YOU WOULD HURT THEM IN RETURN.
YOU CLAIM TO BE WHAT YOU'RE NOT, AND YOU'D BRING HARM BY DOING SO.

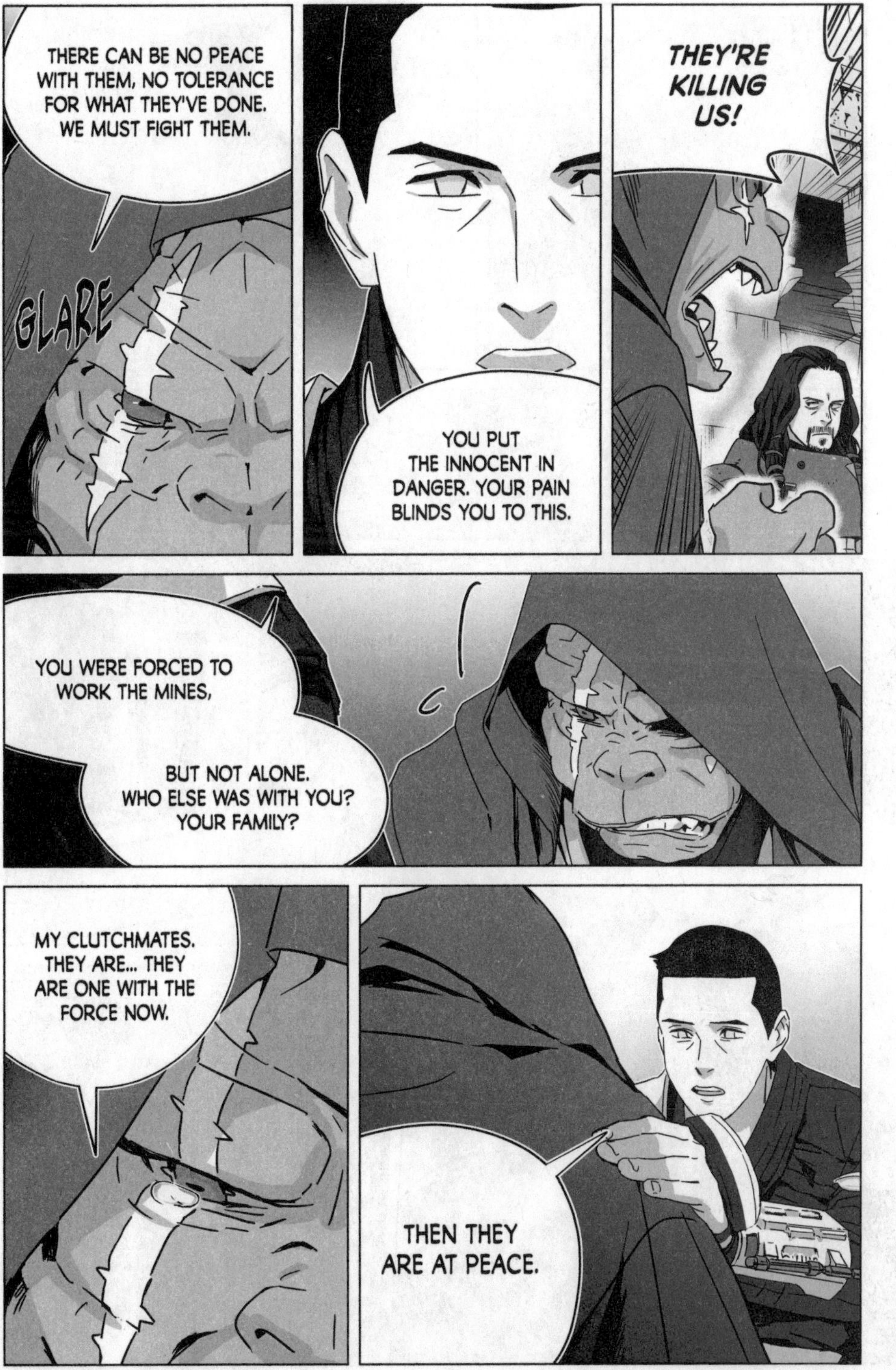

THERE CAN BE NO PEACE WITH THEM, NO TOLERANCE FOR WHAT THEY'VE DONE. WE MUST FIGHT THEM.
GLARE
YOU PUT THE INNOCENT IN DANGER. YOUR PAIN BLINDS YOU TO THIS.
THEY'RE KILLING US!
YOU WERE FORCED TO WORK THE MINES,
BUT NOT ALONE. WHO ELSE WAS WITH YOU? YOUR FAMILY?
MY CLUTCHMATES. THEY ARE... THEY ARE ONE WITH THE FORCE NOW.
THEN THEY ARE AT PEACE.

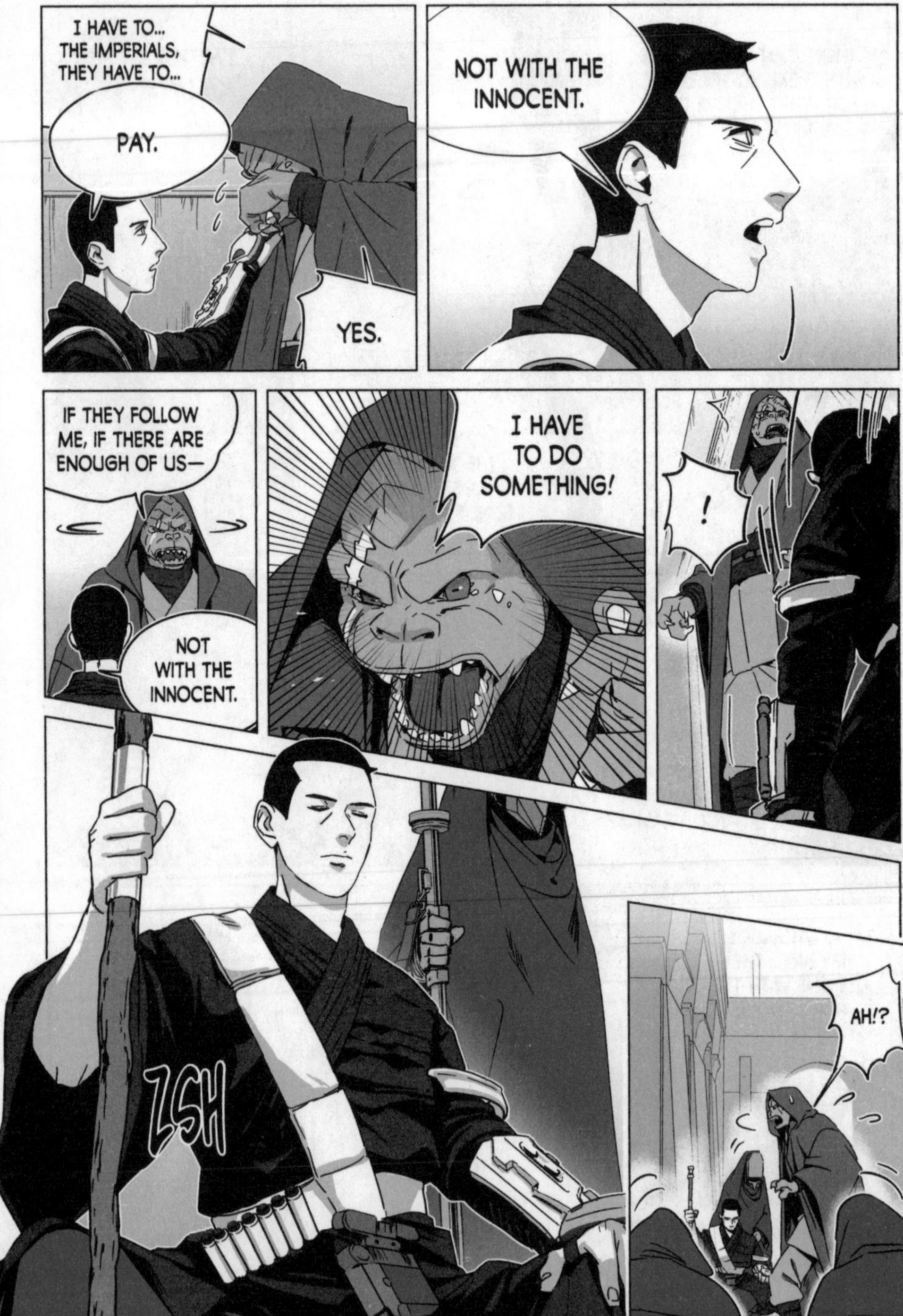
I HAVE TO... THE IMPERIALS, THEY HAVE TO...
PAY.
YES.
NOT WITH THE INNOCENT.
IF THEY FOLLOW ME, IF THERE ARE ENOUGH OF US—
NOT WITH THE INNOCENT.
I HAVE TO DO SOMETHING!
!
ZSH
AH!?
KWSH
SWSH

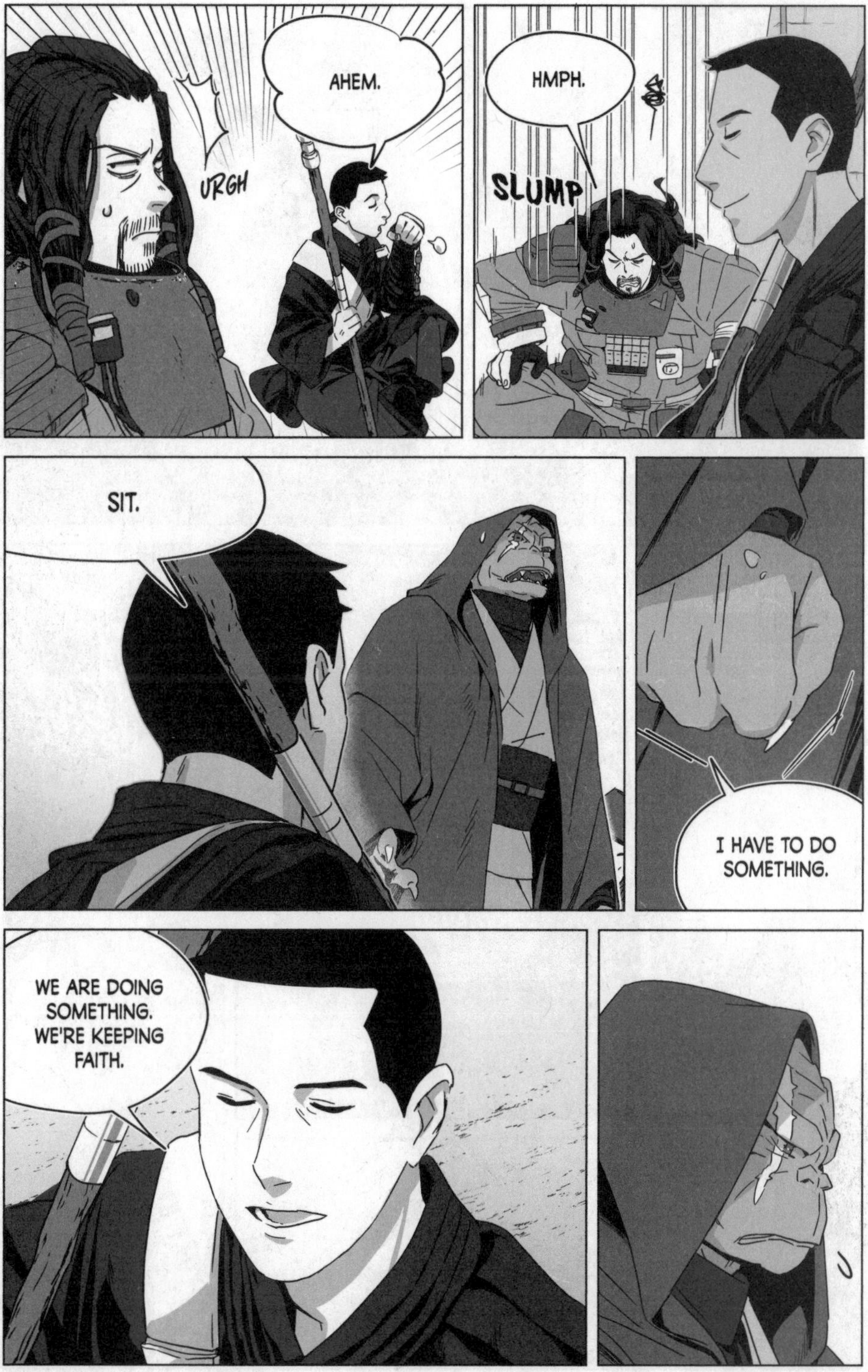
URGH
AHEM.
HMPH.
SLUMP
SIT.
I HAVE TO DO SOMETHING.
WE ARE DOING SOMETHING. WE'RE KEEPING FAITH.

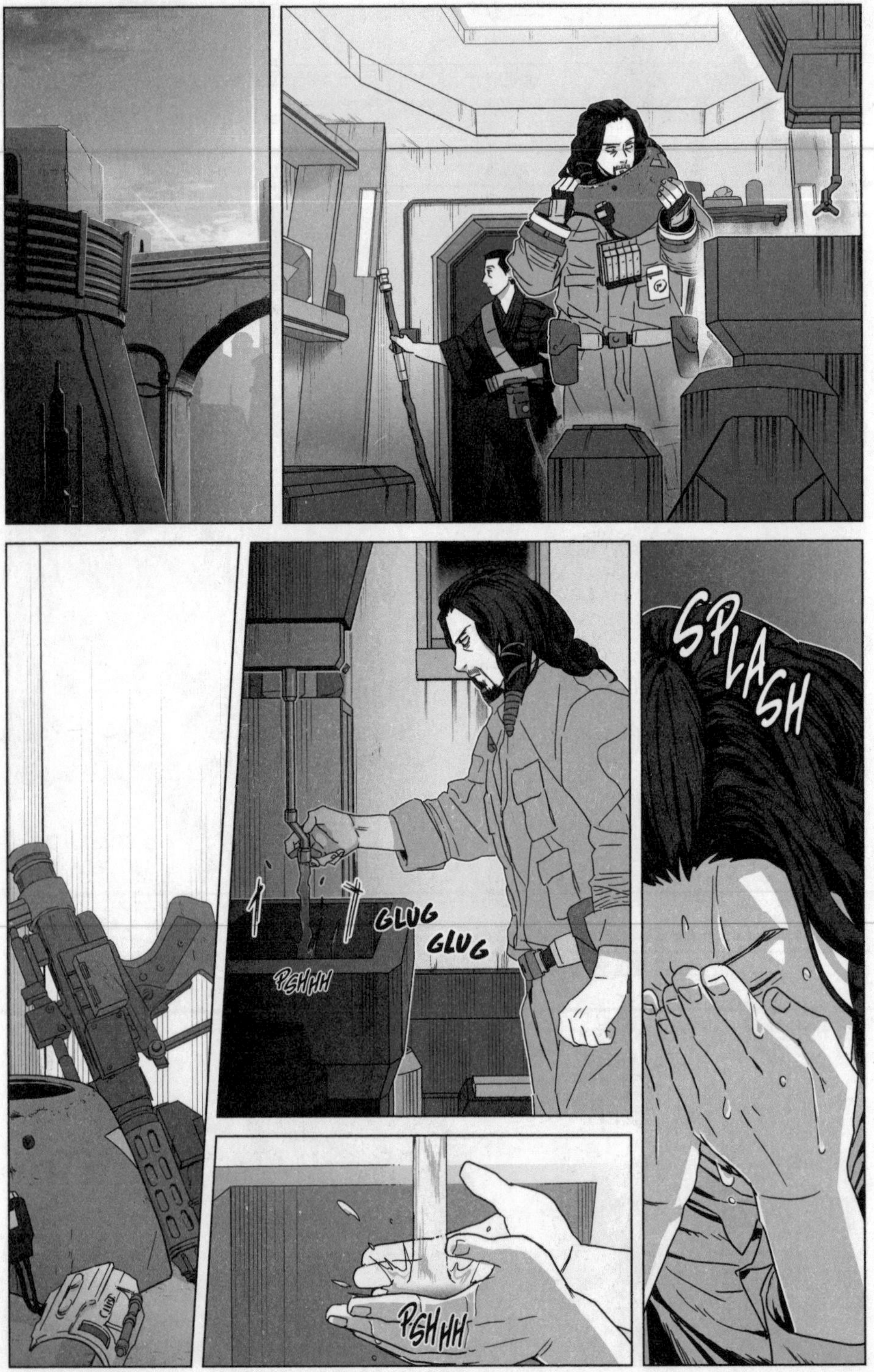
GLUG
GLUG
PSHHH
PSHHH
SPLASH

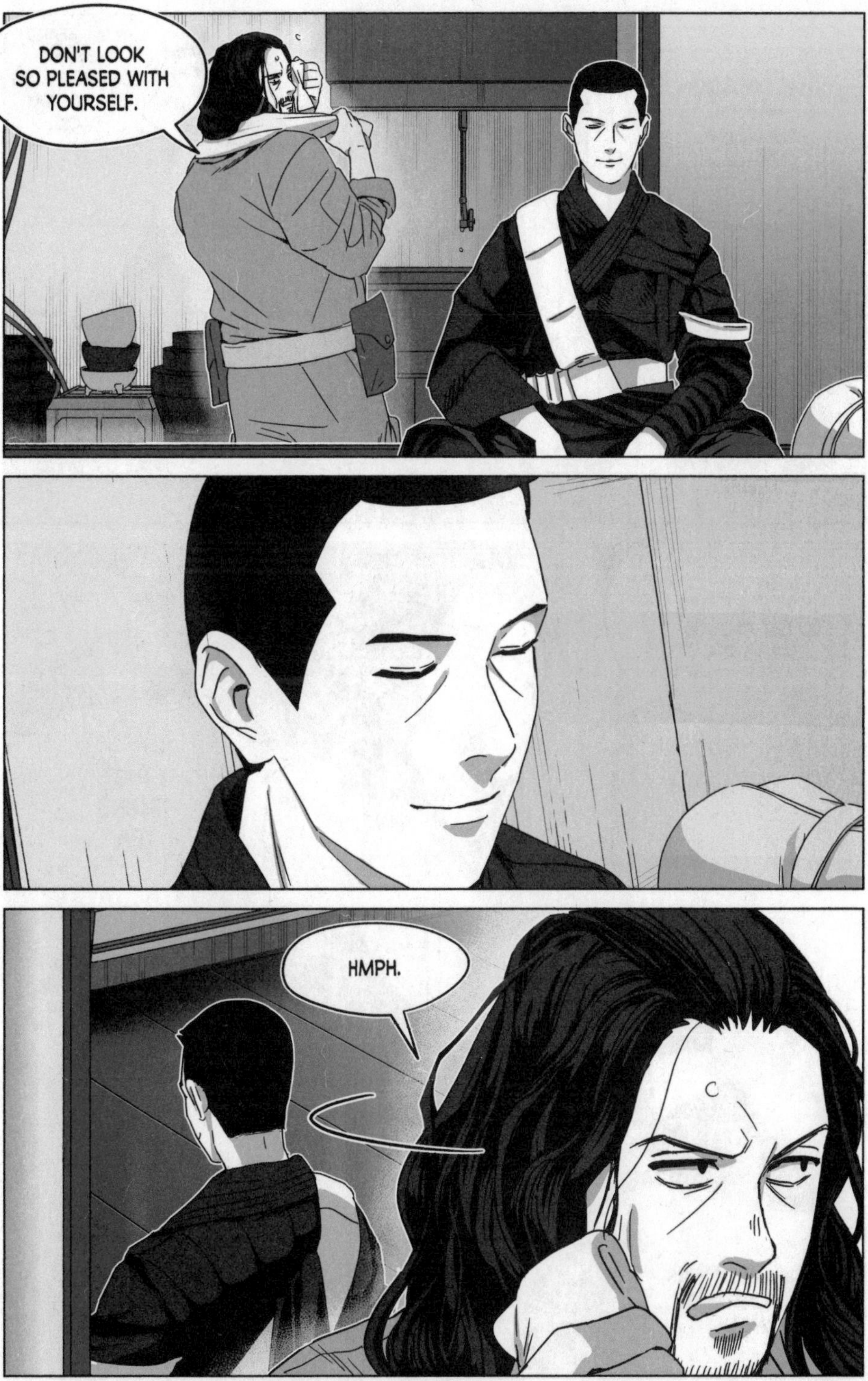
DON'T LOOK SO PLEASED WITH YOURSELF.
HMPH.

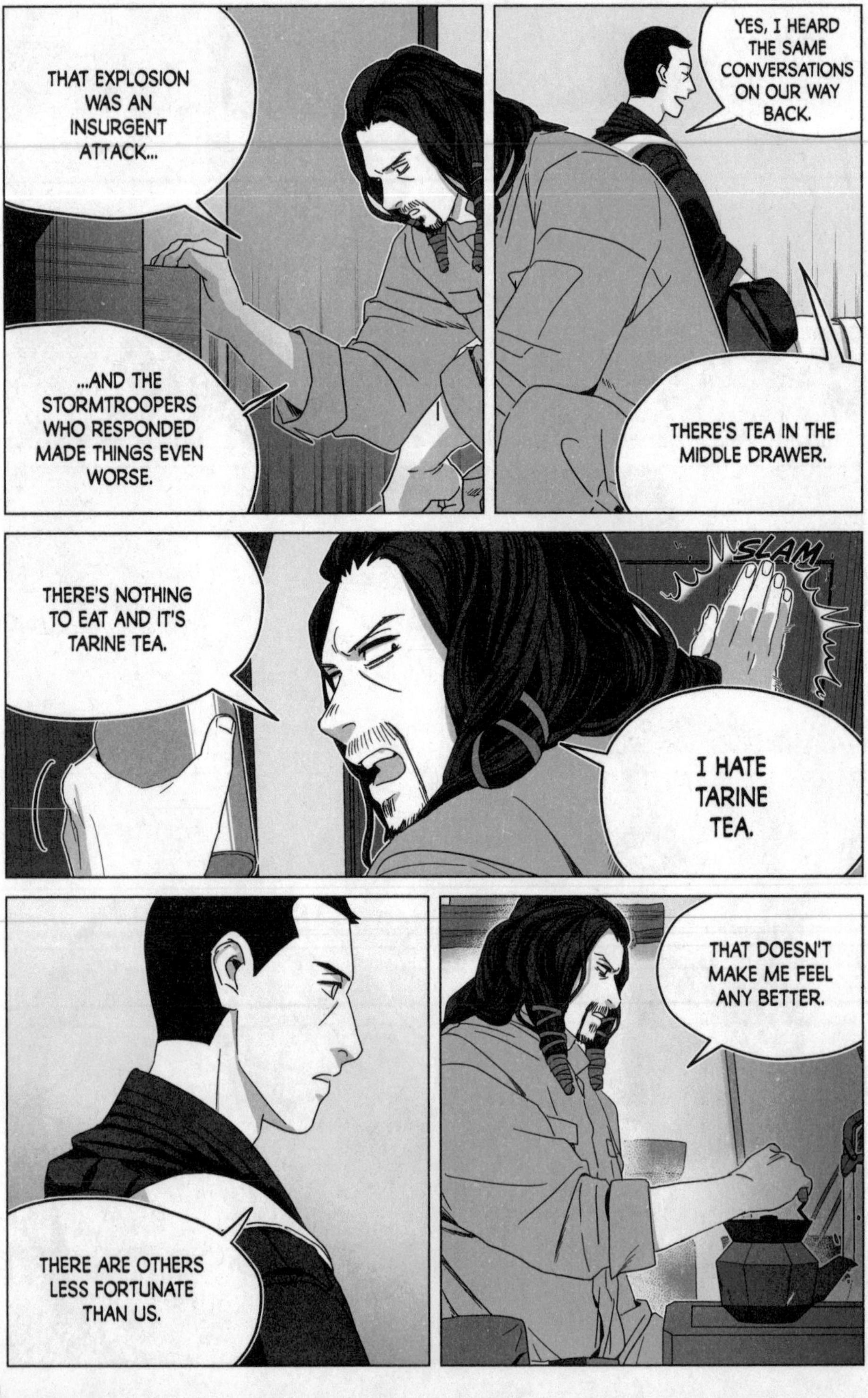
THAT EXPLOSION WAS AN INSURGENT ATTACK...
...AND THE STORMTROOPERS WHO RESPONDED MADE THINGS EVEN WORSE.
YES, I HEARD THE SAME CONVERSATIONS ON OUR WAY BACK.
THERE'S TEA IN THE MIDDLE DRAWER.
THERE'S NOTHING TO EAT AND IT'S TARINE TEA.
SLAM
I HATE TARINE TEA.
THERE ARE OTHERS LESS FORTUNATE THAN US.
THAT DOESN'T MAKE ME FEEL ANY BETTER.

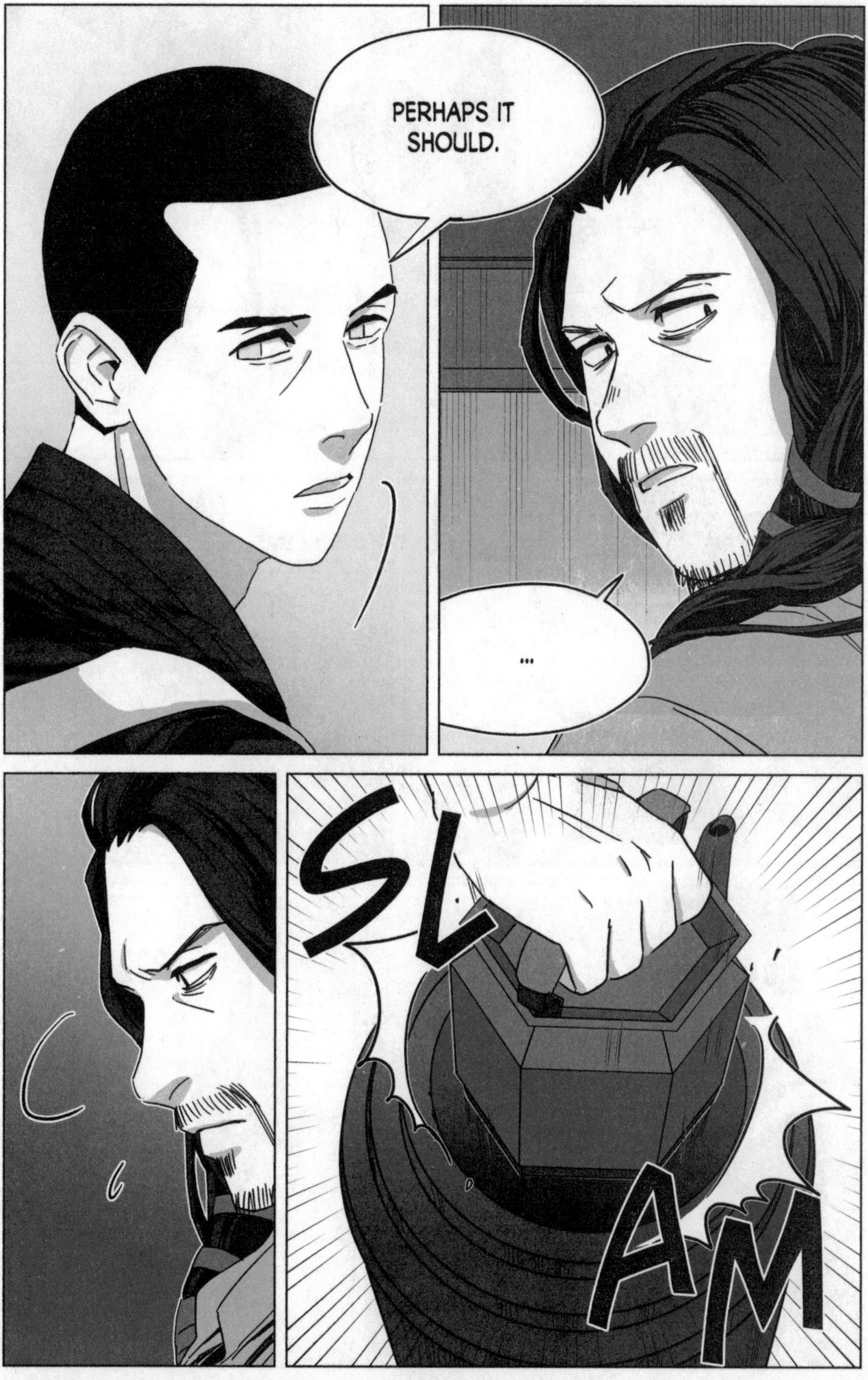
PERHAPS IT SHOULD.
...
SLAM

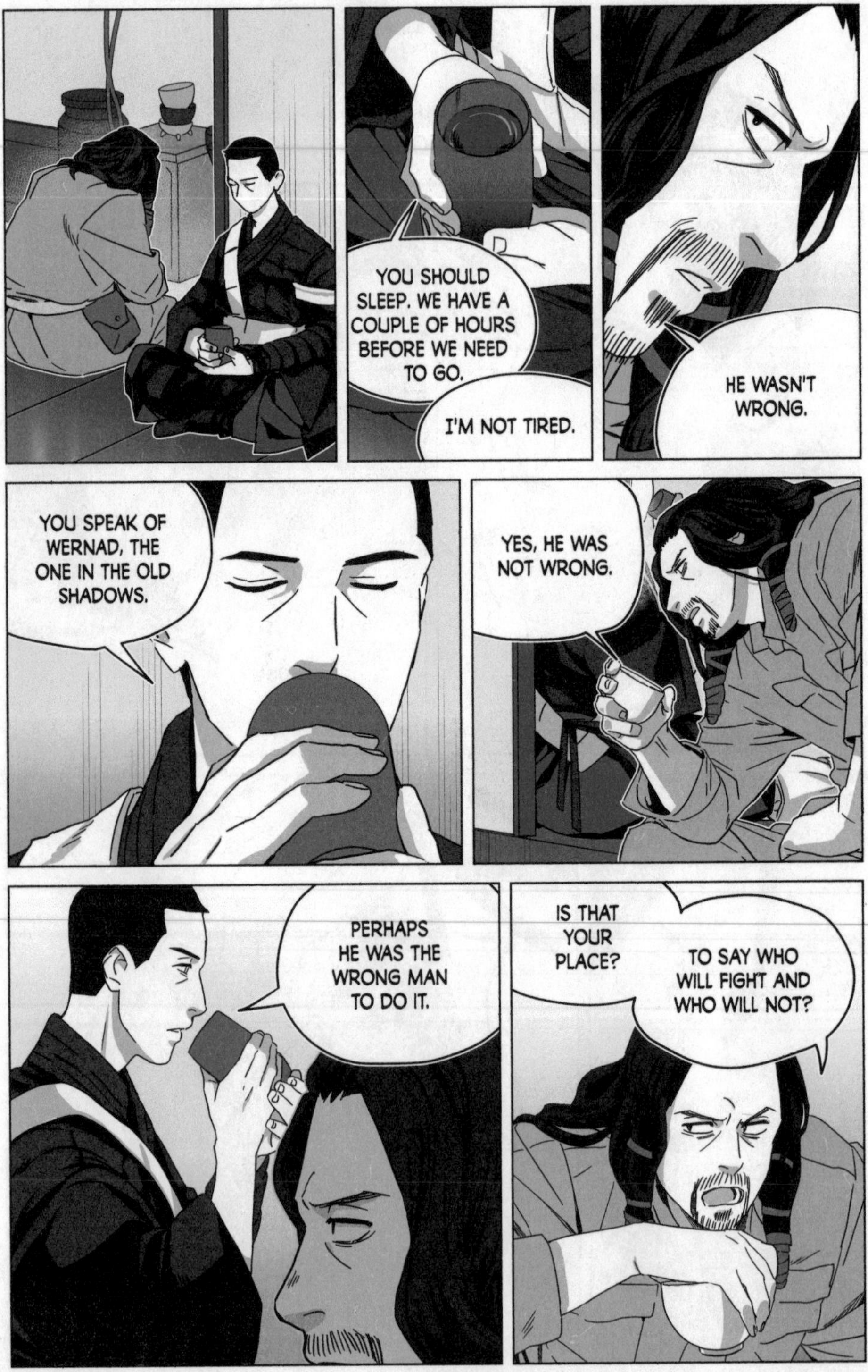
YOU SHOULD SLEEP. WE HAVE A COUPLE OF HOURS BEFORE WE NEED TO GO.
I'M NOT TIRED.
HE WASN'T WRONG.
YOU SPEAK OF WERNAD, THE ONE IN THE OLD SHADOWS.
YES, HE WAS NOT WRONG.
PERHAPS HE WAS THE WRONG MAN TO DO IT.
IS THAT YOUR PLACE?
TO SAY WHO WILL FIGHT AND WHO WILL NOT?

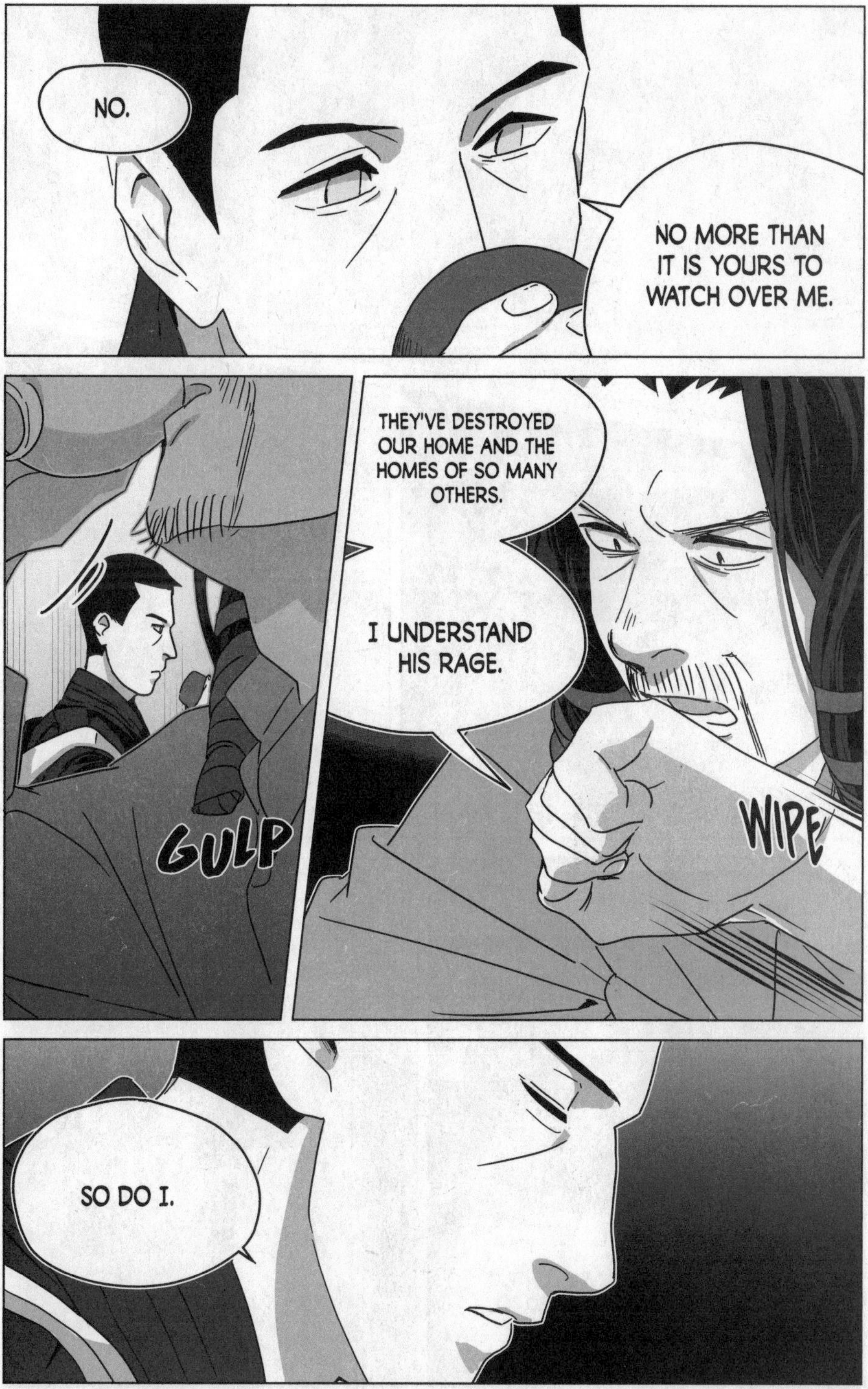
NO.
NO MORE THAN IT IS YOURS TO WATCH OVER ME.
GULP
THEY'VE DESTROYED OUR HOME AND THE HOMES OF SO MANY OTHERS.
I UNDERSTAND HIS RAGE.
WIPE
SO DO I.

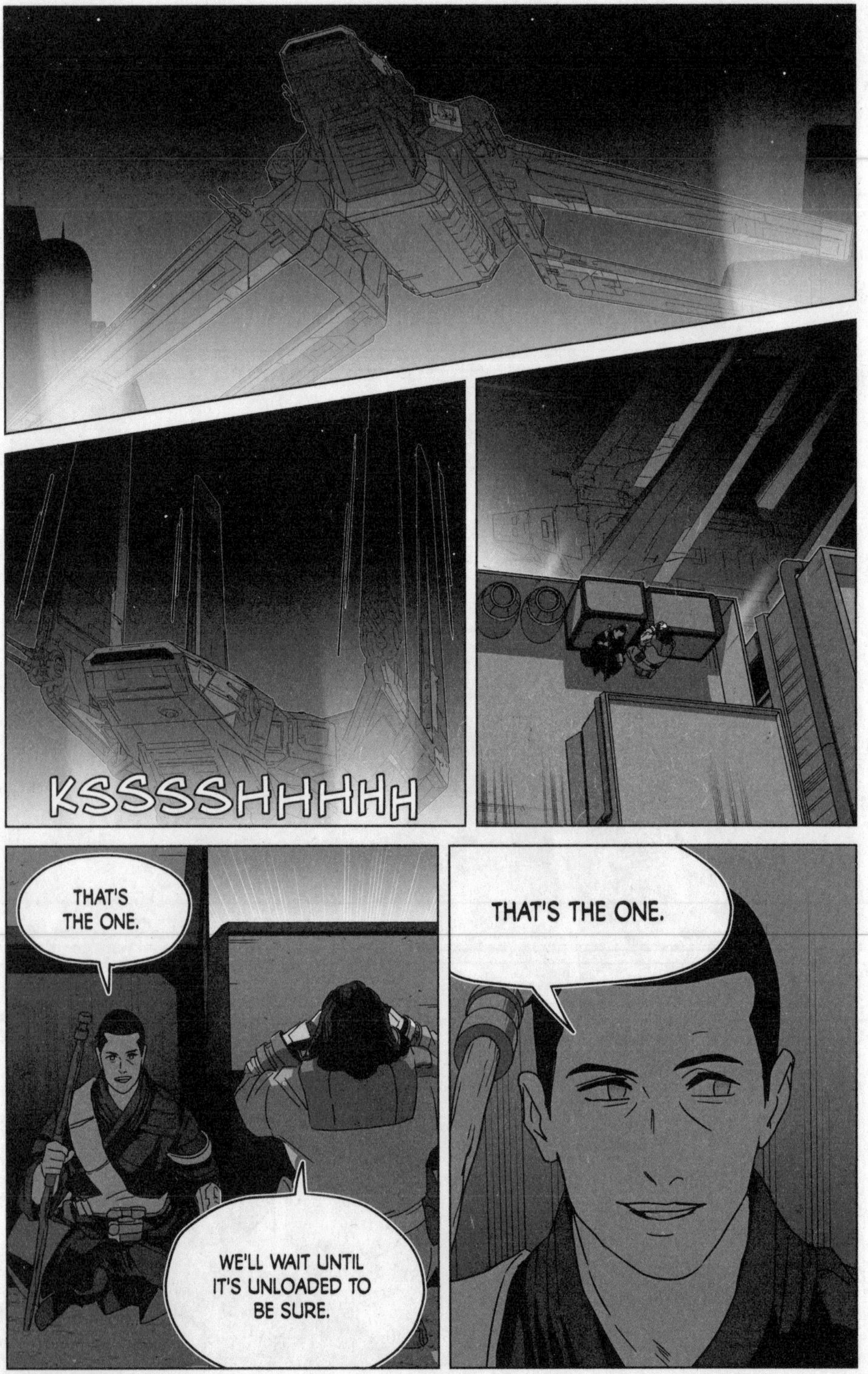
KSSSSHHHHH
THAT'S THE ONE.
WE'LL WAIT UNTIL IT'S UNLOADED TO BE SURE.
THAT'S THE ONE.

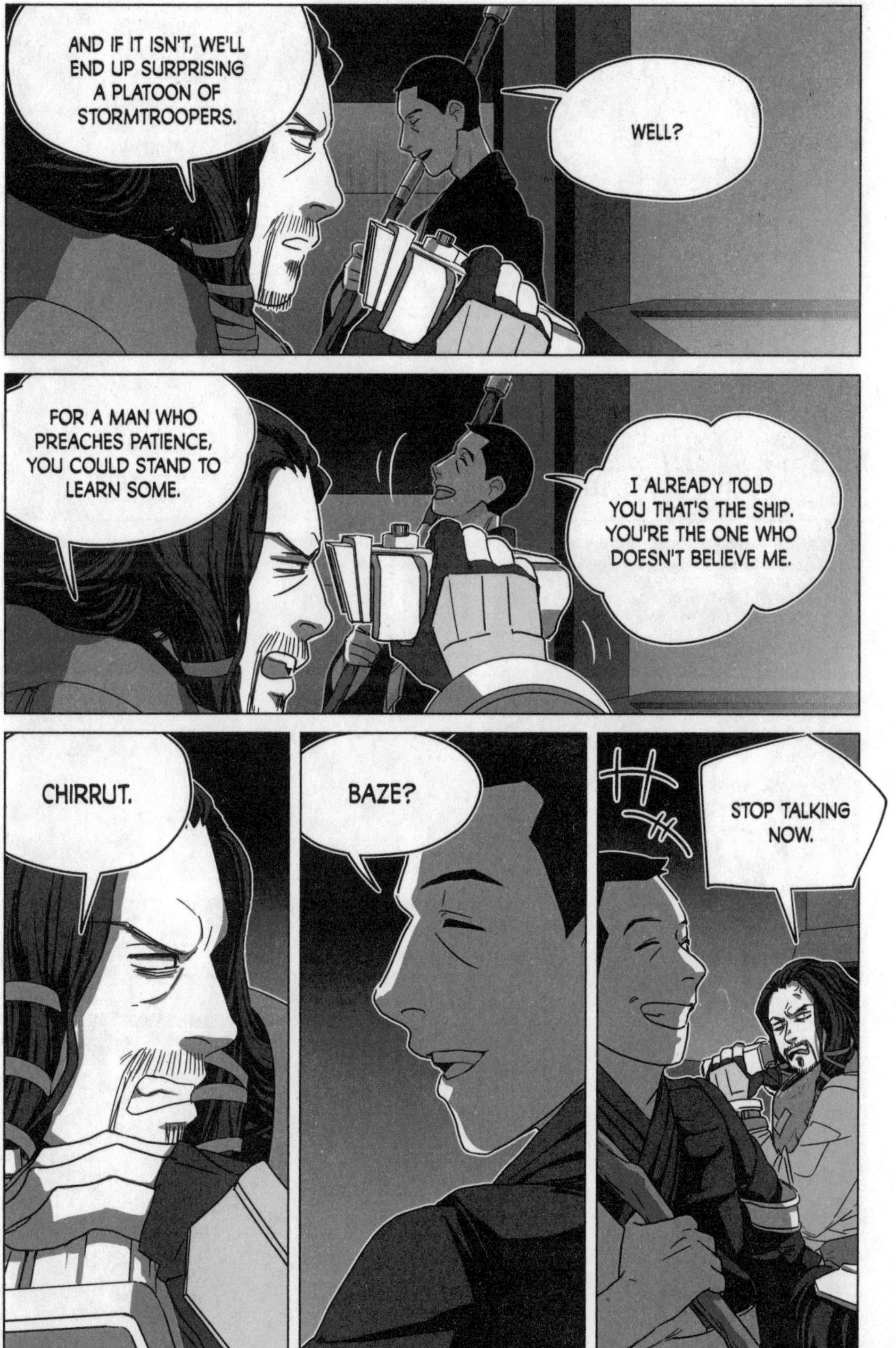
AND IF IT ISN'T, WE'LL END UP SURPRISING A PLATOON OF STORMTROOPERS.
WELL?
FOR A MAN WHO PREACHES PATIENCE, YOU COULD STAND TO LEARN SOME.
I ALREADY TOLD YOU THAT'S THE SHIP. YOU'RE THE ONE WHO DOESN'T BELIEVE ME.
CHIRRUT.
BAZE?
STOP TALKING NOW.

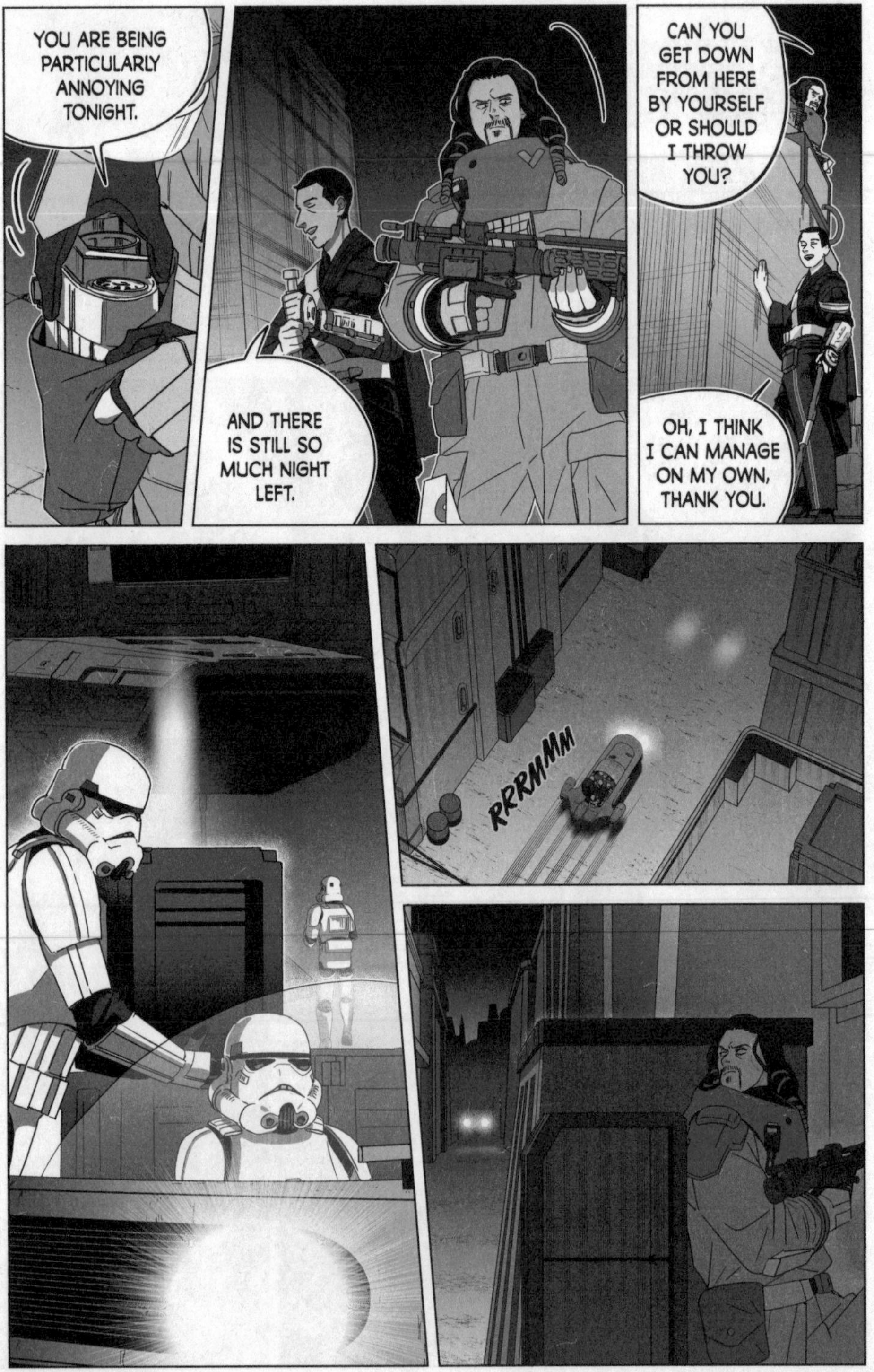
YOU ARE BEING PARTICULARLY ANNOYING TONIGHT.
AND THERE IS STILL SO MUCH NIGHT LEFT.
CAN YOU GET DOWN FROM HERE BY YOURSELF OR SHOULD I THROW YOU?
OH, I THINK I CAN MANAGE ON MY OWN, THANK YOU.
RRRMMM

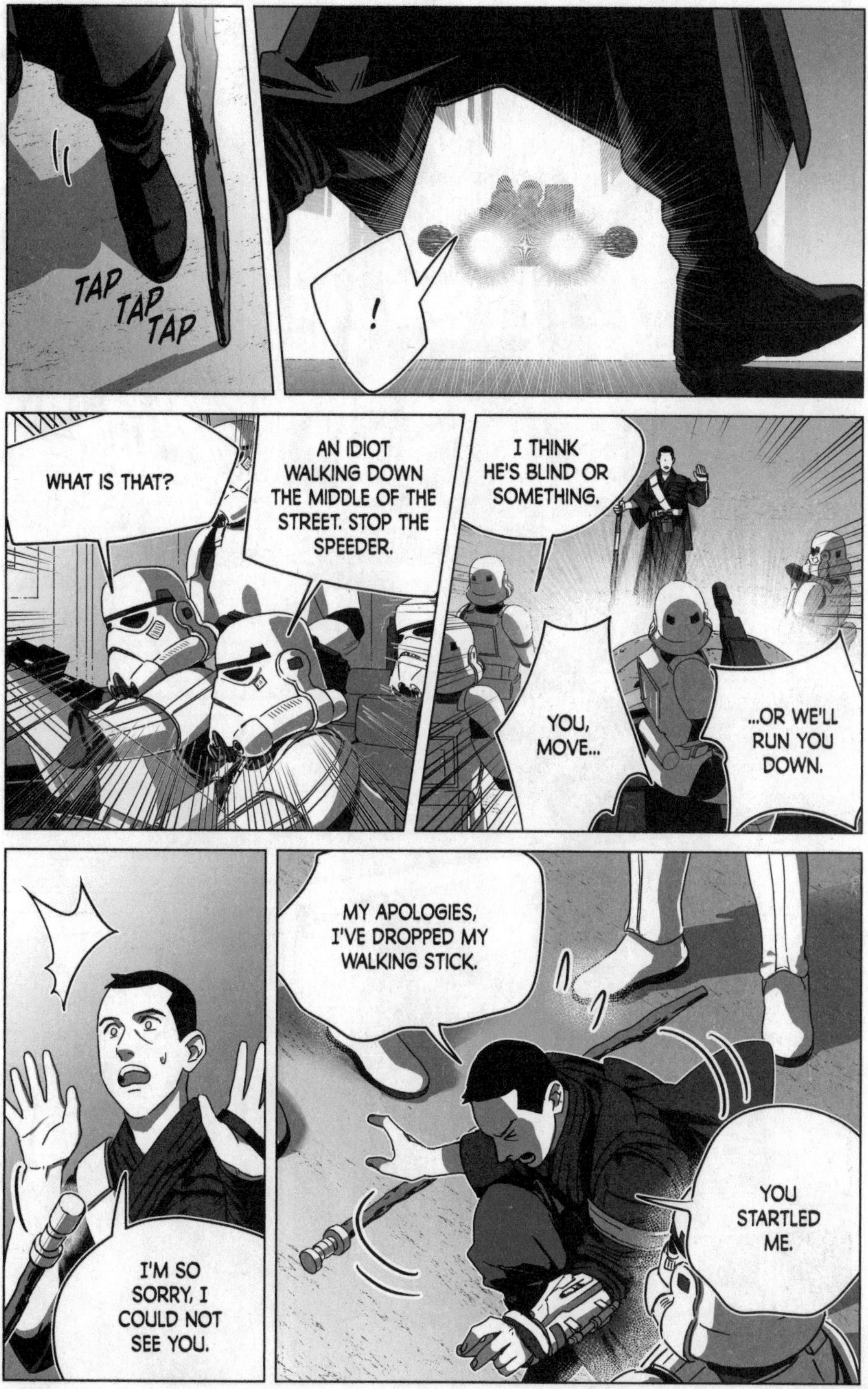

TAP TAP TAP
!
WHAT IS THAT?
AN IDIOT WALKING DOWN THE MIDDLE OF THE STREET. STOP THE SPEEDER.
I THINK HE'S BLIND OR SOMETHING.
YOU, MOVE...
...OR WE'LL RUN YOU DOWN.
I'M SO SORRY, I COULD NOT SEE YOU.
MY APOLOGIES, I'VE DROPPED MY WALKING STICK.
YOU STARTLED ME.

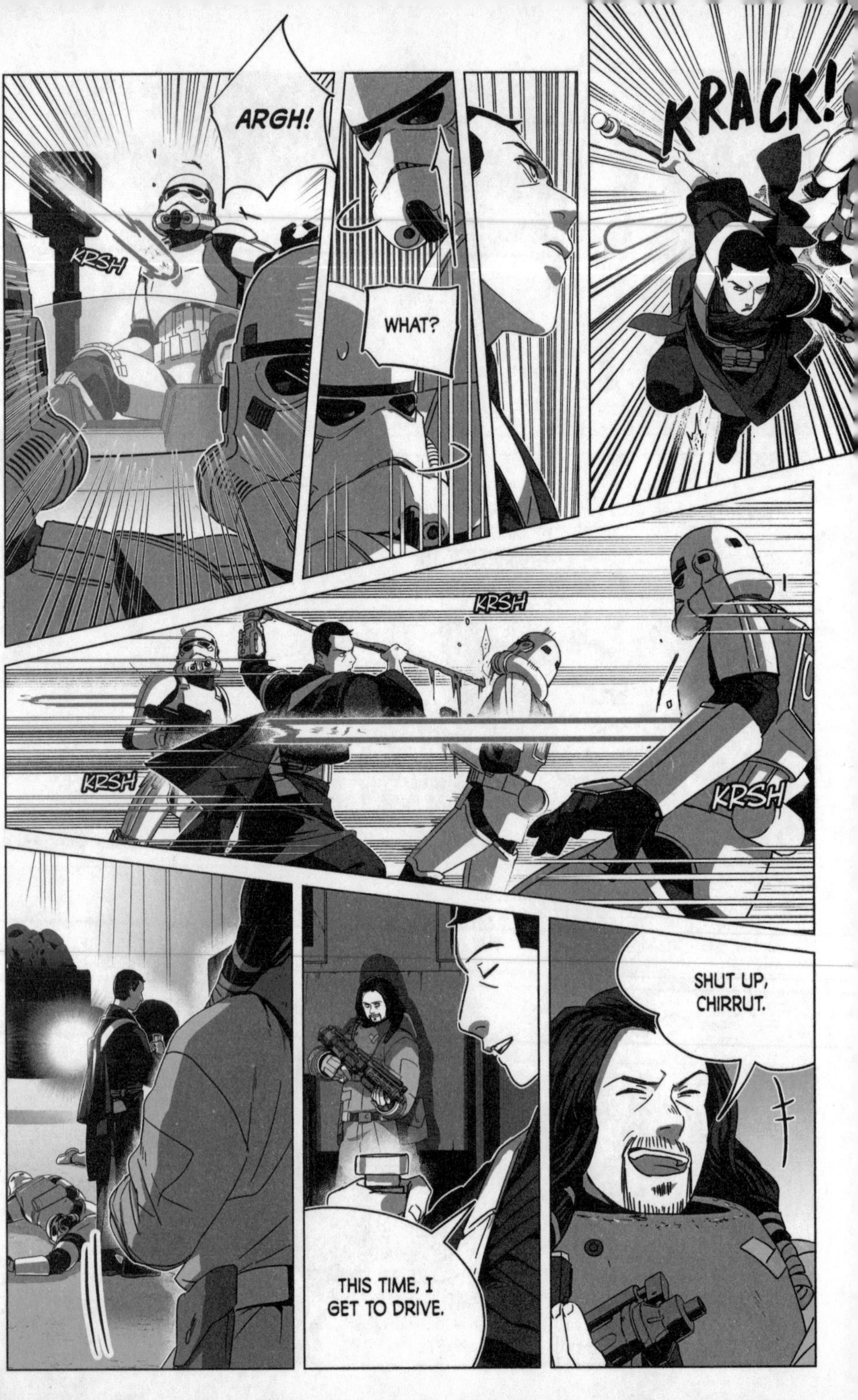
ARGH!
KRSH
WHAT?
KRACK!
KRSH
KRSH
KRSH
SHUT UP, CHIRRUT.
THIS TIME, I GET TO DRIVE.

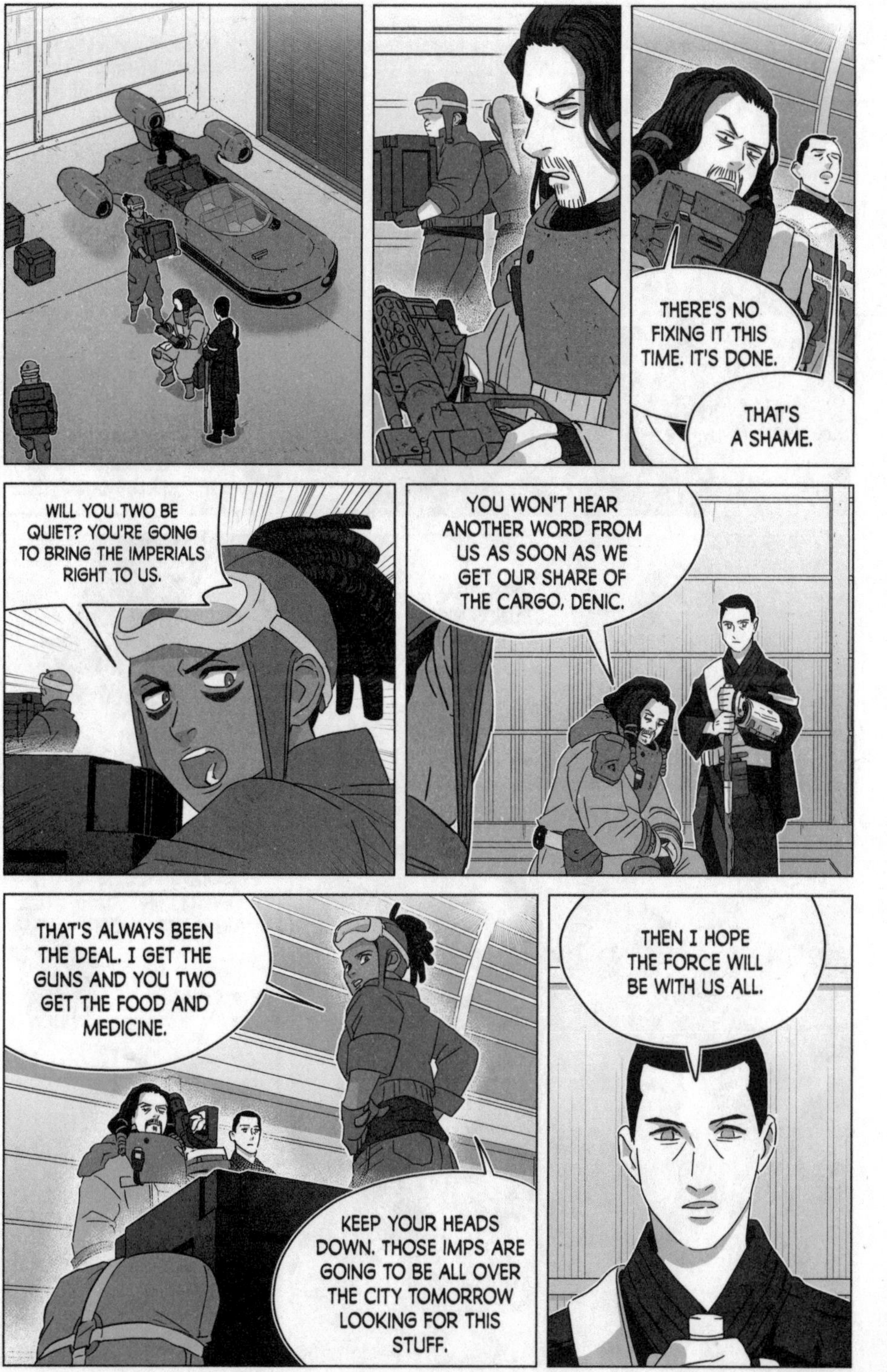
THERE'S NO FIXING IT THIS TIME. IT'S DONE.
THAT'S A SHAME.
WILL YOU TWO BE QUIET? YOU'RE GOING TO BRING THE IMPERIALS RIGHT TO US.
YOU WON'T HEAR ANOTHER WORD FROM US AS SOON AS WE GET OUR SHARE OF THE CARGO, DENIC.
THAT'S ALWAYS BEEN THE DEAL. I GET THE GUNS AND YOU TWO GET THE FOOD AND MEDICINE.
KEEP YOUR HEADS DOWN. THOSE IMPS ARE GOING TO BE ALL OVER THE CITY TOMORROW LOOKING FOR THIS STUFF.
THEN I HOPE THE FORCE WILL BE WITH US ALL.

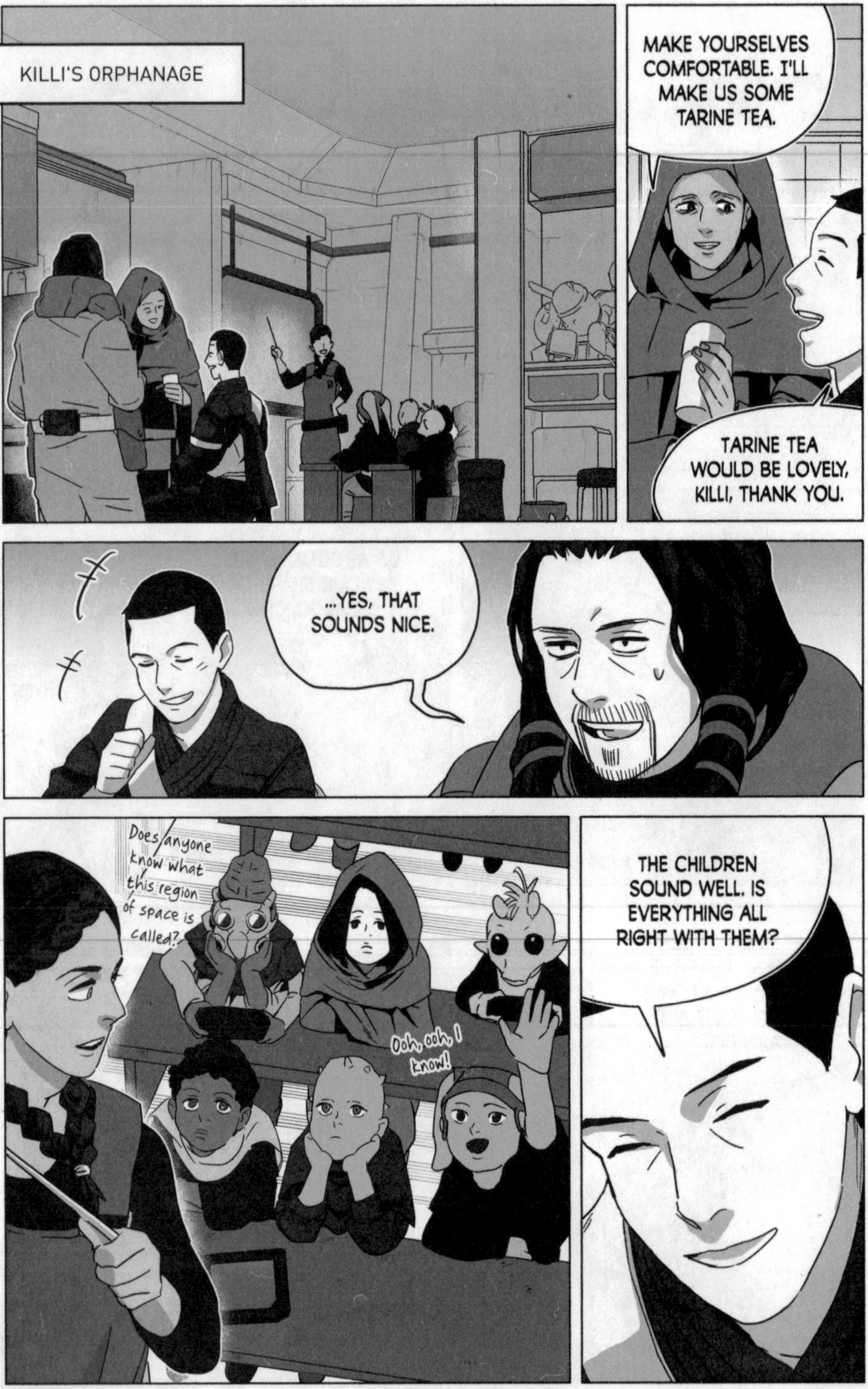
KILLI'S ORPHANAGE
MAKE YOURSELVES COMFORTABLE. I'LL MAKE US SOME TARINE TEA.
TARINE TEA WOULD BE LOVELY, KILLI, THANK YOU.
...YES, THAT SOUNDS NICE.
Does anyone know what this region of space is called?
Ooh, ooh, I know!
THE CHILDREN SOUND WELL. IS EVERYTHING ALL RIGHT WITH THEM?

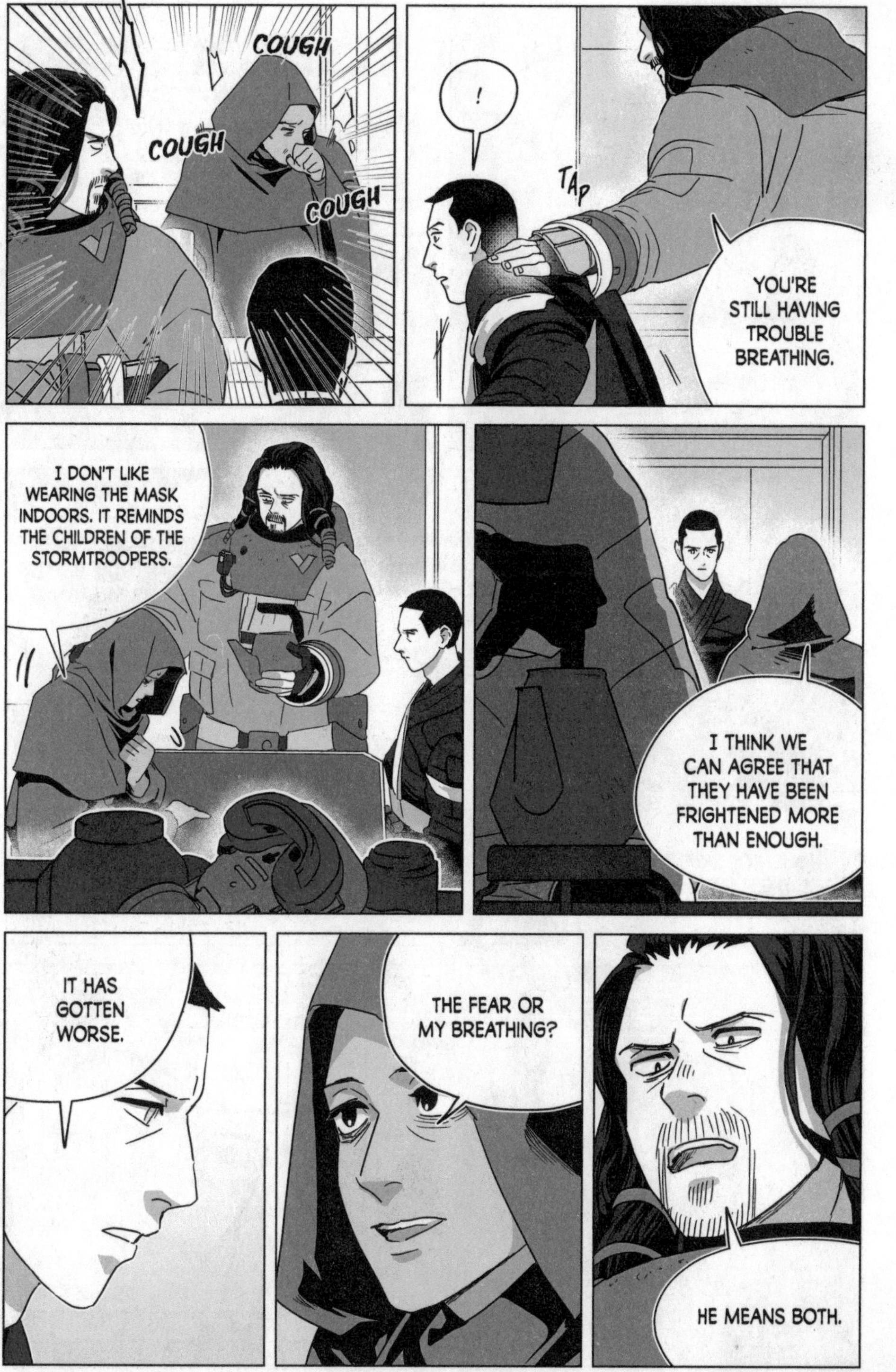
COUGH
COUGH
COUGH
!
TAP
YOU'RE STILL HAVING TROUBLE BREATHING.
I DON'T LIKE WEARING THE MASK INDOORS. IT REMINDS THE CHILDREN OF THE STORMTROOPERS.
I THINK WE CAN AGREE THAT THEY HAVE BEEN FRIGHTENED MORE THAN ENOUGH.
IT HAS GOTTEN WORSE.
THE FEAR OR MY BREATHING?
HE MEANS BOTH.

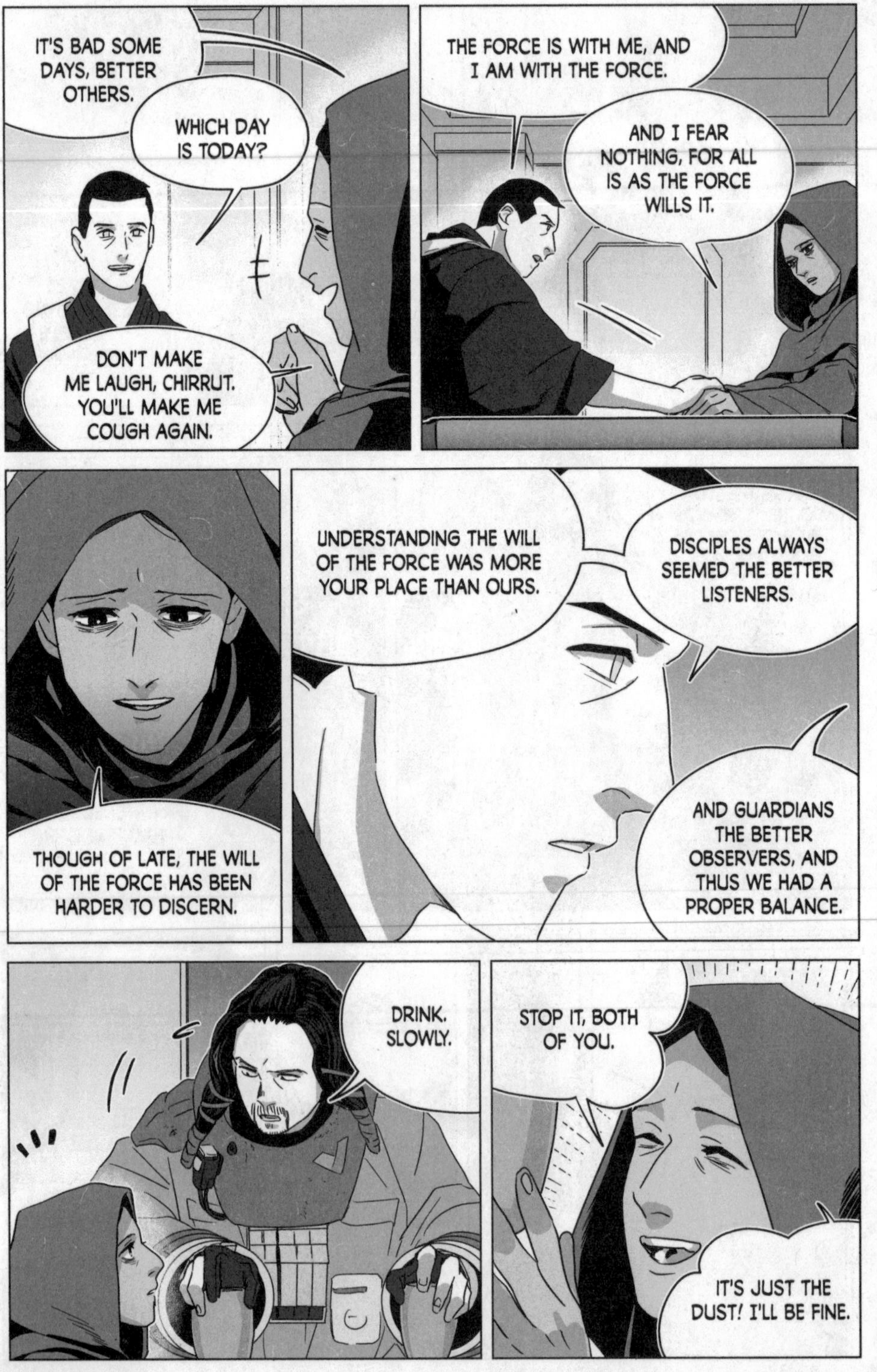

IT'S BAD SOME DAYS, BETTER OTHERS.
WHICH DAY IS TODAY?
DON'T MAKE ME LAUGH, CHIRRUT. YOU'LL MAKE ME COUGH AGAIN.
THE FORCE IS WITH ME, AND I AM WITH THE FORCE.
AND I FEAR NOTHING, FOR ALL IS AS THE FORCE WILLS IT.
THOUGH OF LATE, THE WILL OF THE FORCE HAS BEEN HARDER TO DISCERN.
UNDERSTANDING THE WILL OF THE FORCE WAS MORE YOUR PLACE THAN OURS.
DISCIPLES ALWAYS SEEMED THE BETTER LISTENERS.
AND GUARDIANS THE BETTER OBSERVERS, AND THUS WE HAD A PROPER BALANCE.
DRINK. SLOWLY.
STOP IT, BOTH OF YOU.
IT'S JUST THE DUST! I'LL BE FINE.

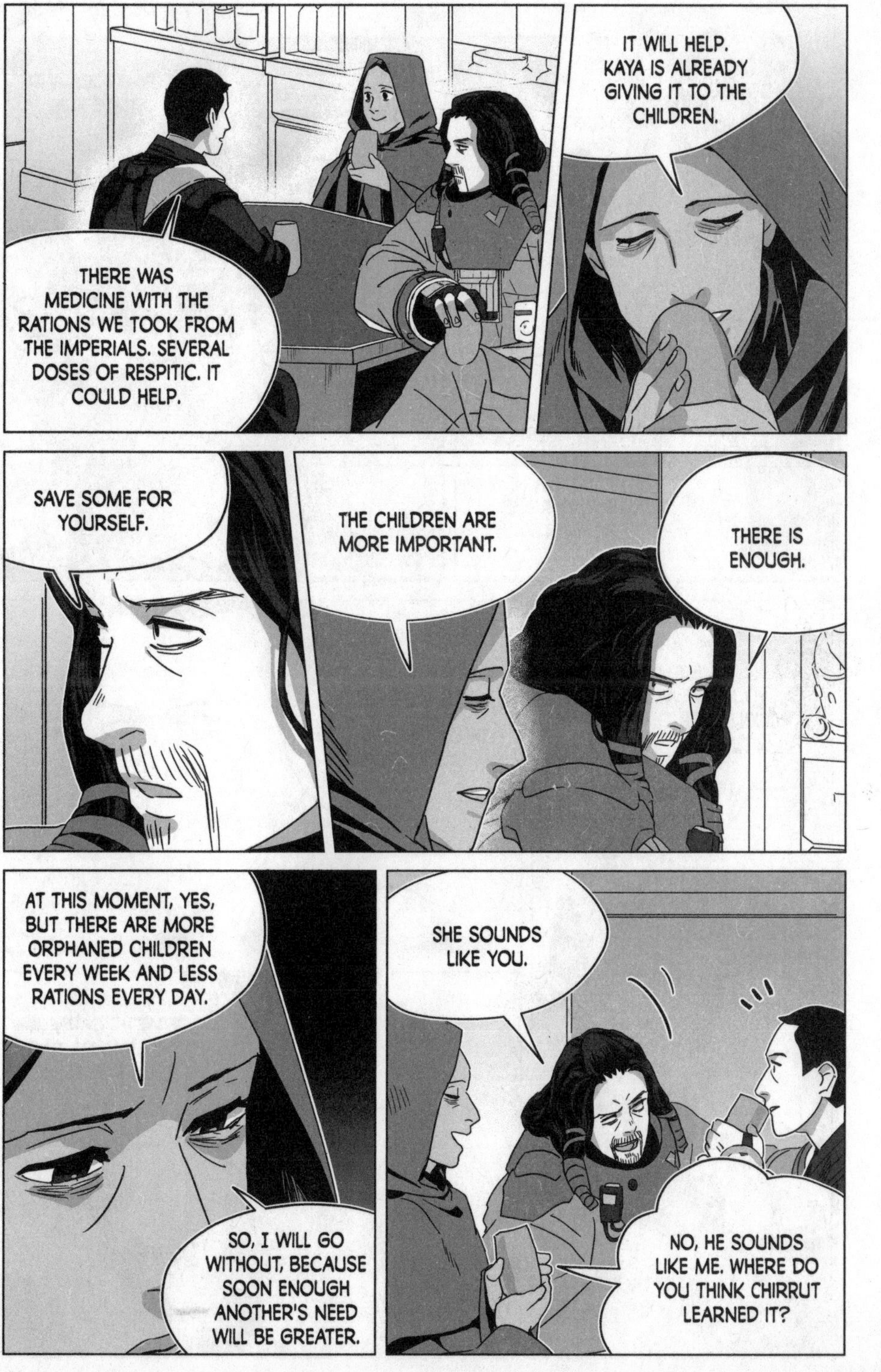
THERE WAS MEDICINE WITH THE RATIONS WE TOOK FROM THE IMPERIALS. SEVERAL DOSES OF RESPITIC. IT COULD HELP.
IT WILL HELP. KAYA IS ALREADY GIVING IT TO THE CHILDREN.
SAVE SOME FOR YOURSELF.
THE CHILDREN ARE MORE IMPORTANT.
THERE IS ENOUGH.
AT THIS MOMENT, YES, BUT THERE ARE MORE ORPHANED CHILDREN EVERY WEEK AND LESS RATIONS EVERY DAY.
SO, I WILL GO WITHOUT, BECAUSE SOON ENOUGH ANOTHER'S NEED WILL BE GREATER.
SHE SOUNDS LIKE YOU.
NO, HE SOUNDS LIKE ME. WHERE DO YOU THINK CHIRRUT LEARNED IT?

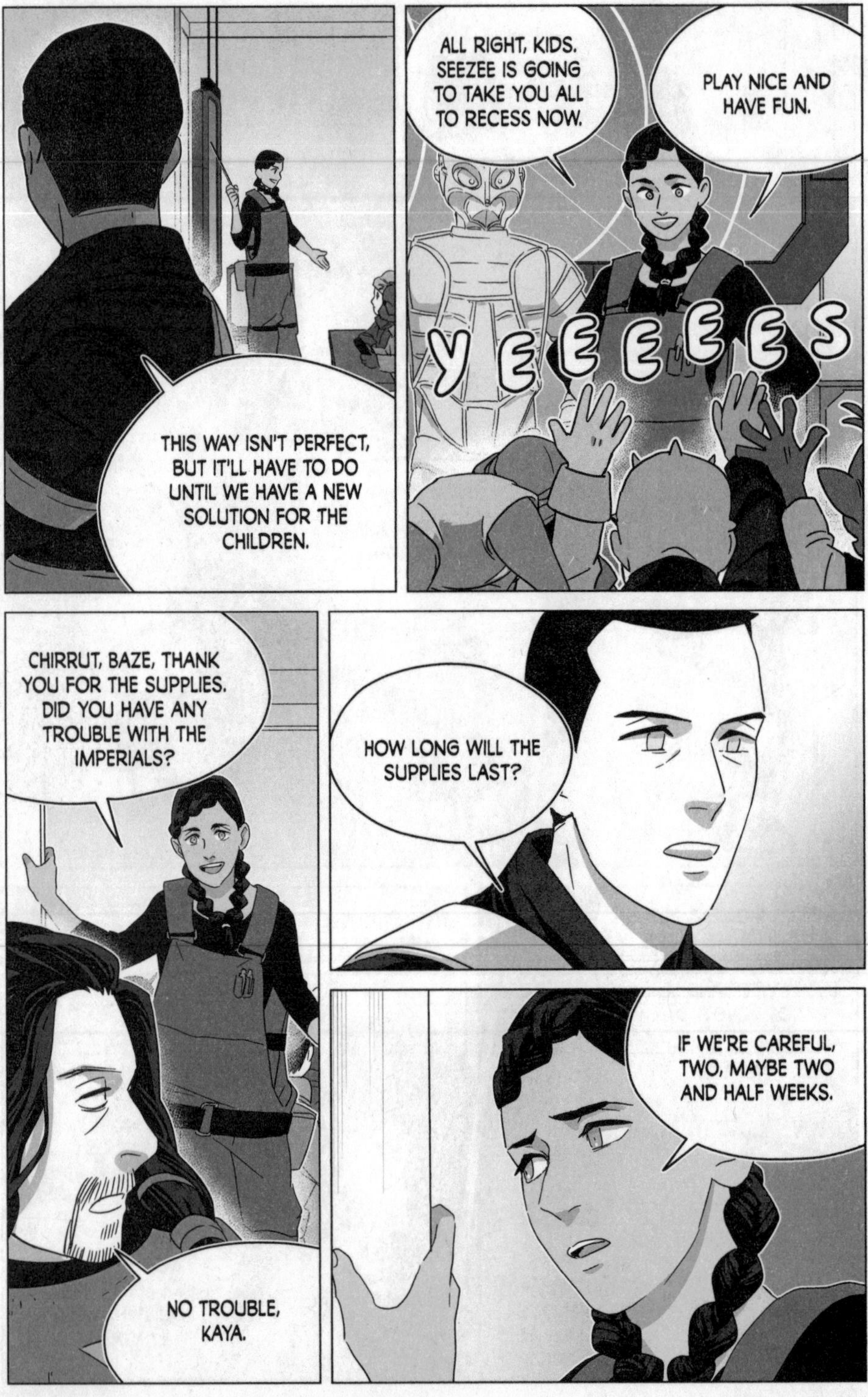
THIS WAY ISN'T PERFECT, BUT IT'LL HAVE TO DO UNTIL WE HAVE A NEW SOLUTION FOR THE CHILDREN.
ALL RIGHT, KIDS. SEEZEE IS GOING TO TAKE YOU ALL TO RECESS NOW.
PLAY NICE AND HAVE FUN.
YEEEEES
CHIRRUT, BAZE, THANK YOU FOR THE SUPPLIES. DID YOU HAVE ANY TROUBLE WITH THE IMPERIALS?
NO TROUBLE, KAYA.
HOW LONG WILL THE SUPPLIES LAST?
IF WE'RE CAREFUL, TWO, MAYBE TWO AND HALF WEEKS.

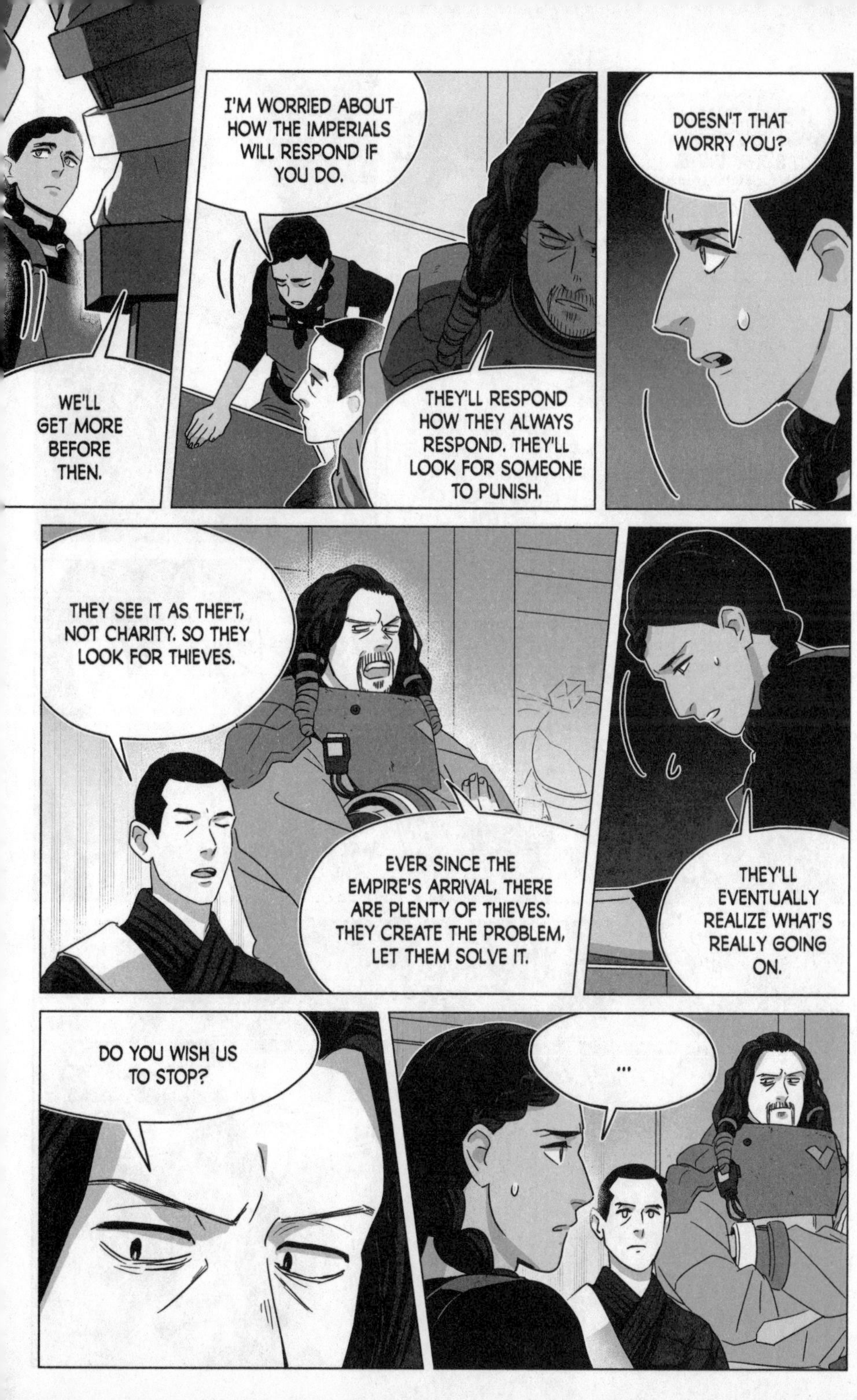
WE'LL GET MORE BEFORE THEN.
I'M WORRIED ABOUT HOW THE IMPERIALS WILL RESPOND IF YOU DO.
THEY'LL RESPOND HOW THEY ALWAYS RESPOND. THEY'LL LOOK FOR SOMEONE TO PUNISH.
DOESN'T THAT WORRY YOU?
THEY SEE IT AS THEFT, NOT CHARITY. SO THEY LOOK FOR THIEVES.
EVER SINCE THE EMPIRE'S ARRIVAL, THERE ARE PLENTY OF THIEVES. THEY CREATE THE PROBLEM, LET THEM SOLVE IT.
THEY'LL EVENTUALLY REALIZE WHAT'S REALLY GOING ON.
DO YOU WISH US TO STOP?
...

IT'S NOT THAT WE WISH YOU TO STOP. IT'S THAT WE'RE CONCERNED WHERE THIS ENDS...

...AND FOR YOUR SAFETY. WHAT HAPPENS IF EITHER ONE OF YOU ARE CAPTURED OR KILLED?

WHAT WOULD YOU RATHER WE DO?

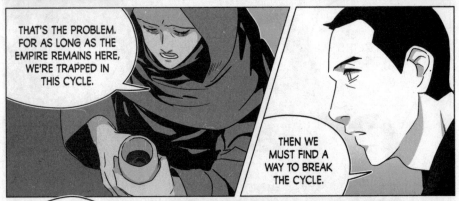

THAT'S THE PROBLEM. FOR AS LONG AS THE EMPIRE REMAINS HERE, WE'RE TRAPPED IN THIS CYCLE.

THEN WE MUST FIND A WAY TO BREAK THE CYCLE.

YES, BEFORE THE CYCLE BREAKS US.

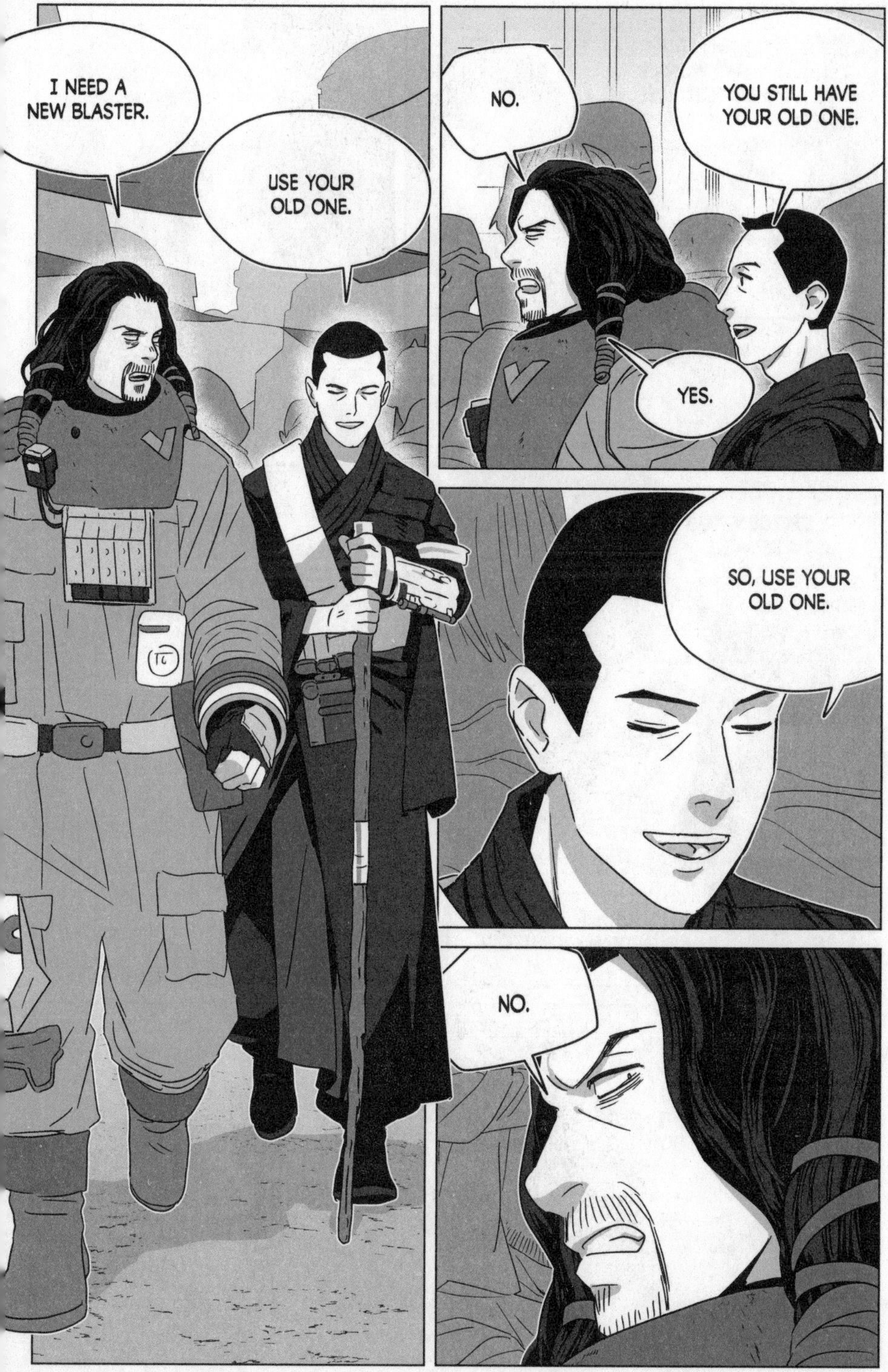
I NEED A NEW BLASTER.
USE YOUR OLD ONE.
NO.
YOU STILL HAVE YOUR OLD ONE.
YES.
SO, USE YOUR OLD ONE.
NO.

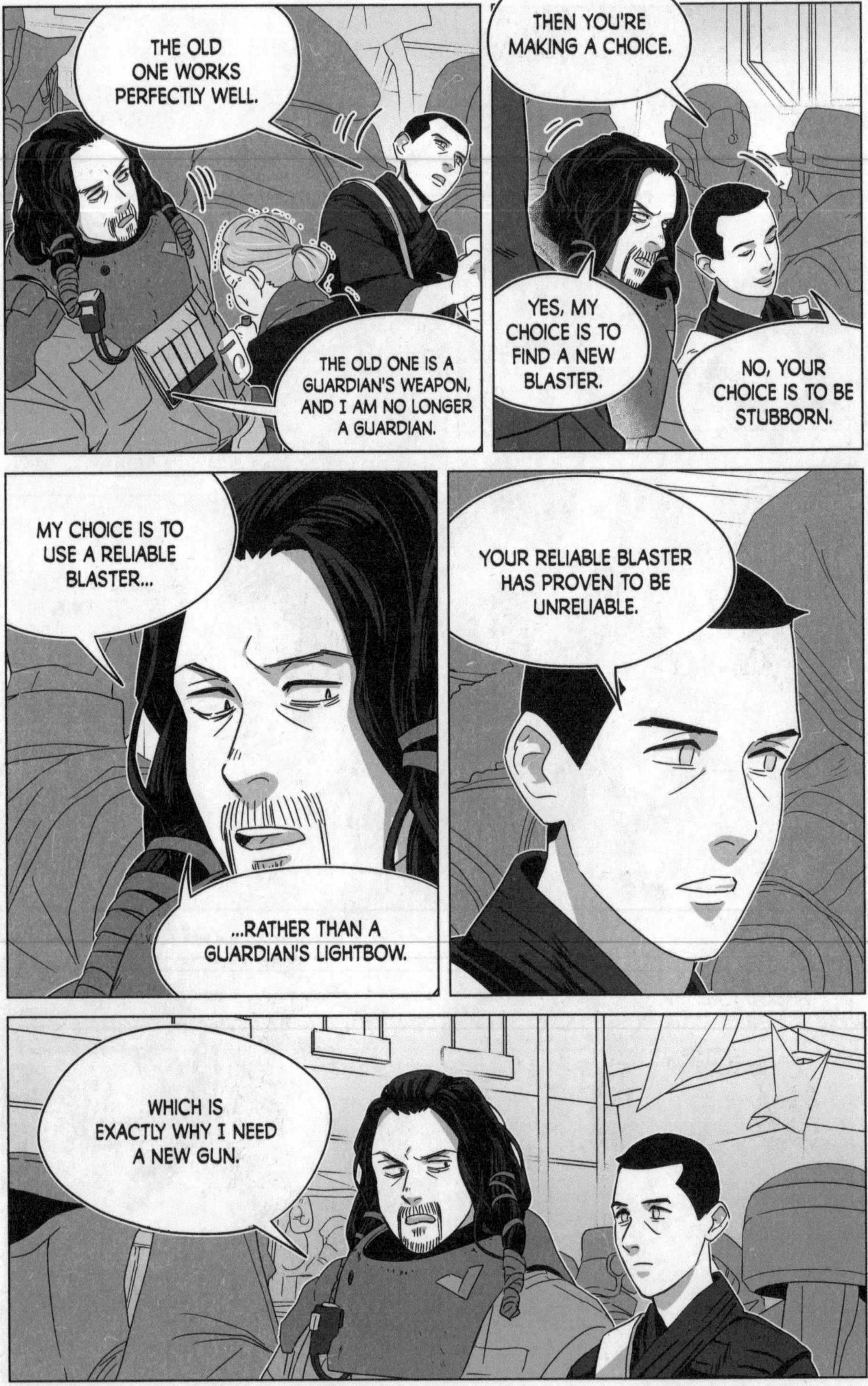
THE OLD ONE WORKS PERFECTLY WELL.
THE OLD ONE IS A GUARDIAN'S WEAPON, AND I AM NO LONGER A GUARDIAN.
THEN YOU'RE MAKING A CHOICE.
YES, MY CHOICE IS TO FIND A NEW BLASTER.
NO, YOUR CHOICE IS TO BE STUBBORN.
MY CHOICE IS TO USE A RELIABLE BLASTER...
...RATHER THAN A GUARDIAN'S LIGHTBOW.
YOUR RELIABLE BLASTER HAS PROVEN TO BE UNRELIABLE.
WHICH IS EXACTLY WHY I NEED A NEW GUN.

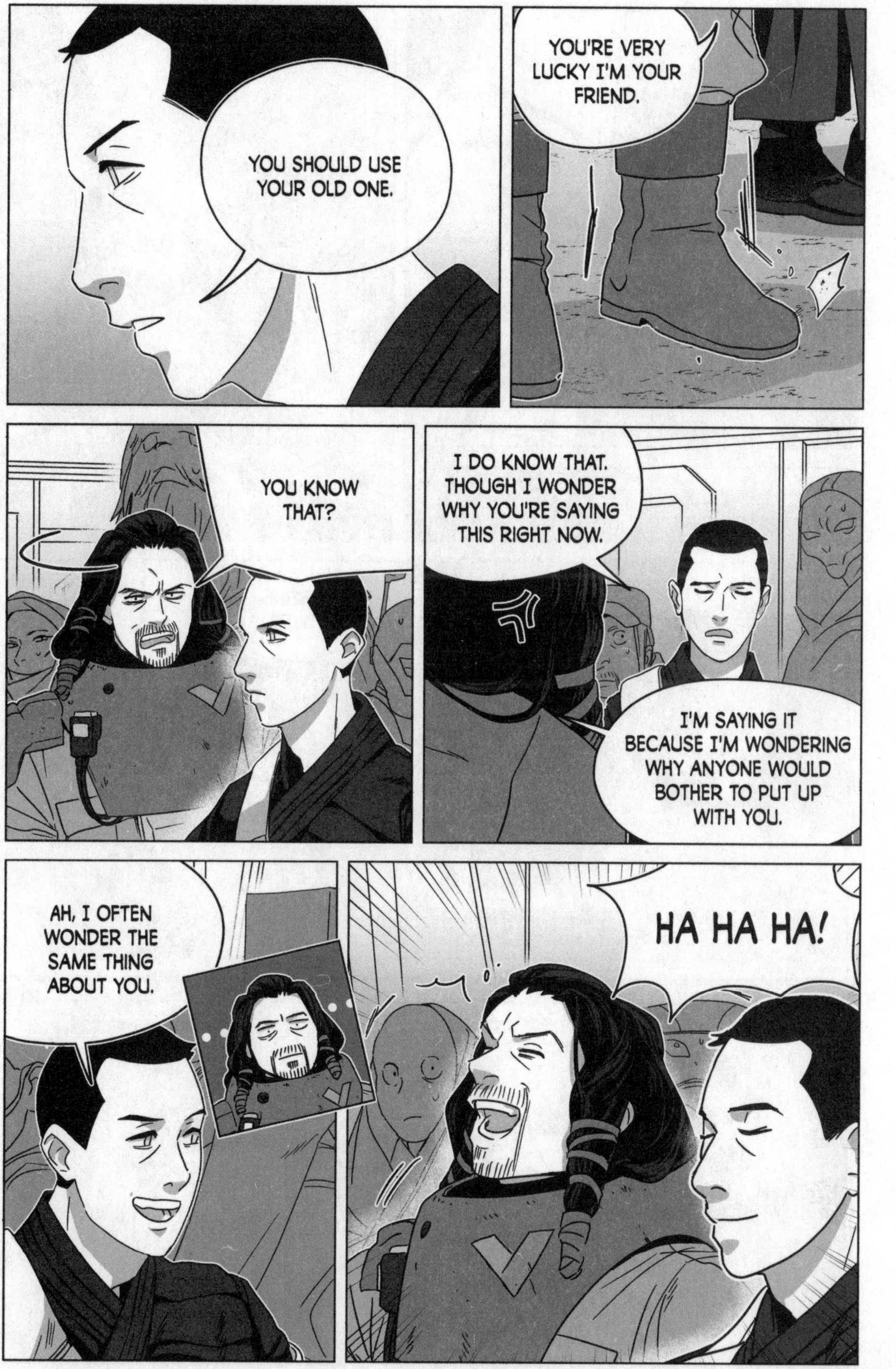
YOU SHOULD USE YOUR OLD ONE.
YOU'RE VERY LUCKY I'M YOUR FRIEND.
YOU KNOW THAT?
I DO KNOW THAT. THOUGH I WONDER WHY YOU'RE SAYING THIS RIGHT NOW.
I'M SAYING IT BECAUSE I'M WONDERING WHY ANYONE WOULD BOTHER TO PUT UP WITH YOU.
AH, I OFTEN WONDER THE SAME THING ABOUT YOU.
HA HA HA!

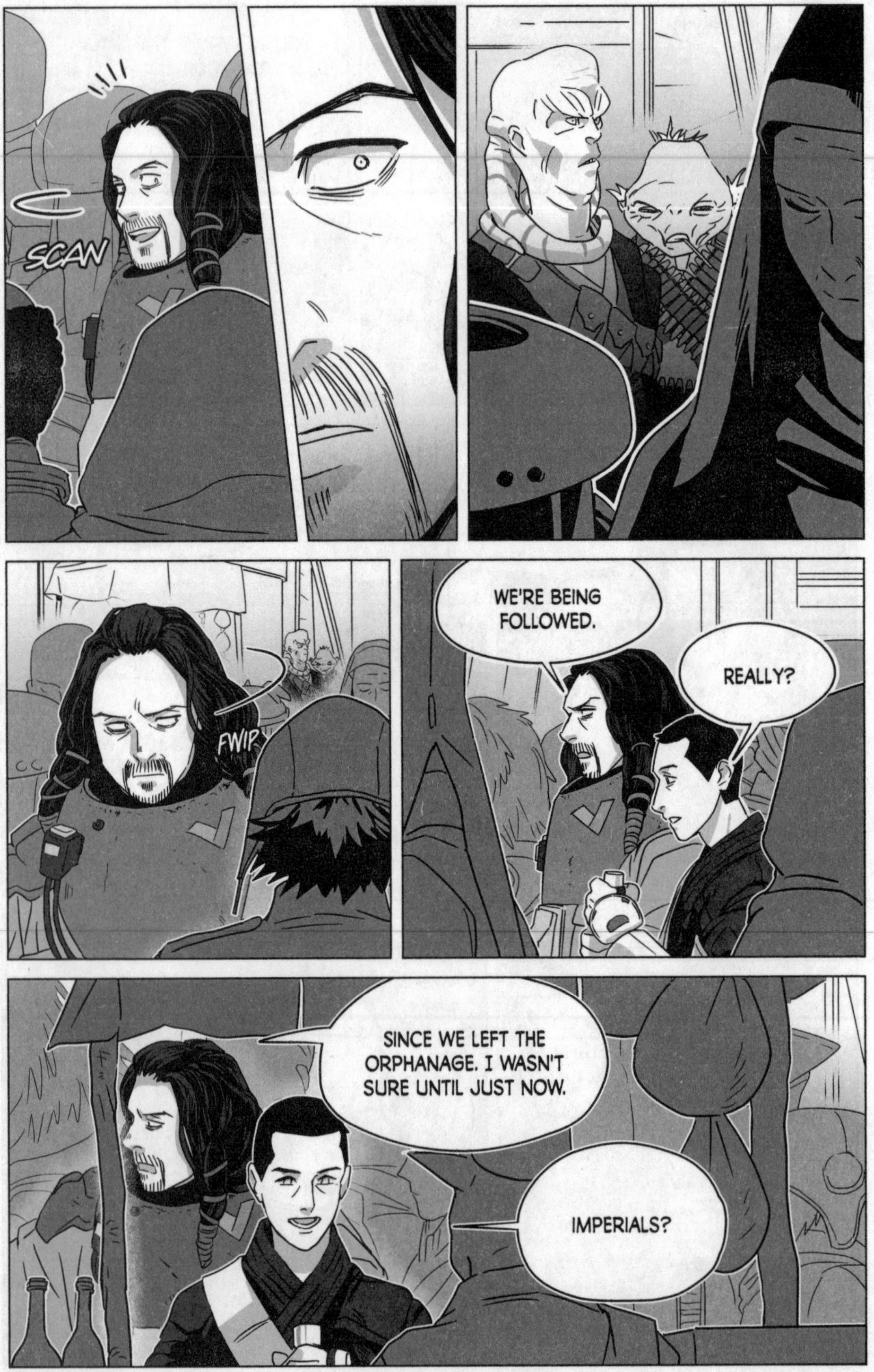
SCAN
FWIP
WE'RE BEING FOLLOWED.
REALLY?
SINCE WE LEFT THE ORPHANAGE. I WASN'T SURE UNTIL JUST NOW.
IMPERIALS?

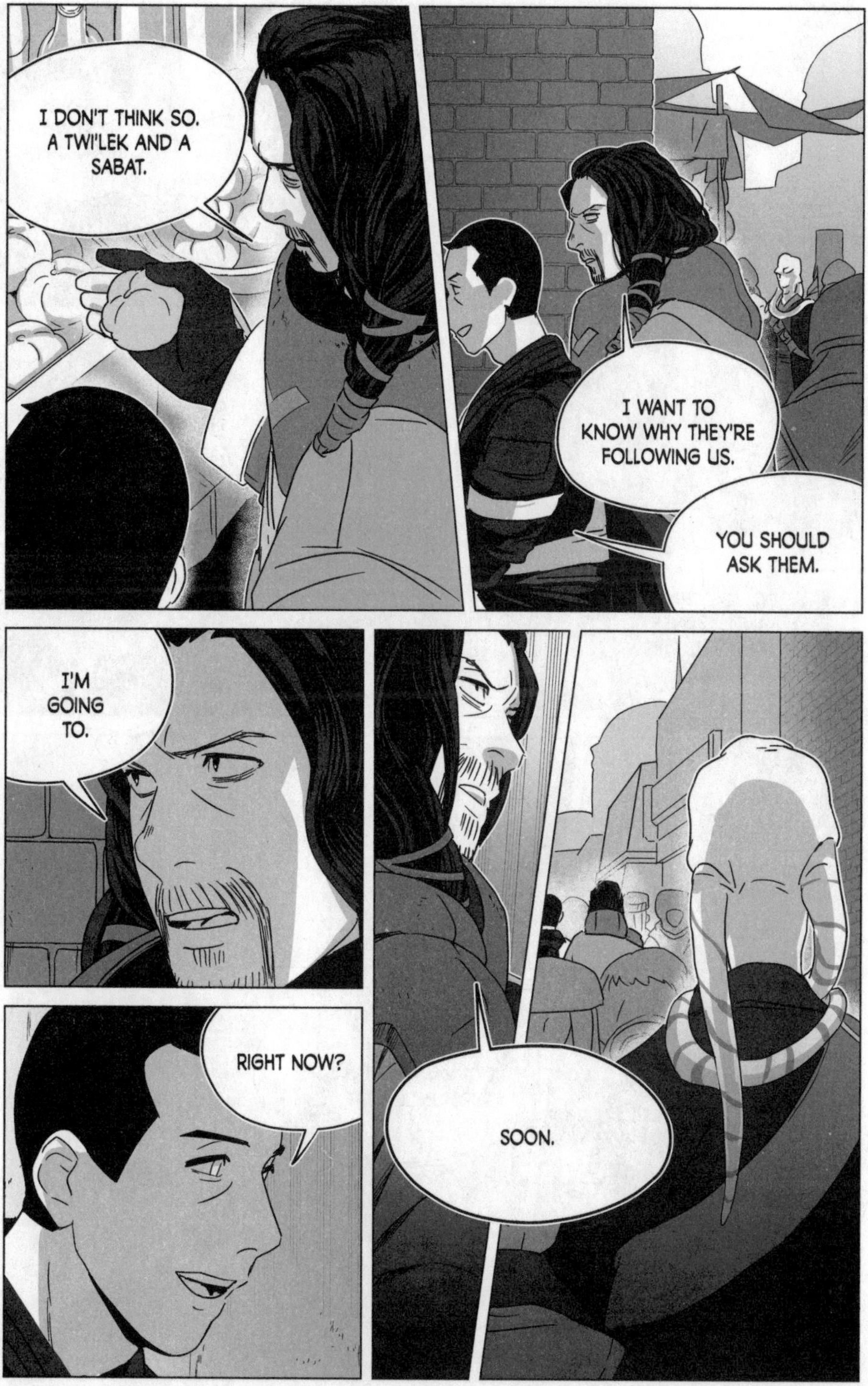
I DON'T THINK SO. A TWI'LEK AND A SABAT.
I WANT TO KNOW WHY THEY'RE FOLLOWING US.
YOU SHOULD ASK THEM.
I'M GOING TO.
RIGHT NOW?
SOON.

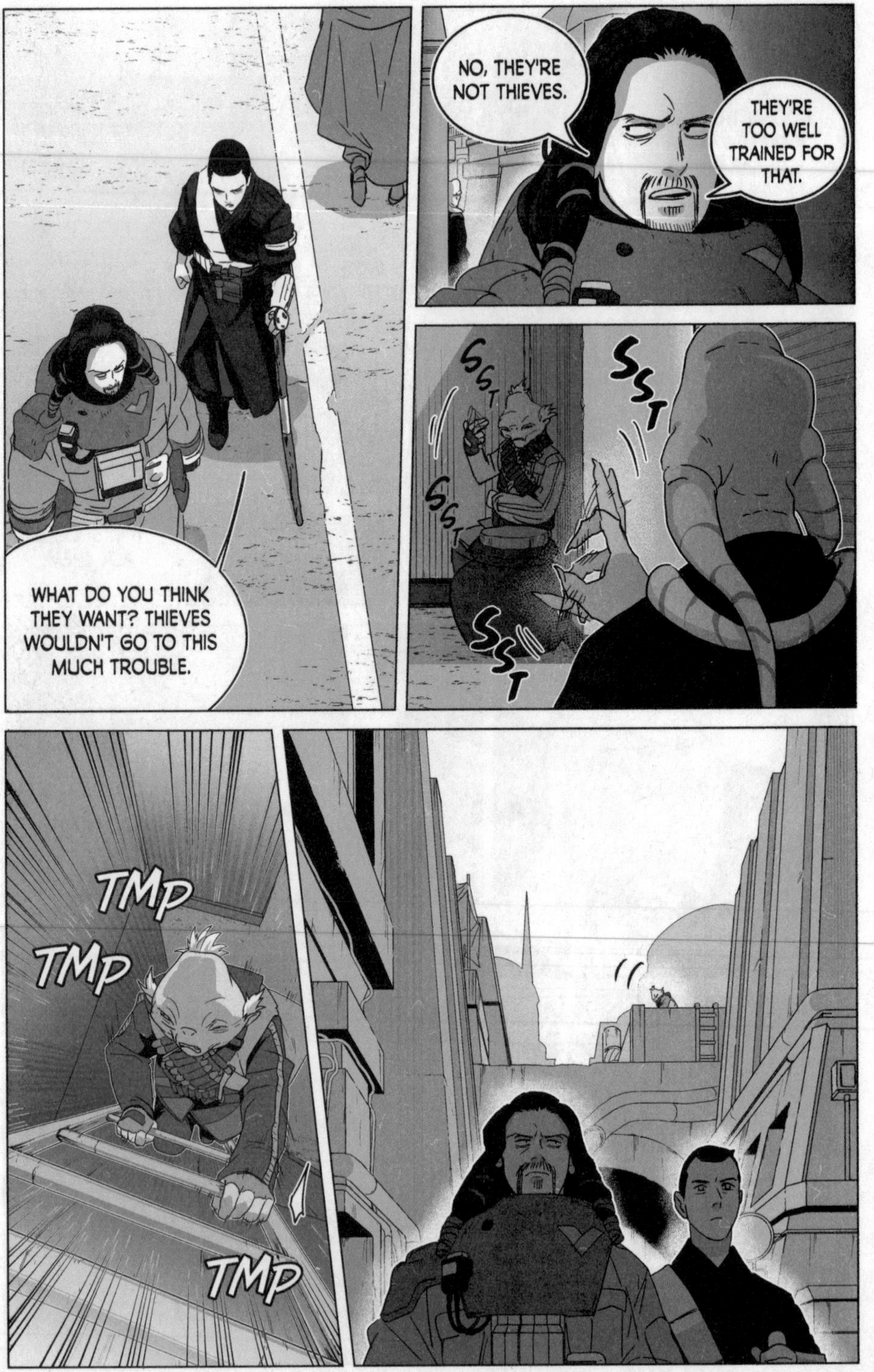
WHAT DO YOU THINK THEY WANT? THIEVES WOULDN'T GO TO THIS MUCH TROUBLE.
NO, THEY'RE NOT THIEVES.
THEY'RE TOO WELL TRAINED FOR THAT.
SST
SST
SST
SST
TMP
TMP
TMP

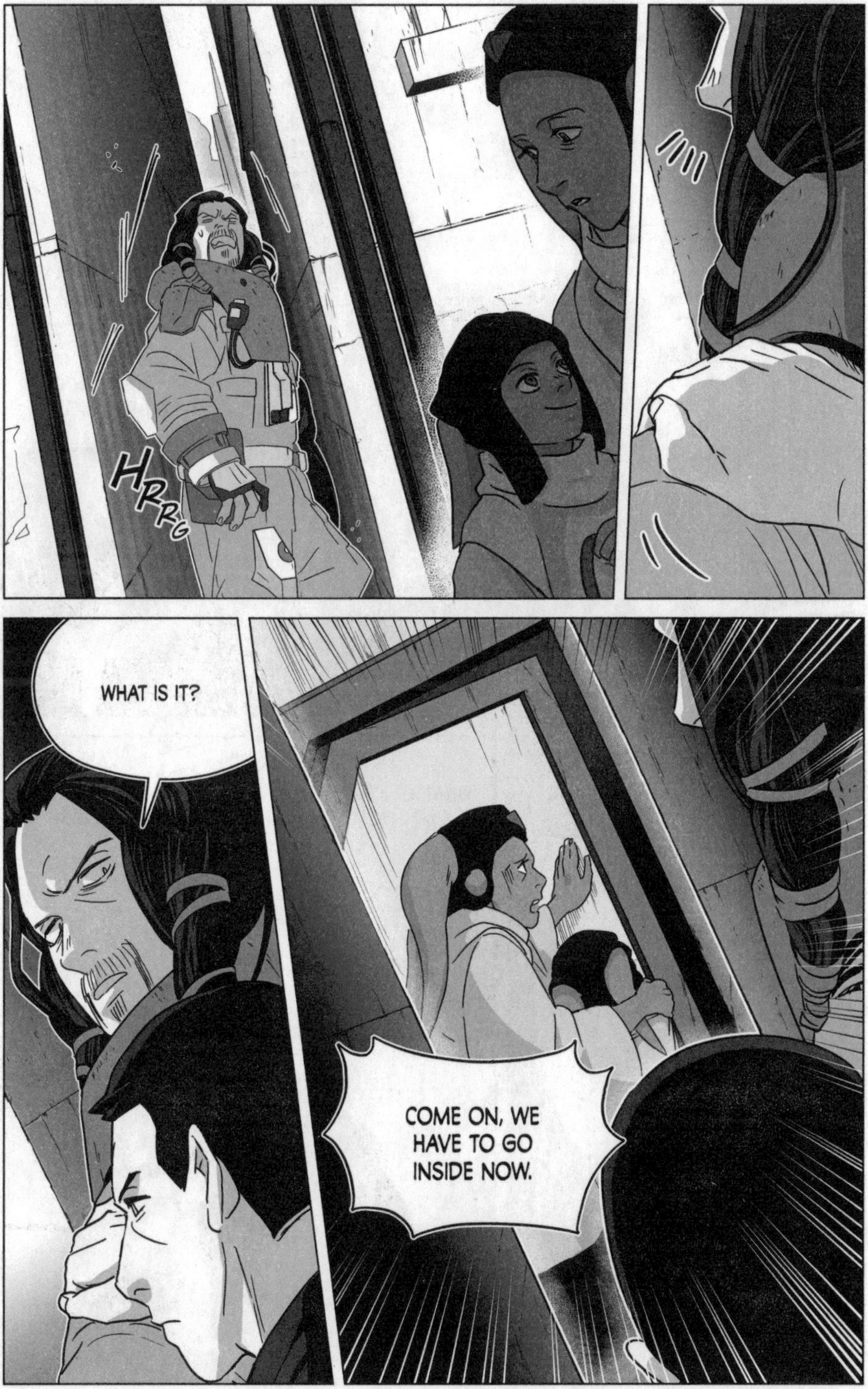
HRRG
WHAT IS IT?
COME ON, WE HAVE TO GO INSIDE NOW.

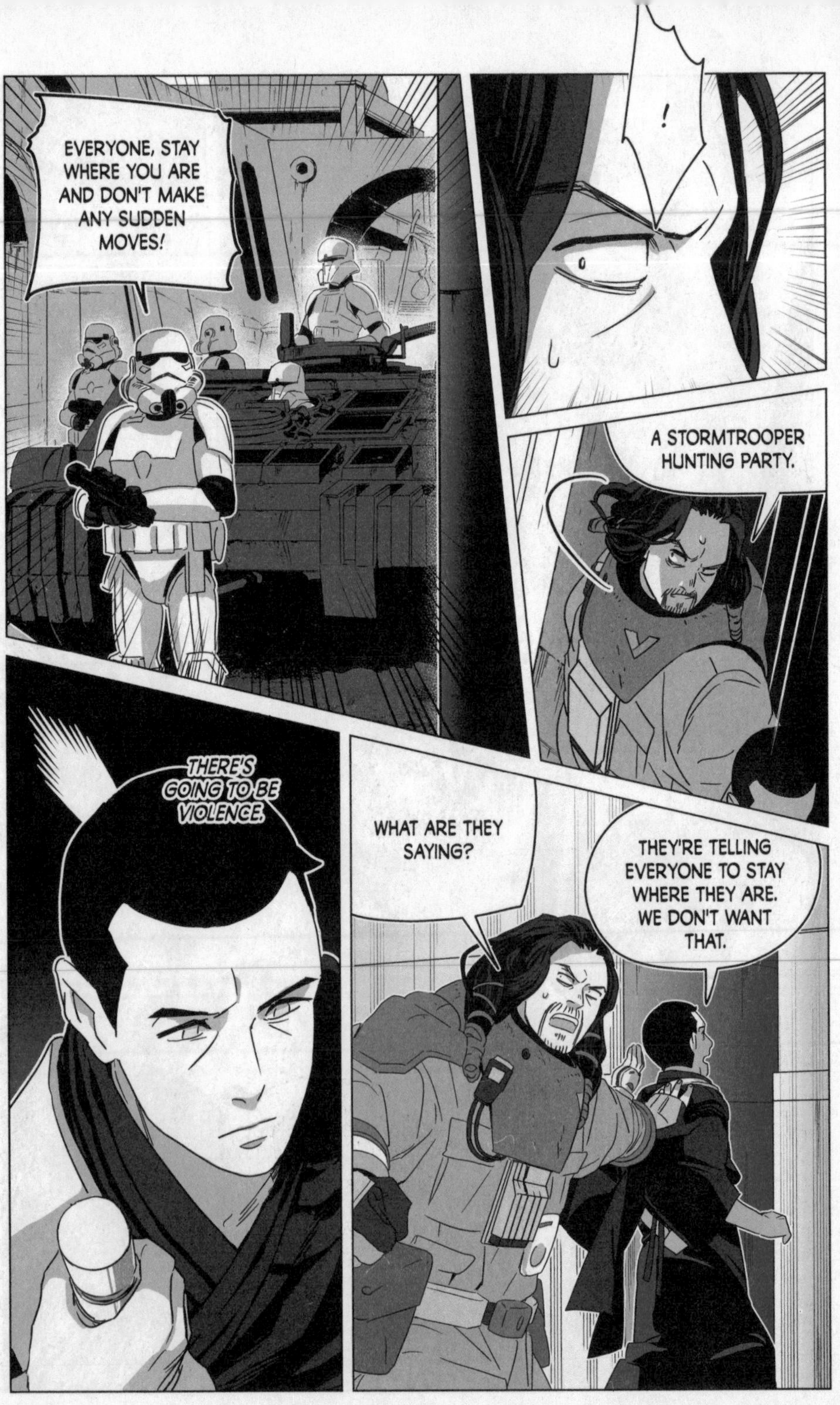
EVERYONE, STAY WHERE YOU ARE AND DON'T MAKE ANY SUDDEN MOVES!
!
A STORMTROOPER HUNTING PARTY.
THERE'S GOING TO BE VIOLENCE.
WHAT ARE THEY SAYING?
THEY'RE TELLING EVERYONE TO STAY WHERE THEY ARE. WE DON'T WANT THAT.

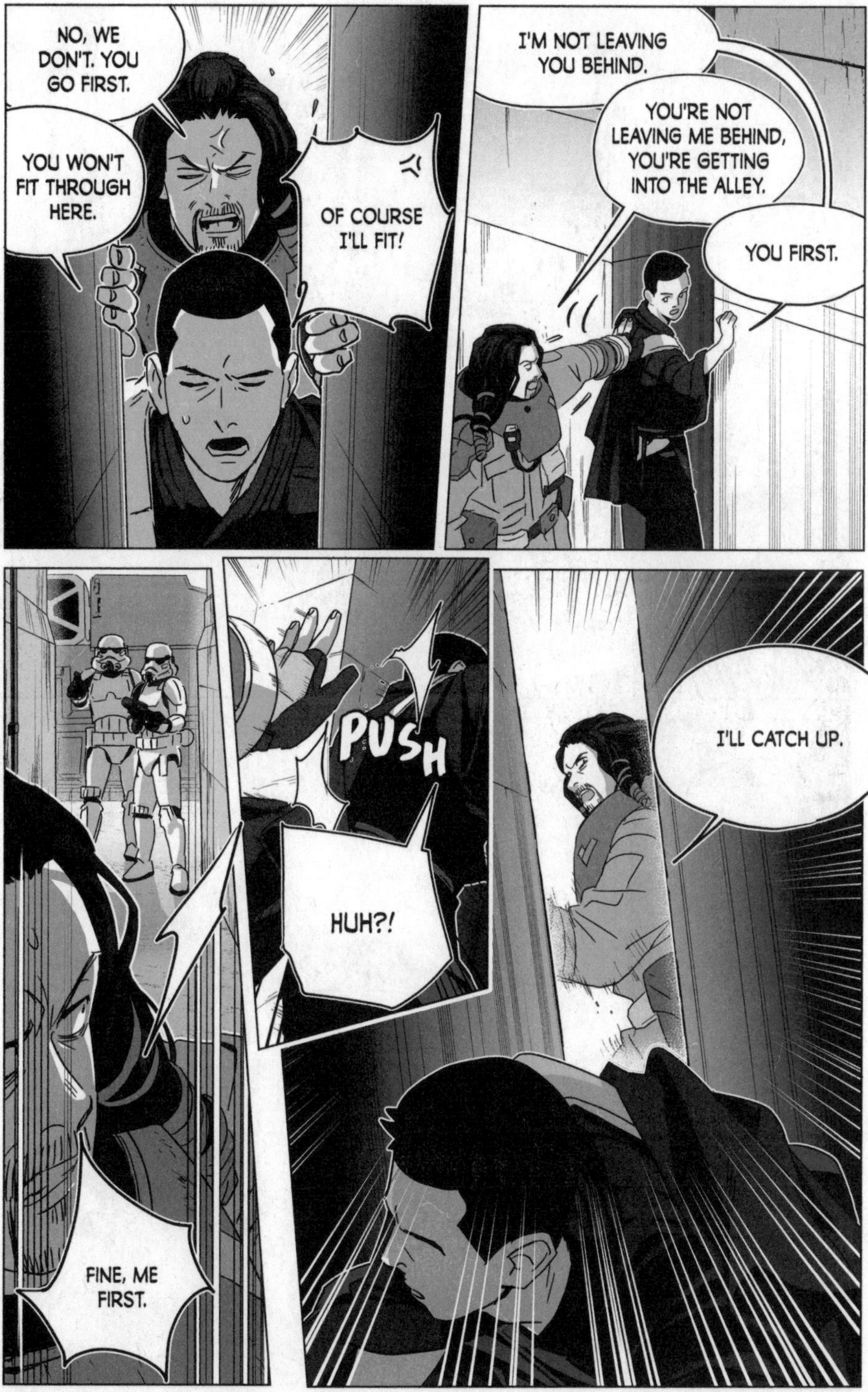
NO, WE DON'T. YOU GO FIRST.
YOU WON'T FIT THROUGH HERE.
OF COURSE I'LL FIT!
I'M NOT LEAVING YOU BEHIND.
YOU'RE NOT LEAVING ME BEHIND, YOU'RE GETTING INTO THE ALLEY.
YOU FIRST.
FINE, ME FIRST.
PUSH
HUH?!
I'LL CATCH UP.

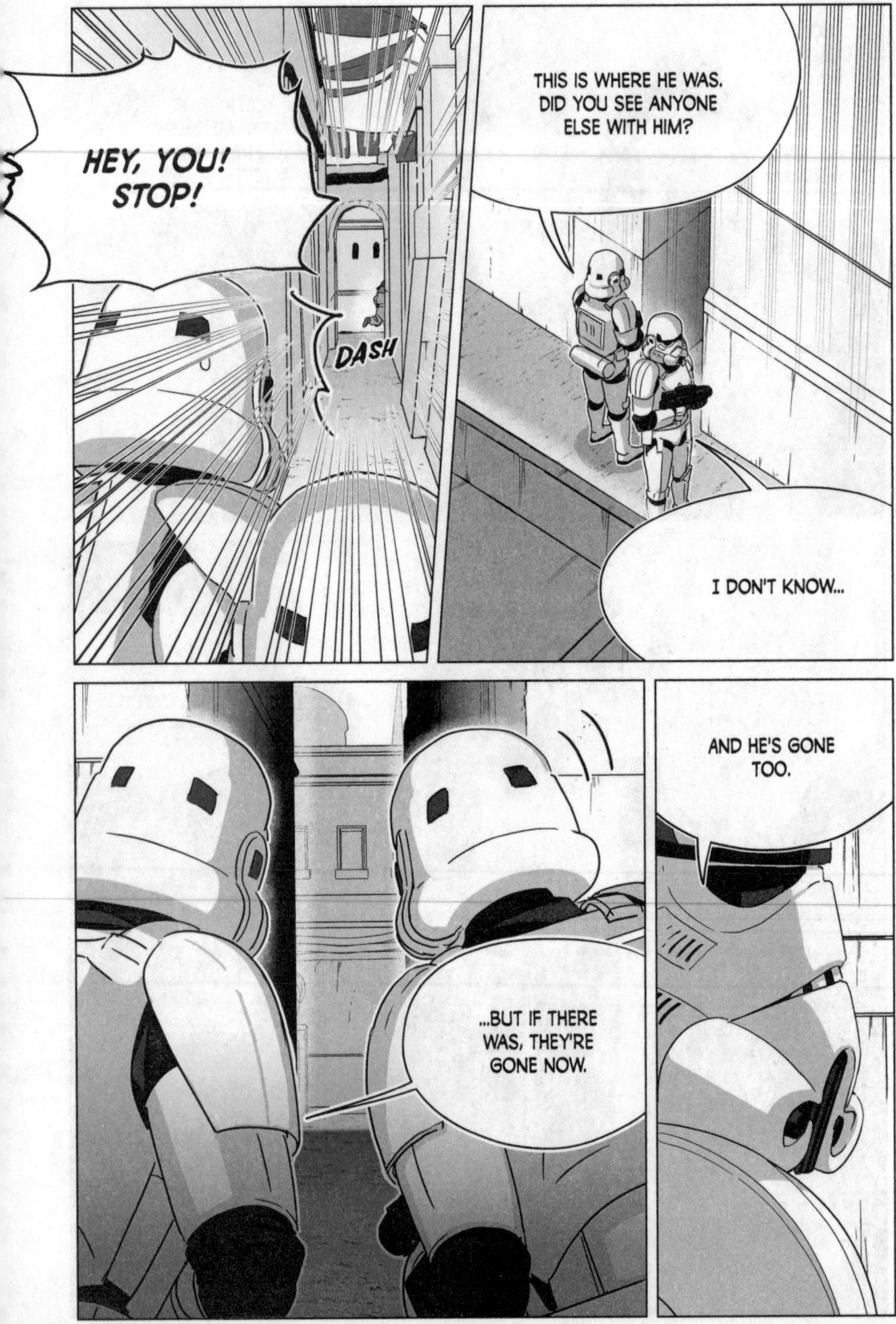
HEY, YOU! STOP!
DASH
THIS IS WHERE HE WAS. DID YOU SEE ANYONE ELSE WITH HIM?
I DON'T KNOW...
...BUT IF THERE WAS, THEY'RE GONE NOW.
AND HE'S GONE TOO.

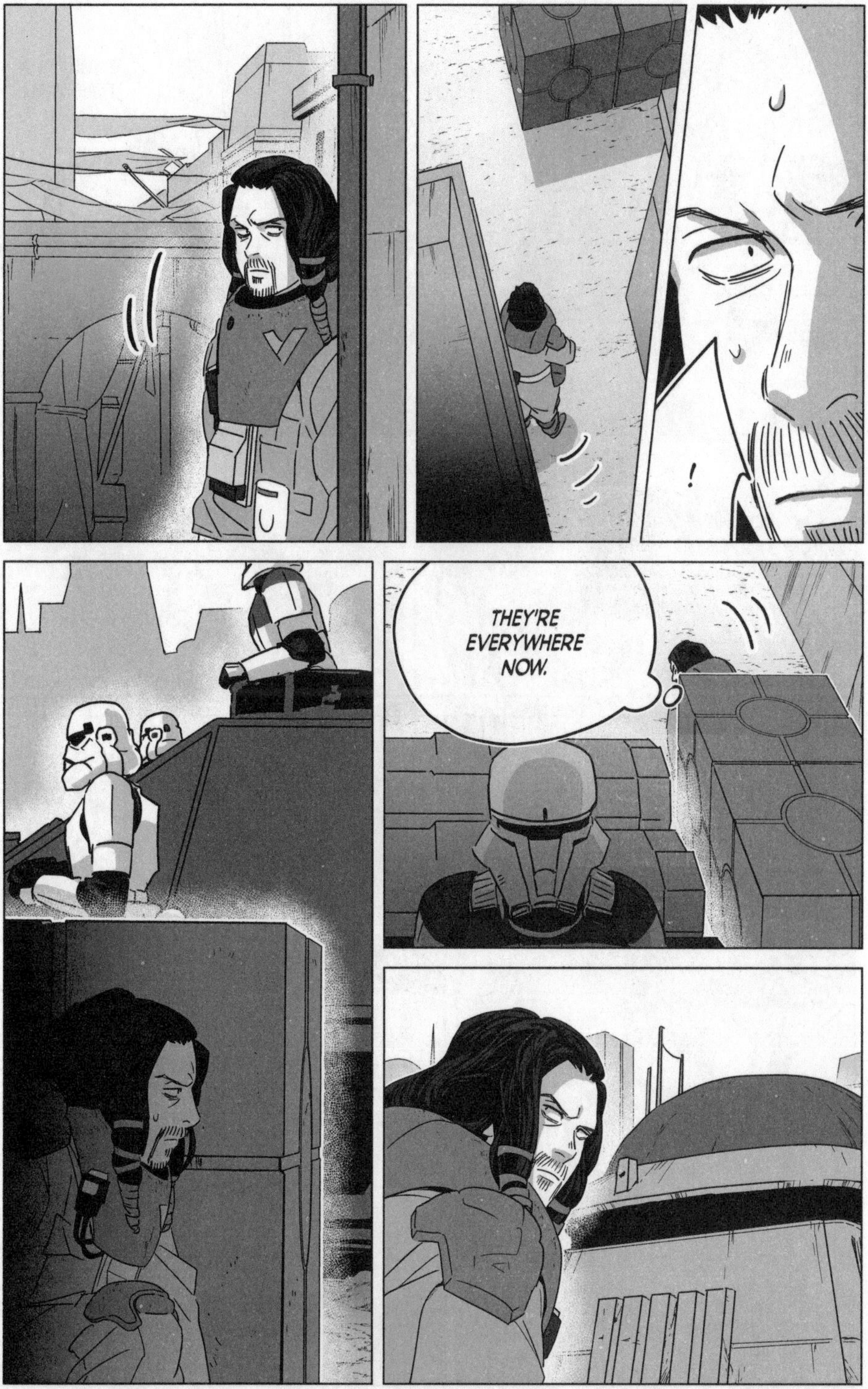
THEY'RE EVERYWHERE NOW.

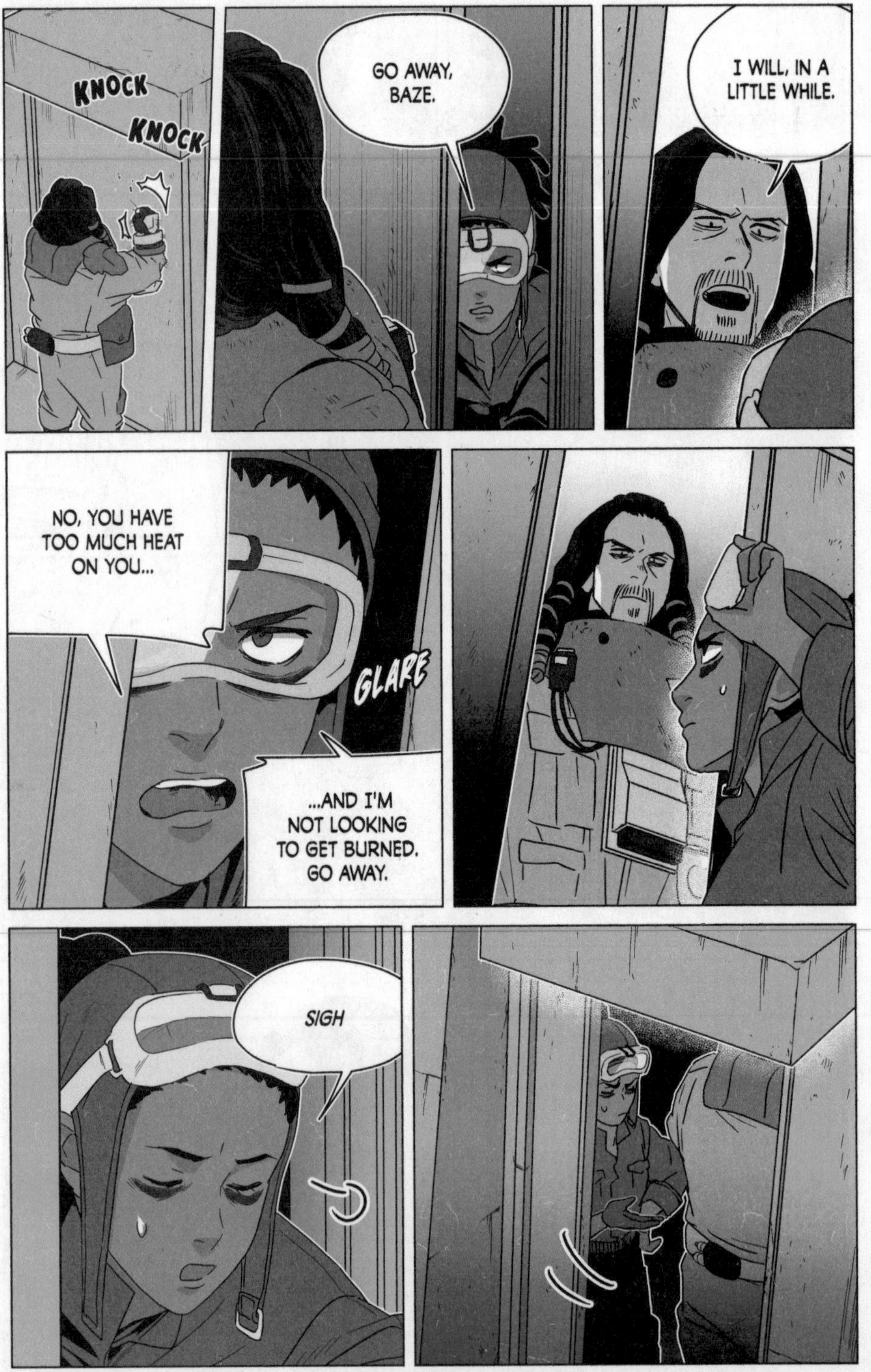
KNOCK
KNOCK
GO AWAY, BAZE.
I WILL, IN A LITTLE WHILE.
NO, YOU HAVE TOO MUCH HEAT ON YOU...
GLARE
...AND I'M NOT LOOKING TO GET BURNED. GO AWAY.
SIGH

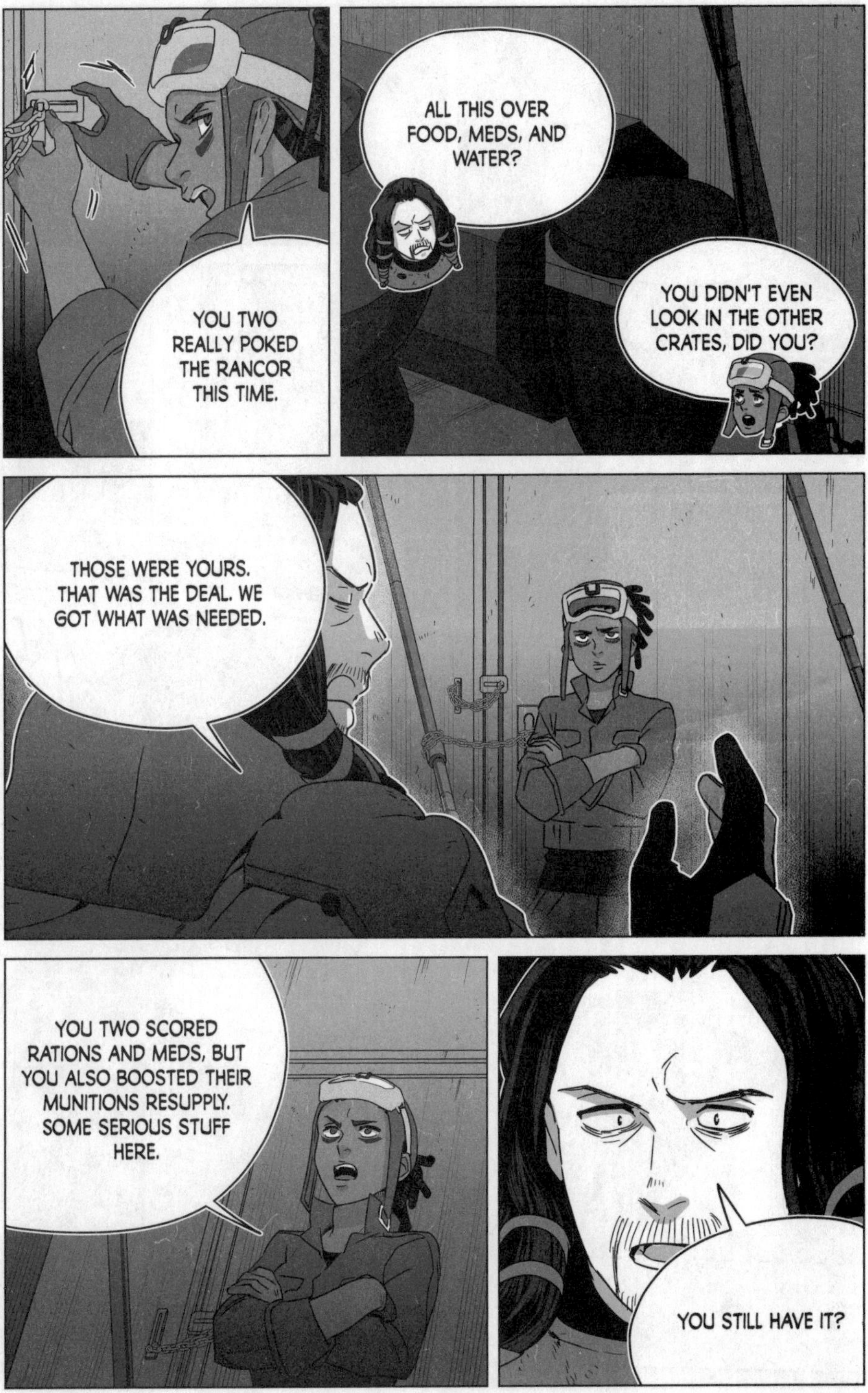
YOU TWO REALLY POKED THE RANCOR THIS TIME.
ALL THIS OVER FOOD, MEDS, AND WATER?
YOU DIDN'T EVEN LOOK IN THE OTHER CRATES, DID YOU?
THOSE WERE YOURS. THAT WAS THE DEAL. WE GOT WHAT WAS NEEDED.
YOU TWO SCORED RATIONS AND MEDS, BUT YOU ALSO BOOSTED THEIR MUNITIONS RESUPPLY. SOME SERIOUS STUFF HERE.
YOU STILL HAVE IT?

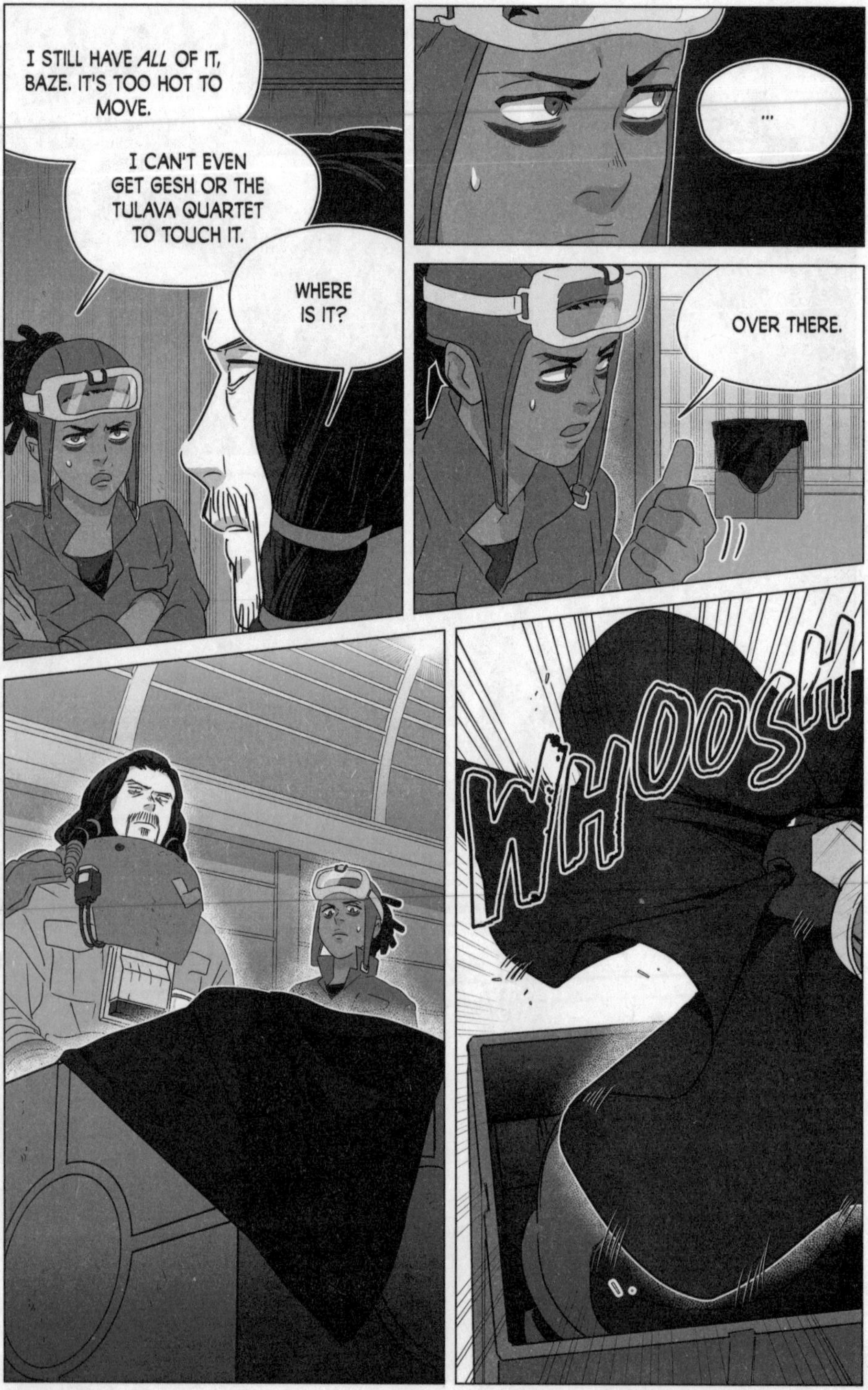
I STILL HAVE *ALL* OF IT, BAZE. IT'S TOO HOT TO MOVE.
I CAN'T EVEN GET GESH OR THE TULAVA QUARTET TO TOUCH IT.
WHERE IS IT?
...
OVER THERE.
WHOOSH

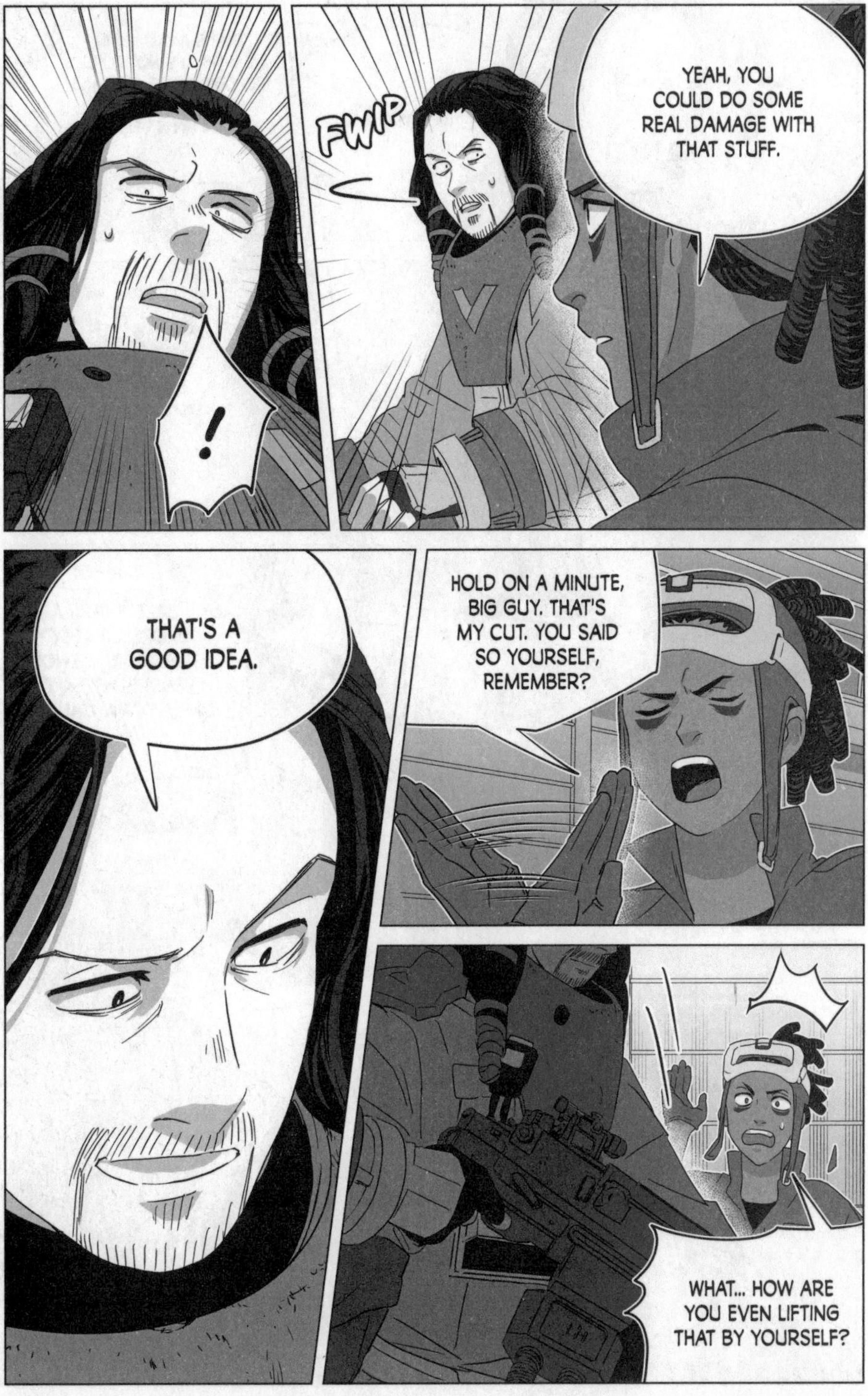
!
FWIP
YEAH, YOU COULD DO SOME REAL DAMAGE WITH THAT STUFF.
THAT'S A GOOD IDEA.
HOLD ON A MINUTE, BIG GUY. THAT'S MY CUT. YOU SAID SO YOURSELF, REMEMBER?
WHAT... HOW ARE YOU EVEN LIFTING THAT BY YOURSELF?

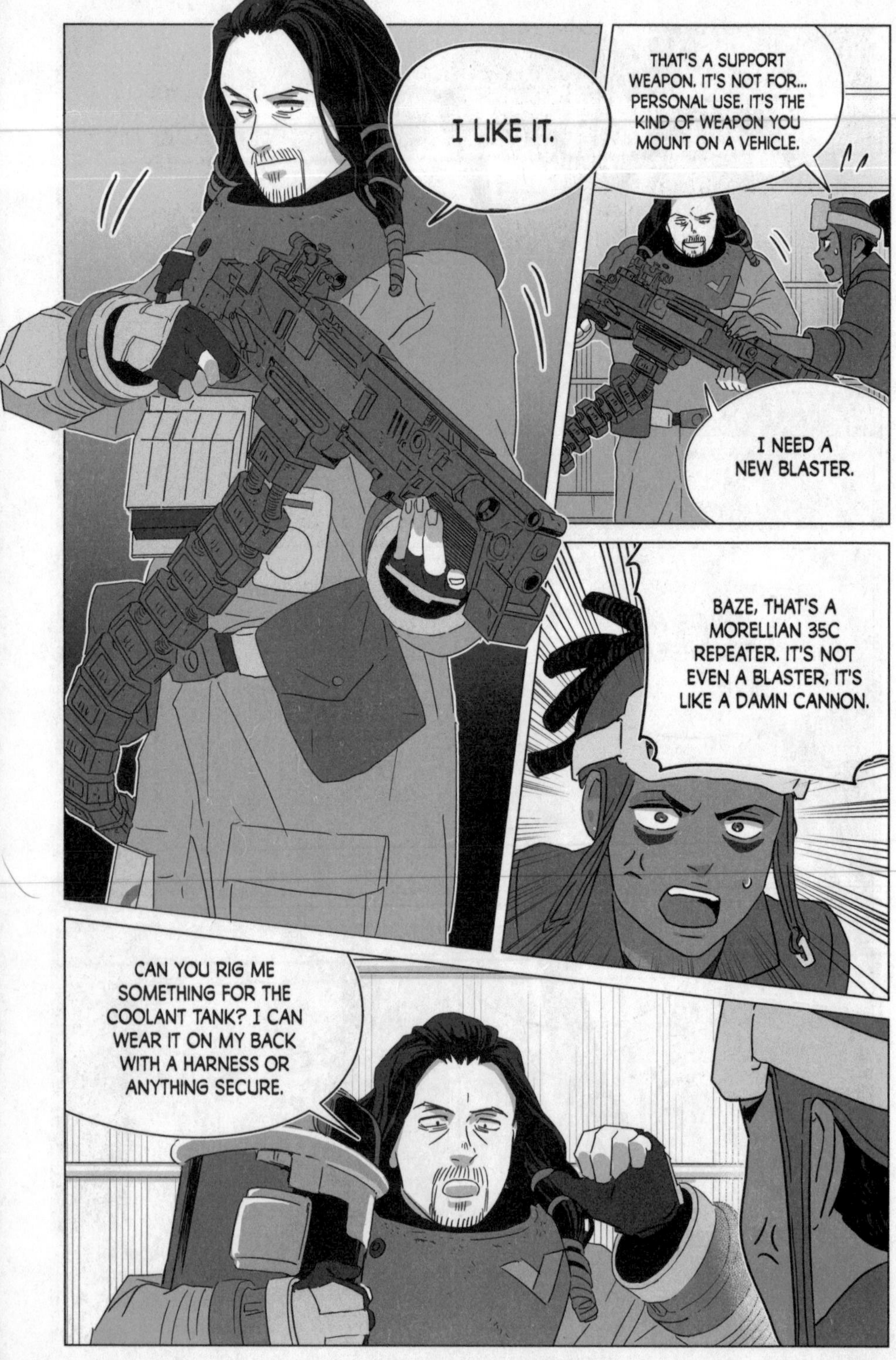
I LIKE IT.
THAT'S A SUPPORT WEAPON. IT'S NOT FOR... PERSONAL USE. IT'S THE KIND OF WEAPON YOU MOUNT ON A VEHICLE.
I NEED A NEW BLASTER.
BAZE, THAT'S A MORELLIAN 35C REPEATER. IT'S NOT EVEN A BLASTER, IT'S LIKE A DAMN CANNON.
CAN YOU RIG ME SOMETHING FOR THE COOLANT TANK? I CAN WEAR IT ON MY BACK WITH A HARNESS OR ANYTHING SECURE.

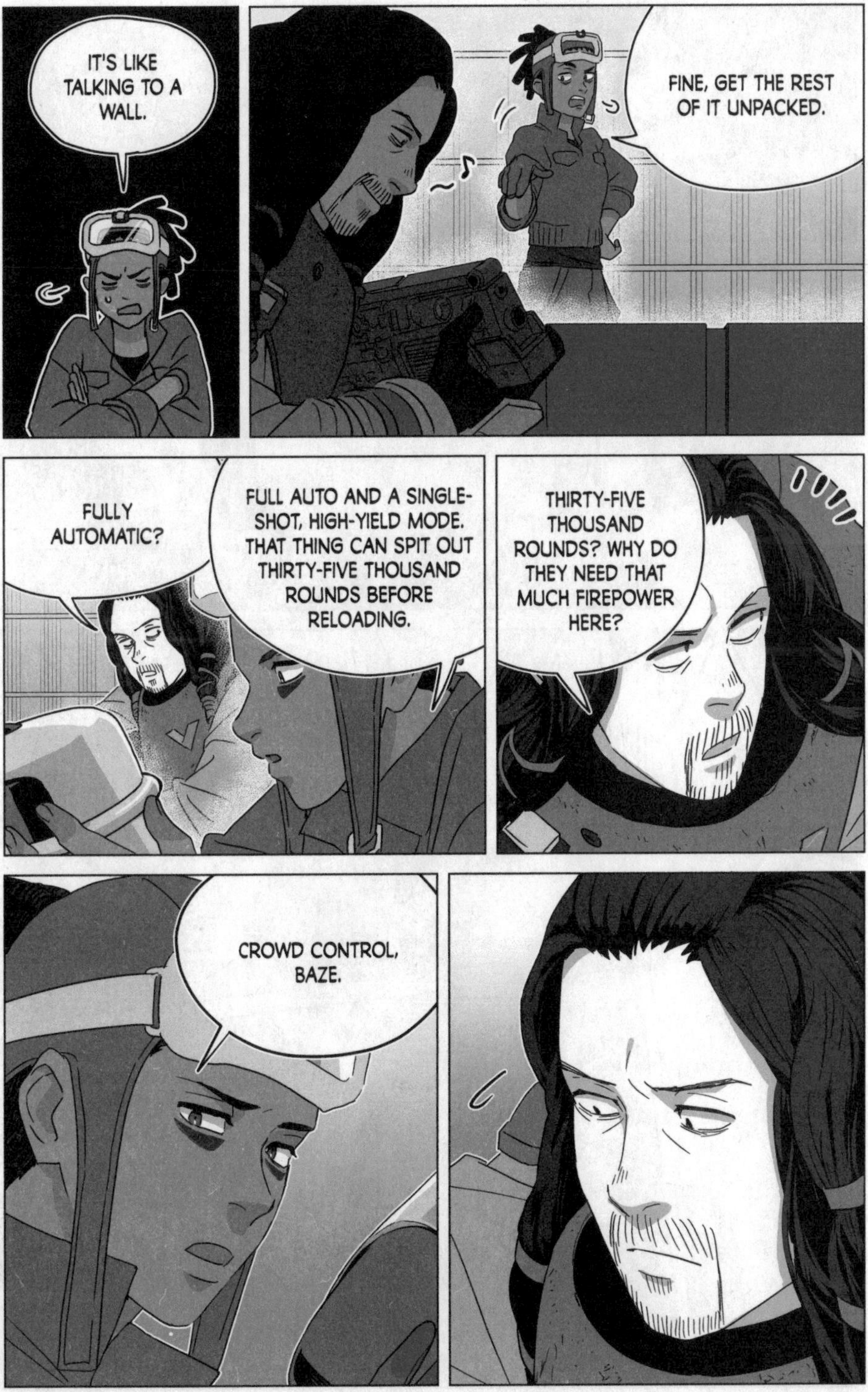
IT'S LIKE TALKING TO A WALL.
FINE, GET THE REST OF IT UNPACKED.
FULLY AUTOMATIC?
FULL AUTO AND A SINGLE-SHOT, HIGH-YIELD MODE. THAT THING CAN SPIT OUT THIRTY-FIVE THOUSAND ROUNDS BEFORE RELOADING.
THIRTY-FIVE THOUSAND ROUNDS? WHY DO THEY NEED THAT MUCH FIREPOWER HERE?
CROWD CONTROL, BAZE.

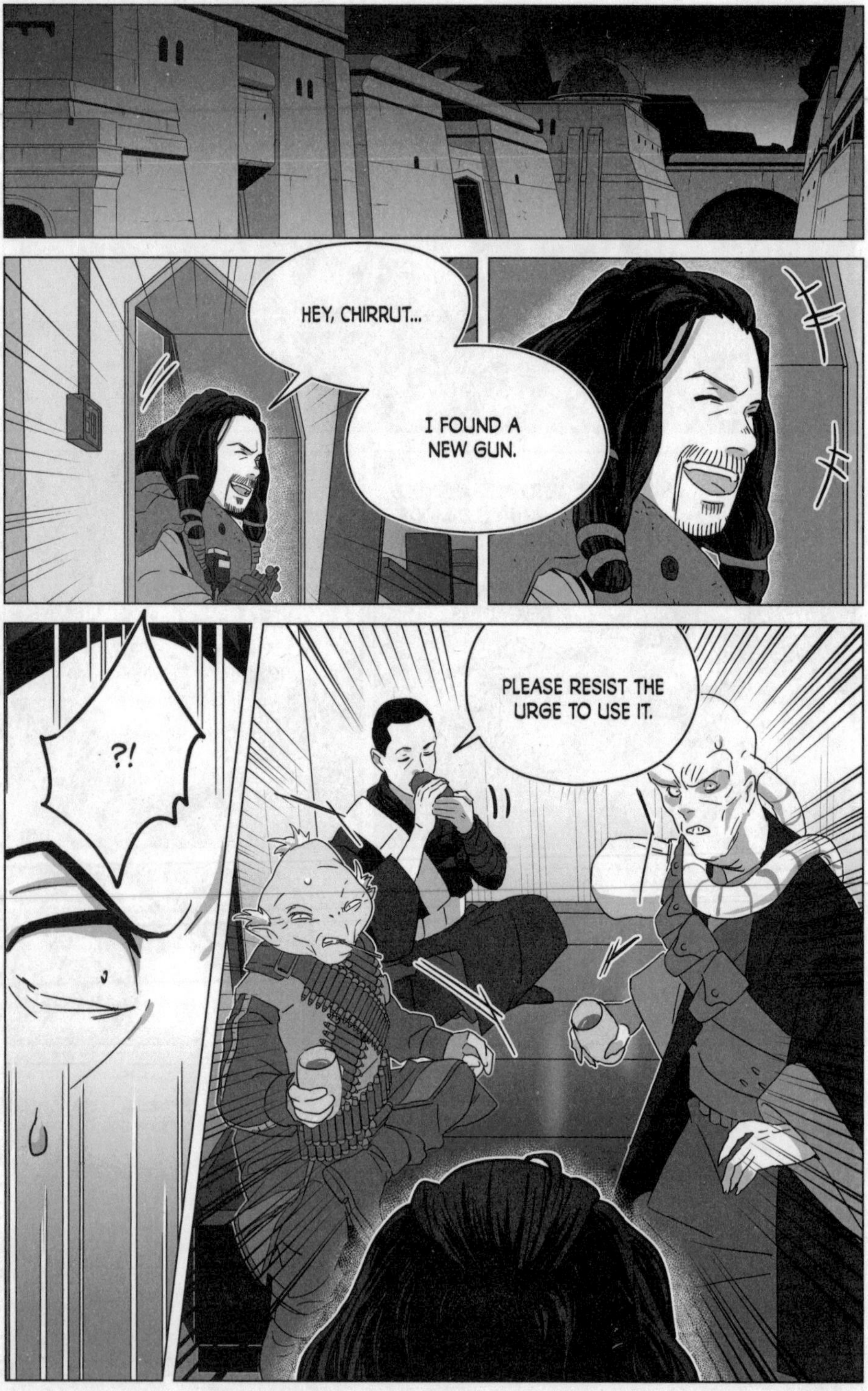

HEY, CHIRRUT...
I FOUND A NEW GUN.
?!
PLEASE RESIST THE URGE TO USE IT.

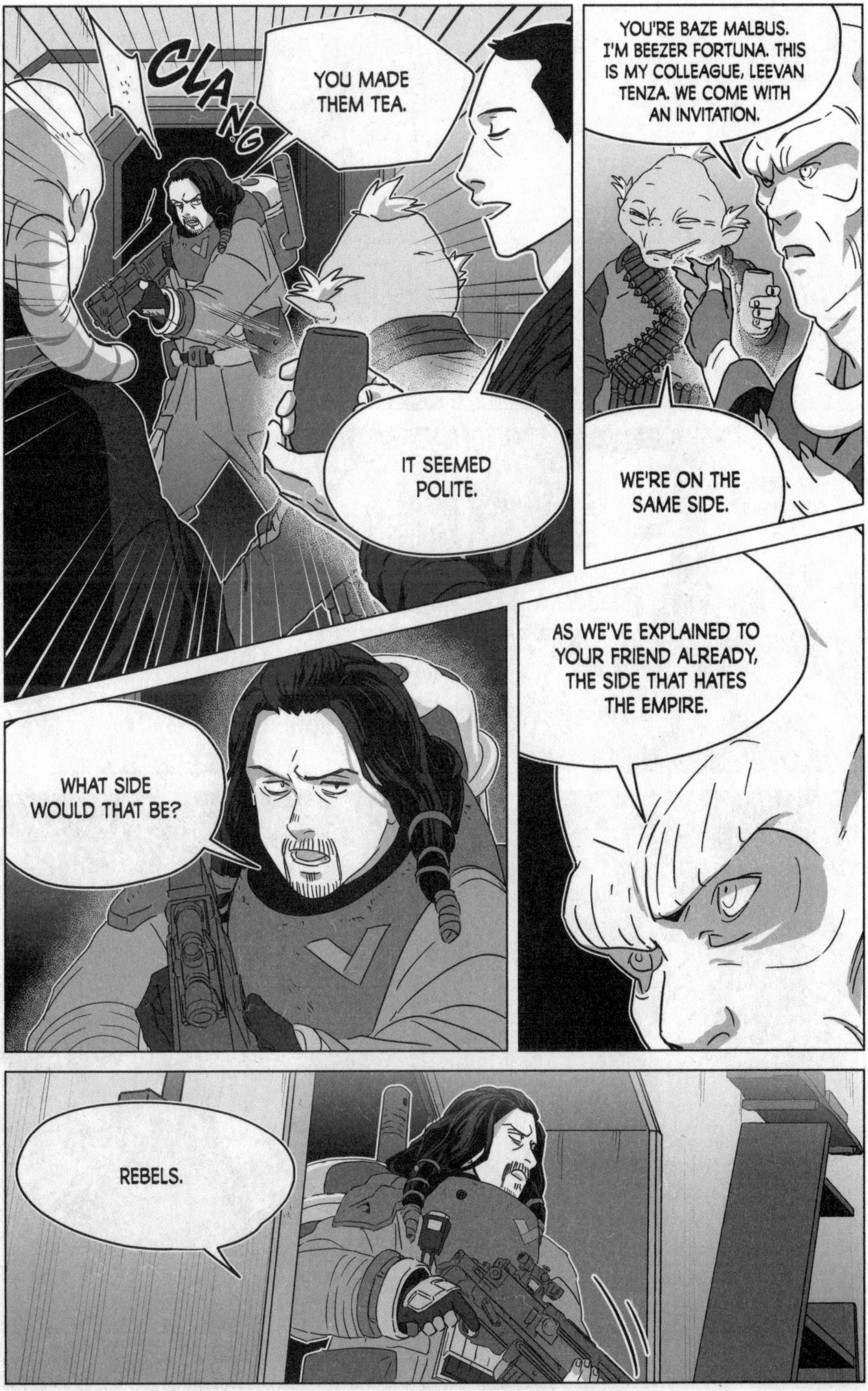
CLANG
YOU MADE THEM TEA.
IT SEEMED POLITE.
YOU'RE BAZE MALBUS. I'M BEEZER FORTUNA. THIS IS MY COLLEAGUE, LEEVAN TENZA. WE COME WITH AN INVITATION.
WE'RE ON THE SAME SIDE.
WHAT SIDE WOULD THAT BE?
AS WE'VE EXPLAINED TO YOUR FRIEND ALREADY, THE SIDE THAT HATES THE EMPIRE.
REBELS.

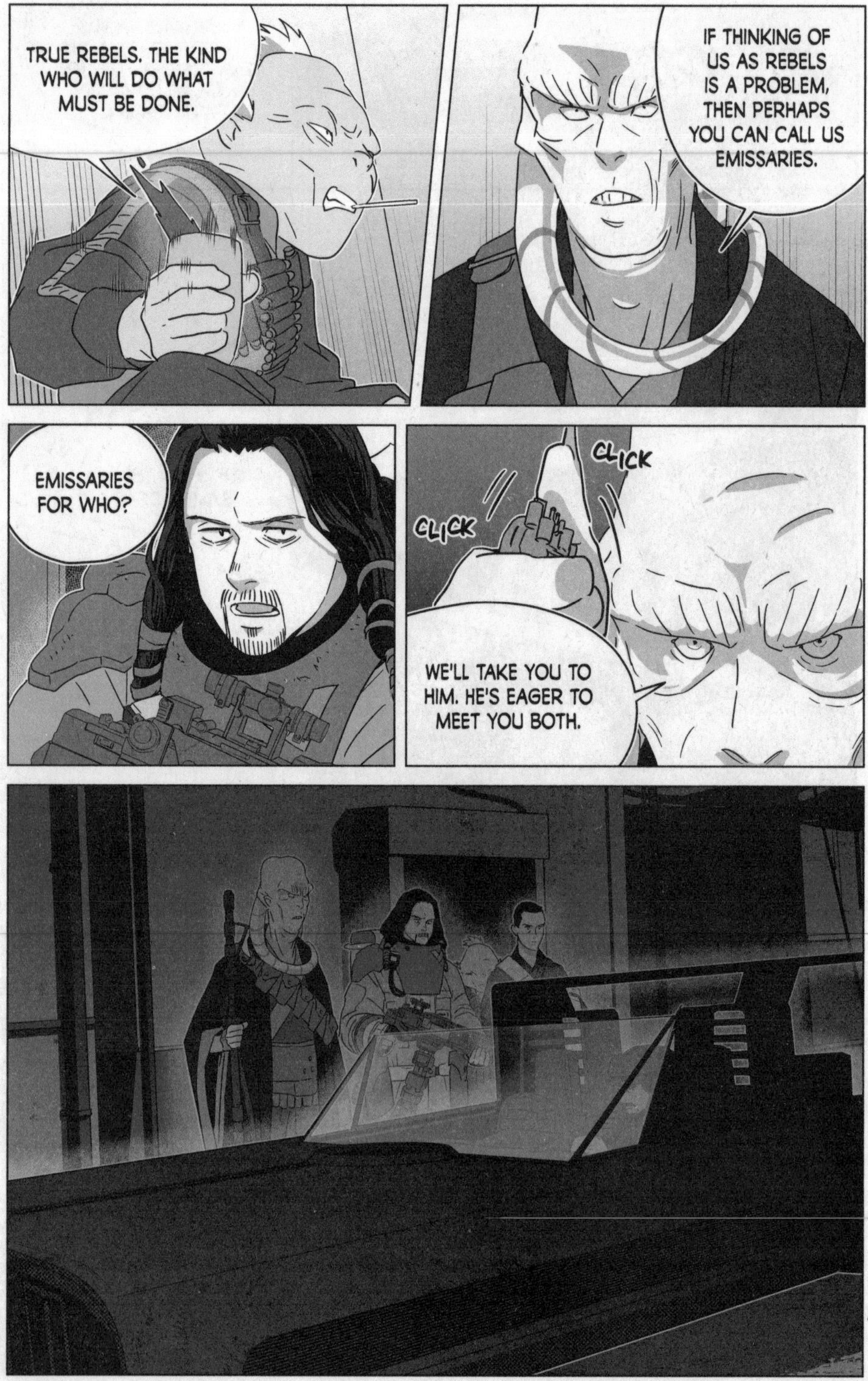
TRUE REBELS. THE KIND WHO WILL DO WHAT MUST BE DONE.
IF THINKING OF US AS REBELS IS A PROBLEM, THEN PERHAPS YOU CAN CALL US EMISSARIES.
EMISSARIES FOR WHO?
CLICK
CLICK
WE'LL TAKE YOU TO HIM. HE'S EAGER TO MEET YOU BOTH.

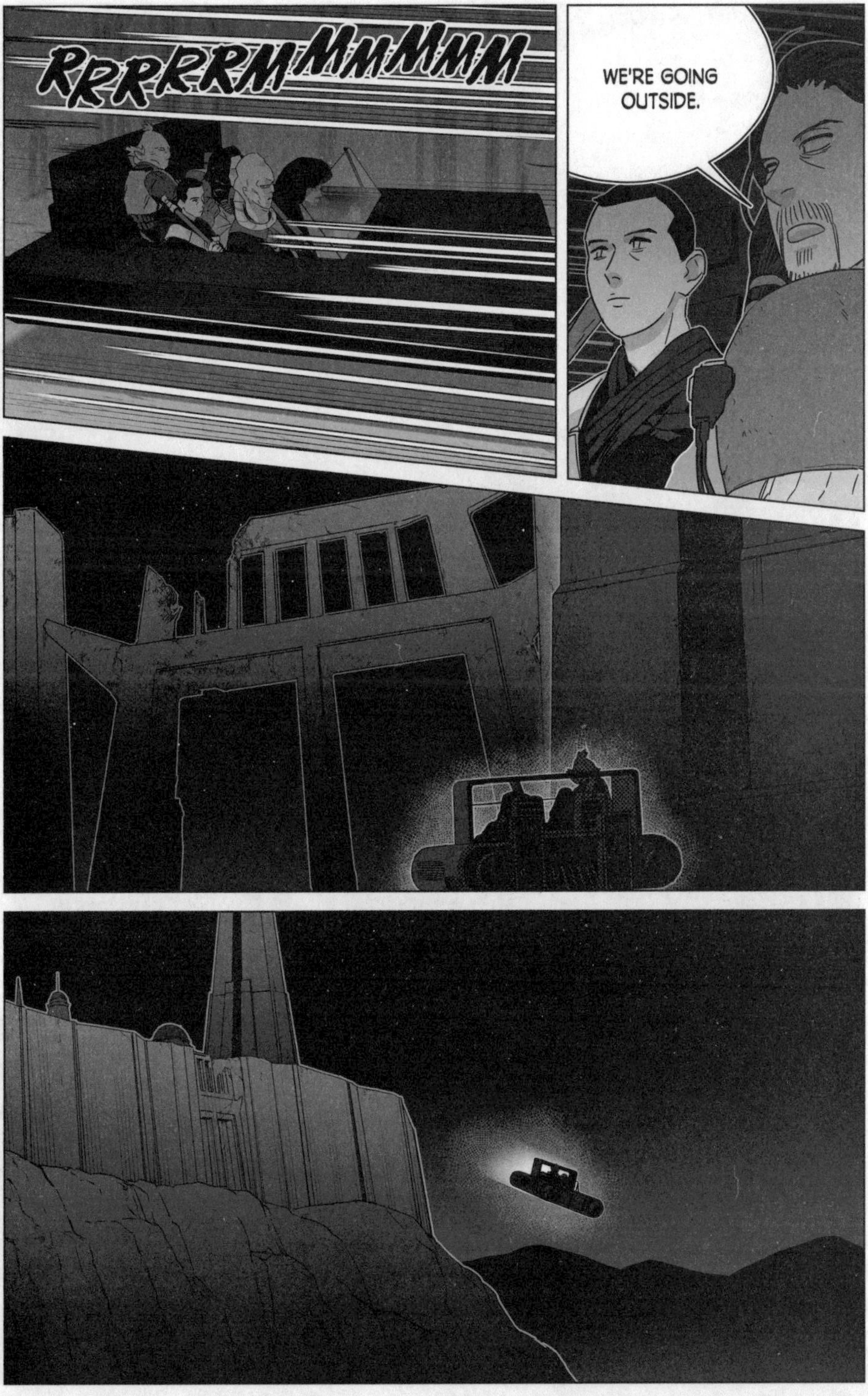
RRRRRMMMMMM
WE'RE GOING OUTSIDE.

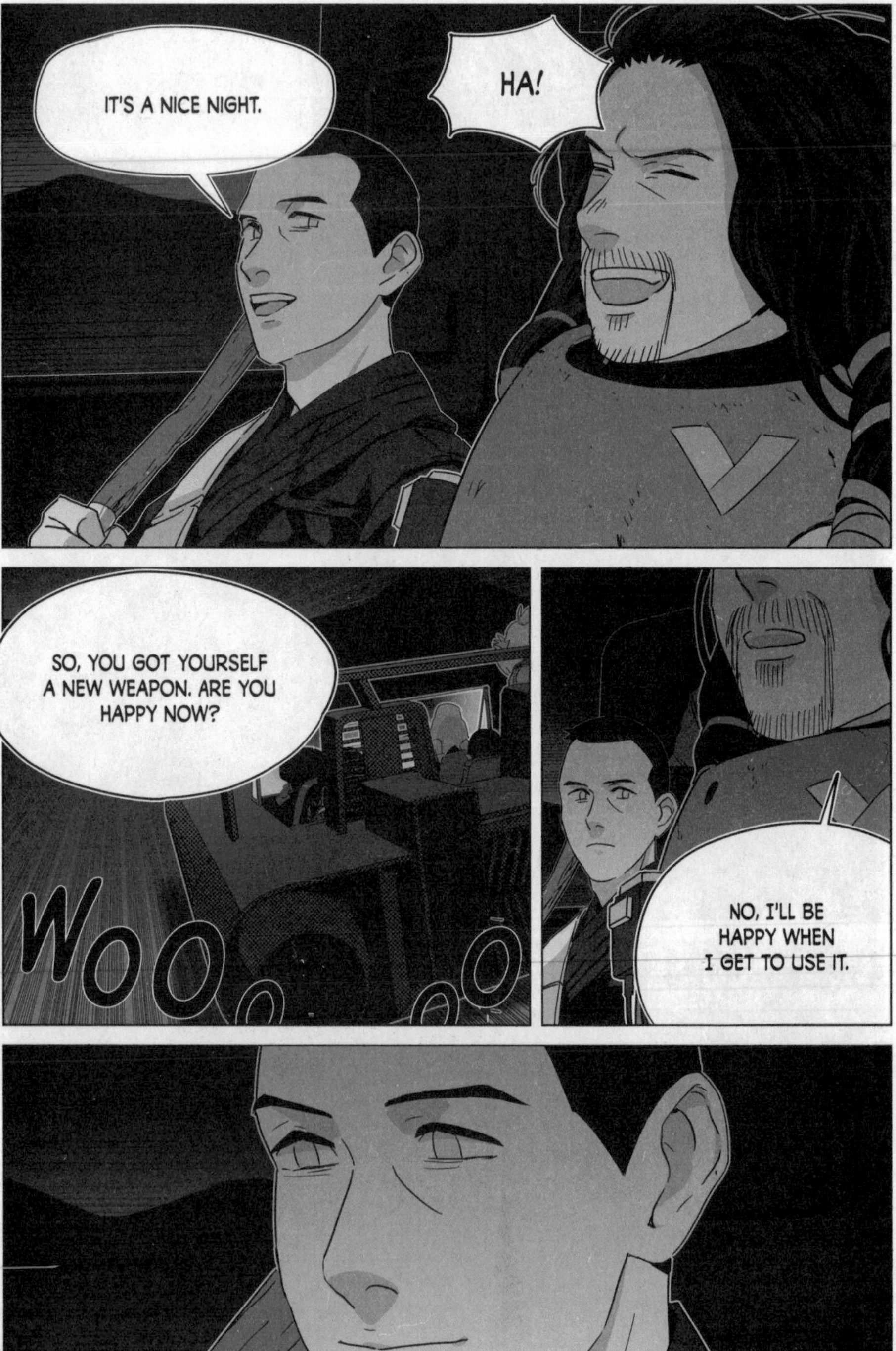
IT'S A NICE NIGHT.
HA!
SO, YOU GOT YOURSELF A NEW WEAPON. ARE YOU HAPPY NOW?
WOOOOO
NO, I'LL BE HAPPY WHEN I GET TO USE IT.

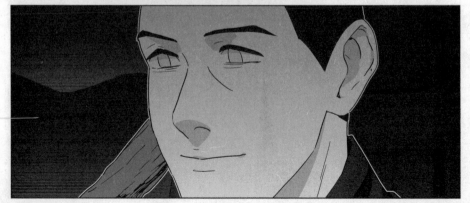

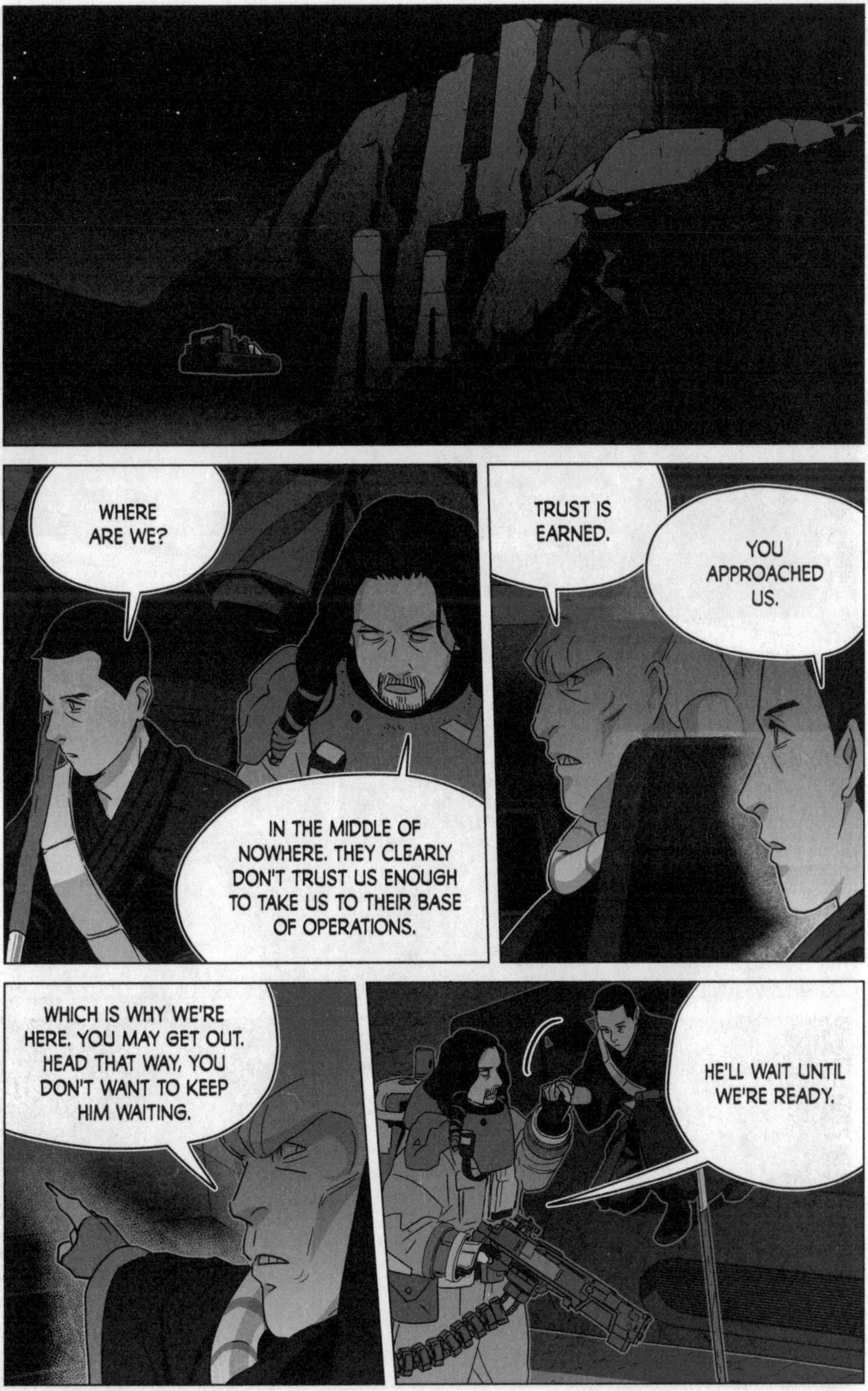
WHERE ARE WE?
IN THE MIDDLE OF NOWHERE. THEY CLEARLY DON'T TRUST US ENOUGH TO TAKE US TO THEIR BASE OF OPERATIONS.
TRUST IS EARNED.
YOU APPROACHED US.
WHICH IS WHY WE'RE HERE. YOU MAY GET OUT. HEAD THAT WAY, YOU DON'T WANT TO KEEP HIM WAITING.
HE'LL WAIT UNTIL WE'RE READY.

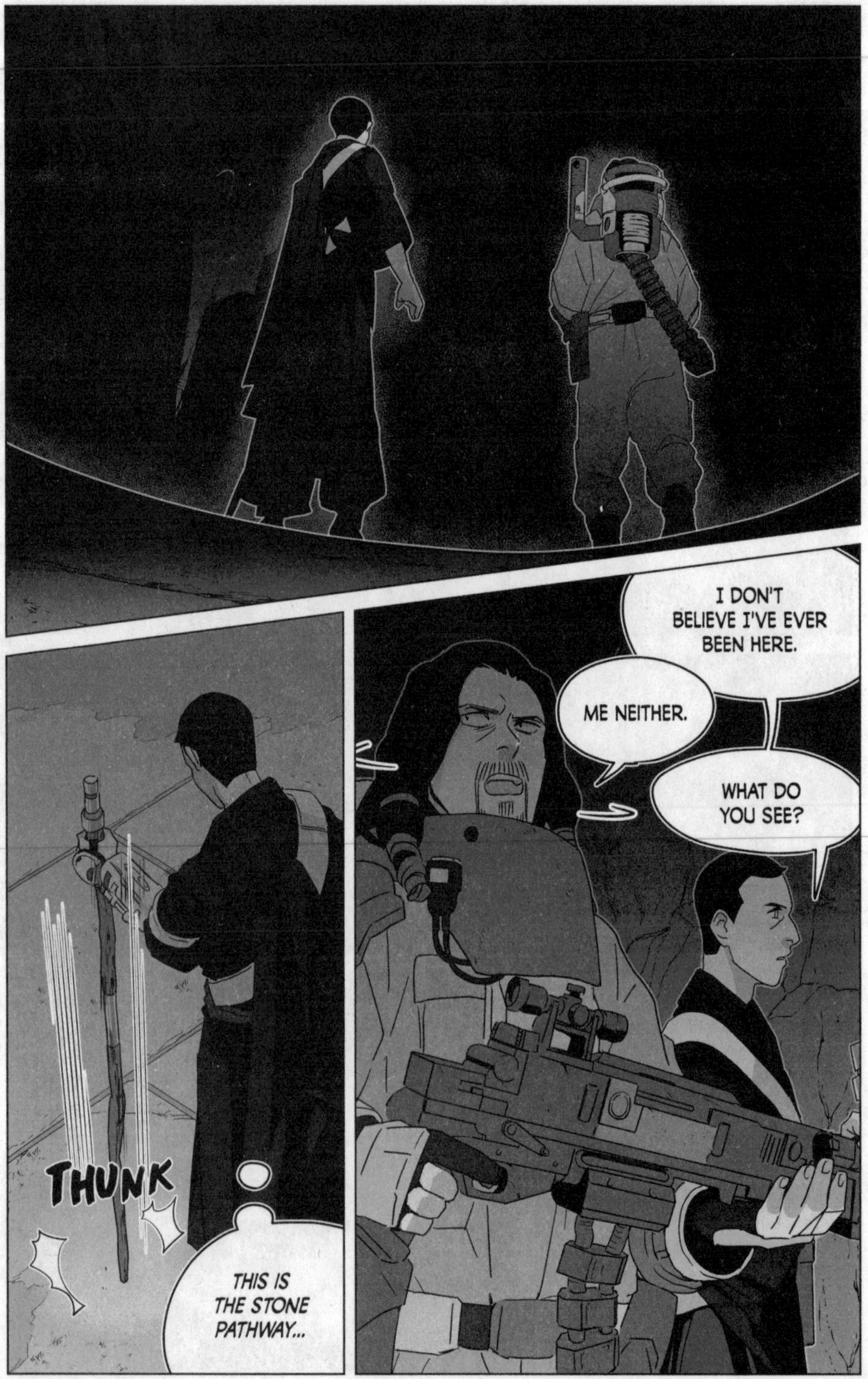
THUNK
THIS IS THE STONE PATHWAY...
I DON'T BELIEVE I'VE EVER BEEN HERE.
ME NEITHER.
WHAT DO YOU SEE?

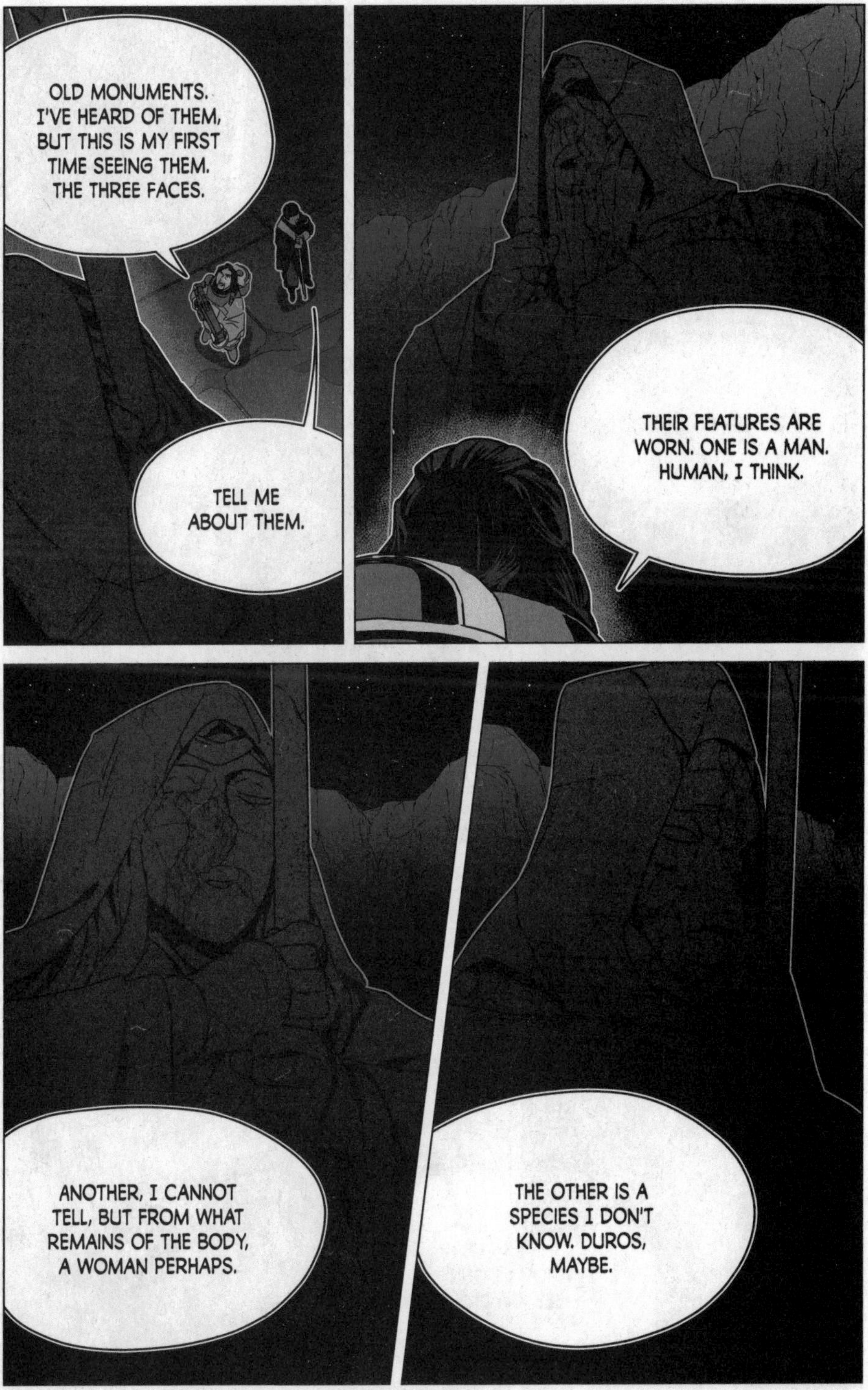
OLD MONUMENTS. I'VE HEARD OF THEM, BUT THIS IS MY FIRST TIME SEEING THEM. THE THREE FACES.
TELL ME ABOUT THEM.
THEIR FEATURES ARE WORN. ONE IS A MAN. HUMAN, I THINK.
ANOTHER, I CANNOT TELL, BUT FROM WHAT REMAINS OF THE BODY, A WOMAN PERHAPS.
THE OTHER IS A SPECIES I DON'T KNOW. DUROS, MAYBE.

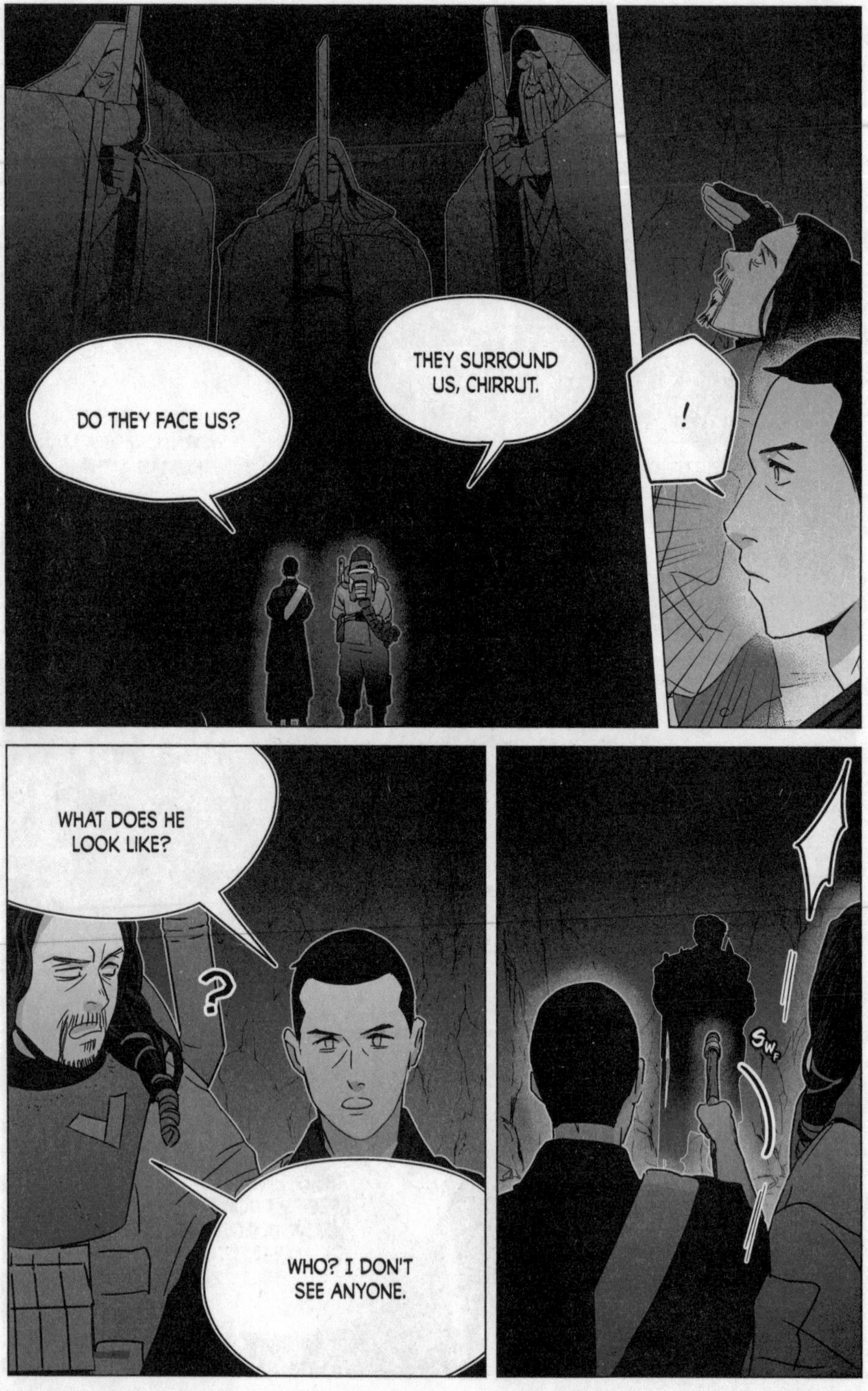
DO THEY FACE US?
THEY SURROUND US, CHIRRUT.
!
WHAT DOES HE LOOK LIKE?
?
WHO? I DON'T SEE ANYONE.
SWF

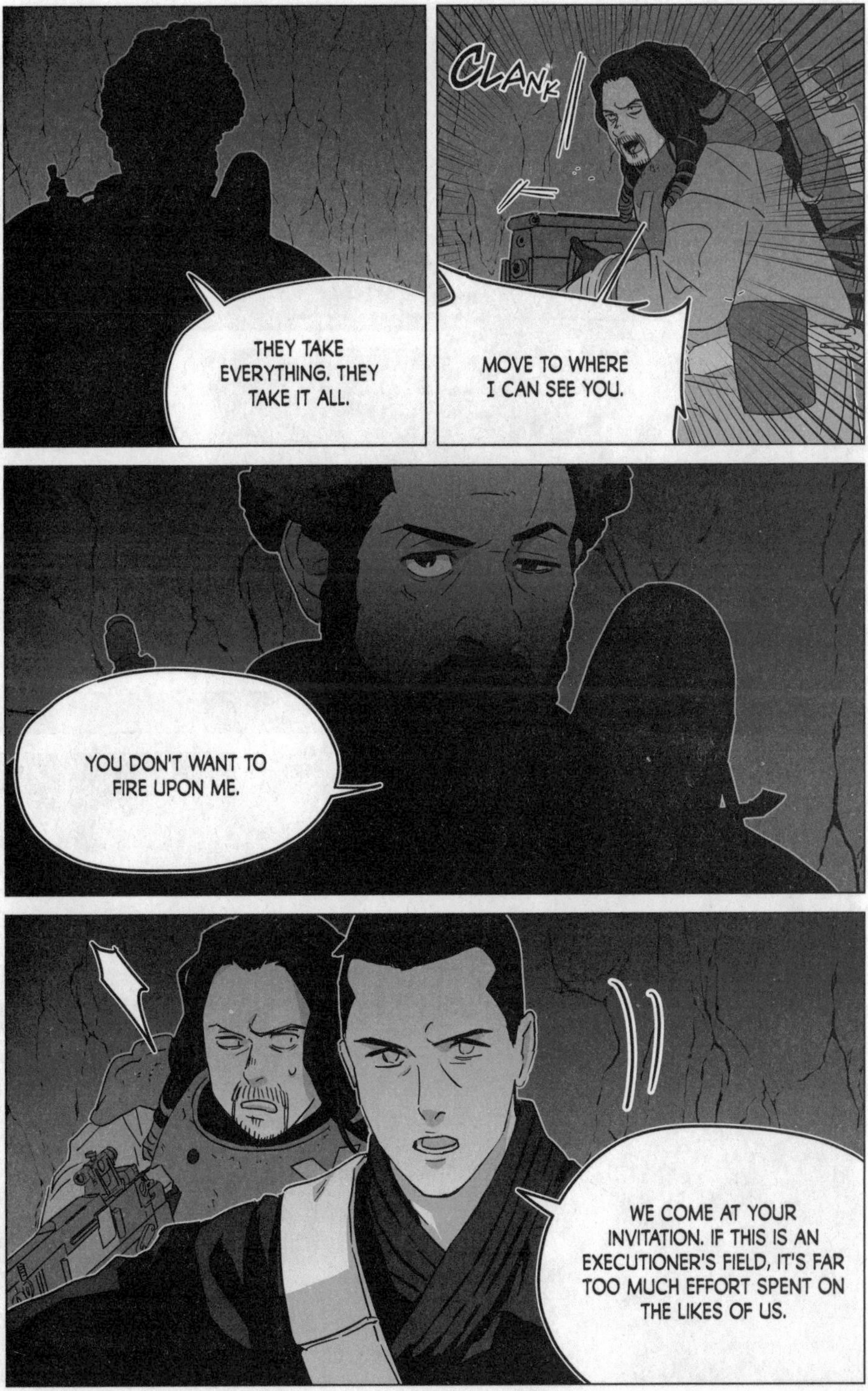
THEY TAKE EVERYTHING. THEY TAKE IT ALL.
CLANK
MOVE TO WHERE I CAN SEE YOU.
YOU DON'T WANT TO FIRE UPON ME.
WE COME AT YOUR INVITATION. IF THIS IS AN EXECUTIONER'S FIELD, IT'S FAR TOO MUCH EFFORT SPENT ON THE LIKES OF US.

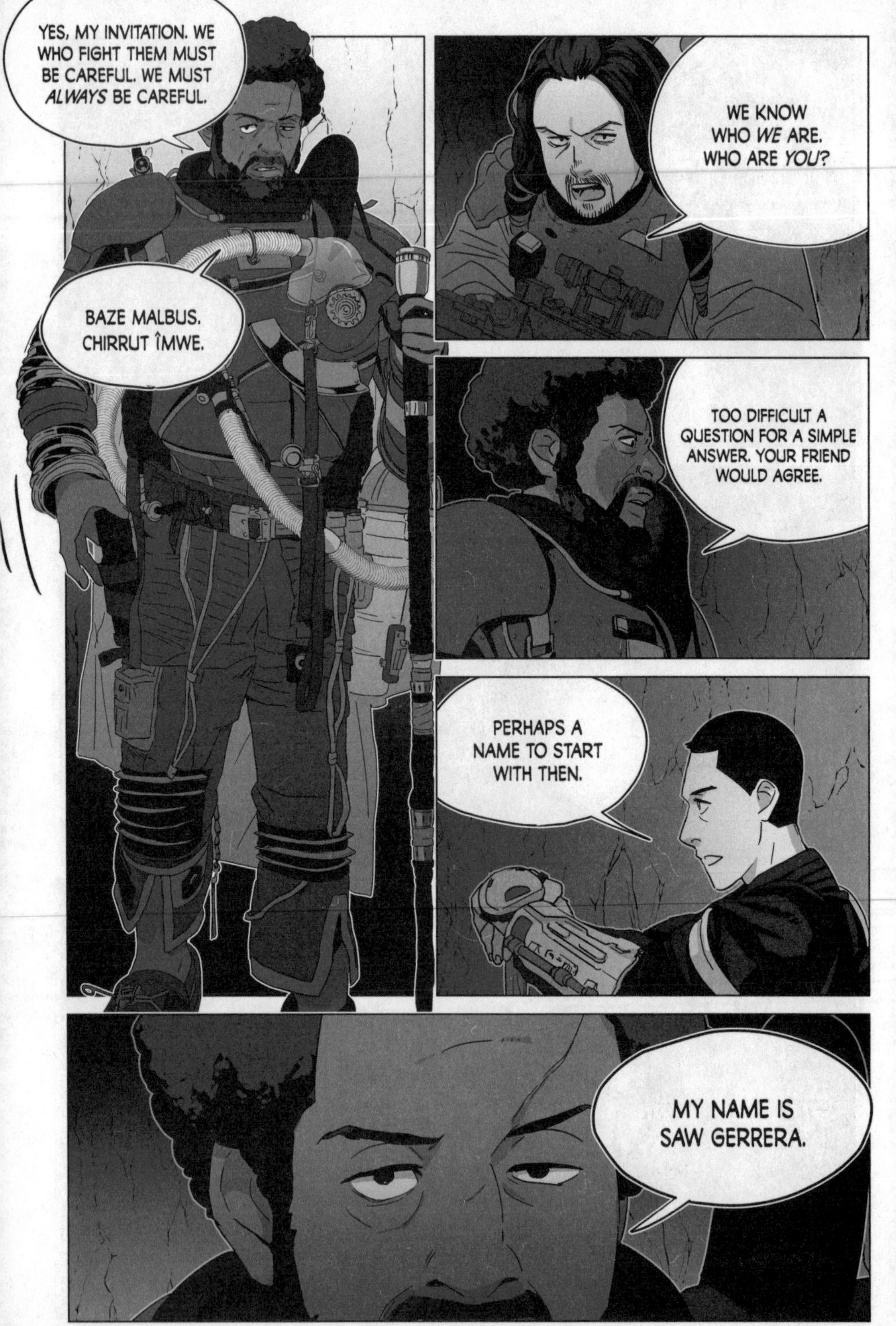
YES, MY INVITATION. WE WHO FIGHT THEM MUST BE CAREFUL. WE MUST *ALWAYS* BE CAREFUL.
BAZE MALBUS. CHIRRUT ÎMWE.
WE KNOW WHO *WE* ARE. WHO ARE *YOU*?
TOO DIFFICULT A QUESTION FOR A SIMPLE ANSWER. YOUR FRIEND WOULD AGREE.
PERHAPS A NAME TO START WITH THEN.
MY NAME IS SAW GERRERA.

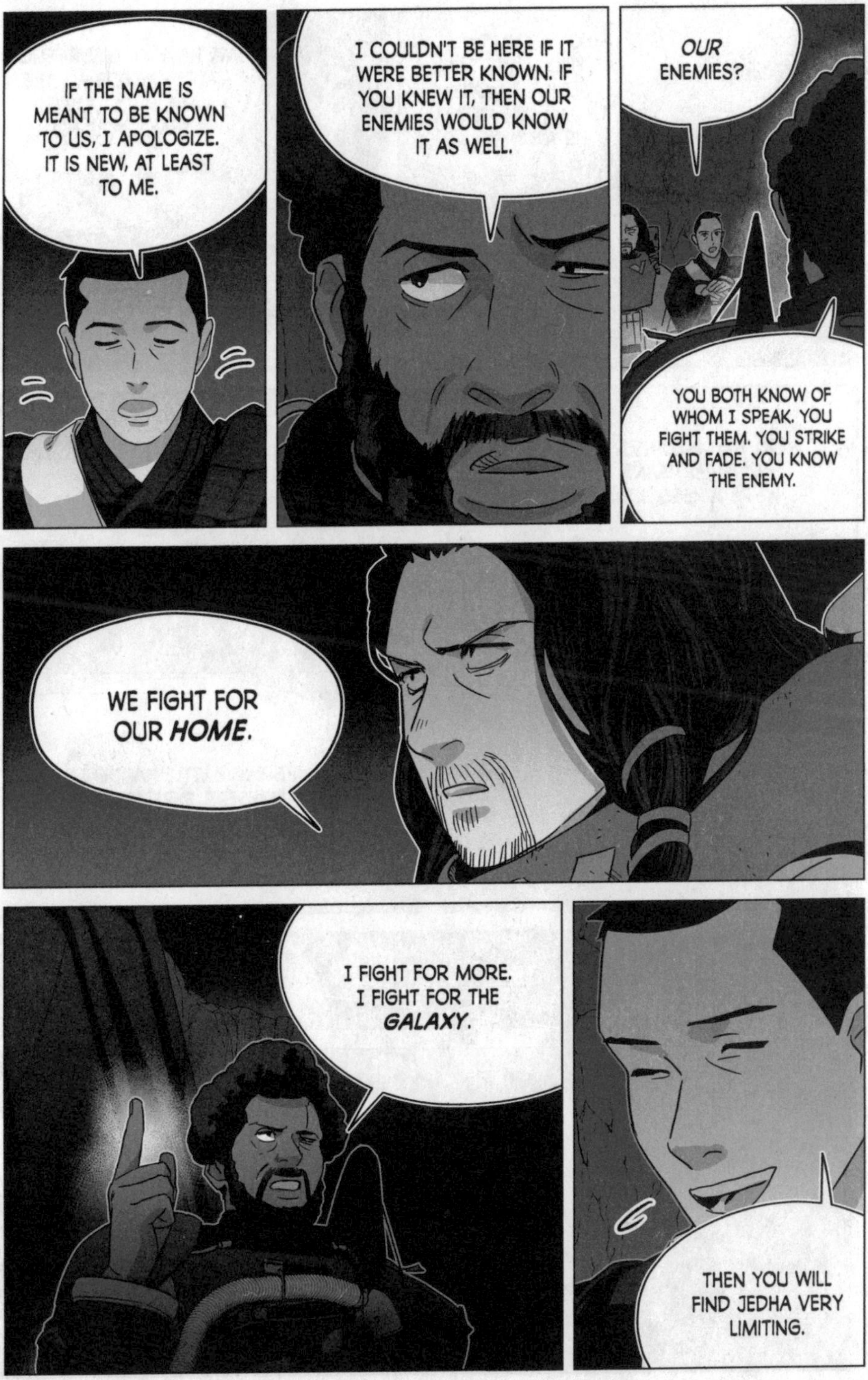
IF THE NAME IS MEANT TO BE KNOWN TO US, I APOLOGIZE. IT IS NEW, AT LEAST TO ME.
I COULDN'T BE HERE IF IT WERE BETTER KNOWN. IF YOU KNEW IT, THEN OUR ENEMIES WOULD KNOW IT AS WELL.
OUR ENEMIES?
YOU BOTH KNOW OF WHOM I SPEAK. YOU FIGHT THEM. YOU STRIKE AND FADE. YOU KNOW THE ENEMY.
WE FIGHT FOR OUR ***HOME***.
I FIGHT FOR MORE. I FIGHT FOR THE ***GALAXY***.
THEN YOU WILL FIND JEDHA VERY LIMITING.

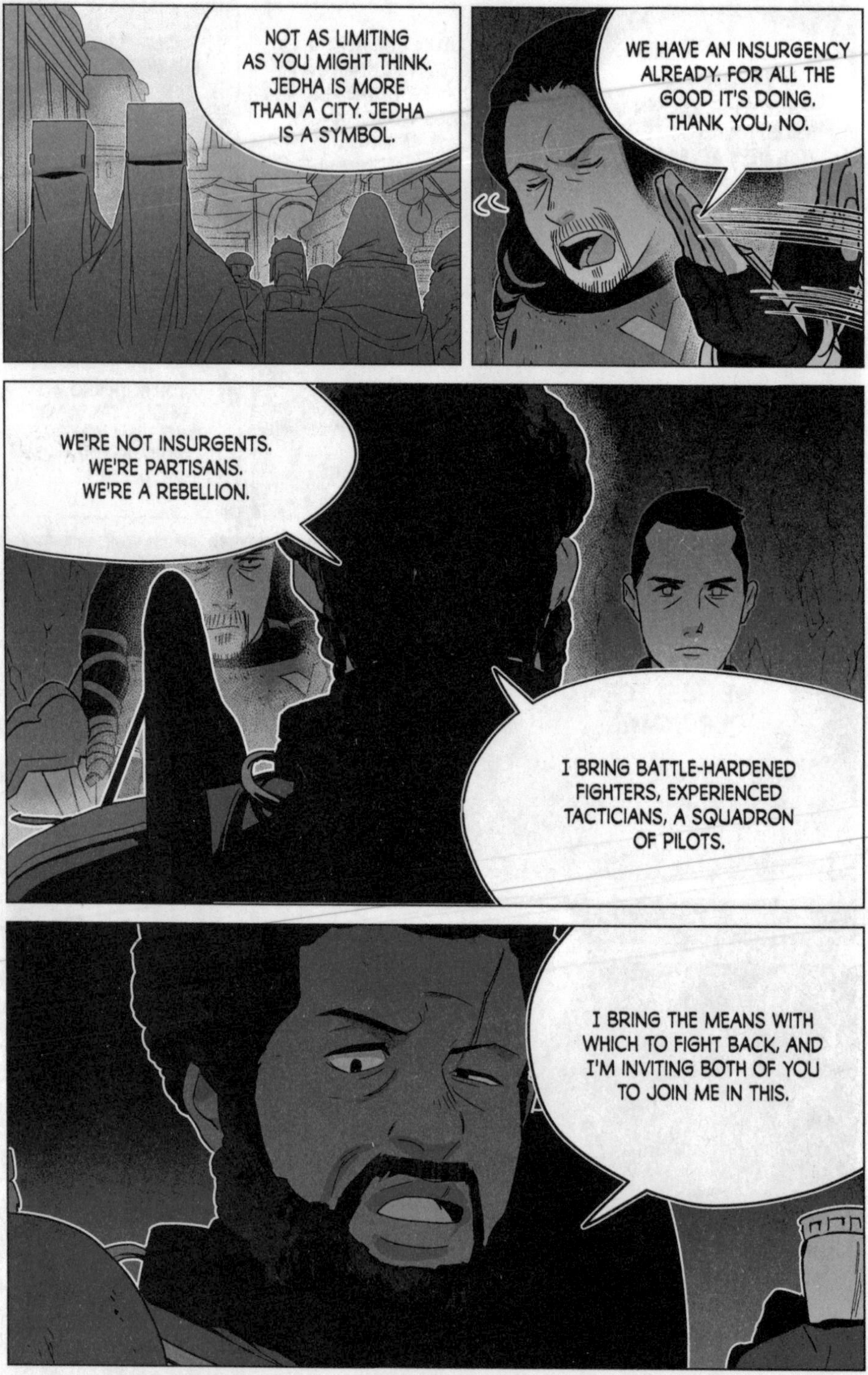
NOT AS LIMITING AS YOU MIGHT THINK. JEDHA IS MORE THAN A CITY. JEDHA IS A SYMBOL.
WE HAVE AN INSURGENCY ALREADY. FOR ALL THE GOOD IT'S DOING. THANK YOU, NO.
WE'RE NOT INSURGENTS. WE'RE PARTISANS. WE'RE A REBELLION.
I BRING BATTLE-HARDENED FIGHTERS, EXPERIENCED TACTICIANS, A SQUADRON OF PILOTS.
I BRING THE MEANS WITH WHICH TO FIGHT BACK, AND I'M INVITING BOTH OF YOU TO JOIN ME IN THIS.

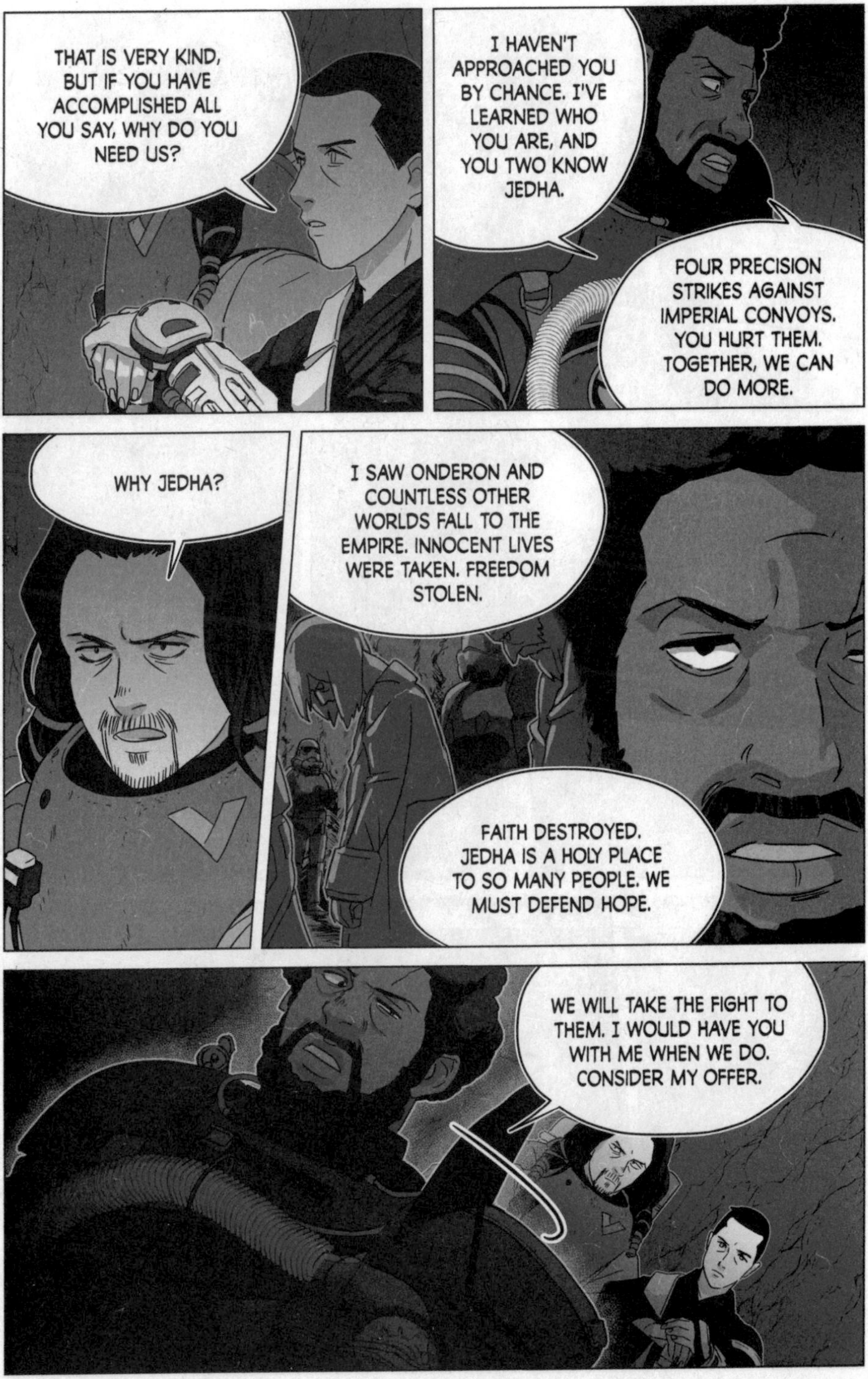
THAT IS VERY KIND, BUT IF YOU HAVE ACCOMPLISHED ALL YOU SAY, WHY DO YOU NEED US?
I HAVEN'T APPROACHED YOU BY CHANCE. I'VE LEARNED WHO YOU ARE, AND YOU TWO KNOW JEDHA.
FOUR PRECISION STRIKES AGAINST IMPERIAL CONVOYS. YOU HURT THEM. TOGETHER, WE CAN DO MORE.
WHY JEDHA?
I SAW ONDERON AND COUNTLESS OTHER WORLDS FALL TO THE EMPIRE. INNOCENT LIVES WERE TAKEN. FREEDOM STOLEN.
FAITH DESTROYED. JEDHA IS A HOLY PLACE TO SO MANY PEOPLE. WE MUST DEFEND HOPE.
WE WILL TAKE THE FIGHT TO THEM. I WOULD HAVE YOU WITH ME WHEN WE DO. CONSIDER MY OFFER.

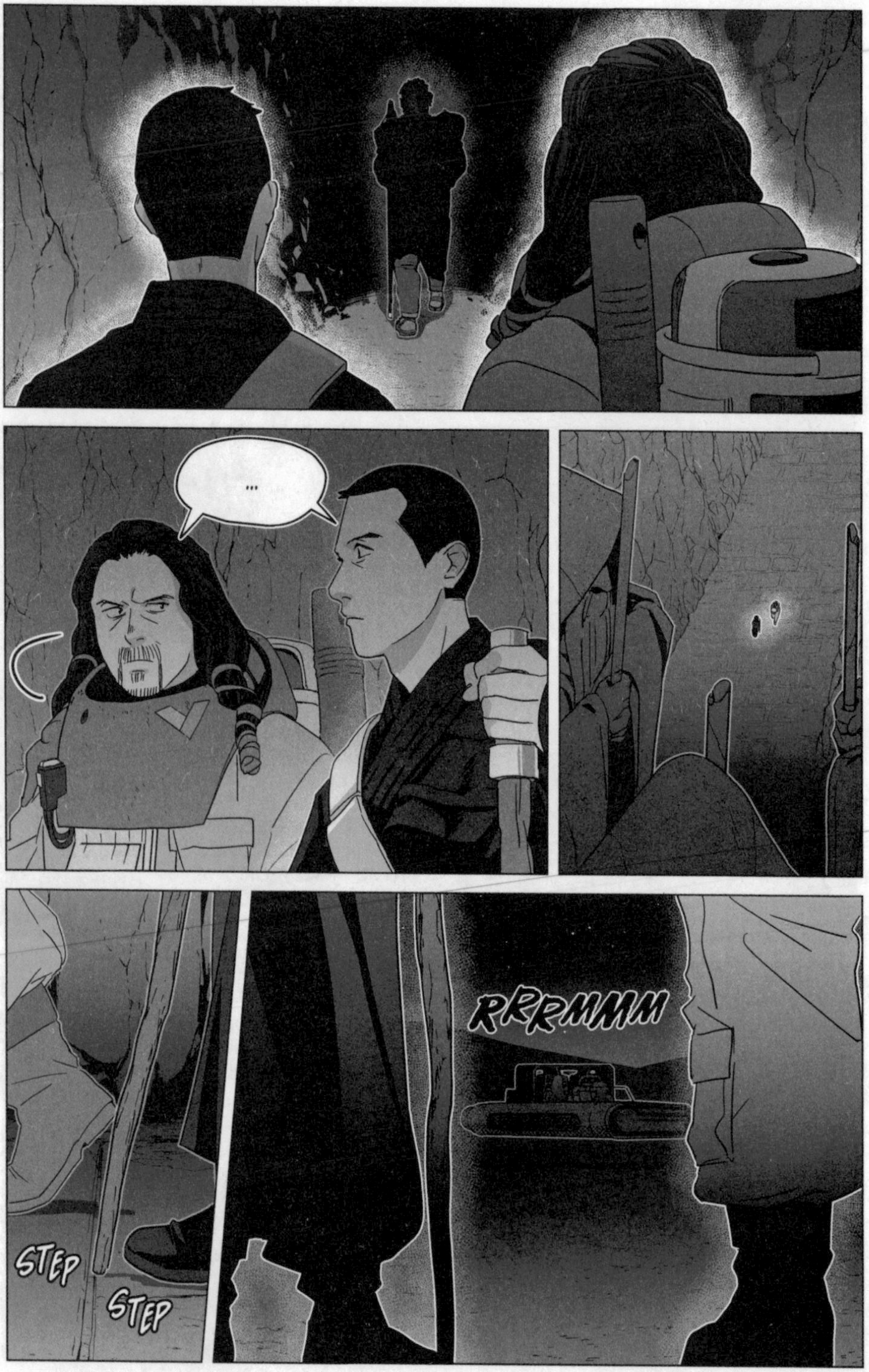
...
RRRMMM
STEP
STEP

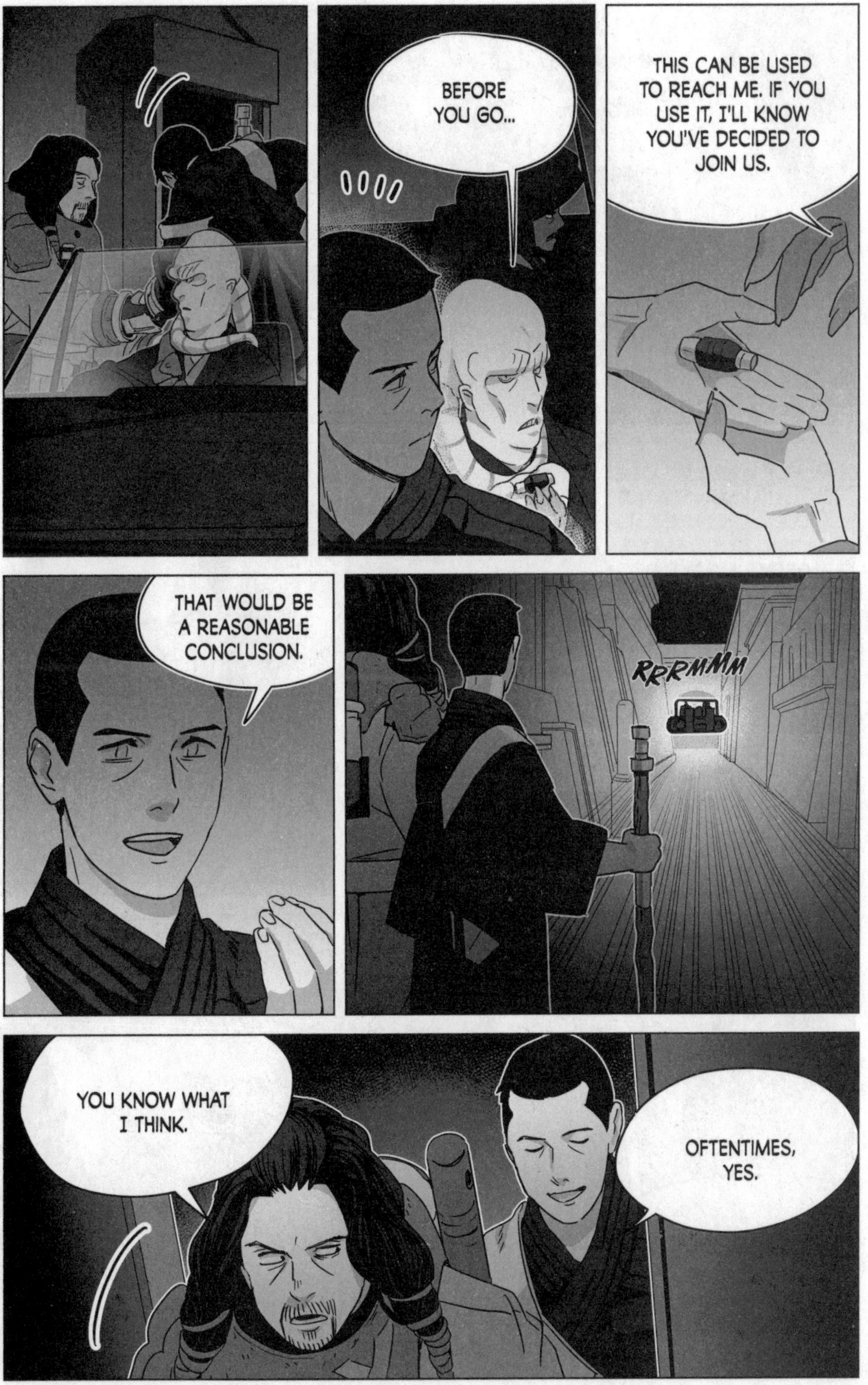
BEFORE YOU GO...
THIS CAN BE USED TO REACH ME. IF YOU USE IT, I'LL KNOW YOU'VE DECIDED TO JOIN US.
THAT WOULD BE A REASONABLE CONCLUSION.
RRRMMM
YOU KNOW WHAT I THINK.
OFTENTIMES, YES.

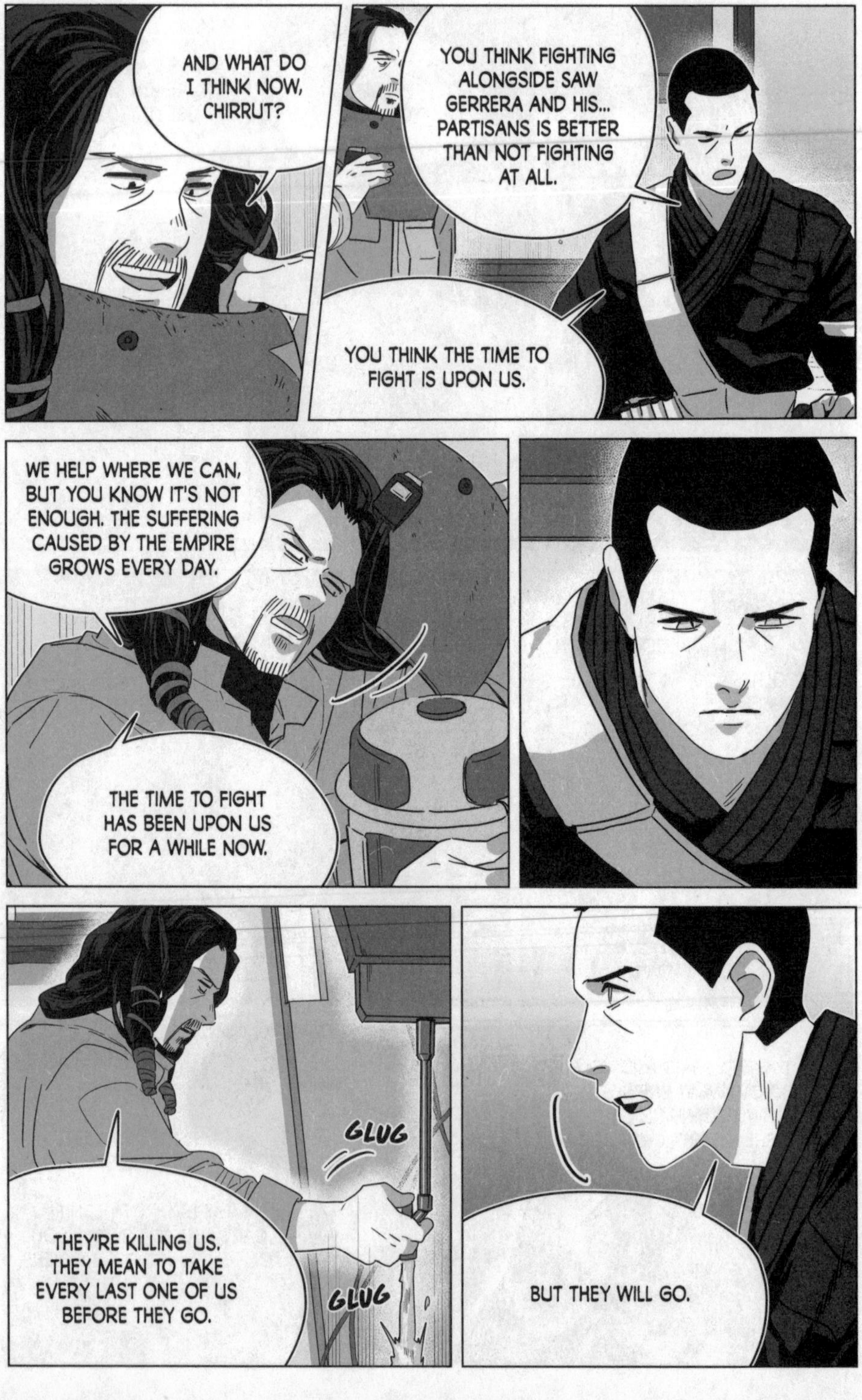
AND WHAT DO I THINK NOW, CHIRRUT?
YOU THINK FIGHTING ALONGSIDE SAW GERRERA AND HIS... PARTISANS IS BETTER THAN NOT FIGHTING AT ALL.
YOU THINK THE TIME TO FIGHT IS UPON US.
WE HELP WHERE WE CAN, BUT YOU KNOW IT'S NOT ENOUGH. THE SUFFERING CAUSED BY THE EMPIRE GROWS EVERY DAY.
THE TIME TO FIGHT HAS BEEN UPON US FOR A WHILE NOW.
THEY'RE KILLING US. THEY MEAN TO TAKE EVERY LAST ONE OF US BEFORE THEY GO.
GLUG
GLUG
BUT THEY WILL GO.

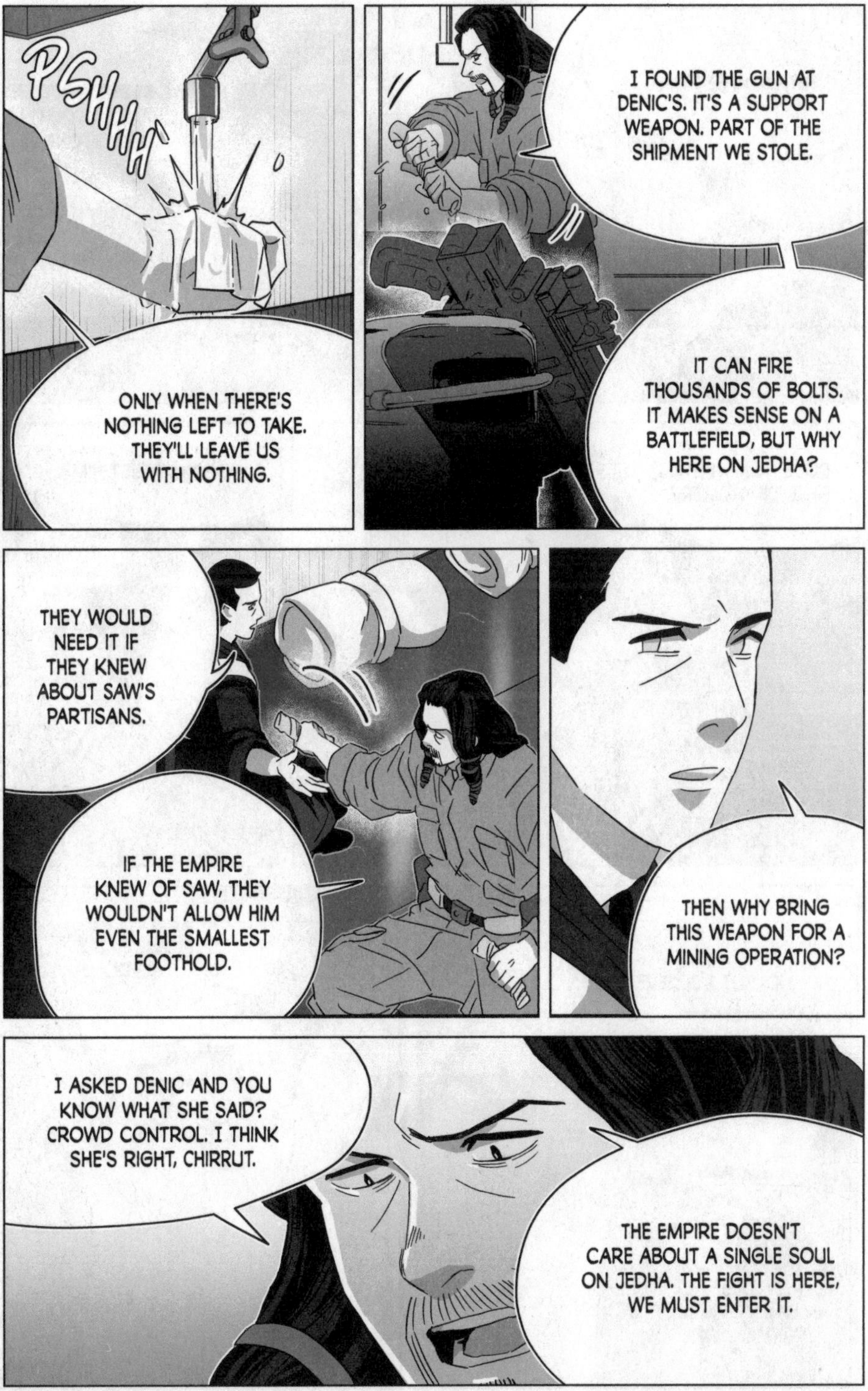
PSHHH
ONLY WHEN THERE'S NOTHING LEFT TO TAKE. THEY'LL LEAVE US WITH NOTHING.
I FOUND THE GUN AT DENIC'S. IT'S A SUPPORT WEAPON. PART OF THE SHIPMENT WE STOLE.
IT CAN FIRE THOUSANDS OF BOLTS. IT MAKES SENSE ON A BATTLEFIELD, BUT WHY HERE ON JEDHA?
THEY WOULD NEED IT IF THEY KNEW ABOUT SAW'S PARTISANS.
IF THE EMPIRE KNEW OF SAW, THEY WOULDN'T ALLOW HIM EVEN THE SMALLEST FOOTHOLD.
THEN WHY BRING THIS WEAPON FOR A MINING OPERATION?
I ASKED DENIC AND YOU KNOW WHAT SHE SAID? CROWD CONTROL. I THINK SHE'S RIGHT, CHIRRUT.
THE EMPIRE DOESN'T CARE ABOUT A SINGLE SOUL ON JEDHA. THE FIGHT IS HERE, WE MUST ENTER IT.

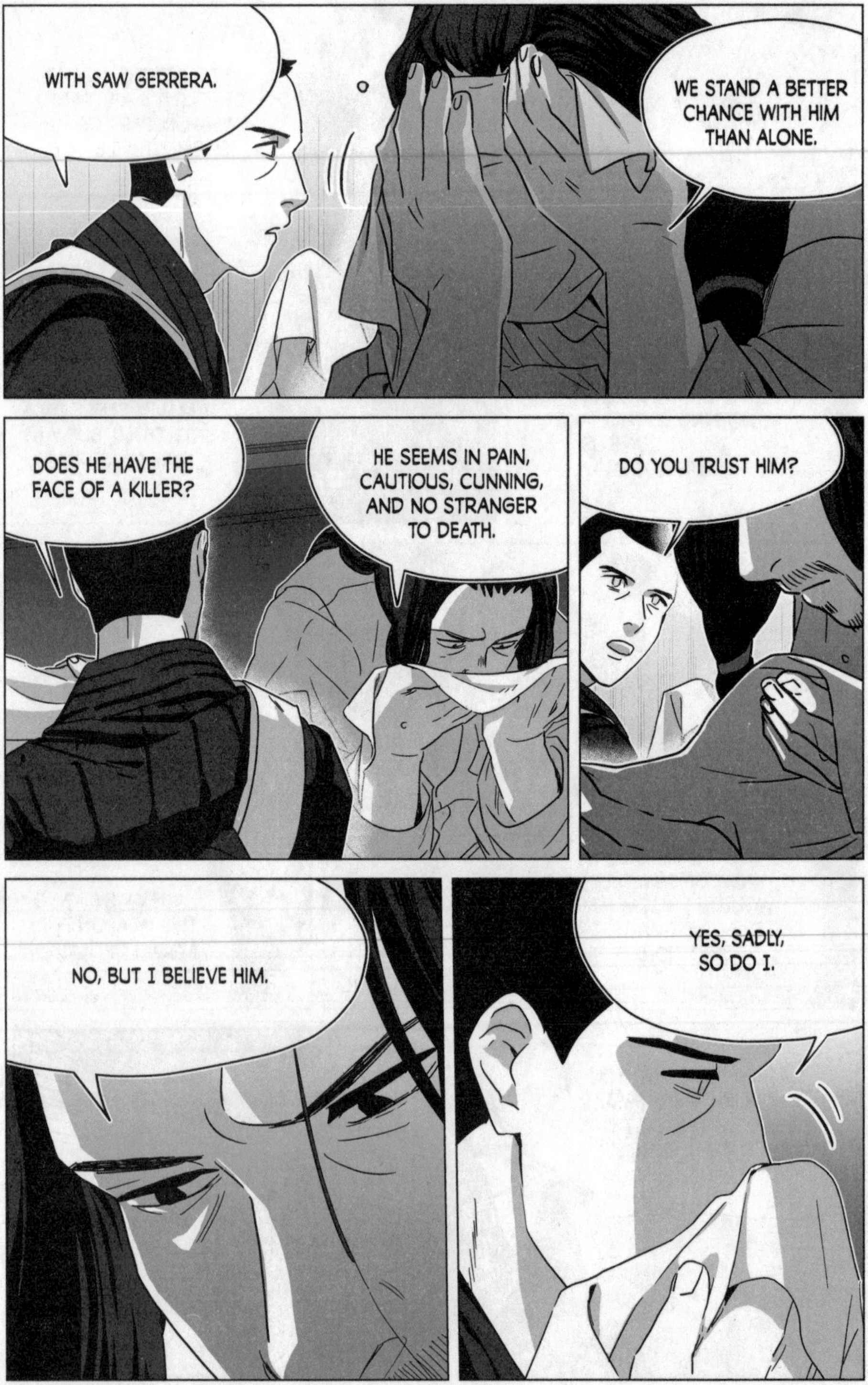
WITH SAW GERRERA.
WE STAND A BETTER CHANCE WITH HIM THAN ALONE.
DOES HE HAVE THE FACE OF A KILLER?
HE SEEMS IN PAIN, CAUTIOUS, CUNNING, AND NO STRANGER TO DEATH.
DO YOU TRUST HIM?
NO, BUT I BELIEVE HIM.
YES, SADLY, SO DO I.

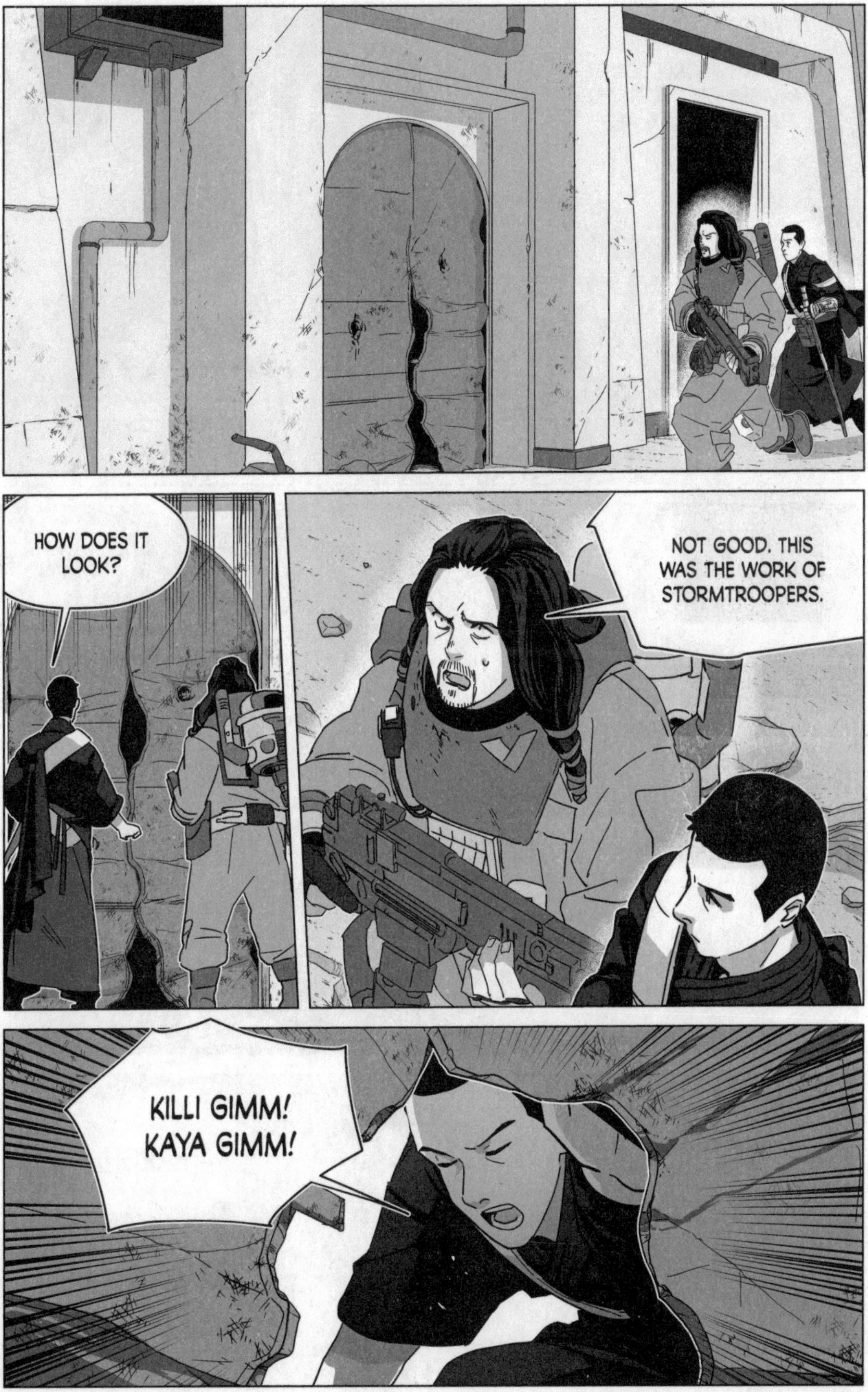
HOW DOES IT LOOK?
NOT GOOD. THIS WAS THE WORK OF STORMTROOPERS.
KILLI GIMM! KAYA GIMM!

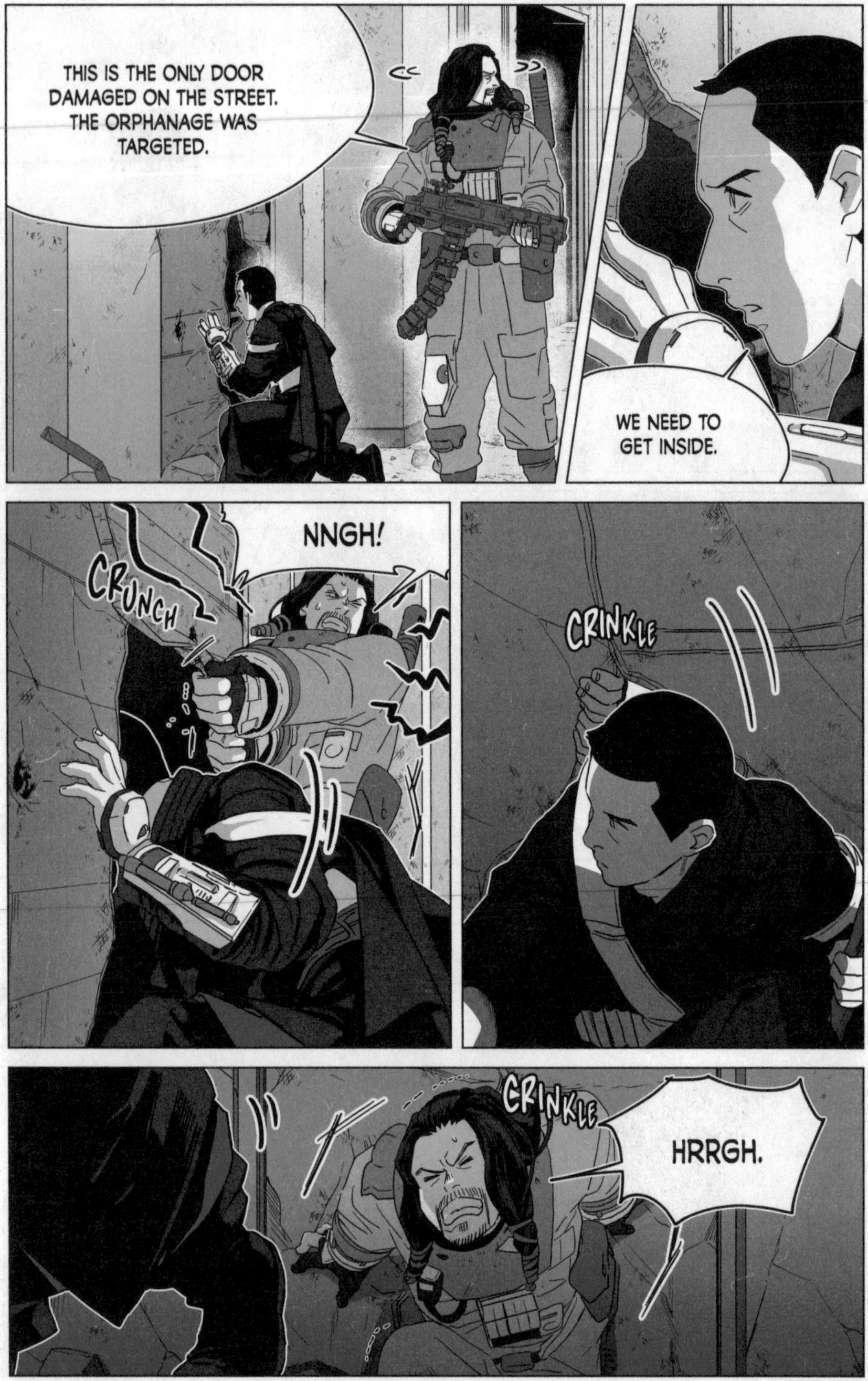
THIS IS THE ONLY DOOR DAMAGED ON THE STREET. THE ORPHANAGE WAS TARGETED.
WE NEED TO GET INSIDE.
NNGH!
CRUNCH
CRINKLE
CRINKLE
HRRGH.

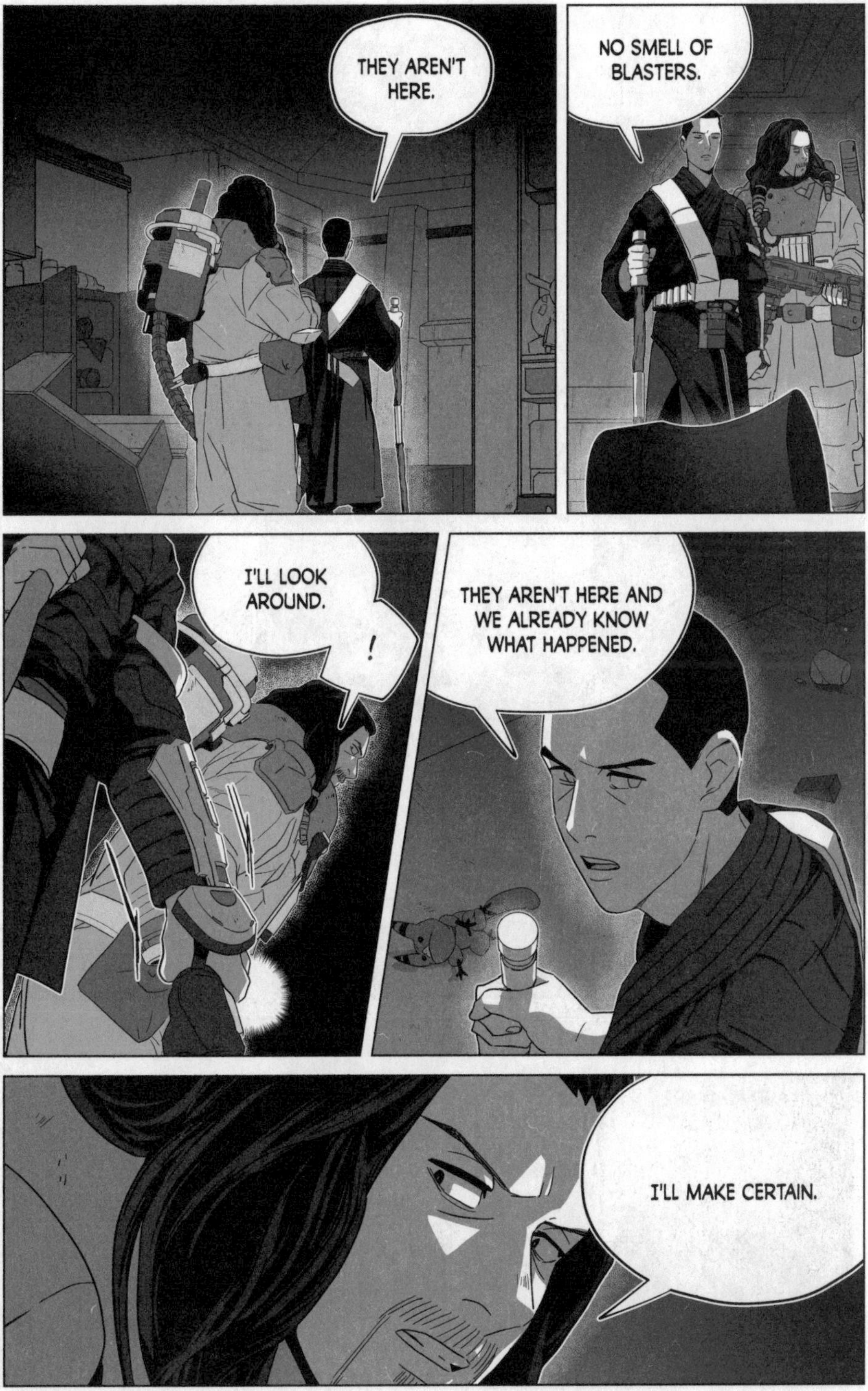
THEY AREN'T HERE.
NO SMELL OF BLASTERS.
I'LL LOOK AROUND.
!
THEY AREN'T HERE AND WE ALREADY KNOW WHAT HAPPENED.
I'LL MAKE CERTAIN.

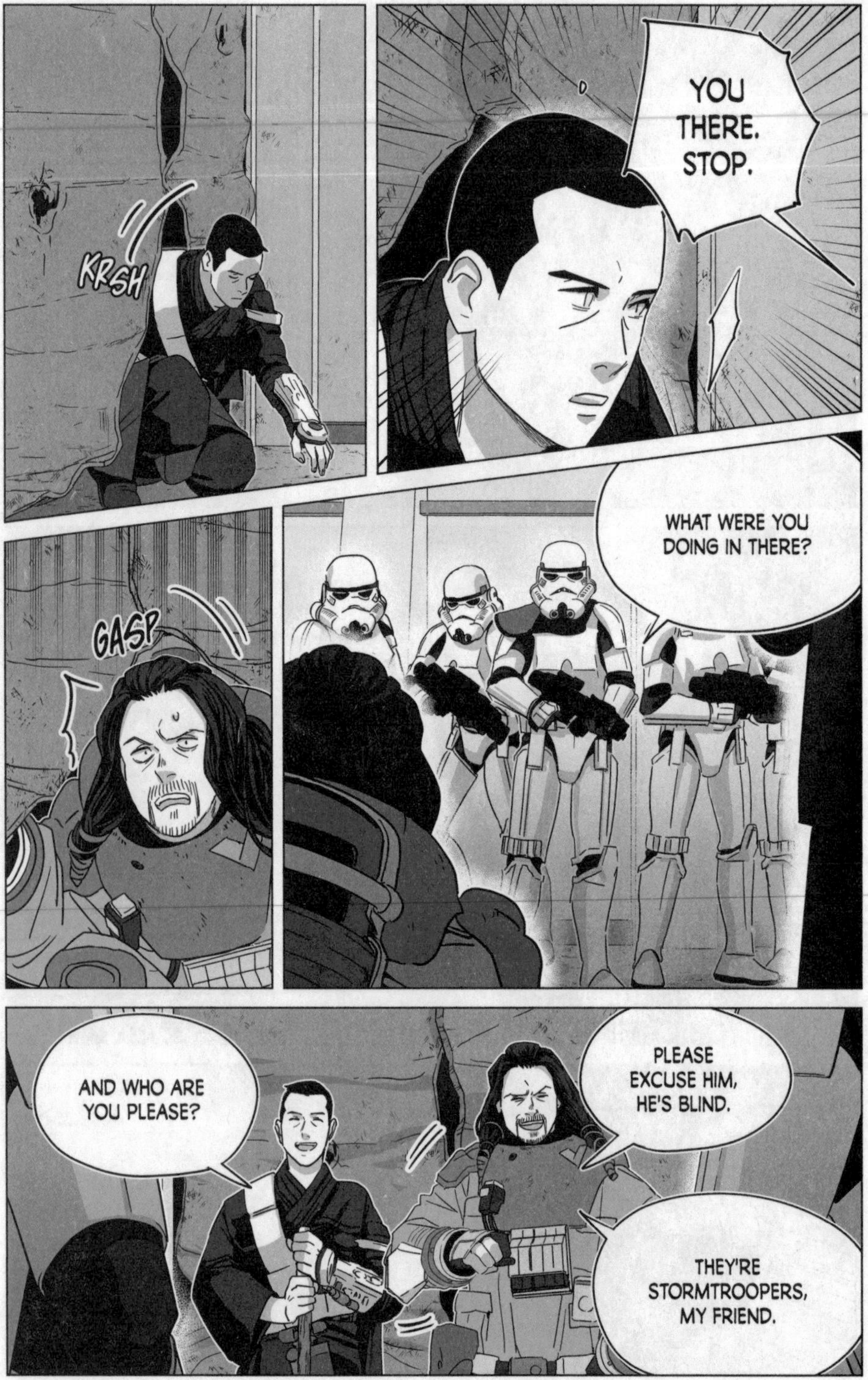
KRSH
YOU THERE. STOP.
GASP
WHAT WERE YOU DOING IN THERE?
AND WHO ARE YOU PLEASE?
PLEASE EXCUSE HIM, HE'S BLIND.
THEY'RE STORMTROOPERS, MY FRIEND.

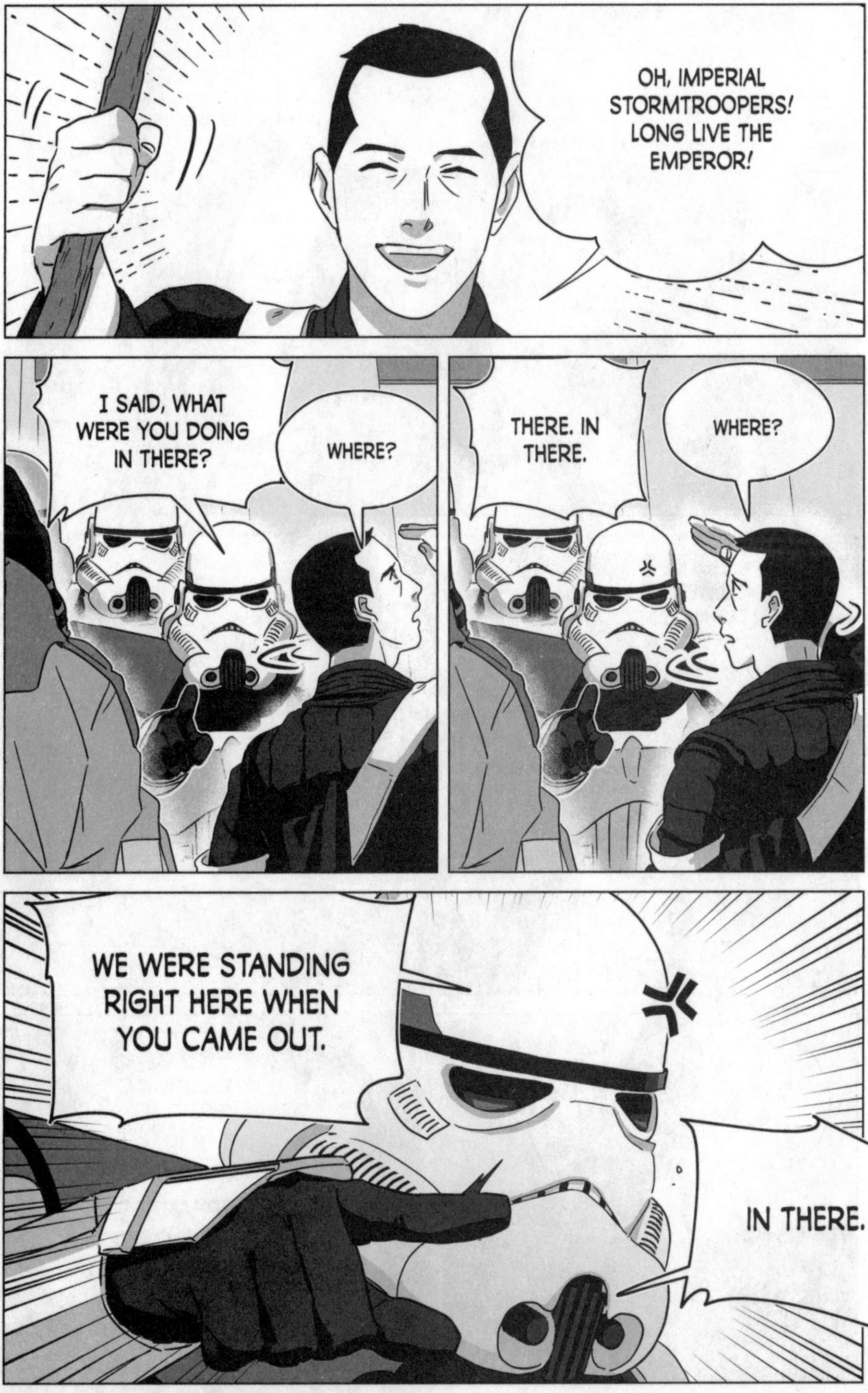
OH, IMPERIAL STORMTROOPERS! LONG LIVE THE EMPEROR!
I SAID, WHAT WERE YOU DOING IN THERE?
WHERE?
THERE. IN THERE.
WHERE?
WE WERE STANDING RIGHT HERE WHEN YOU CAME OUT.
IN THERE.

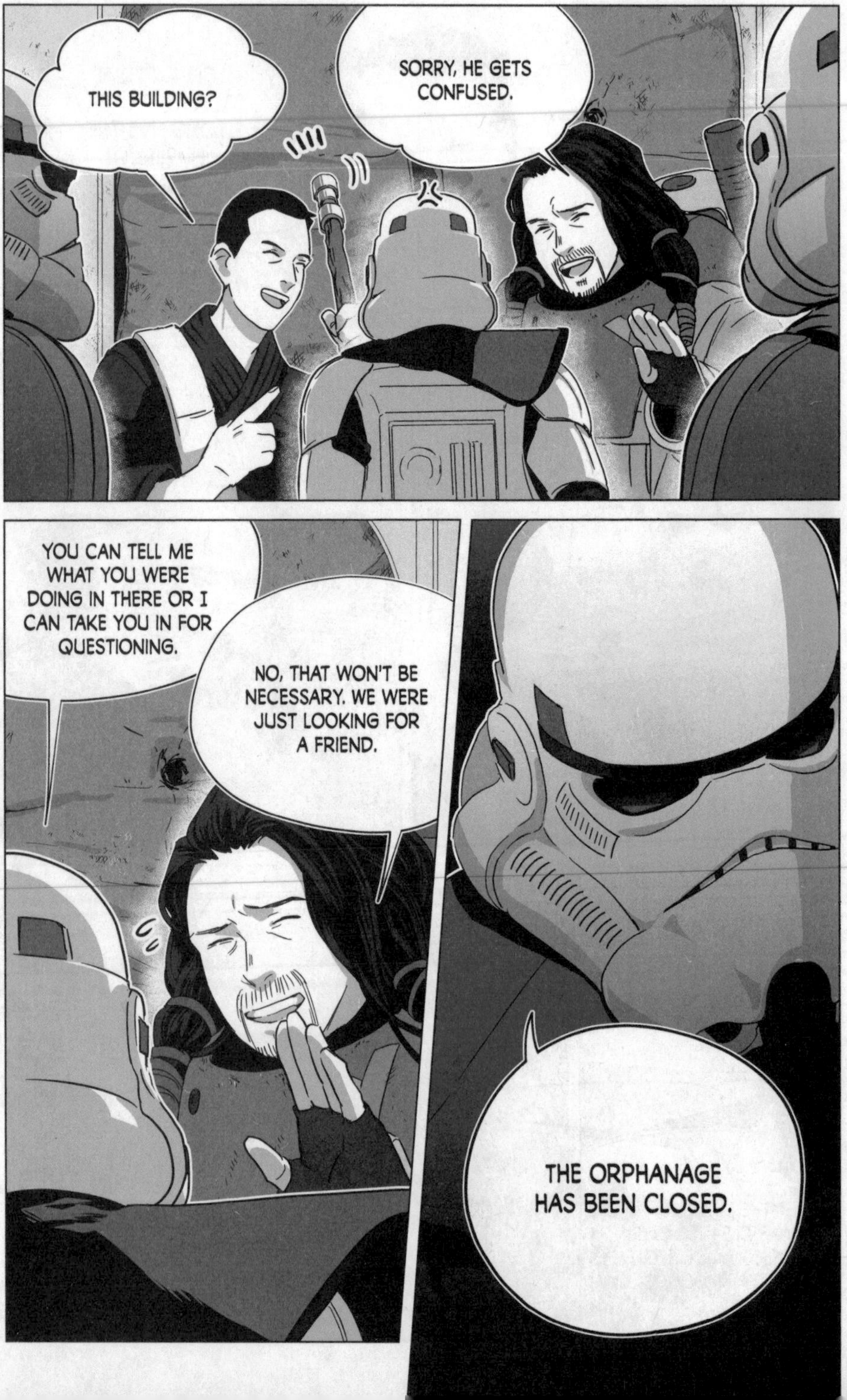
THIS BUILDING?
SORRY, HE GETS CONFUSED.
YOU CAN TELL ME WHAT YOU WERE DOING IN THERE OR I CAN TAKE YOU IN FOR QUESTIONING.
NO, THAT WON'T BE NECESSARY. WE WERE JUST LOOKING FOR A FRIEND.
THE ORPHANAGE HAS BEEN CLOSED.

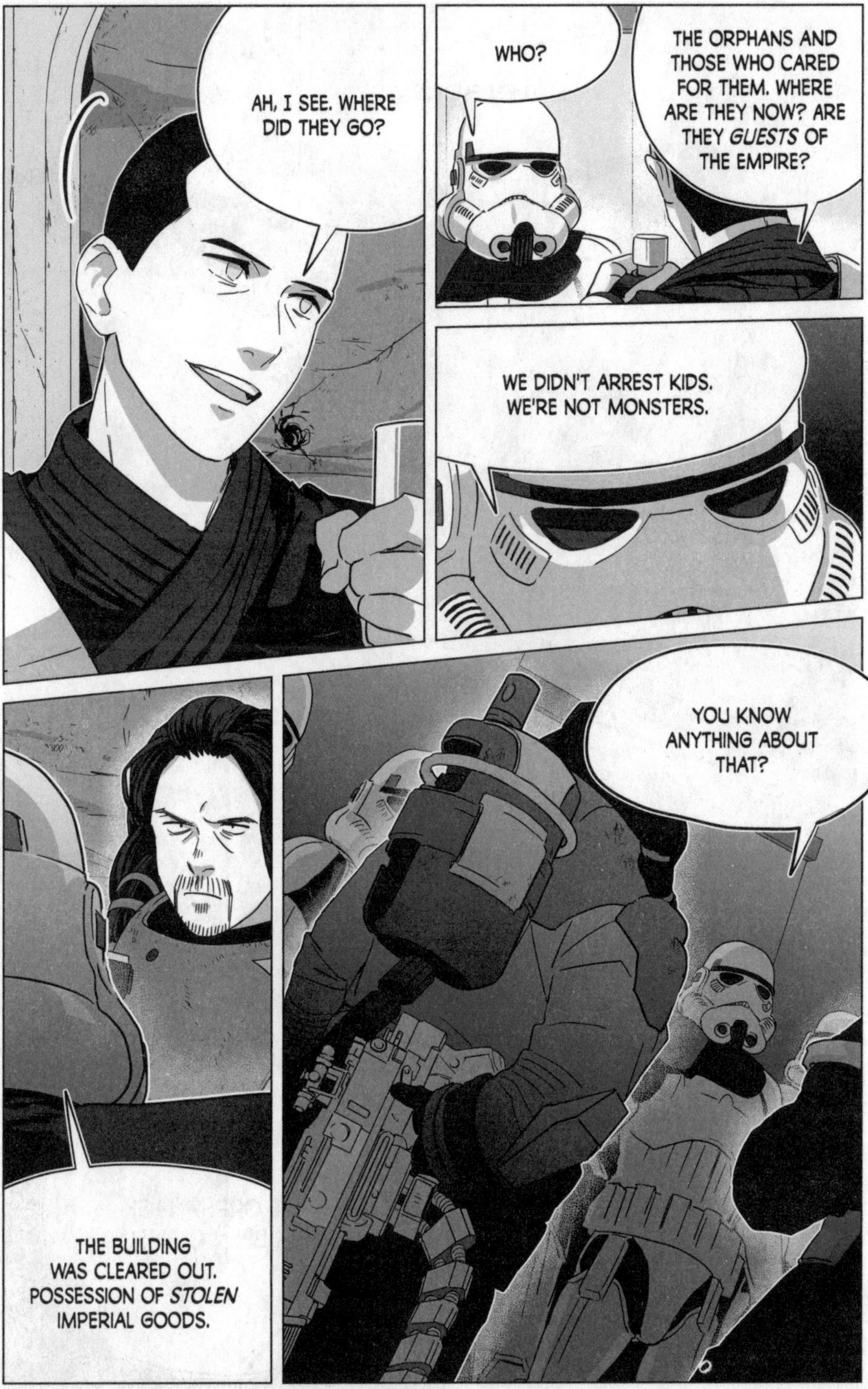
AH, I SEE. WHERE DID THEY GO?
WHO?
THE ORPHANS AND THOSE WHO CARED FOR THEM. WHERE ARE THEY NOW? ARE THEY *GUESTS* OF THE EMPIRE?
WE DIDN'T ARREST KIDS. WE'RE NOT MONSTERS.
THE BUILDING WAS CLEARED OUT. POSSESSION OF *STOLEN* IMPERIAL GOODS.
YOU KNOW ANYTHING ABOUT THAT?

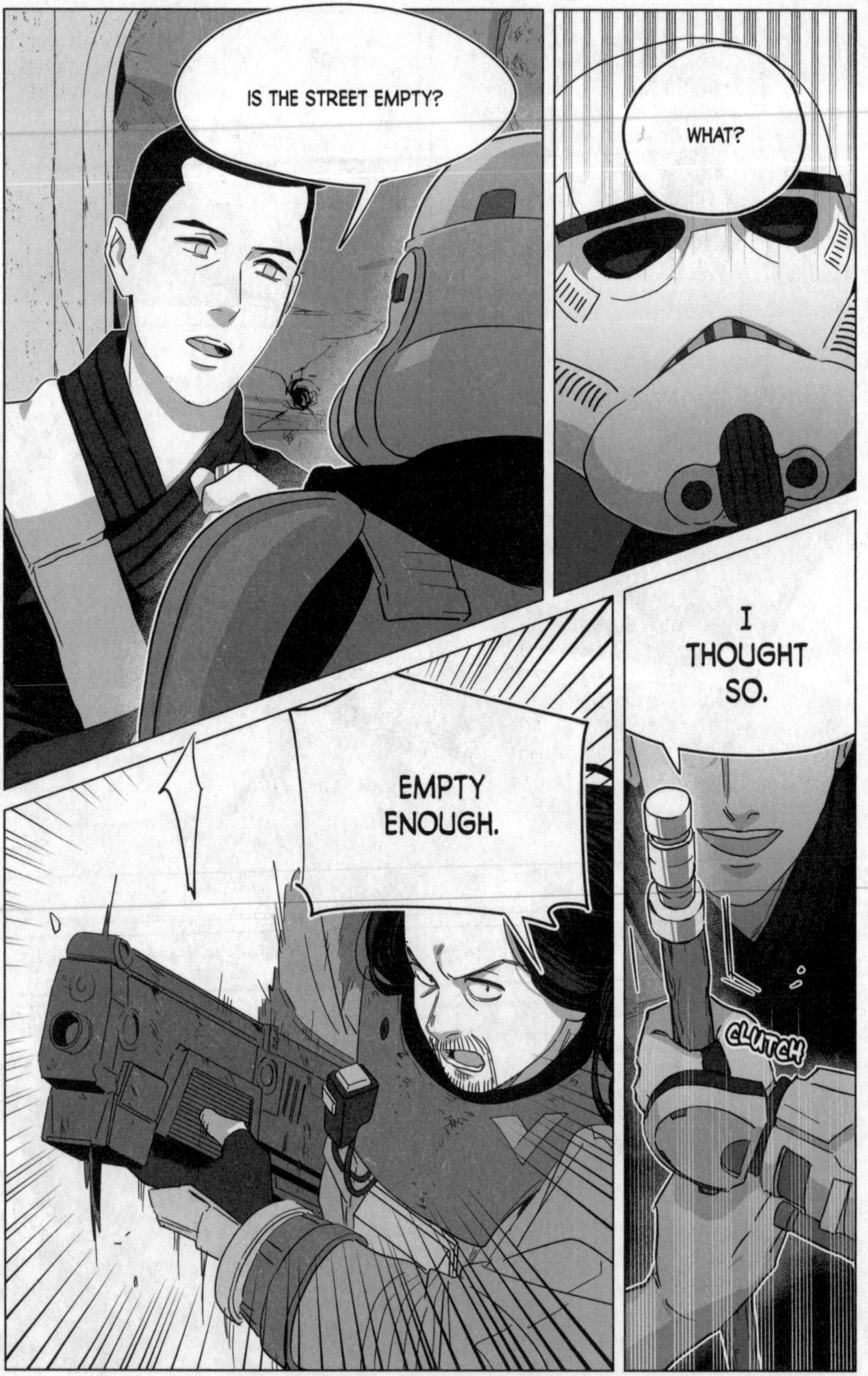
IS THE STREET EMPTY?
WHAT?
EMPTY ENOUGH.
I THOUGHT SO.
CLUTCH

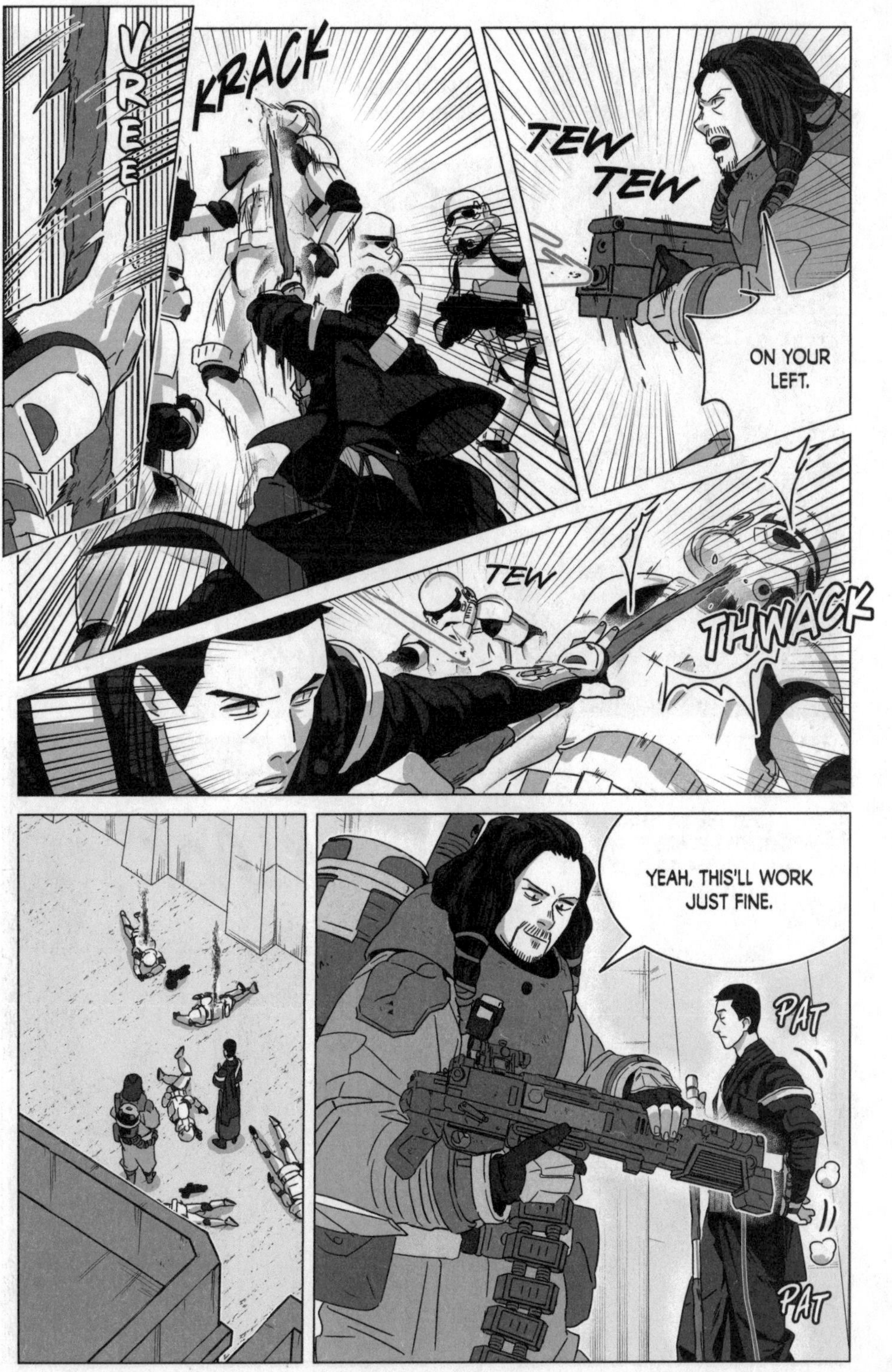

VREE
KRACK
TEW TEW
ON YOUR LEFT.
TEW
THWACK
YEAH, THIS'LL WORK JUST FINE.
PAT
PAT

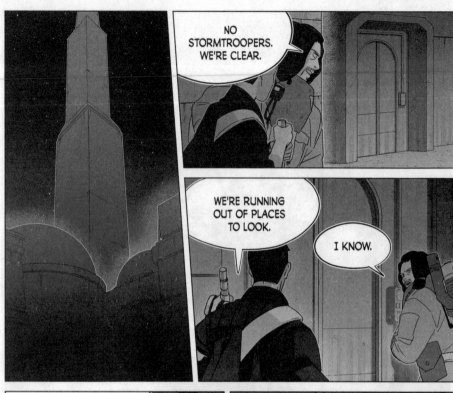

NO STORMTROOPERS. WE'RE CLEAR.

WE'RE RUNNING OUT OF PLACES TO LOOK.

I KNOW.

I TOLD THE SISTERS ABOUT THIS PLACE SOME TIME AGO. MAYBE THEY REMEMBERED IT.

BZZZZ

KLACK

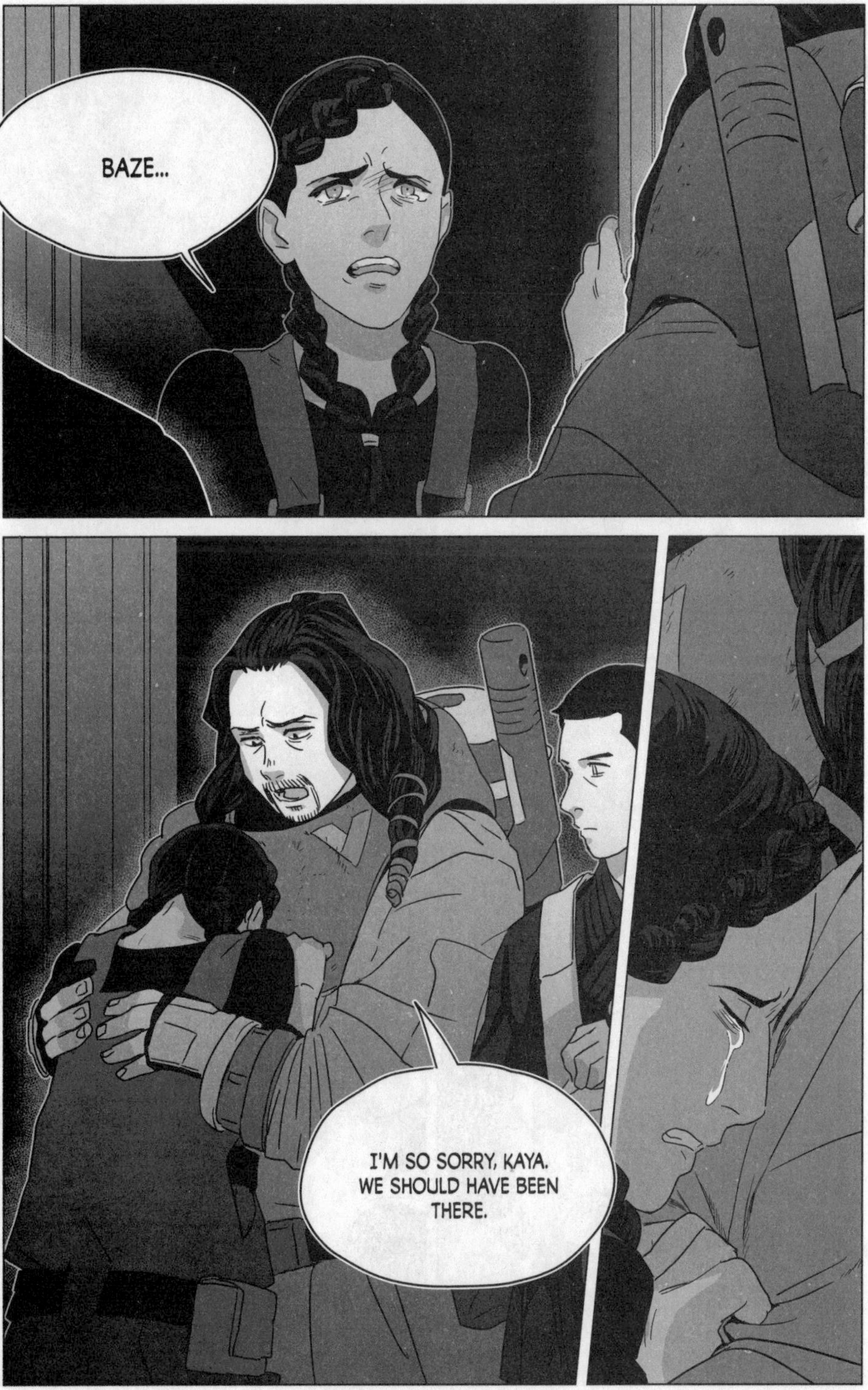
BAZE...
I'M SO SORRY, KAYA. WE SHOULD HAVE BEEN THERE.

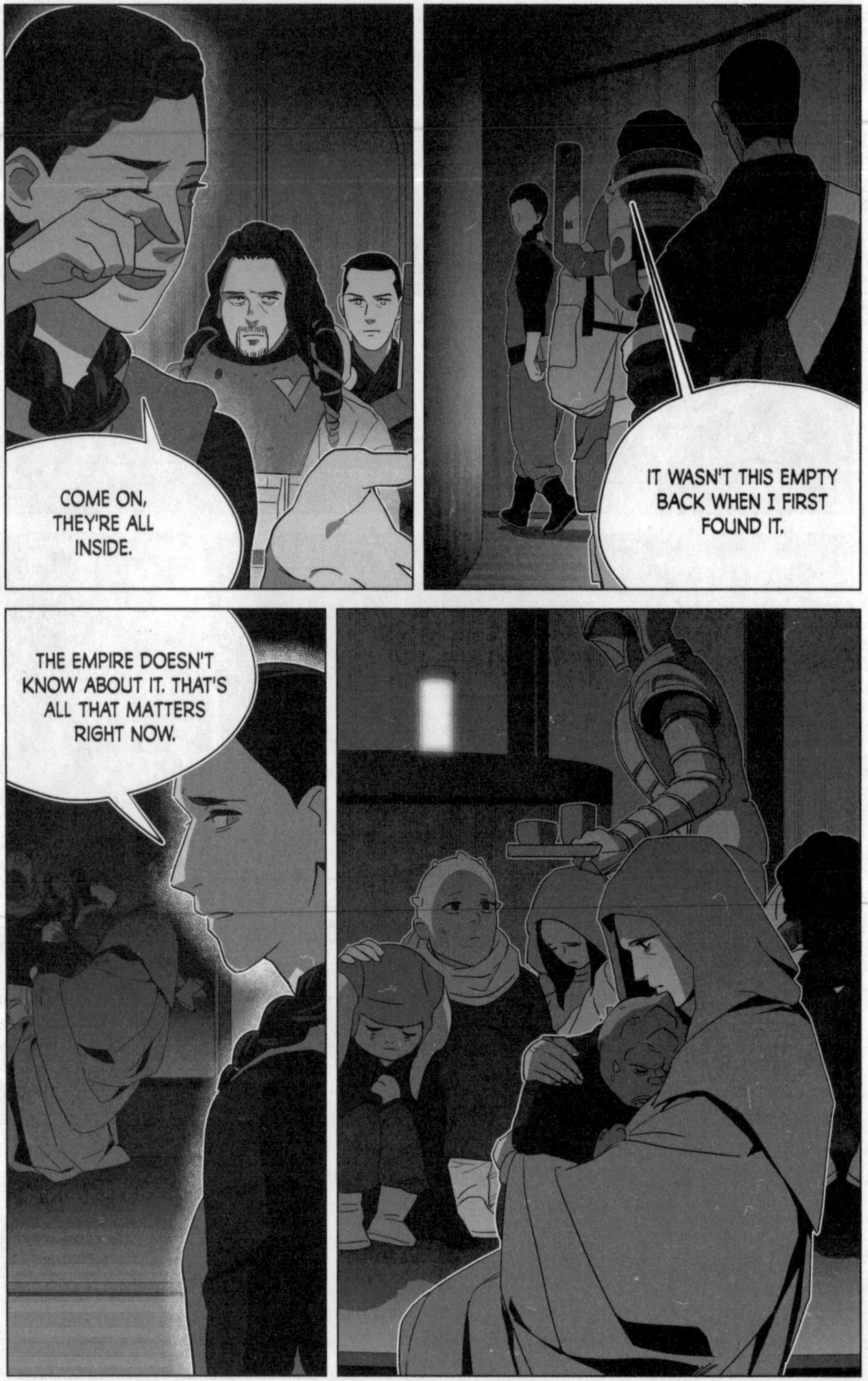
COME ON, THEY'RE ALL INSIDE.
IT WASN'T THIS EMPTY BACK WHEN I FIRST FOUND IT.
THE EMPIRE DOESN'T KNOW ABOUT IT. THAT'S ALL THAT MATTERS RIGHT NOW.

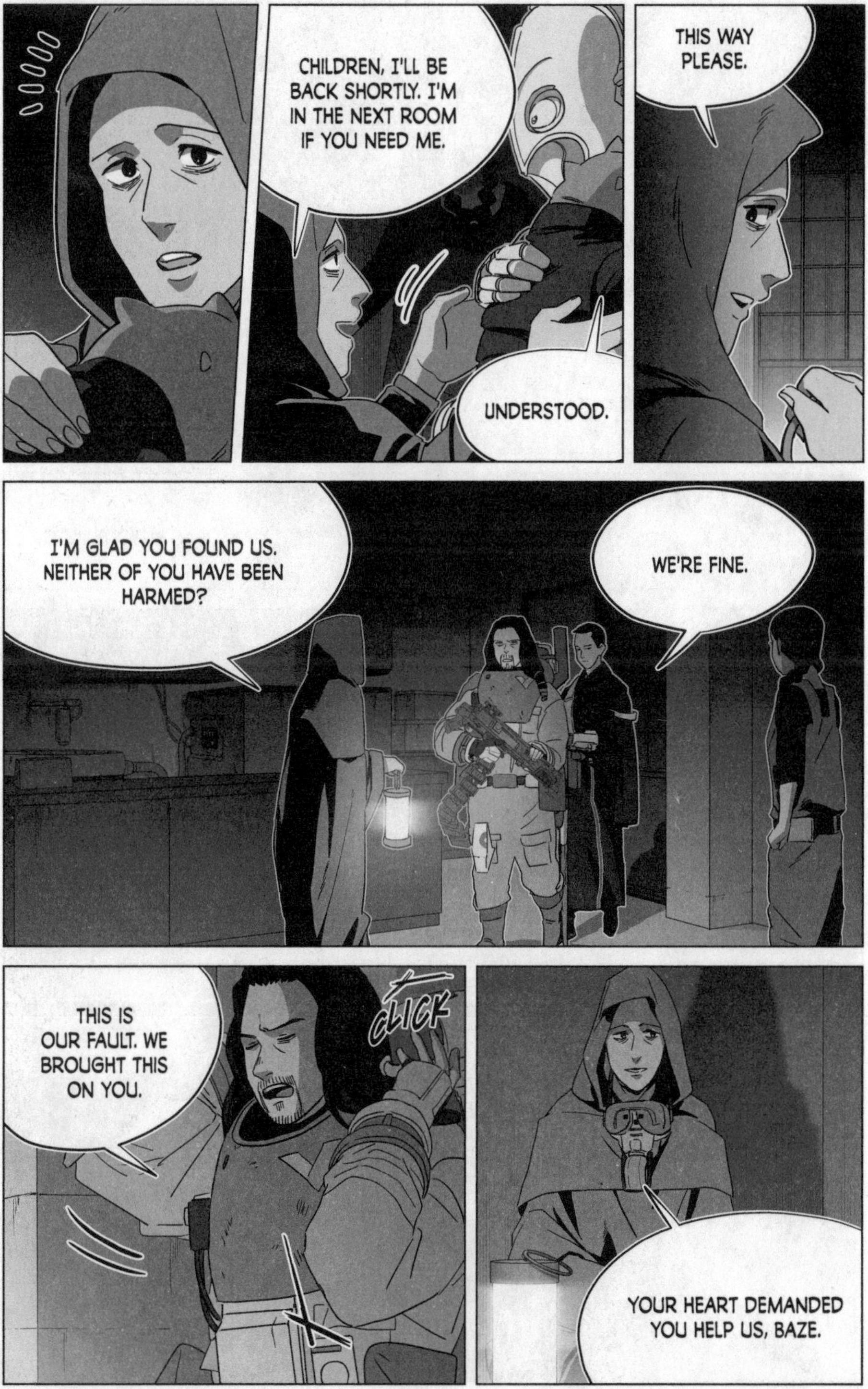

CHILDREN, I'LL BE BACK SHORTLY. I'M IN THE NEXT ROOM IF YOU NEED ME.
UNDERSTOOD.
THIS WAY PLEASE.
I'M GLAD YOU FOUND US. NEITHER OF YOU HAVE BEEN HARMED?
WE'RE FINE.
THIS IS OUR FAULT. WE BROUGHT THIS ON YOU.
CLICK
YOUR HEART DEMANDED YOU HELP US, BAZE.

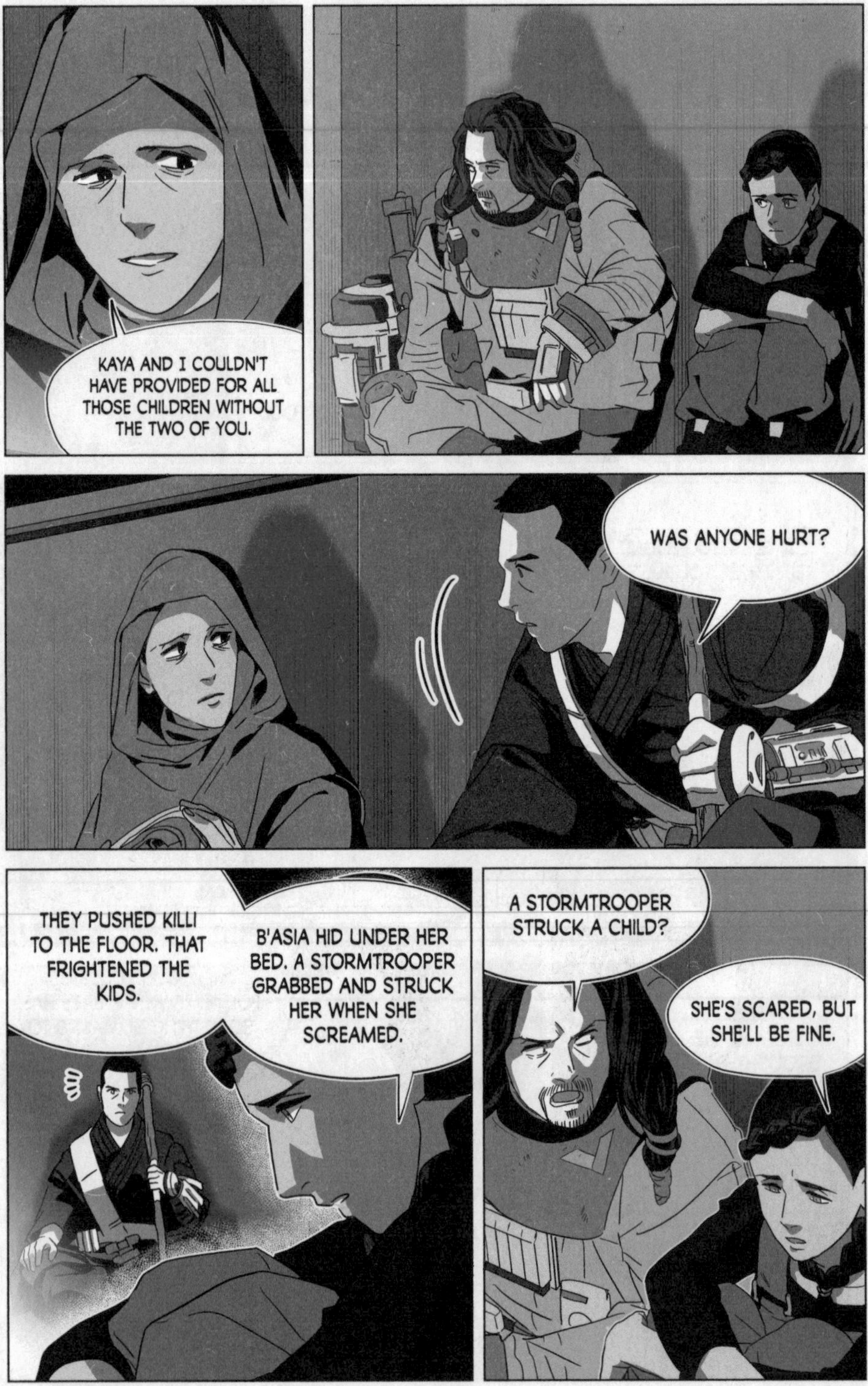
KAYA AND I COULDN'T HAVE PROVIDED FOR ALL THOSE CHILDREN WITHOUT THE TWO OF YOU.
WAS ANYONE HURT?
THEY PUSHED KILLI TO THE FLOOR. THAT FRIGHTENED THE KIDS.
B'ASIA HID UNDER HER BED. A STORMTROOPER GRABBED AND STRUCK HER WHEN SHE SCREAMED.
A STORMTROOPER STRUCK A CHILD?
SHE'S SCARED, BUT SHE'LL BE FINE.

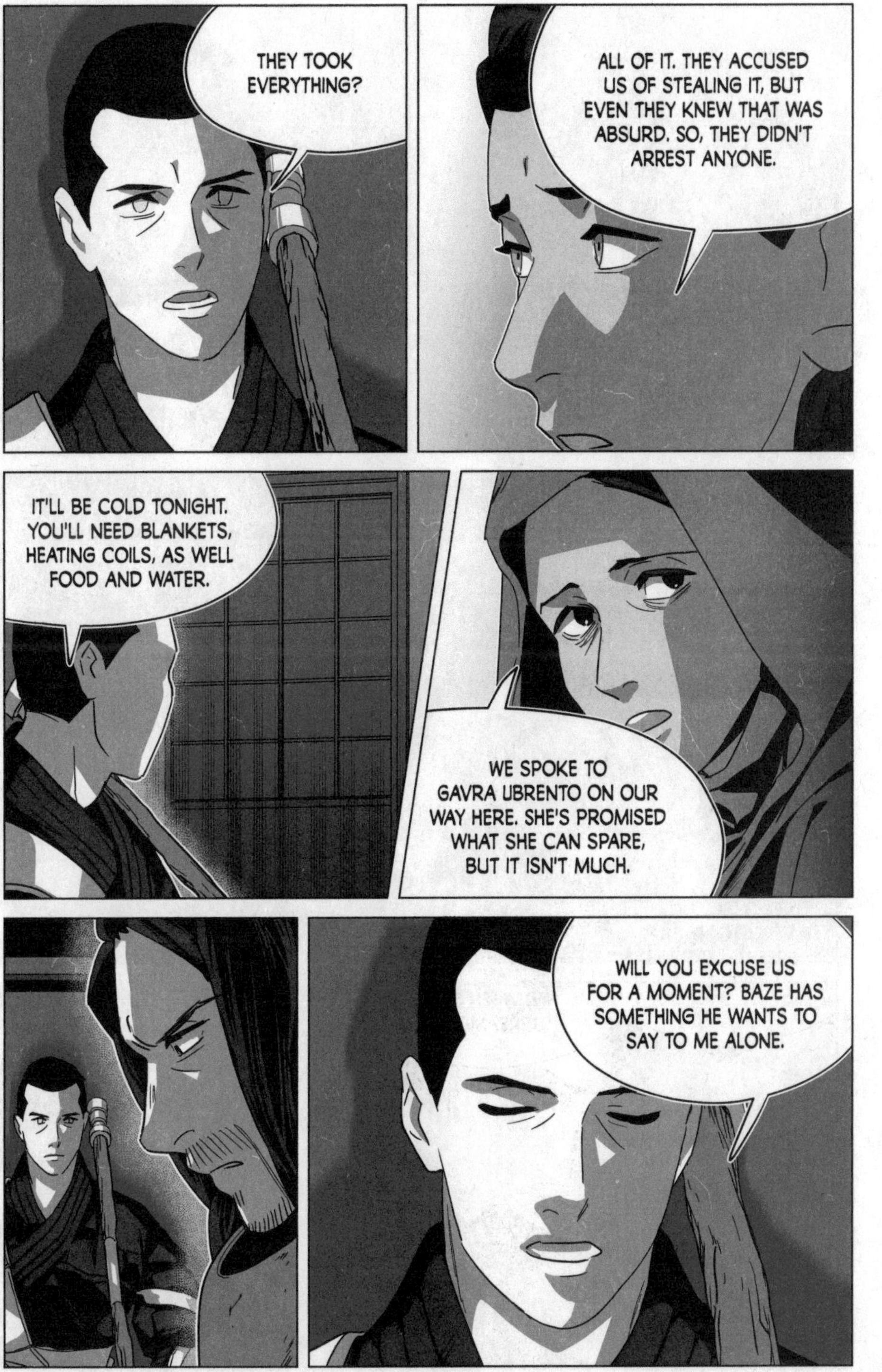
THEY TOOK EVERYTHING?
ALL OF IT. THEY ACCUSED US OF STEALING IT, BUT EVEN THEY KNEW THAT WAS ABSURD. SO, THEY DIDN'T ARREST ANYONE.
IT'LL BE COLD TONIGHT. YOU'LL NEED BLANKETS, HEATING COILS, AS WELL FOOD AND WATER.
WE SPOKE TO GAVRA UBRENTO ON OUR WAY HERE. SHE'S PROMISED WHAT SHE CAN SPARE, BUT IT ISN'T MUCH.
WILL YOU EXCUSE US FOR A MOMENT? BAZE HAS SOMETHING HE WANTS TO SAY TO ME ALONE.

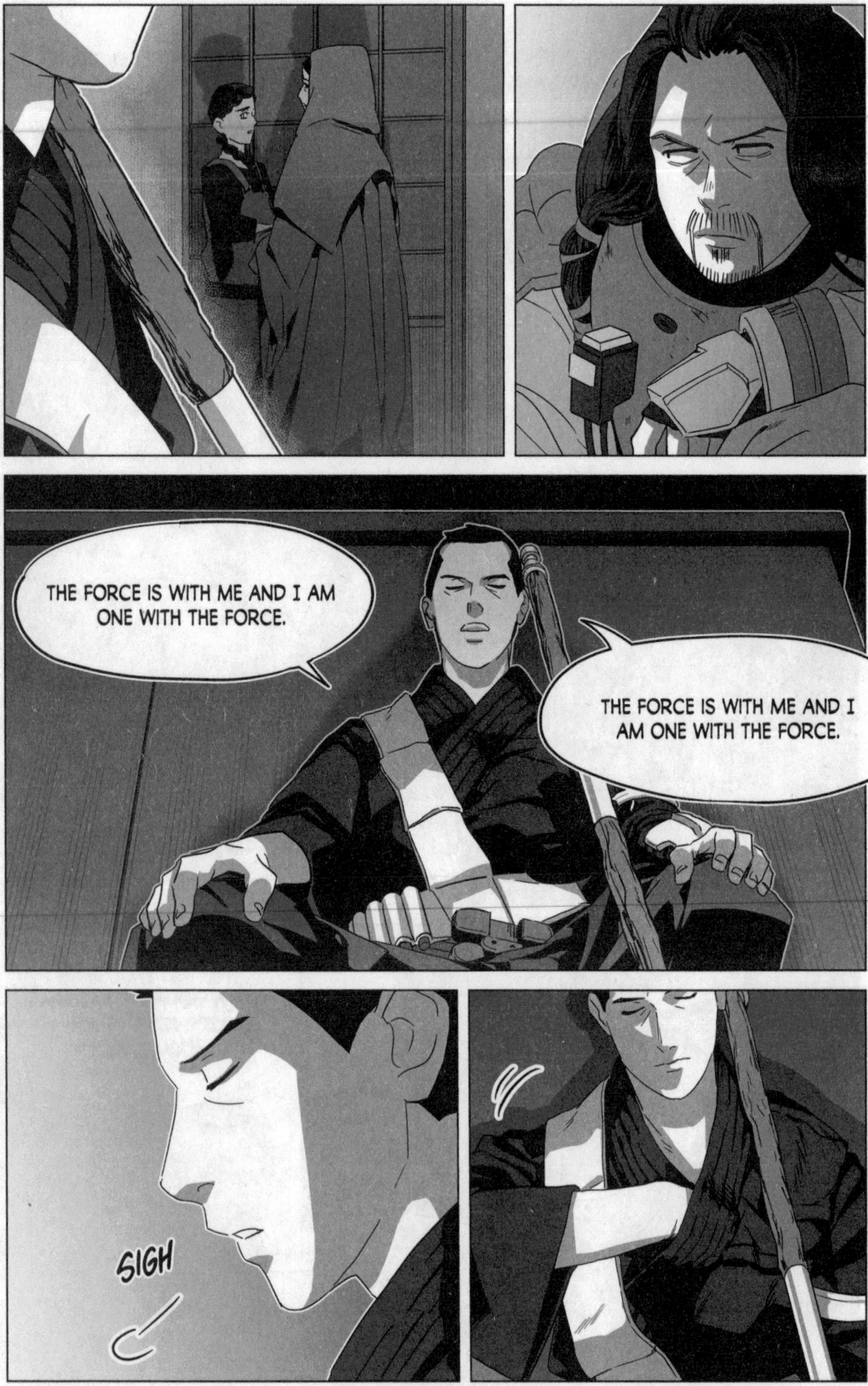
THE FORCE IS WITH ME AND I AM ONE WITH THE FORCE.
THE FORCE IS WITH ME AND I AM ONE WITH THE FORCE.
SIGH

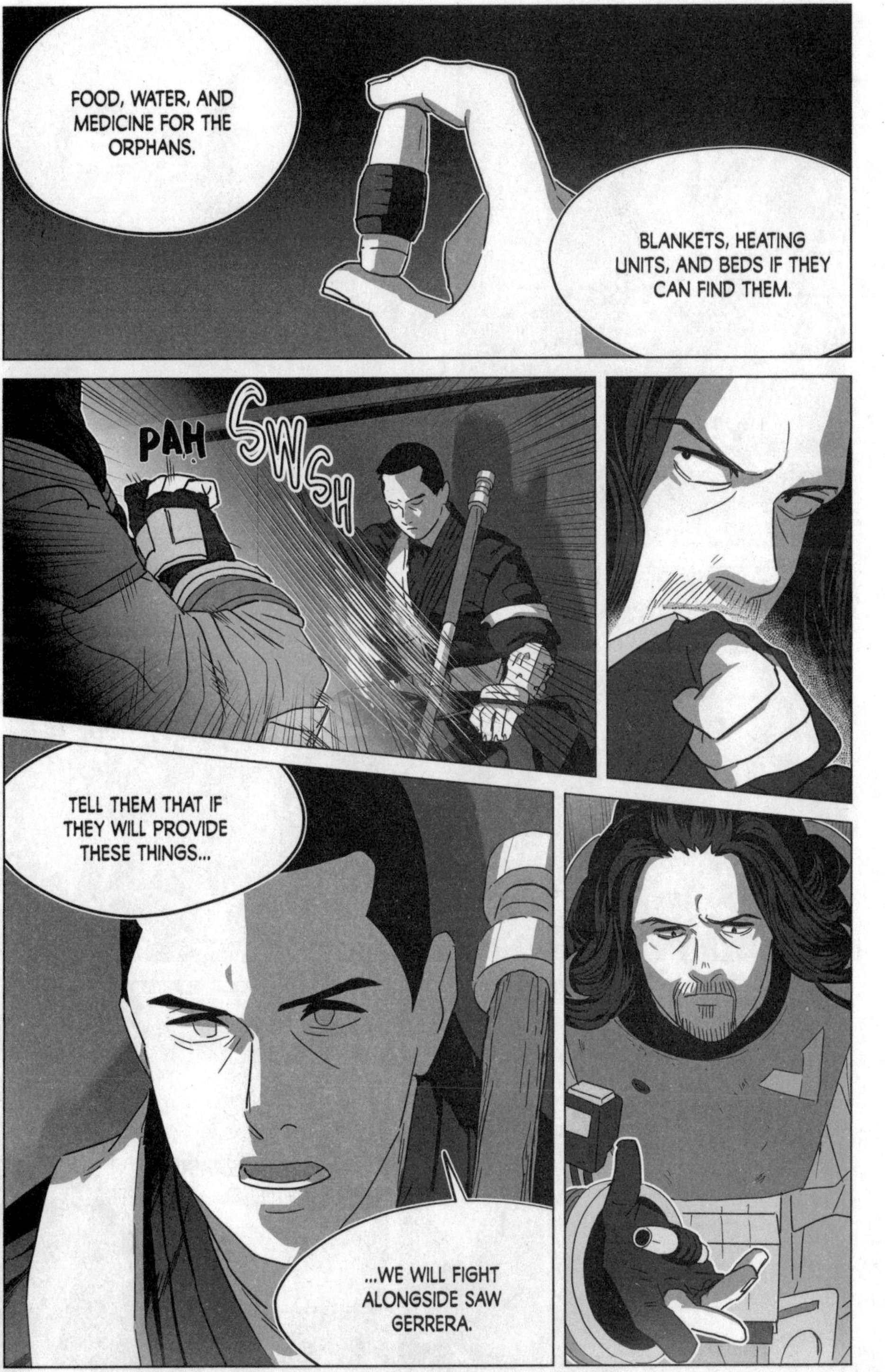

FOOD, WATER, AND MEDICINE FOR THE ORPHANS.
BLANKETS, HEATING UNITS, AND BEDS IF THEY CAN FIND THEM.
PAH
SWSH
TELL THEM THAT IF THEY WILL PROVIDE THESE THINGS...
...WE WILL FIGHT ALONGSIDE SAW GERRERA.

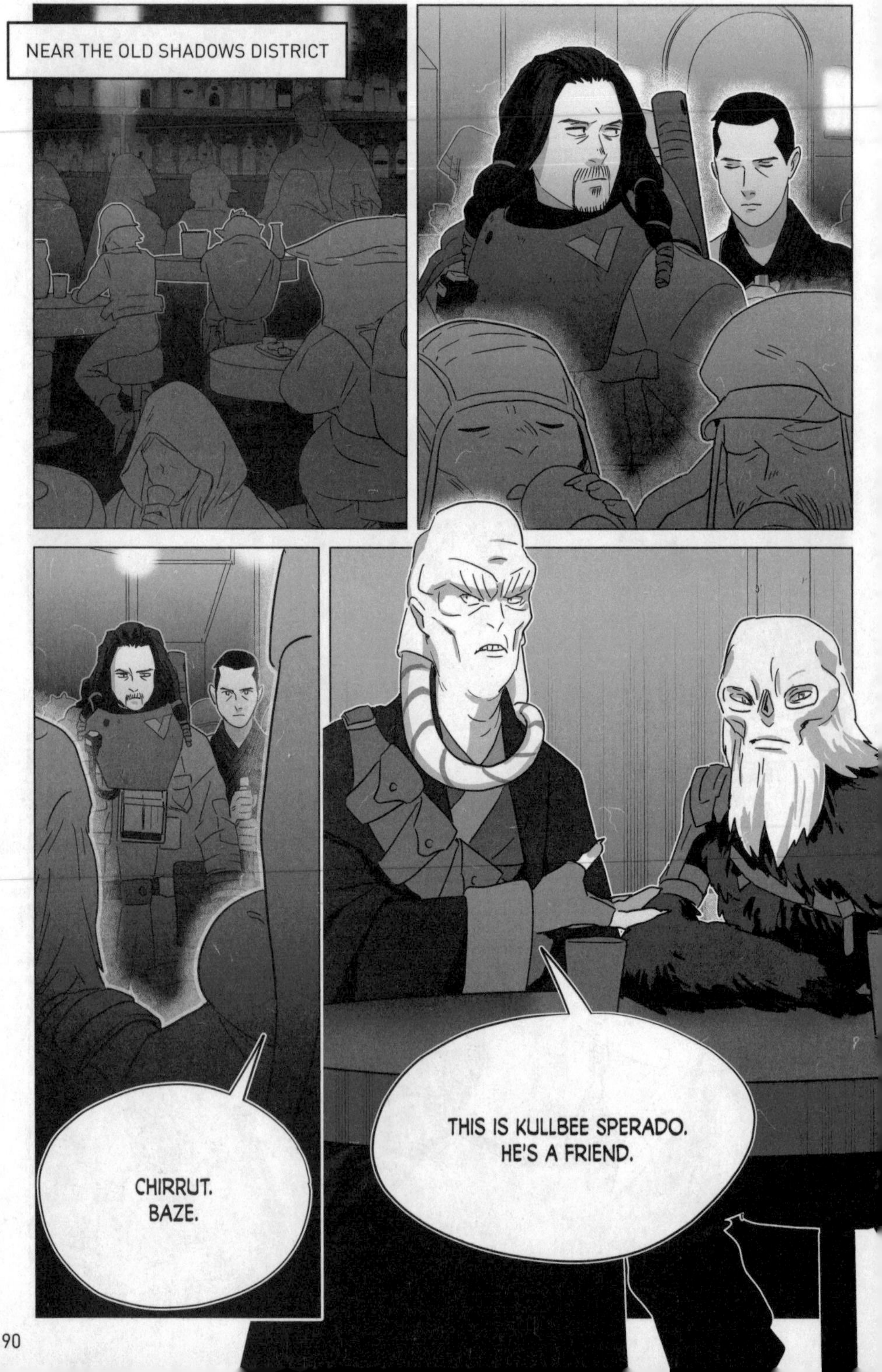
NEAR THE OLD SHADOWS DISTRICT
CHIRRUT. BAZE.
THIS IS KULLBEE SPERADO. HE'S A FRIEND.

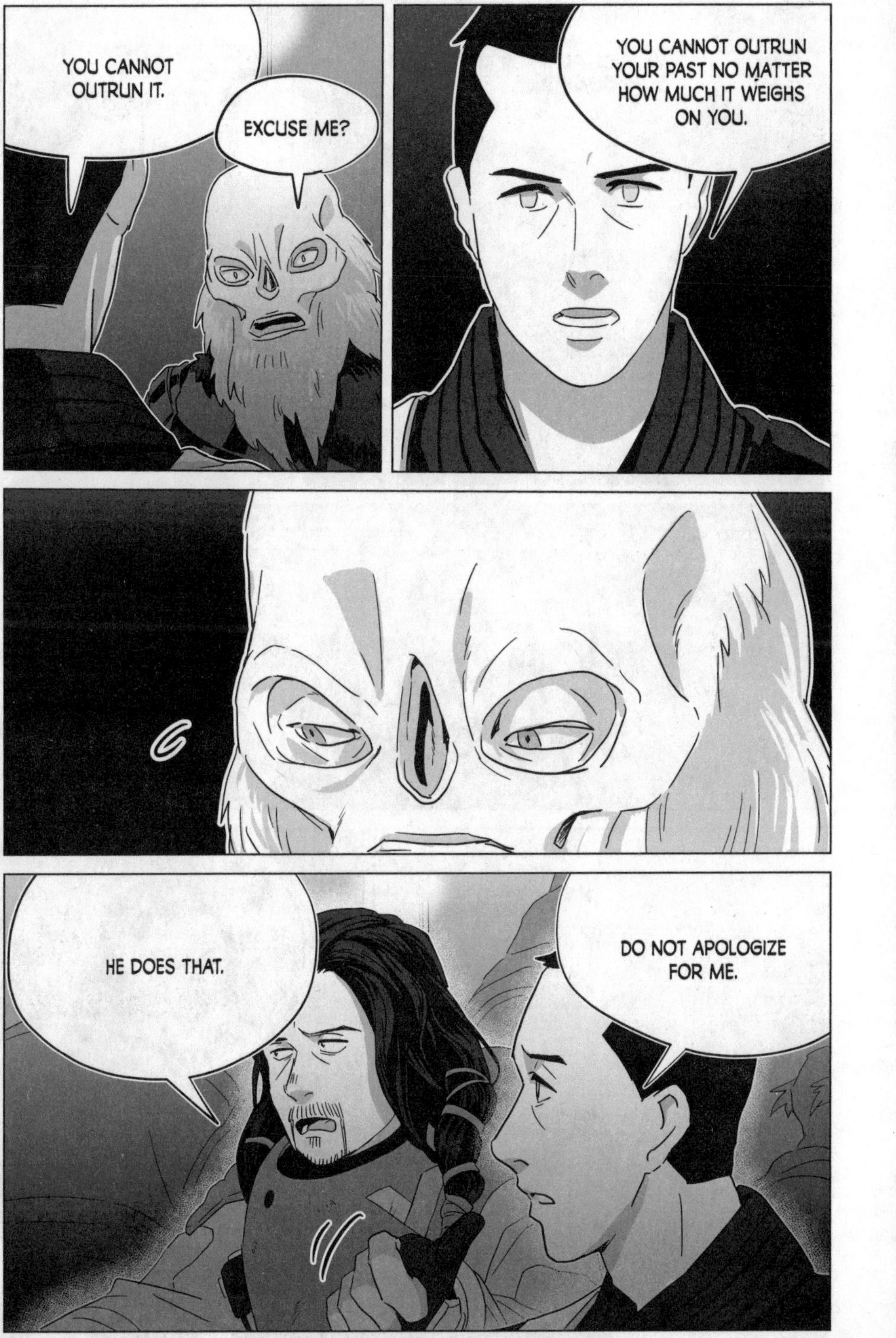

YOU CANNOT OUTRUN IT.
EXCUSE ME?
YOU CANNOT OUTRUN YOUR PAST NO MATTER HOW MUCH IT WEIGHS ON YOU.
HE DOES THAT.
DO NOT APOLOGIZE FOR ME.

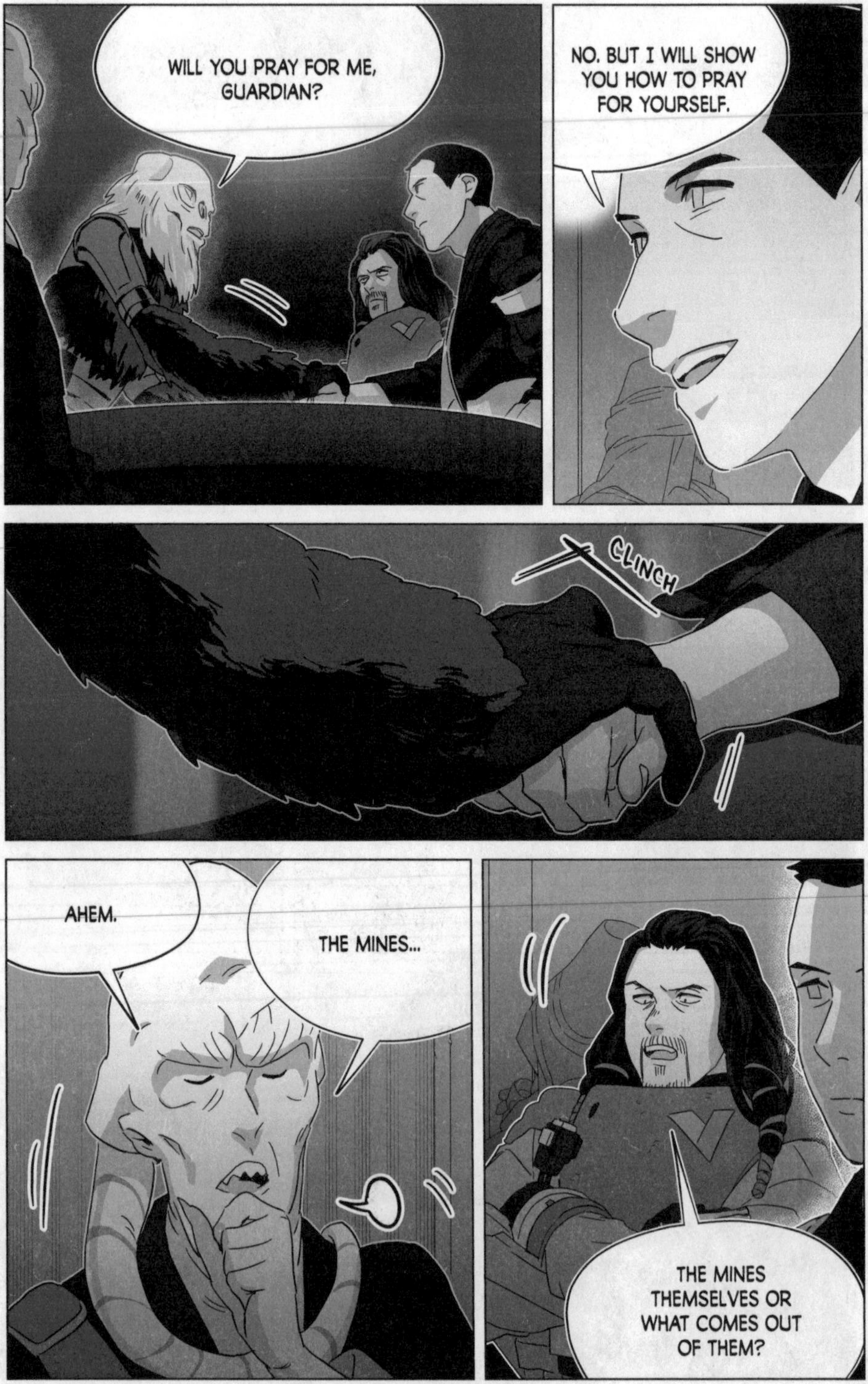
WILL YOU PRAY FOR ME, GUARDIAN?
NO. BUT I WILL SHOW YOU HOW TO PRAY FOR YOURSELF.
CLINCH
AHEM.
THE MINES...
THE MINES THEMSELVES OR WHAT COMES OUT OF THEM?

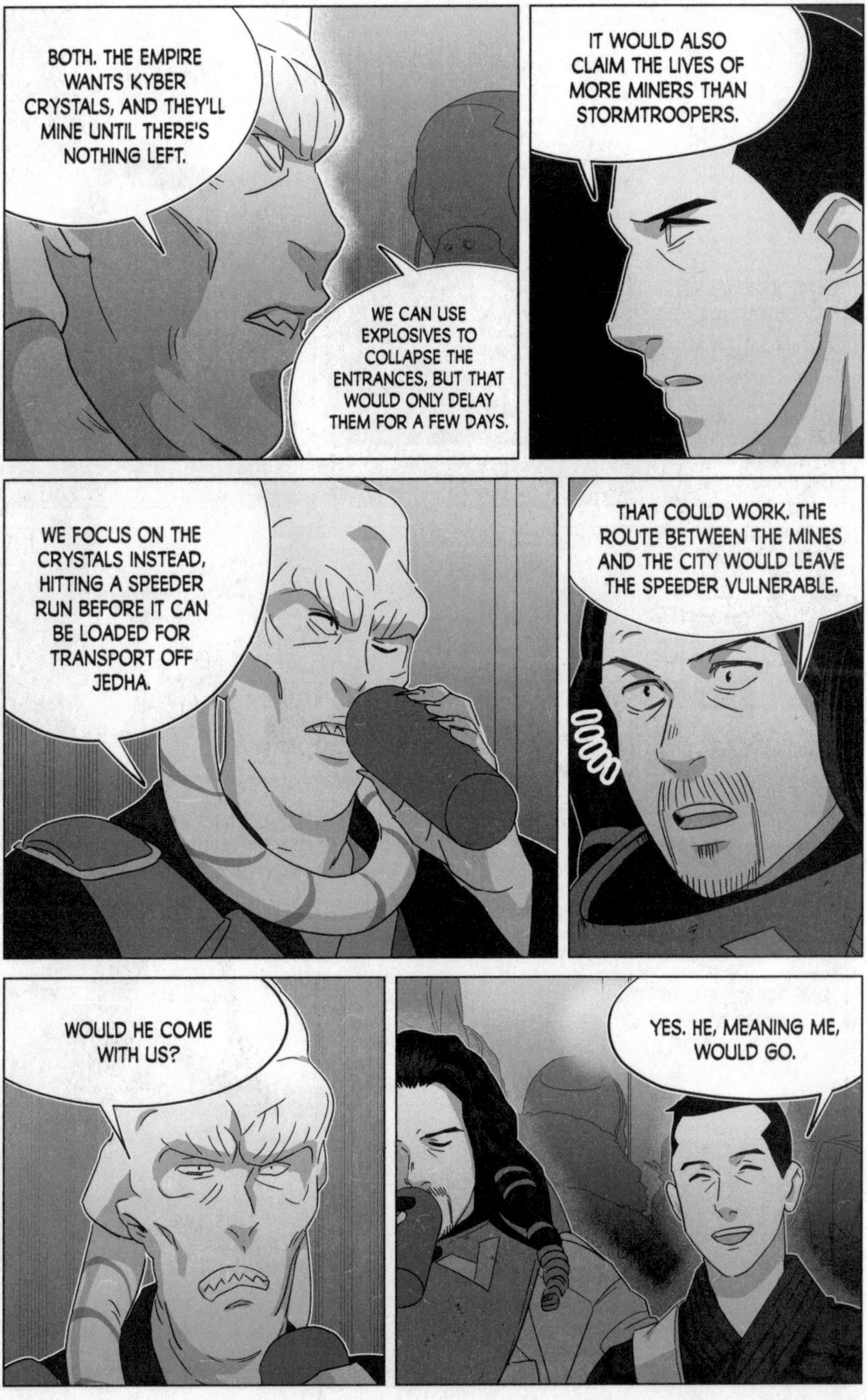
BOTH. THE EMPIRE WANTS KYBER CRYSTALS, AND THEY'LL MINE UNTIL THERE'S NOTHING LEFT.
WE CAN USE EXPLOSIVES TO COLLAPSE THE ENTRANCES, BUT THAT WOULD ONLY DELAY THEM FOR A FEW DAYS.
IT WOULD ALSO CLAIM THE LIVES OF MORE MINERS THAN STORMTROOPERS.
WE FOCUS ON THE CRYSTALS INSTEAD, HITTING A SPEEDER RUN BEFORE IT CAN BE LOADED FOR TRANSPORT OFF JEDHA.
THAT COULD WORK. THE ROUTE BETWEEN THE MINES AND THE CITY WOULD LEAVE THE SPEEDER VULNERABLE.
WOULD HE COME WITH US?
YES. HE, MEANING ME, WOULD GO.

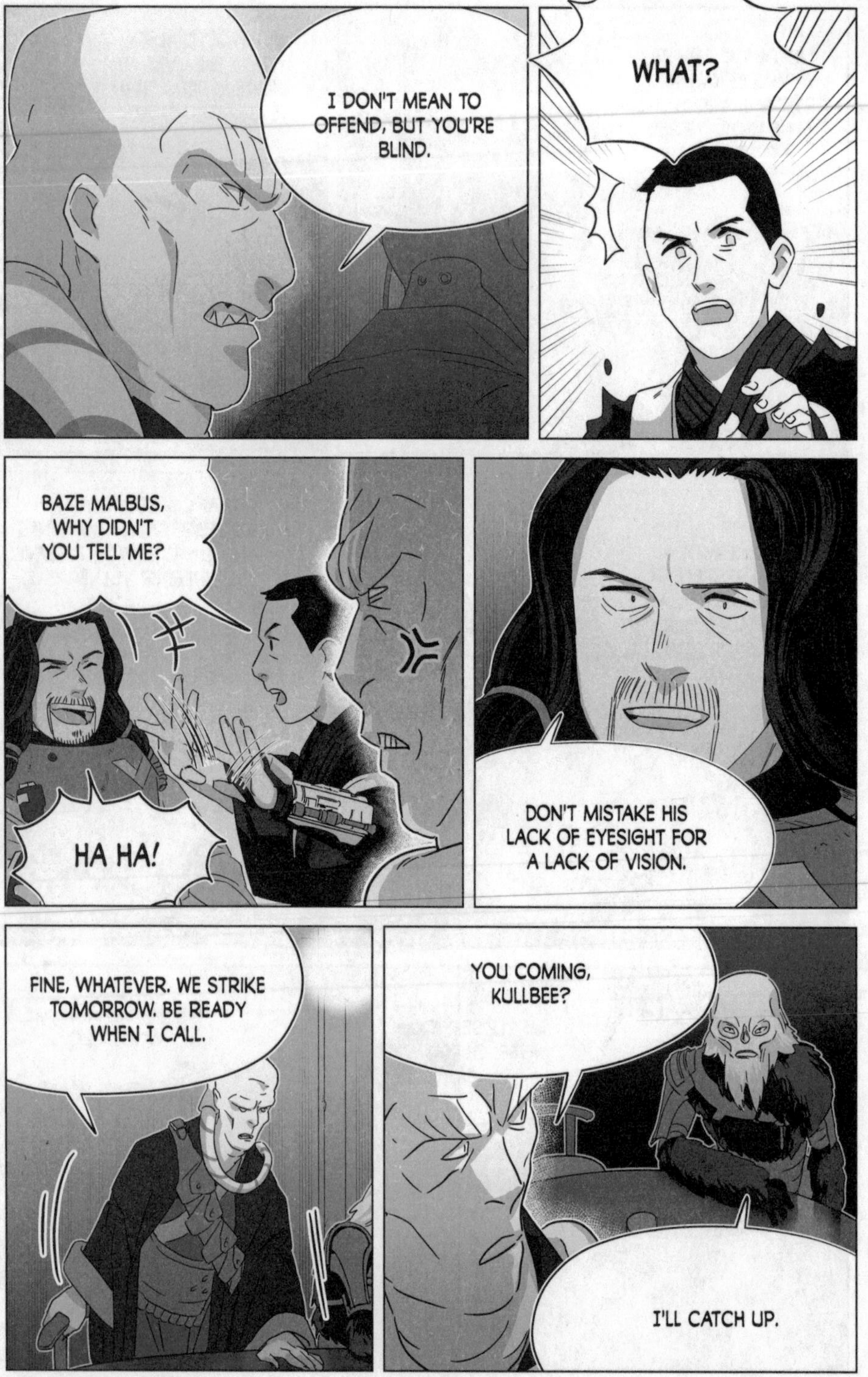
I DON'T MEAN TO OFFEND, BUT YOU'RE BLIND.
WHAT?
BAZE MALBUS, WHY DIDN'T YOU TELL ME?
HA HA!
DON'T MISTAKE HIS LACK OF EYESIGHT FOR A LACK OF VISION.
FINE, WHATEVER. WE STRIKE TOMORROW. BE READY WHEN I CALL.
YOU COMING, KULLBEE?
I'LL CATCH UP.

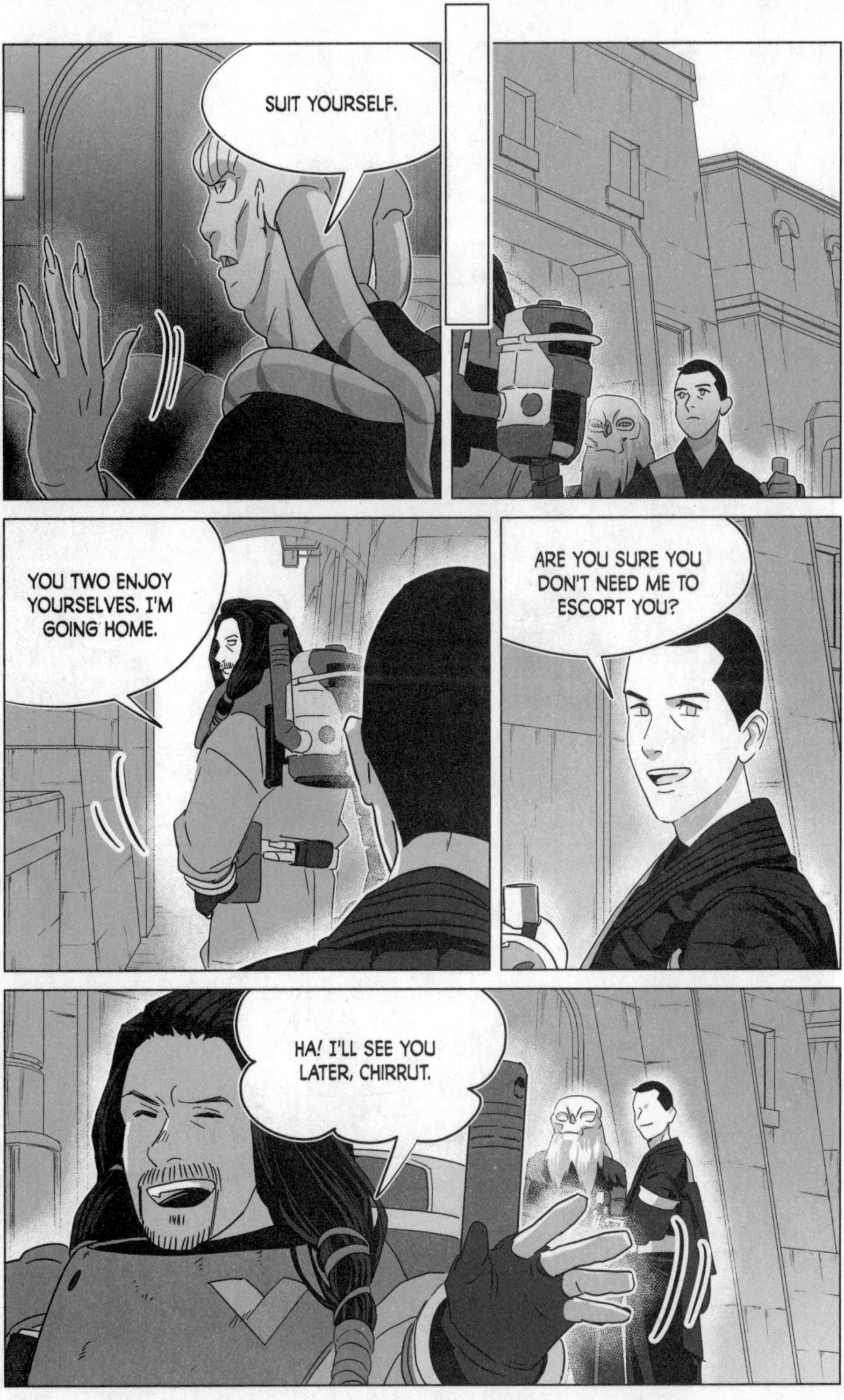
SUIT YOURSELF.
YOU TWO ENJOY YOURSELVES. I'M GOING HOME.
ARE YOU SURE YOU DON'T NEED ME TO ESCORT YOU?
HA! I'LL SEE YOU LATER, CHIRRUT.

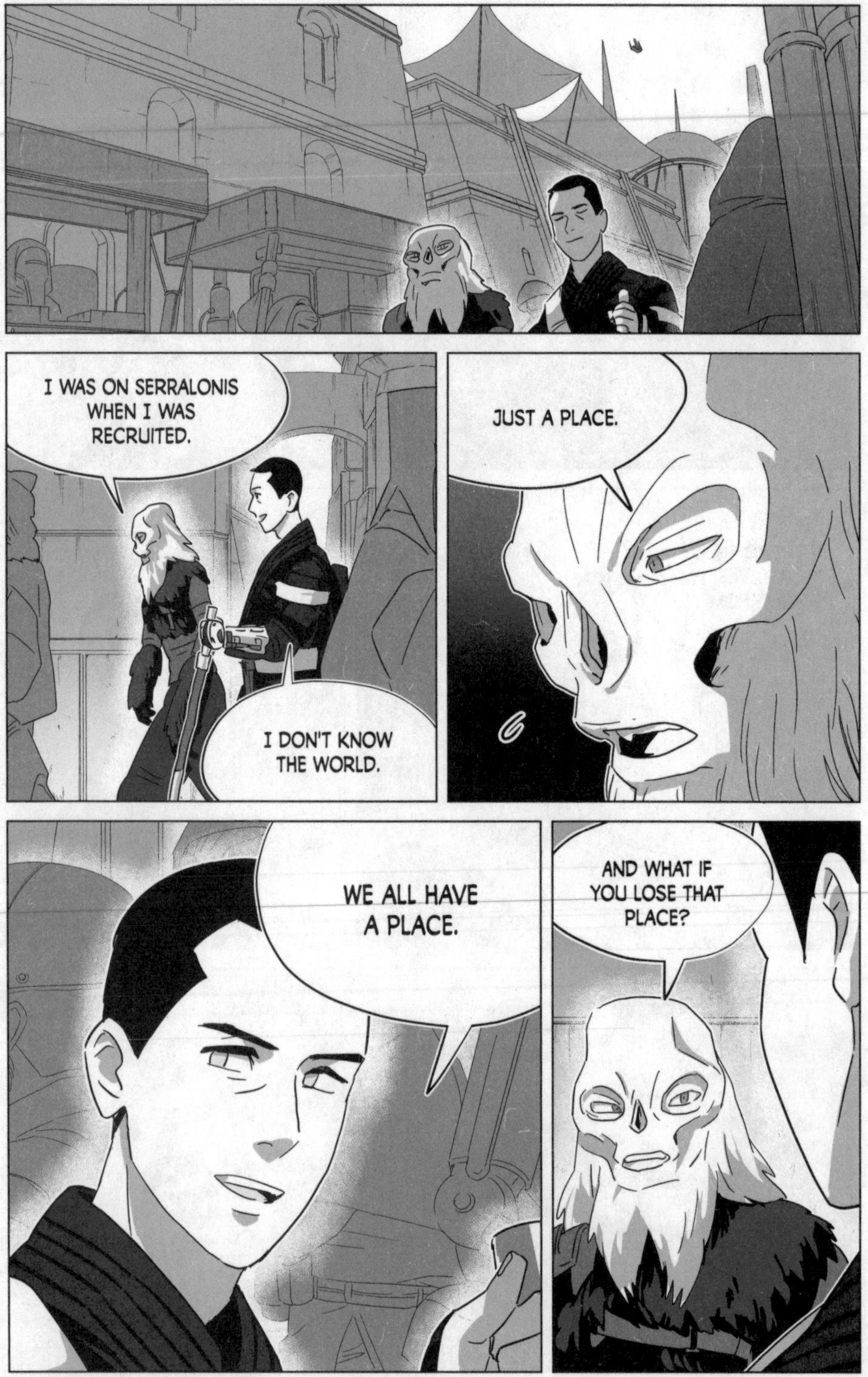
I WAS ON SERRALONIS WHEN I WAS RECRUITED.
I DON'T KNOW THE WORLD.
JUST A PLACE.
WE ALL HAVE A PLACE.
AND WHAT IF YOU LOSE THAT PLACE?

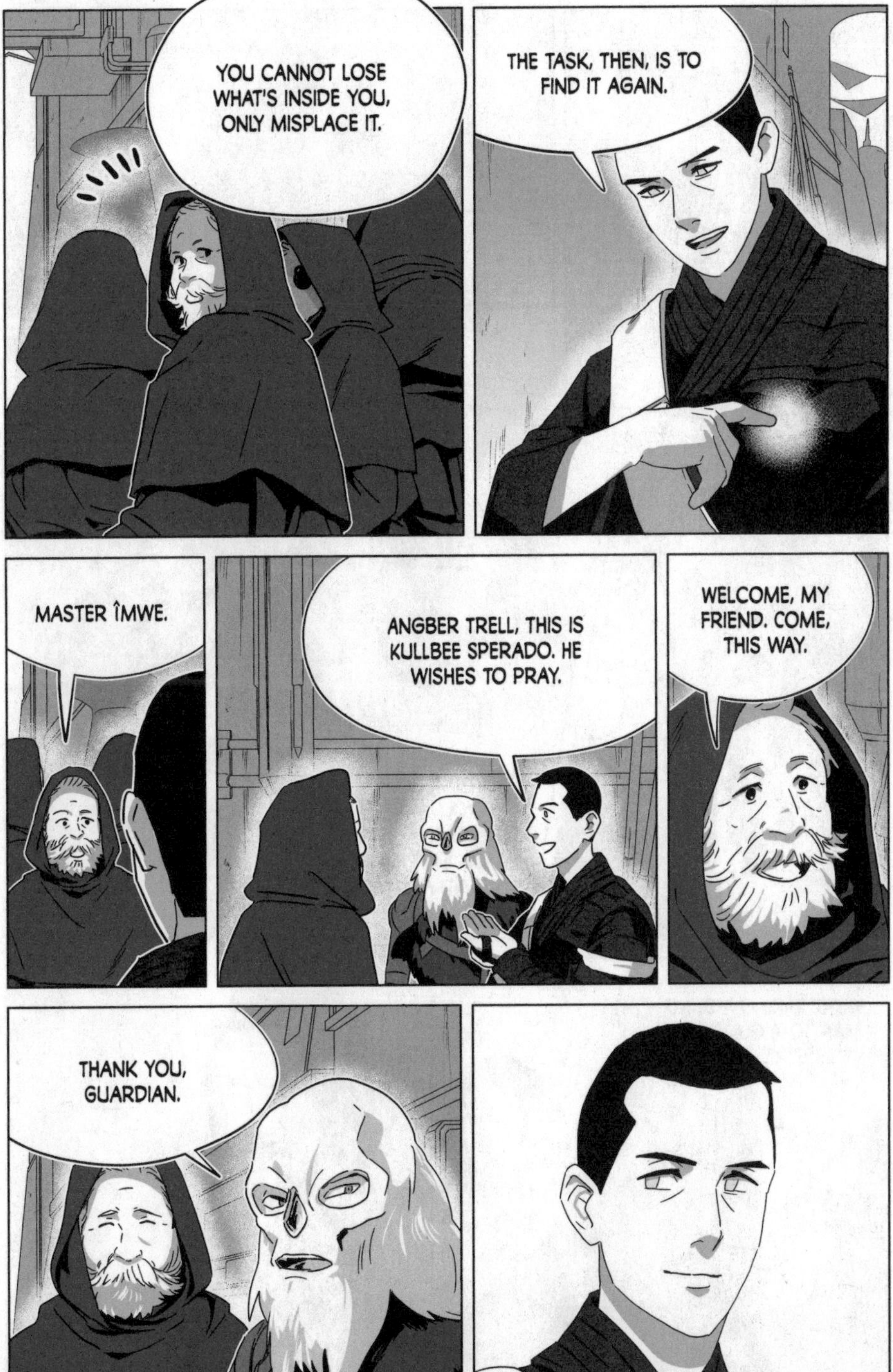
YOU CANNOT LOSE WHAT'S INSIDE YOU, ONLY MISPLACE IT.
THE TASK, THEN, IS TO FIND IT AGAIN.
MASTER ÎMWE.
ANGBER TRELL, THIS IS KULLBEE SPERADO. HE WISHES TO PRAY.
WELCOME, MY FRIEND. COME, THIS WAY.
THANK YOU, GUARDIAN.

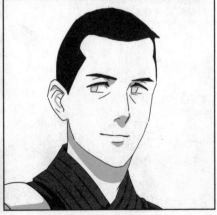

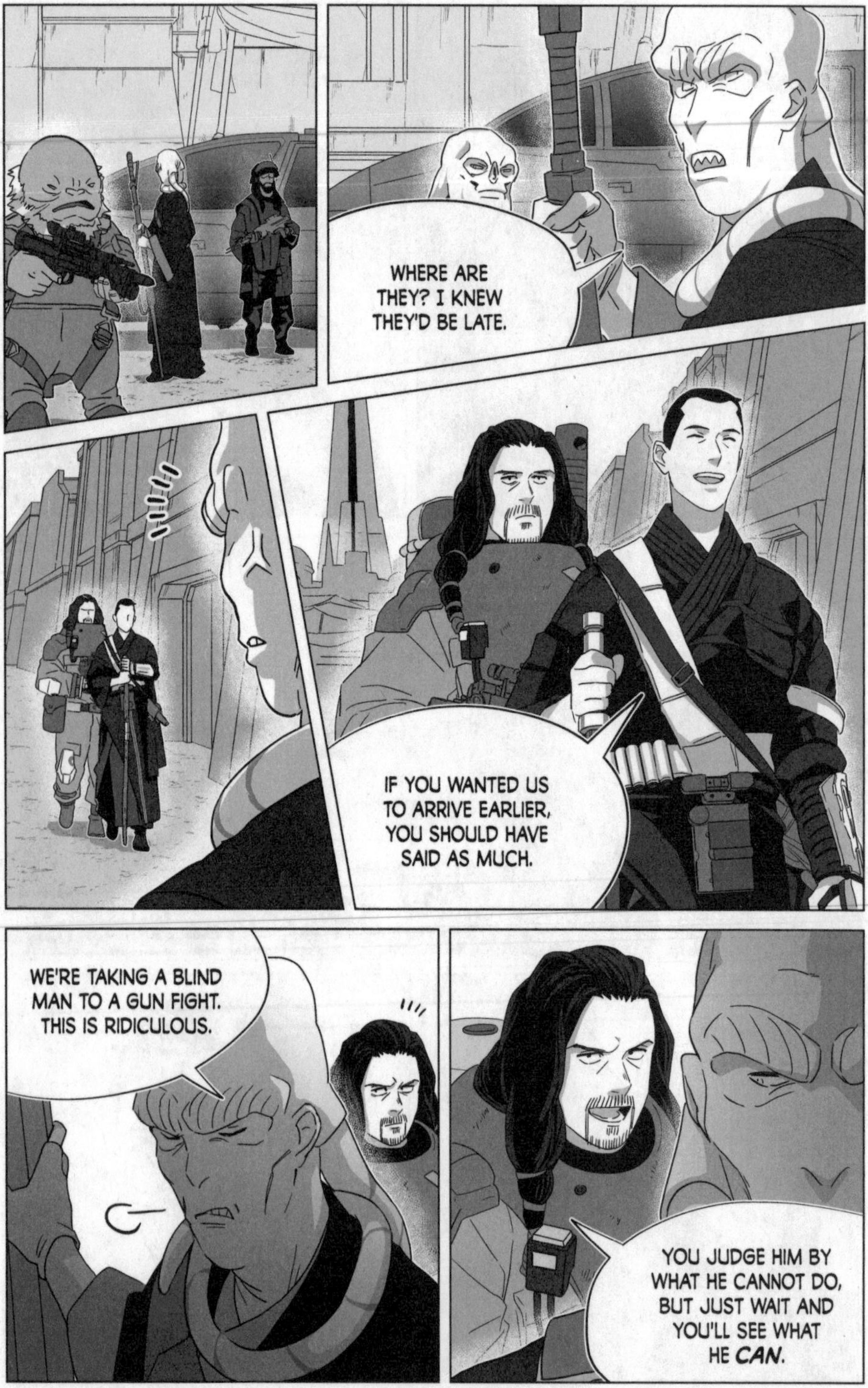
WHERE ARE THEY? I KNEW THEY'D BE LATE.
IF YOU WANTED US TO ARRIVE EARLIER, YOU SHOULD HAVE SAID AS MUCH.
WE'RE TAKING A BLIND MAN TO A GUN FIGHT. THIS IS RIDICULOUS.
YOU JUDGE HIM BY WHAT HE CANNOT DO, BUT JUST WAIT AND YOU'LL SEE WHAT HE ***CAN***.

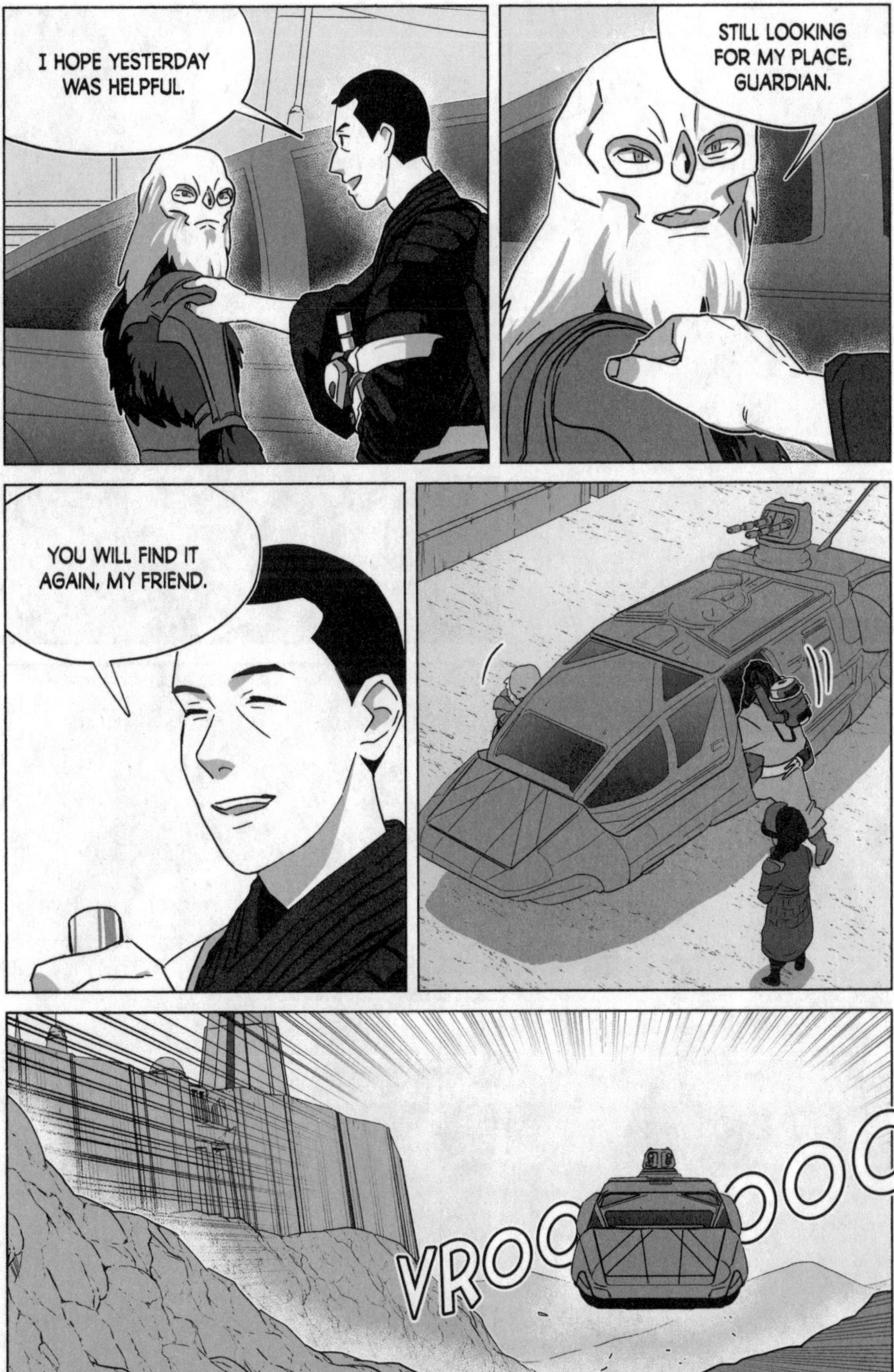
I HOPE YESTERDAY WAS HELPFUL.
STILL LOOKING FOR MY PLACE, GUARDIAN.
YOU WILL FIND IT AGAIN, MY FRIEND.
VROOOOOOO

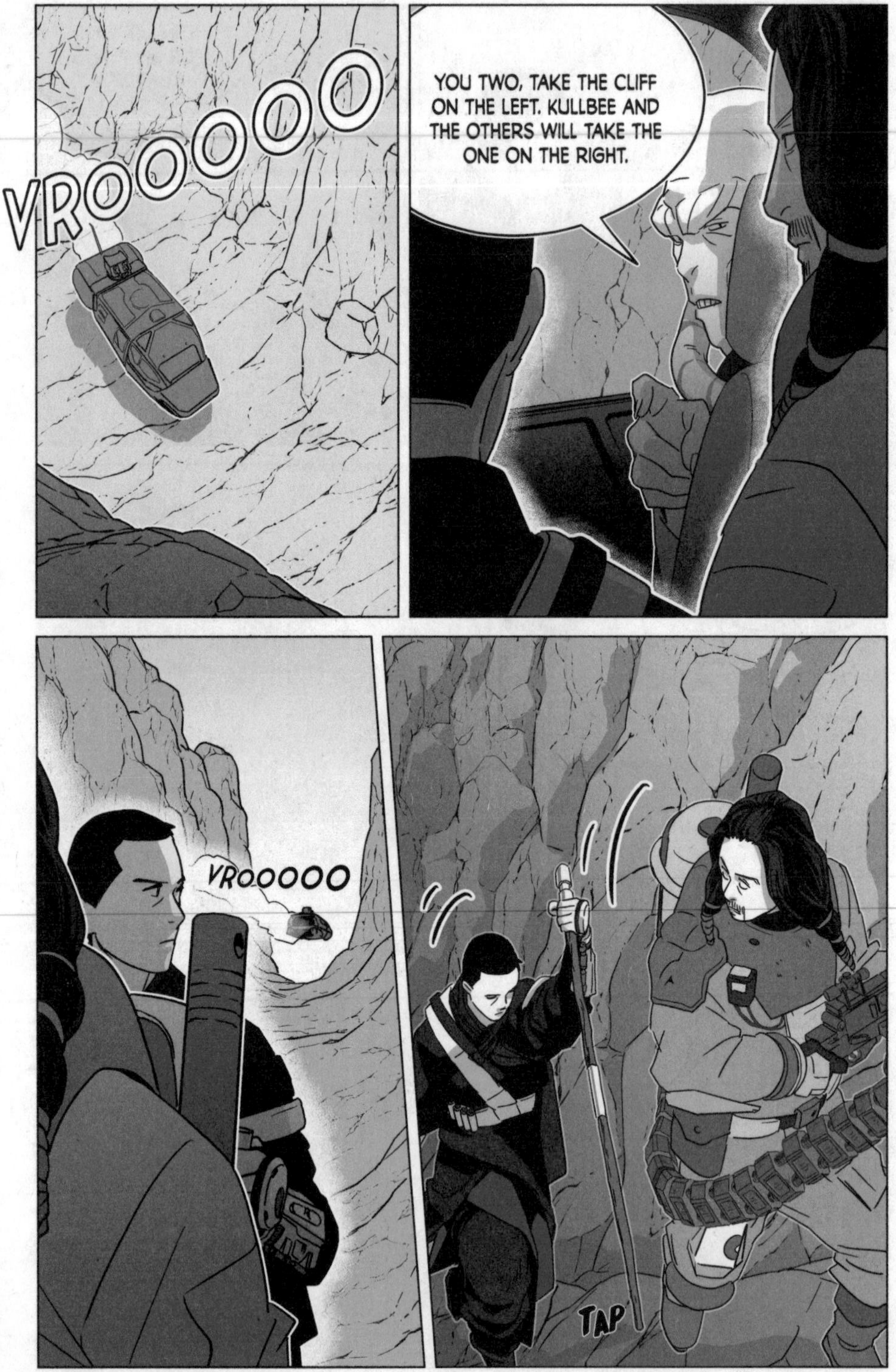
VROOOOOO
YOU TWO, TAKE THE CLIFF ON THE LEFT. KULLBEE AND THE OTHERS WILL TAKE THE ONE ON THE RIGHT.
VROOOOO
TAP

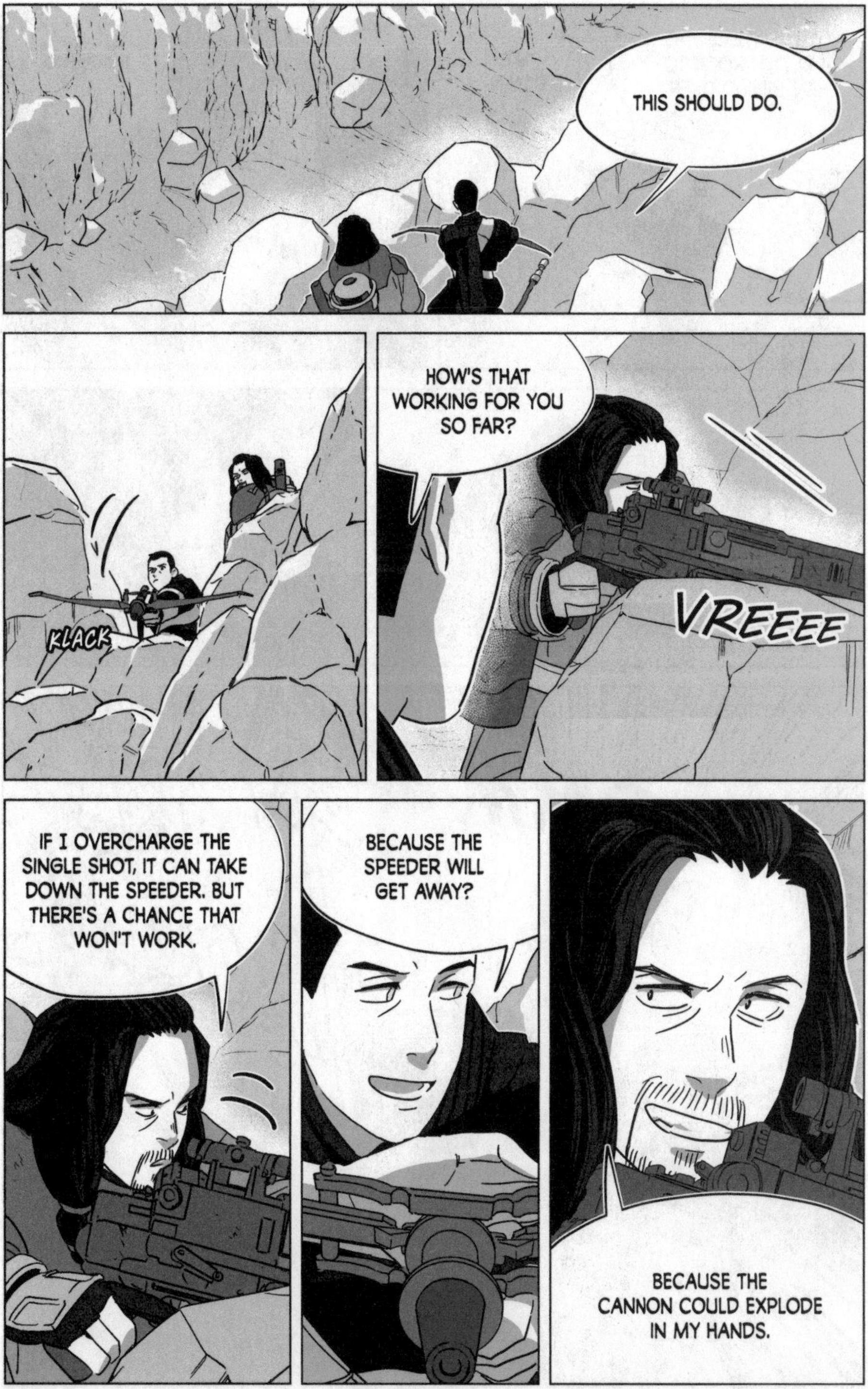
THIS SHOULD DO.
KLACK
HOW'S THAT WORKING FOR YOU SO FAR?
VREEEE
IF I OVERCHARGE THE SINGLE SHOT, IT CAN TAKE DOWN THE SPEEDER. BUT THERE'S A CHANCE THAT WON'T WORK.
BECAUSE THE SPEEDER WILL GET AWAY?
BECAUSE THE CANNON COULD EXPLODE IN MY HANDS.

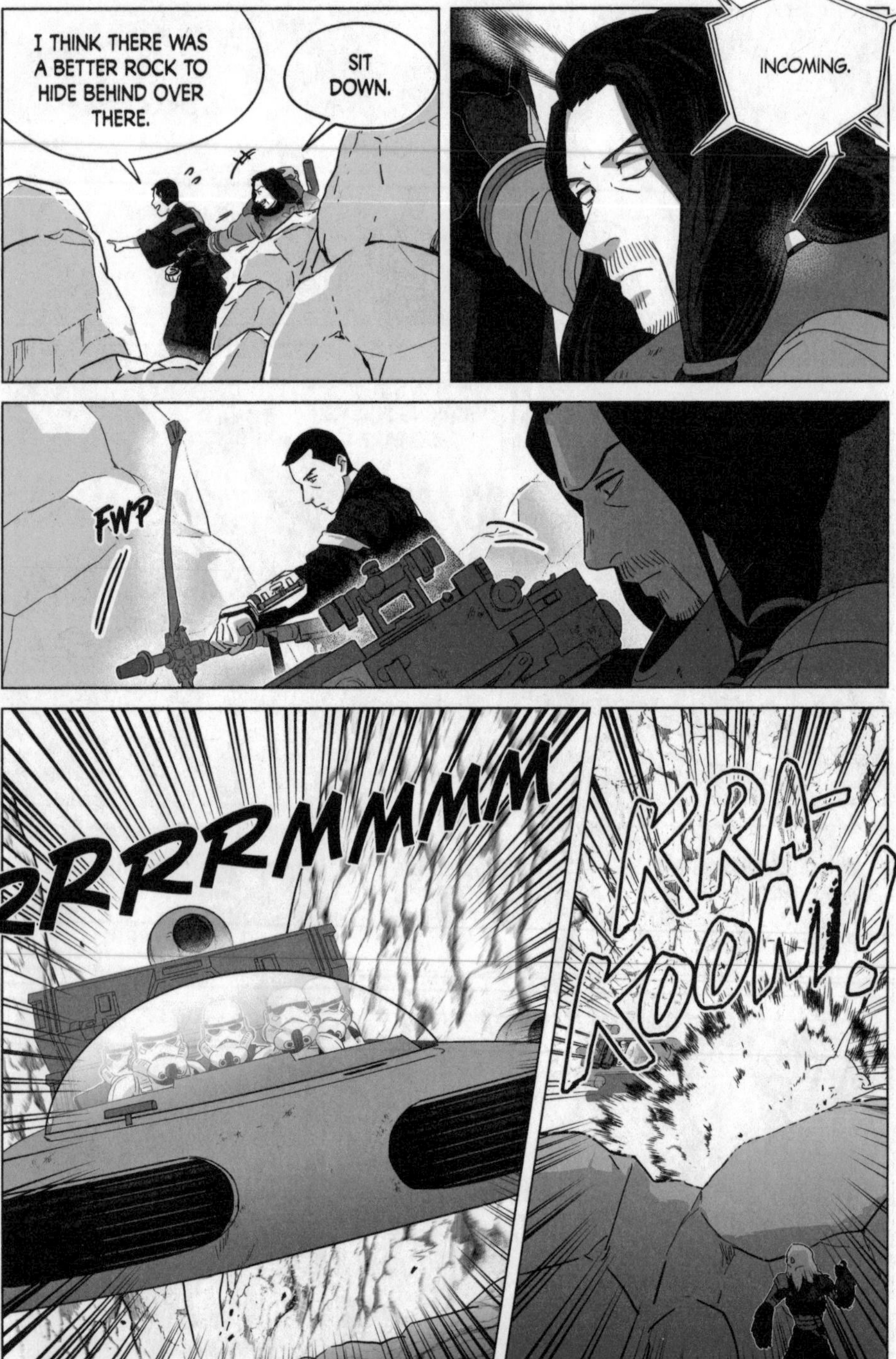
I THINK THERE WAS A BETTER ROCK TO HIDE BEHIND OVER THERE.
SIT DOWN.
INCOMING.
FWP
RRRRMMMMM
KRA-KOOM!

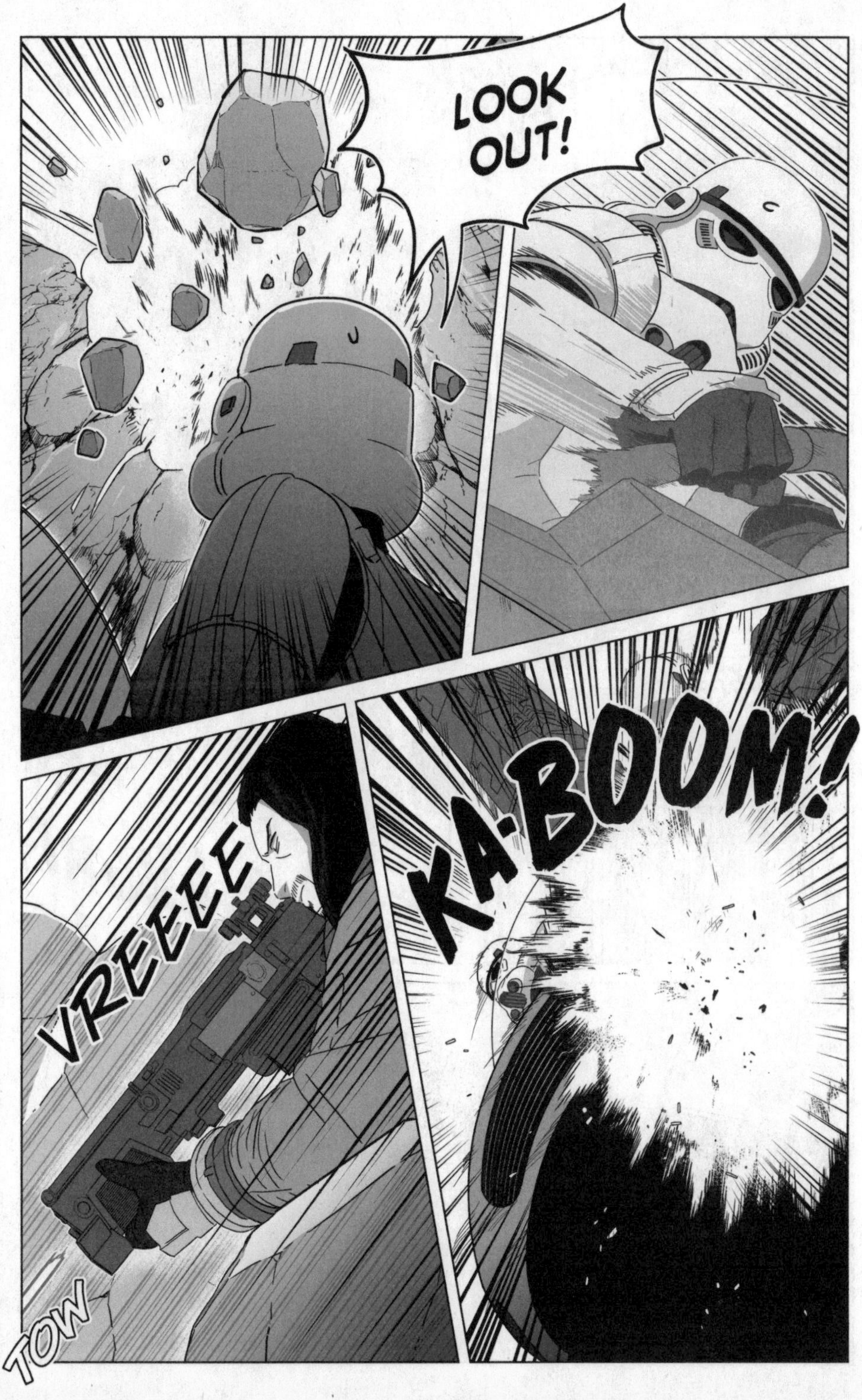
LOOK OUT!
VREEEEE
TOW
KA-BOOM!

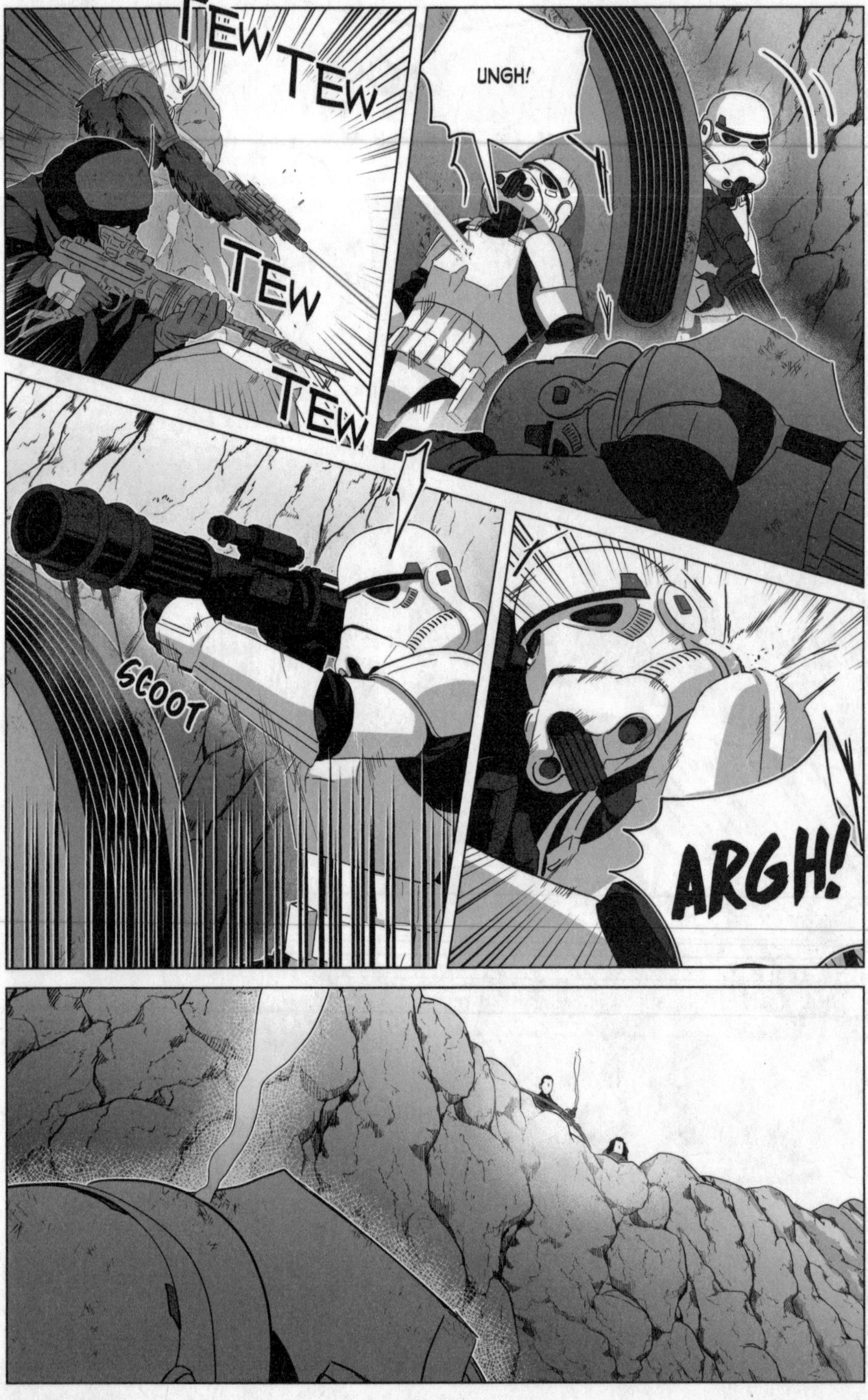
TEW TEW
TEW
TEW
UNGH!
SCOOT
ARGH!

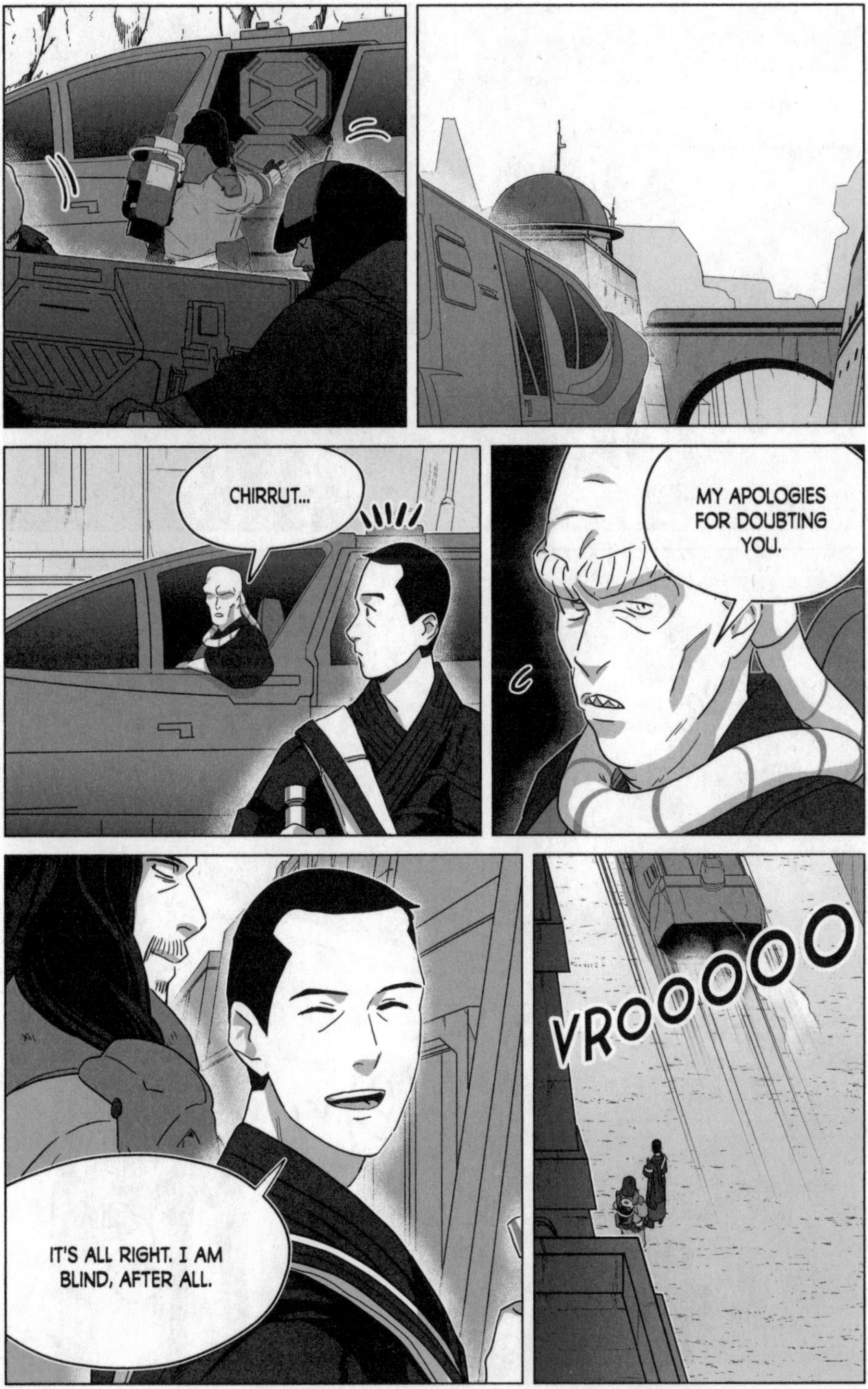

CHIRRUT...
MY APOLOGIES FOR DOUBTING YOU.
IT'S ALL RIGHT. I AM BLIND, AFTER ALL.
VROOOOOO

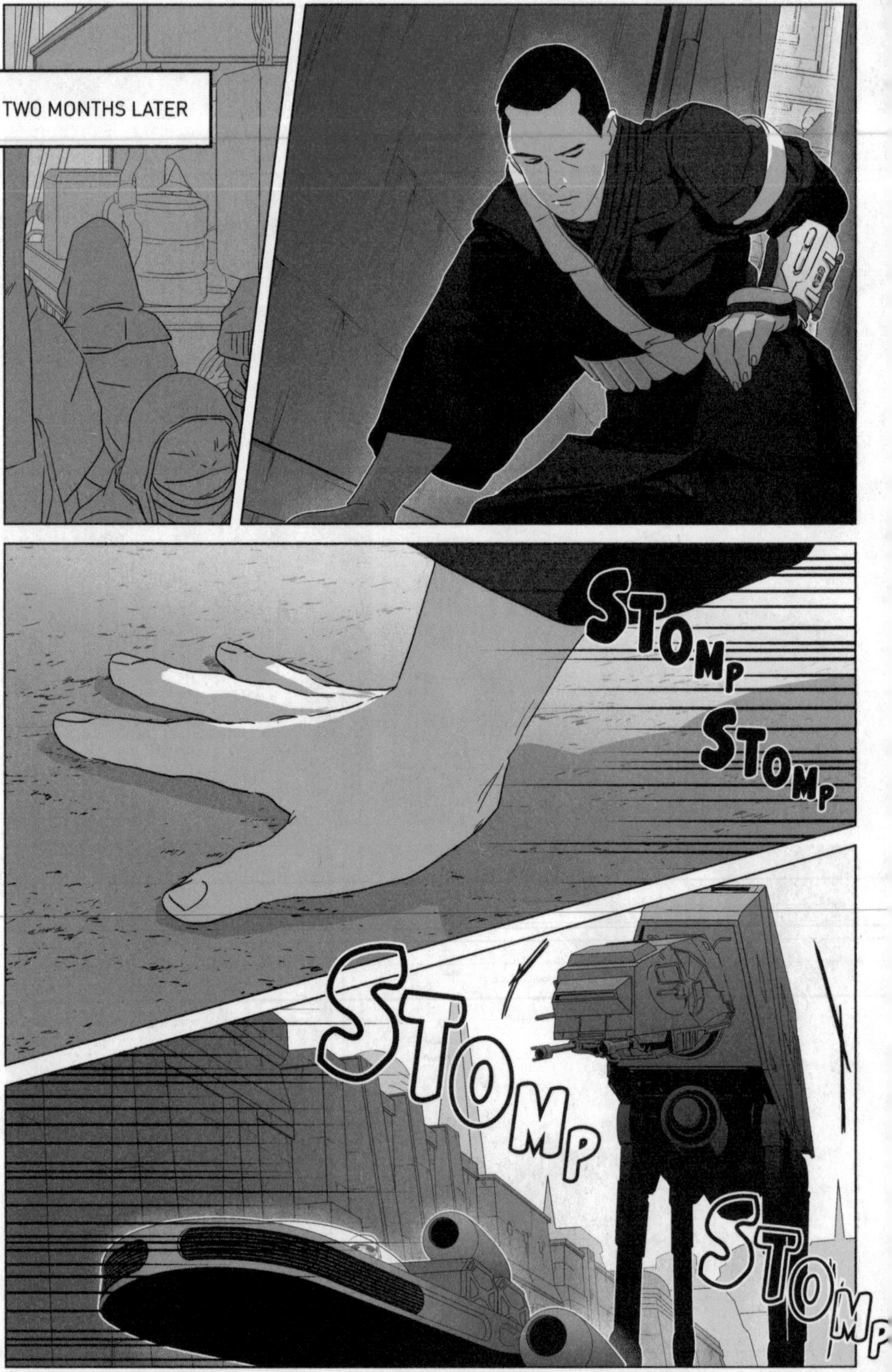
TWO MONTHS LATER
STOMP
STOMP
STOMP
STOMP

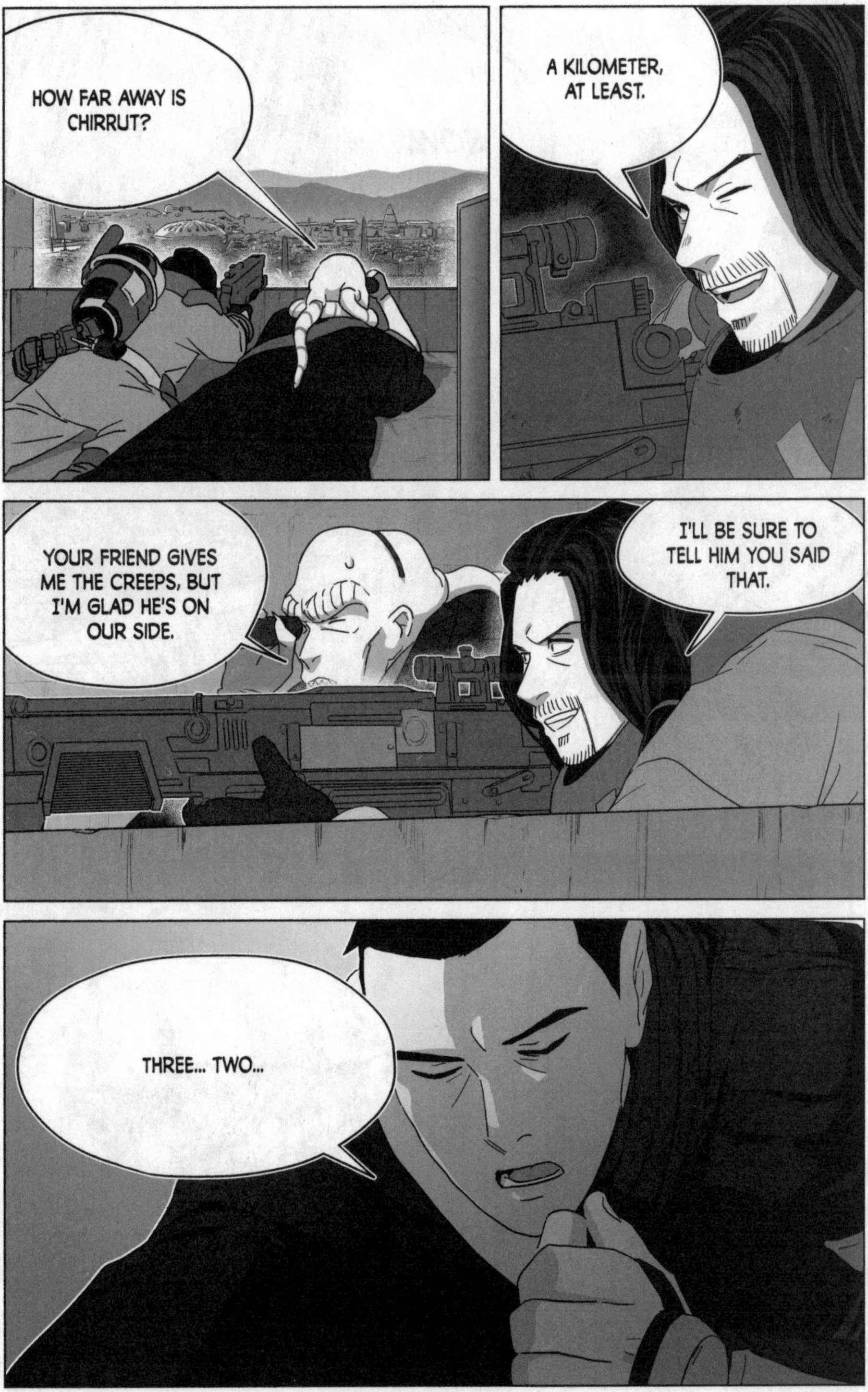
HOW FAR AWAY IS CHIRRUT?
A KILOMETER, AT LEAST.
YOUR FRIEND GIVES ME THE CREEPS, BUT I'M GLAD HE'S ON OUR SIDE.
I'LL BE SURE TO TELL HIM YOU SAID THAT.
THREE... TWO...

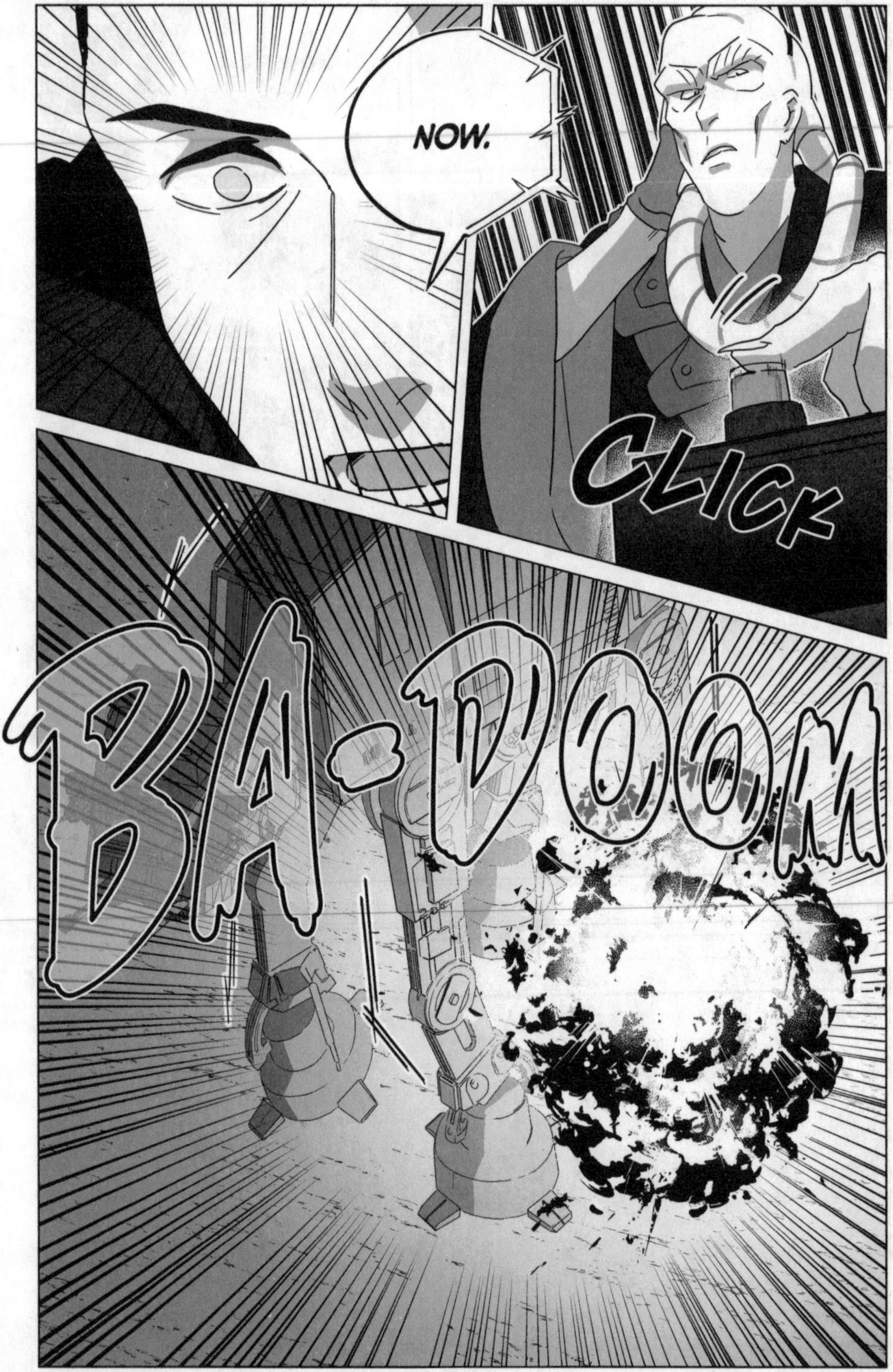
NOW.
CLICK
BA-DOOM

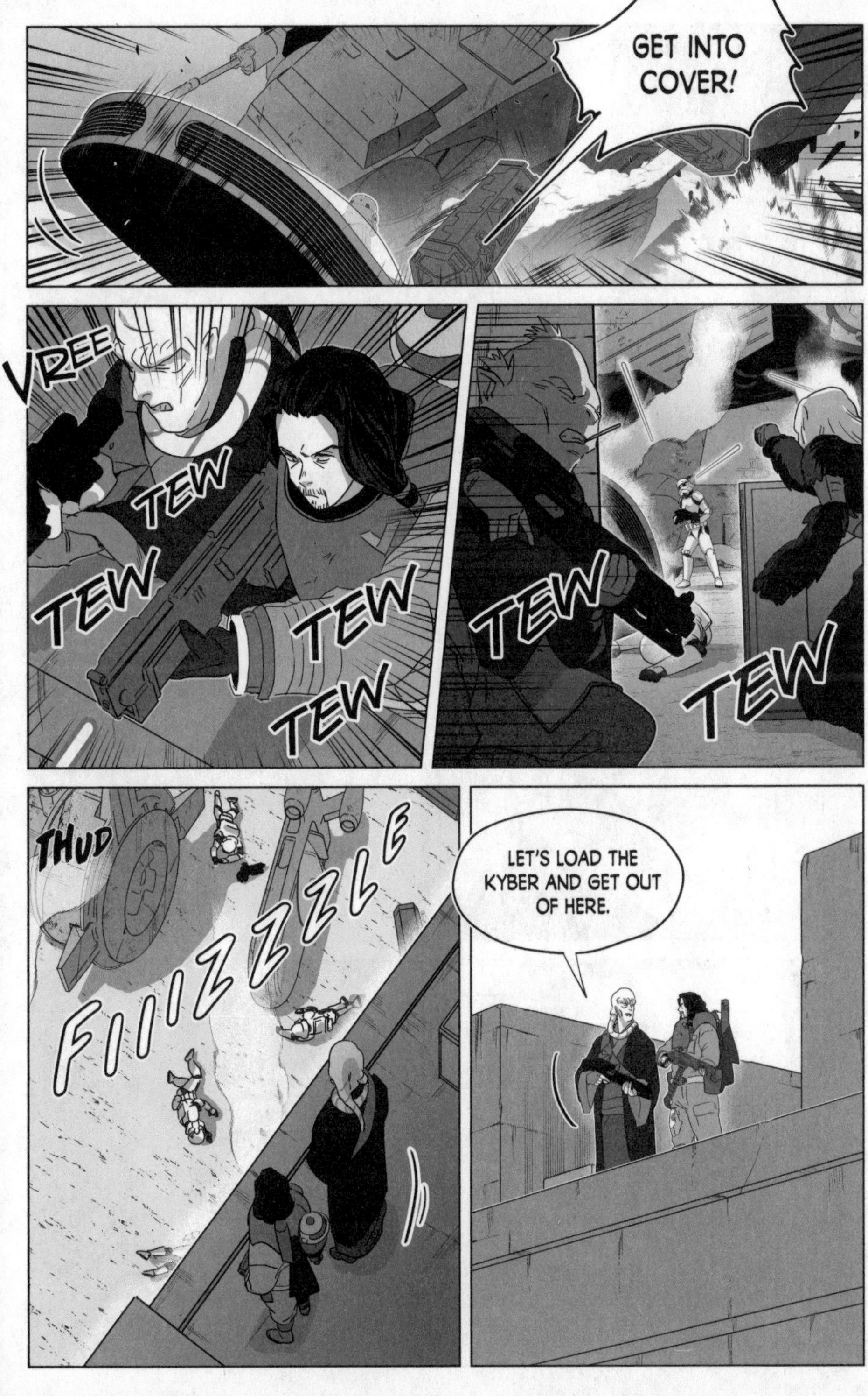
GET INTO COVER!
VREE
TEW
TEW
TEW
TEW
TEW
TEW
TEW
THUD
FIIIZZZZLE
LET'S LOAD THE KYBER AND GET OUT OF HERE.

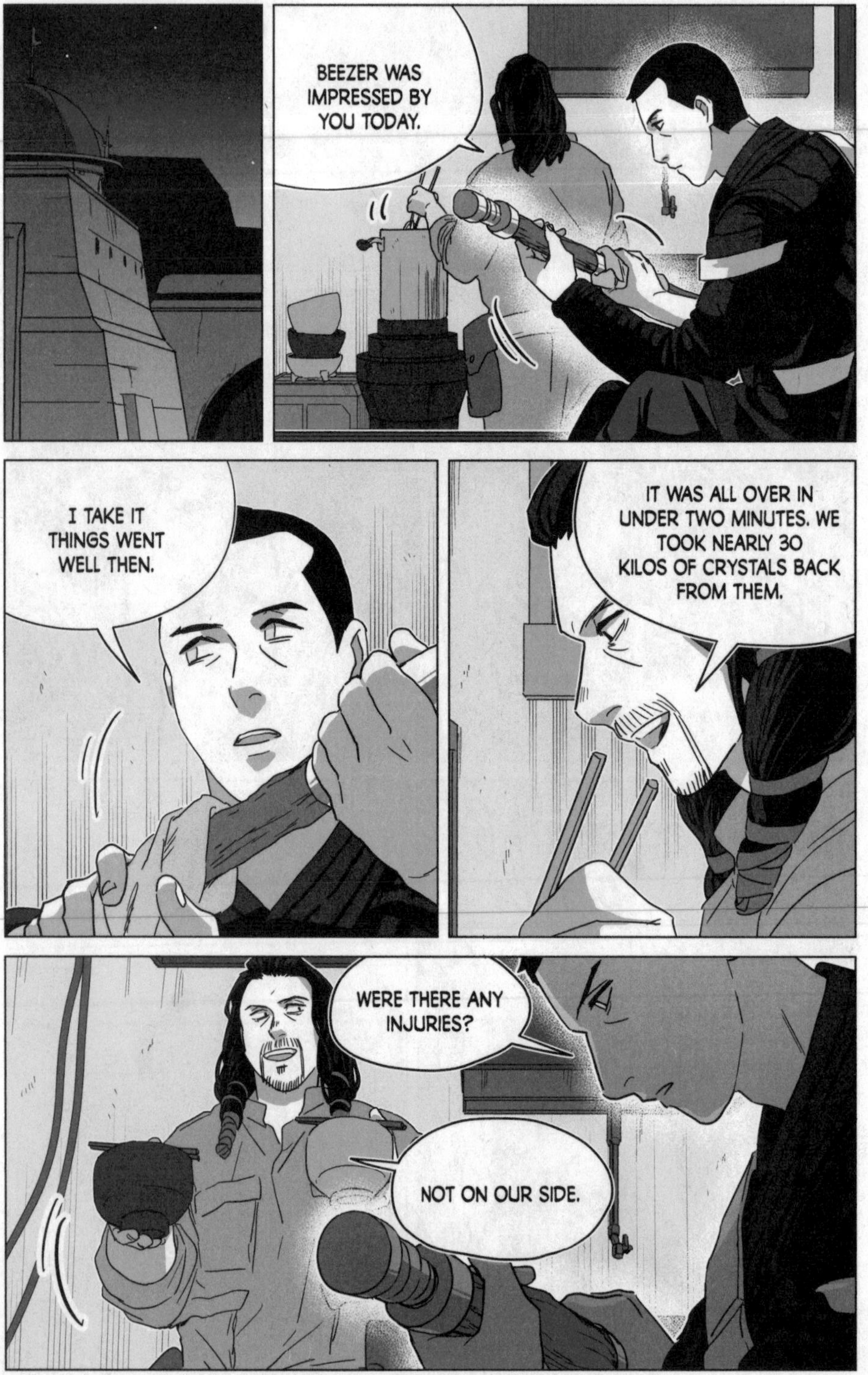
BEEZER WAS IMPRESSED BY YOU TODAY.
I TAKE IT THINGS WENT WELL THEN.
IT WAS ALL OVER IN UNDER TWO MINUTES. WE TOOK NEARLY 30 KILOS OF CRYSTALS BACK FROM THEM.
WERE THERE ANY INJURIES?
NOT ON OUR SIDE.

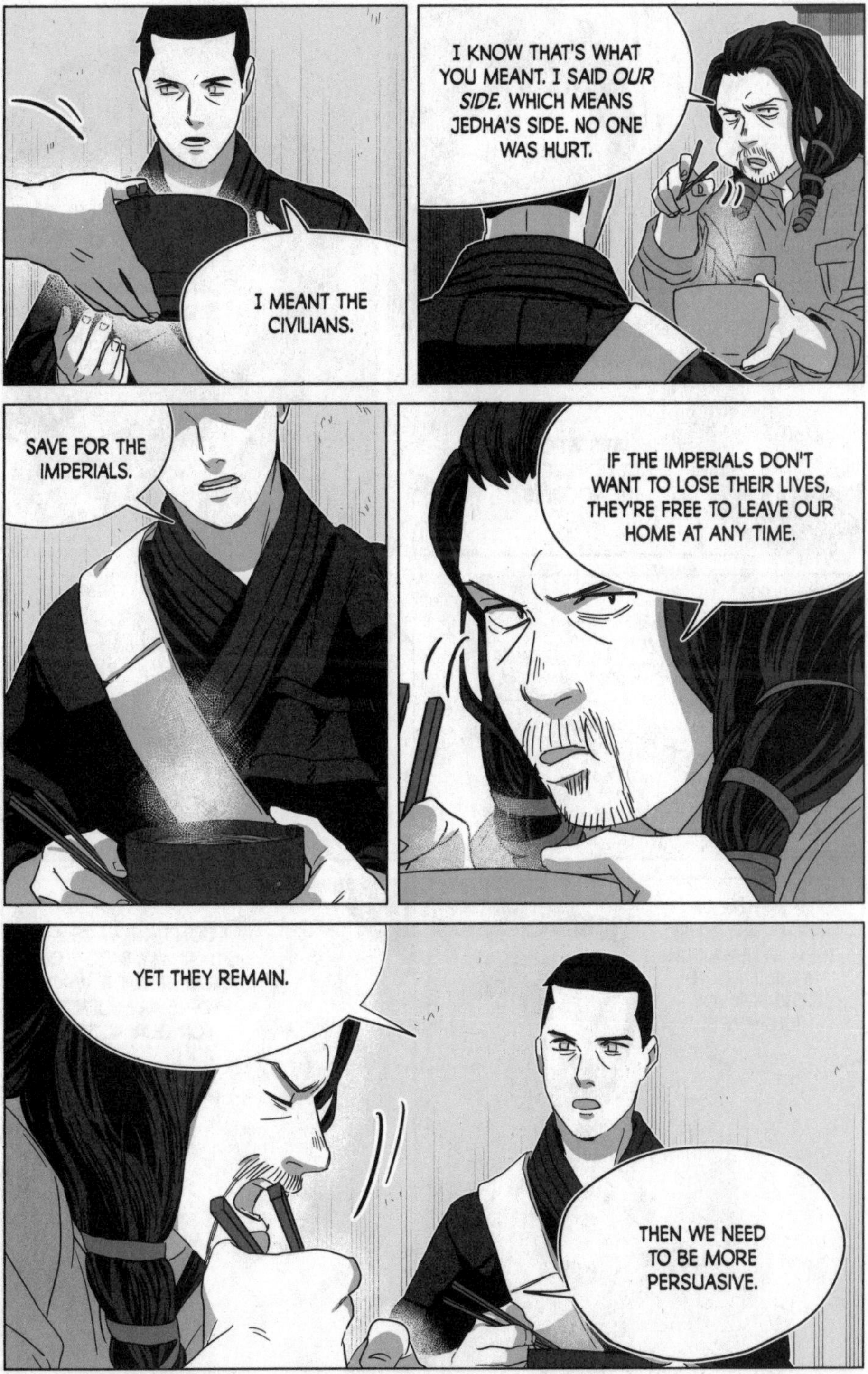
I MEANT THE CIVILIANS.
I KNOW THAT'S WHAT YOU MEANT. I SAID *OUR SIDE.* WHICH MEANS JEDHA'S SIDE. NO ONE WAS HURT.
SAVE FOR THE IMPERIALS.
IF THE IMPERIALS DON'T WANT TO LOSE THEIR LIVES, THEY'RE FREE TO LEAVE OUR HOME AT ANY TIME.
YET THEY REMAIN.
THEN WE NEED TO BE MORE PERSUASIVE.

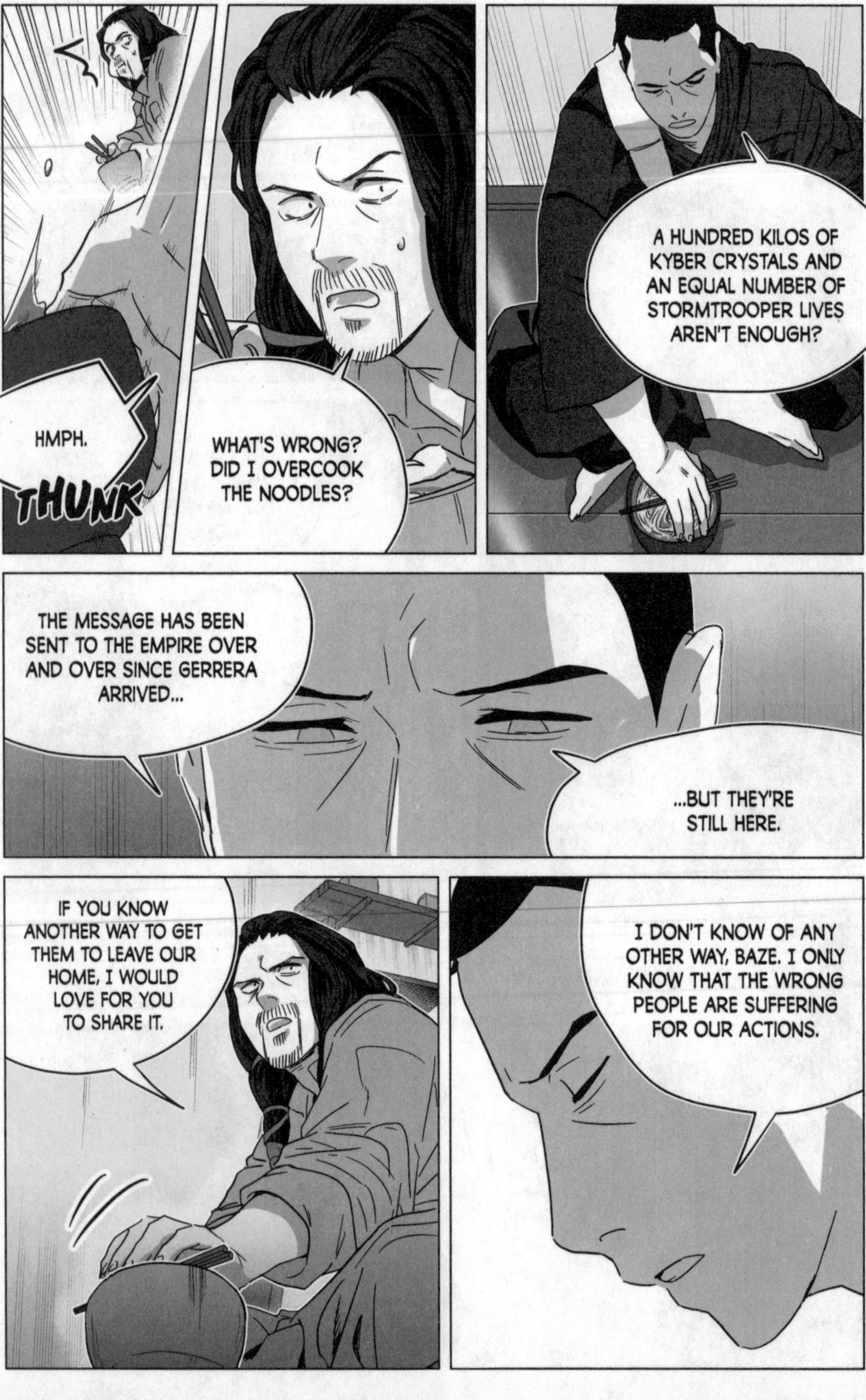
HMPH.
THUNK
WHAT'S WRONG? DID I OVERCOOK THE NOODLES?
A HUNDRED KILOS OF KYBER CRYSTALS AND AN EQUAL NUMBER OF STORMTROOPER LIVES AREN'T ENOUGH?
THE MESSAGE HAS BEEN SENT TO THE EMPIRE OVER AND OVER SINCE GERRERA ARRIVED...
...BUT THEY'RE STILL HERE.
IF YOU KNOW ANOTHER WAY TO GET THEM TO LEAVE OUR HOME, I WOULD LOVE FOR YOU TO SHARE IT.
I DON'T KNOW OF ANY OTHER WAY, BAZE. I ONLY KNOW THAT THE WRONG PEOPLE ARE SUFFERING FOR OUR ACTIONS.

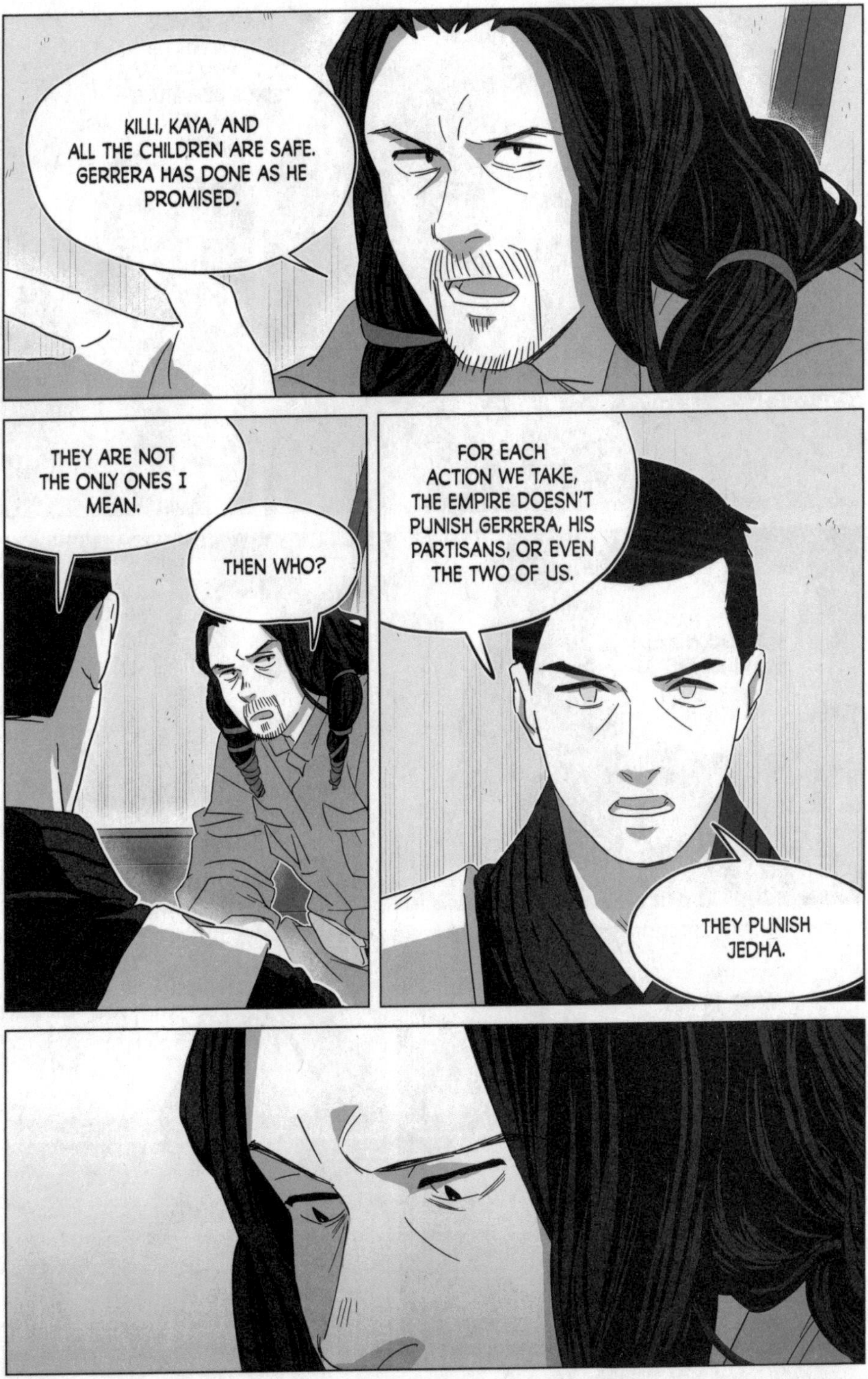
KILLI, KAYA, AND ALL THE CHILDREN ARE SAFE. GERRERA HAS DONE AS HE PROMISED.
THEY ARE NOT THE ONLY ONES I MEAN.
THEN WHO?
FOR EACH ACTION WE TAKE, THE EMPIRE DOESN'T PUNISH GERRERA, HIS PARTISANS, OR EVEN THE TWO OF US.
THEY PUNISH JEDHA.

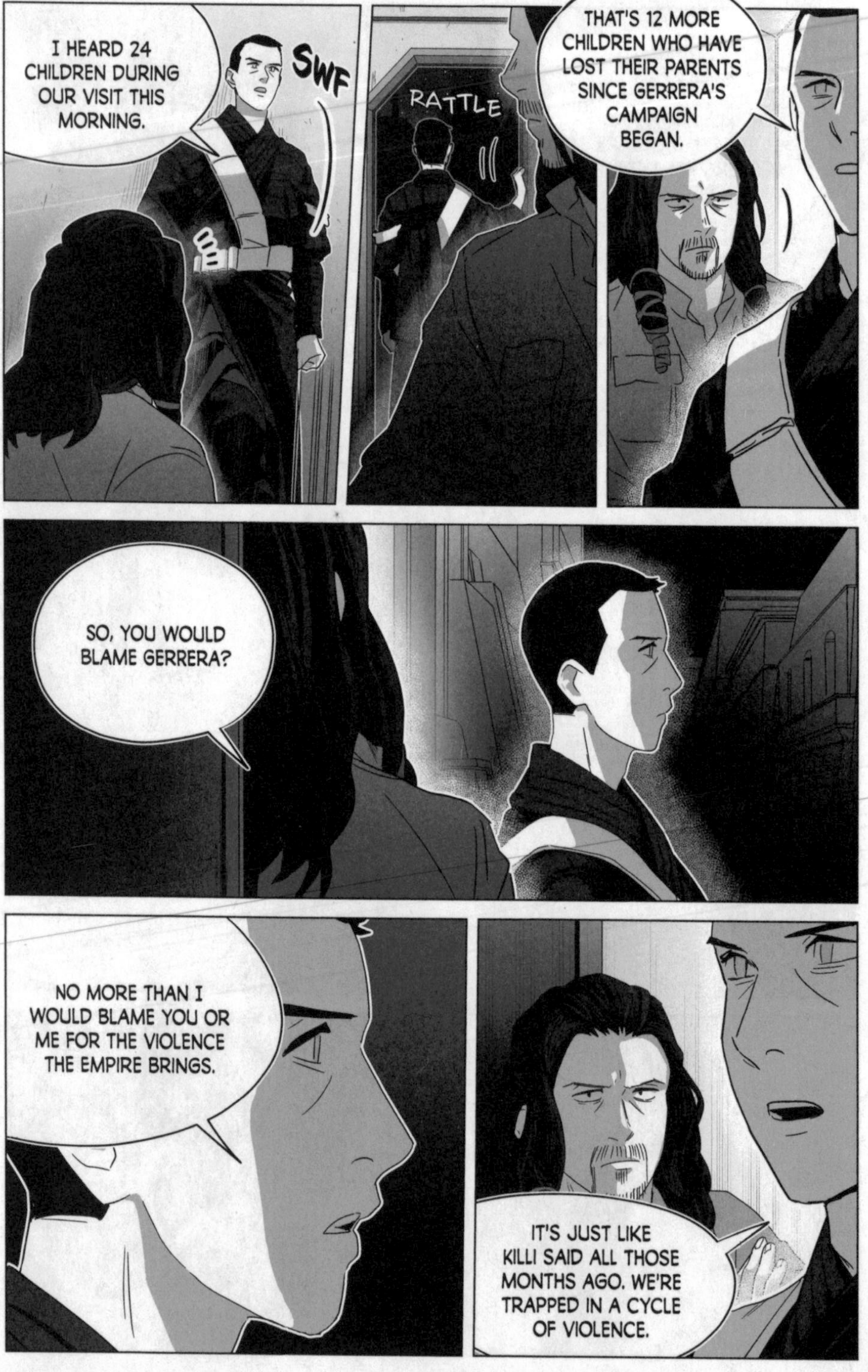
I HEARD 24 CHILDREN DURING OUR VISIT THIS MORNING.
SWF
RATTLE
THAT'S 12 MORE CHILDREN WHO HAVE LOST THEIR PARENTS SINCE GERRERA'S CAMPAIGN BEGAN.
SO, YOU WOULD BLAME GERRERA?
NO MORE THAN I WOULD BLAME YOU OR ME FOR THE VIOLENCE THE EMPIRE BRINGS.
IT'S JUST LIKE KILLI SAID ALL THOSE MONTHS AGO. WE'RE TRAPPED IN A CYCLE OF VIOLENCE.

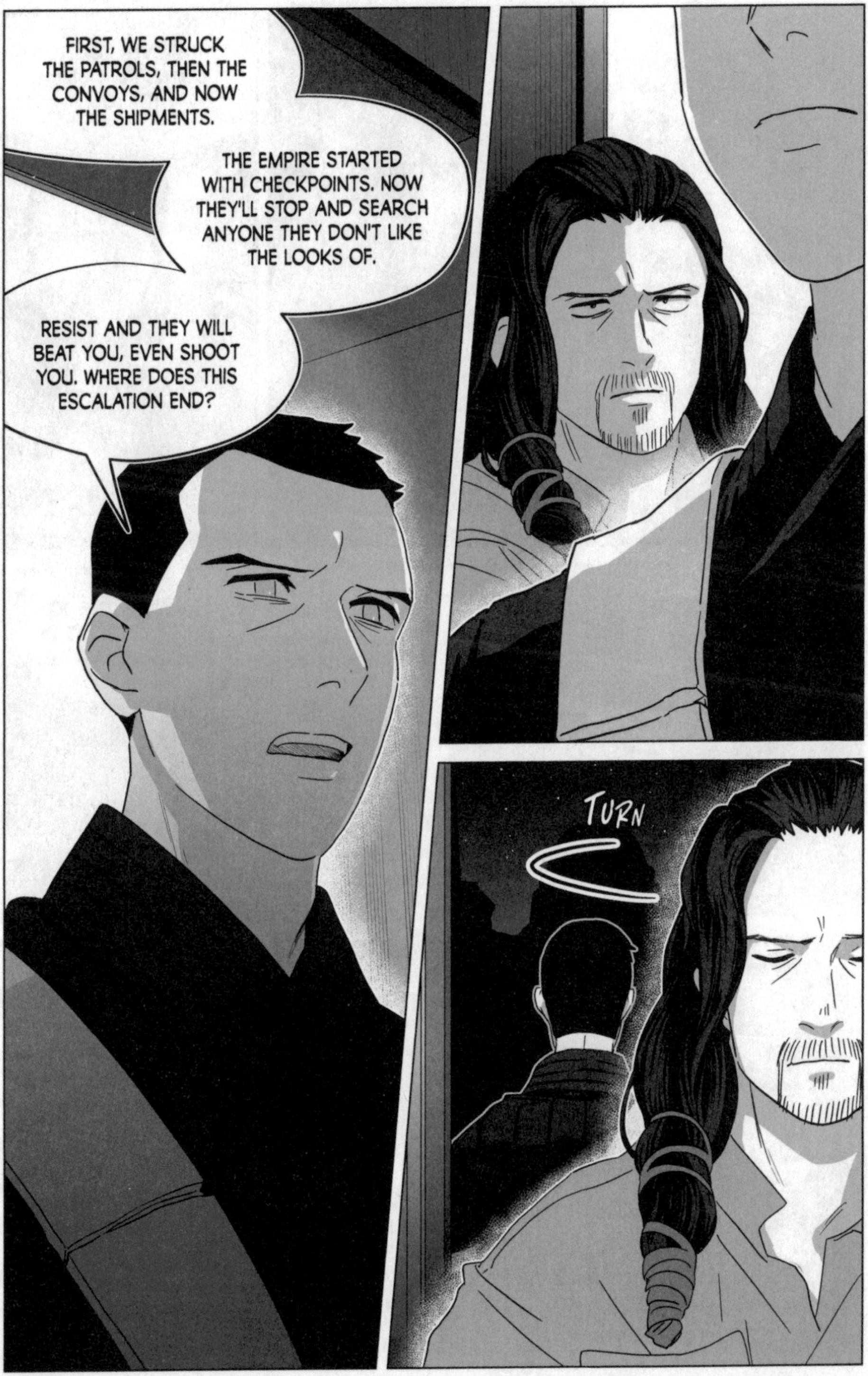
FIRST, WE STRUCK THE PATROLS, THEN THE CONVOYS, AND NOW THE SHIPMENTS.
THE EMPIRE STARTED WITH CHECKPOINTS. NOW THEY'LL STOP AND SEARCH ANYONE THEY DON'T LIKE THE LOOKS OF.
RESIST AND THEY WILL BEAT YOU, EVEN SHOOT YOU. WHERE DOES THIS ESCALATION END?
TURN

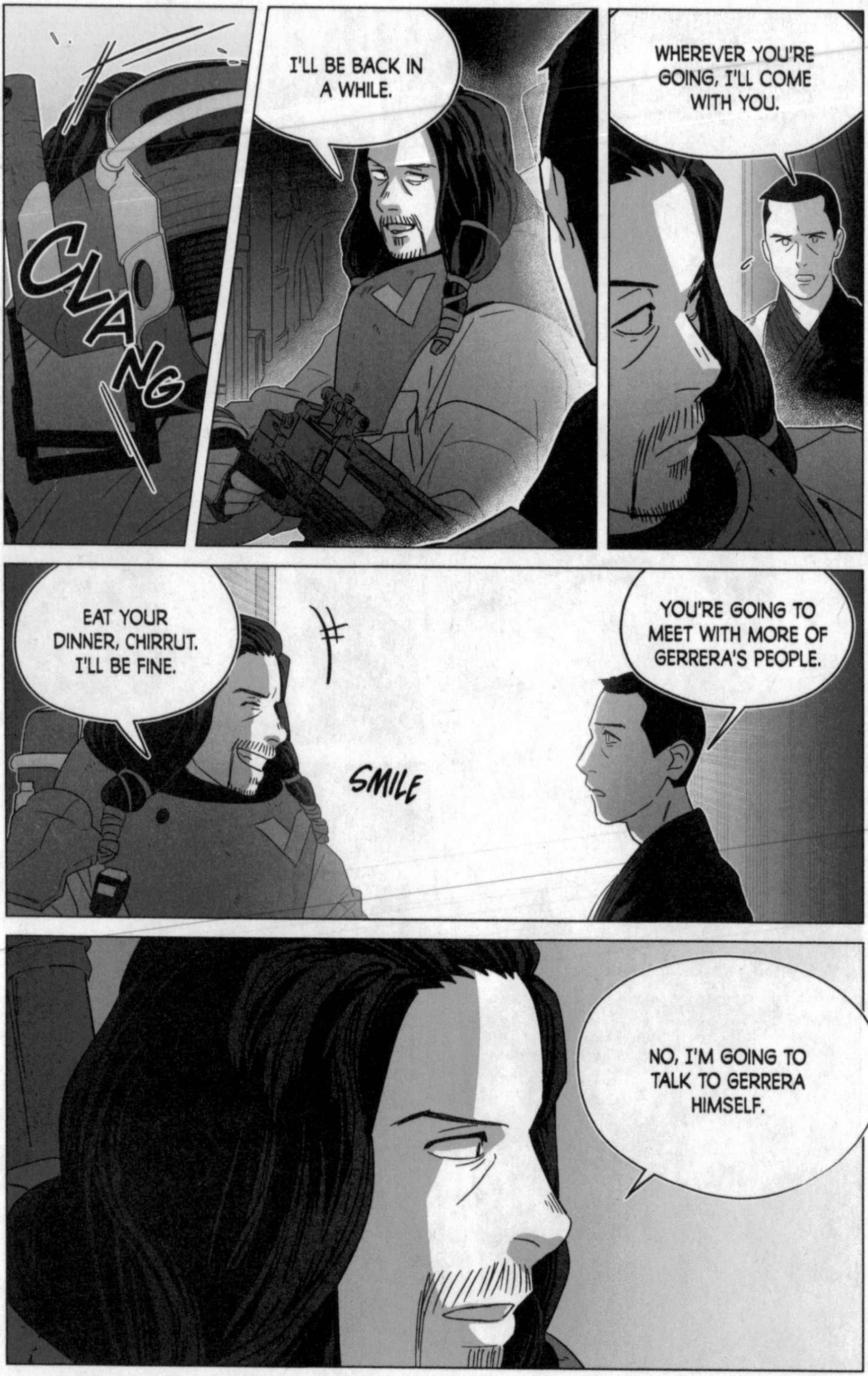
CLANG
I'LL BE BACK IN A WHILE.
WHEREVER YOU'RE GOING, I'LL COME WITH YOU.
EAT YOUR DINNER, CHIRRUT. I'LL BE FINE.
SMILE
YOU'RE GOING TO MEET WITH MORE OF GERRERA'S PEOPLE.
NO, I'M GOING TO TALK TO GERRERA HIMSELF.

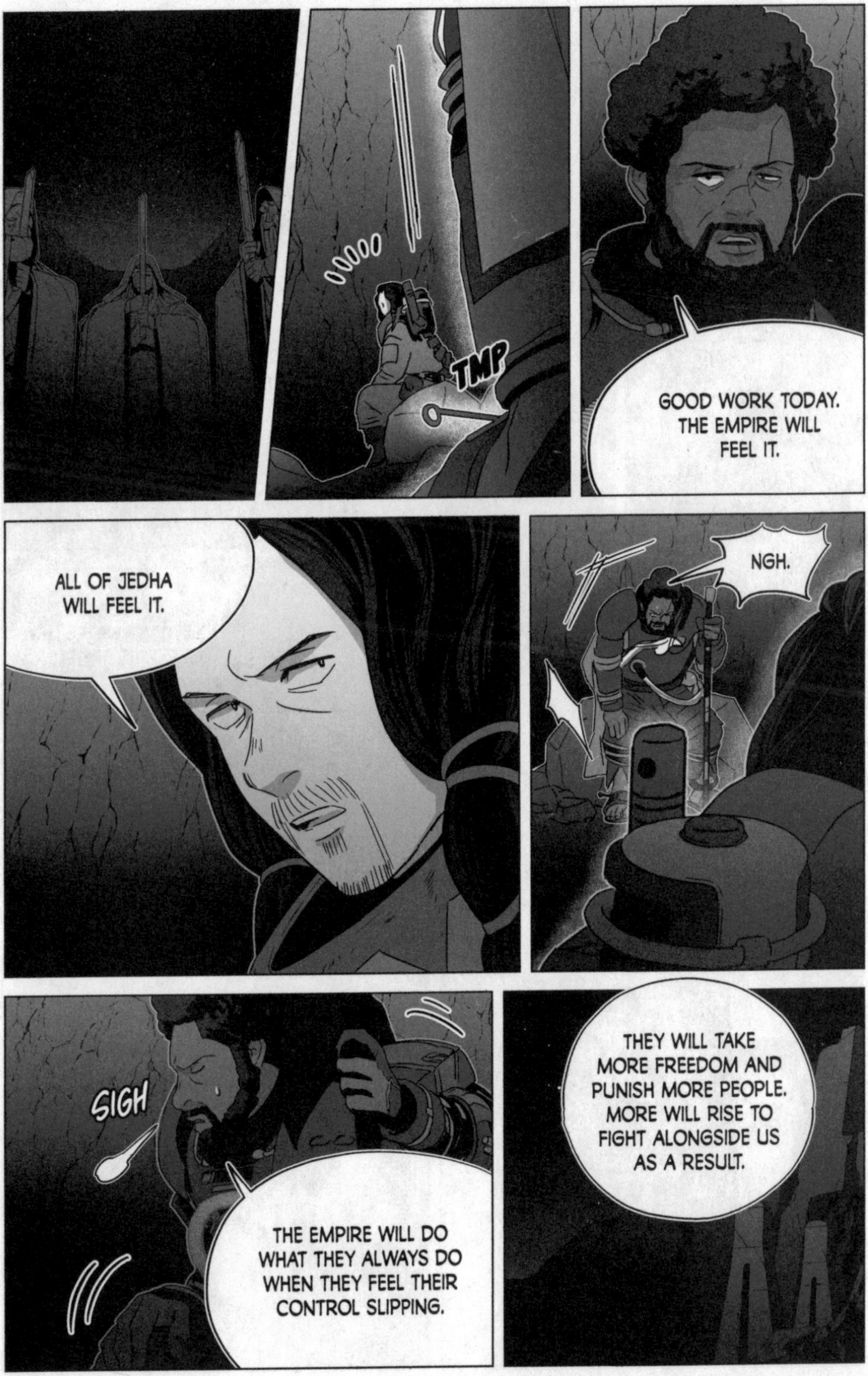

OOOOO
TMP
GOOD WORK TODAY. THE EMPIRE WILL FEEL IT.
ALL OF JEDHA WILL FEEL IT.
NGH.
SIGH
THE EMPIRE WILL DO WHAT THEY ALWAYS DO WHEN THEY FEEL THEIR CONTROL SLIPPING.
THEY WILL TAKE MORE FREEDOM AND PUNISH MORE PEOPLE. MORE WILL RISE TO FIGHT ALONGSIDE US AS A RESULT.

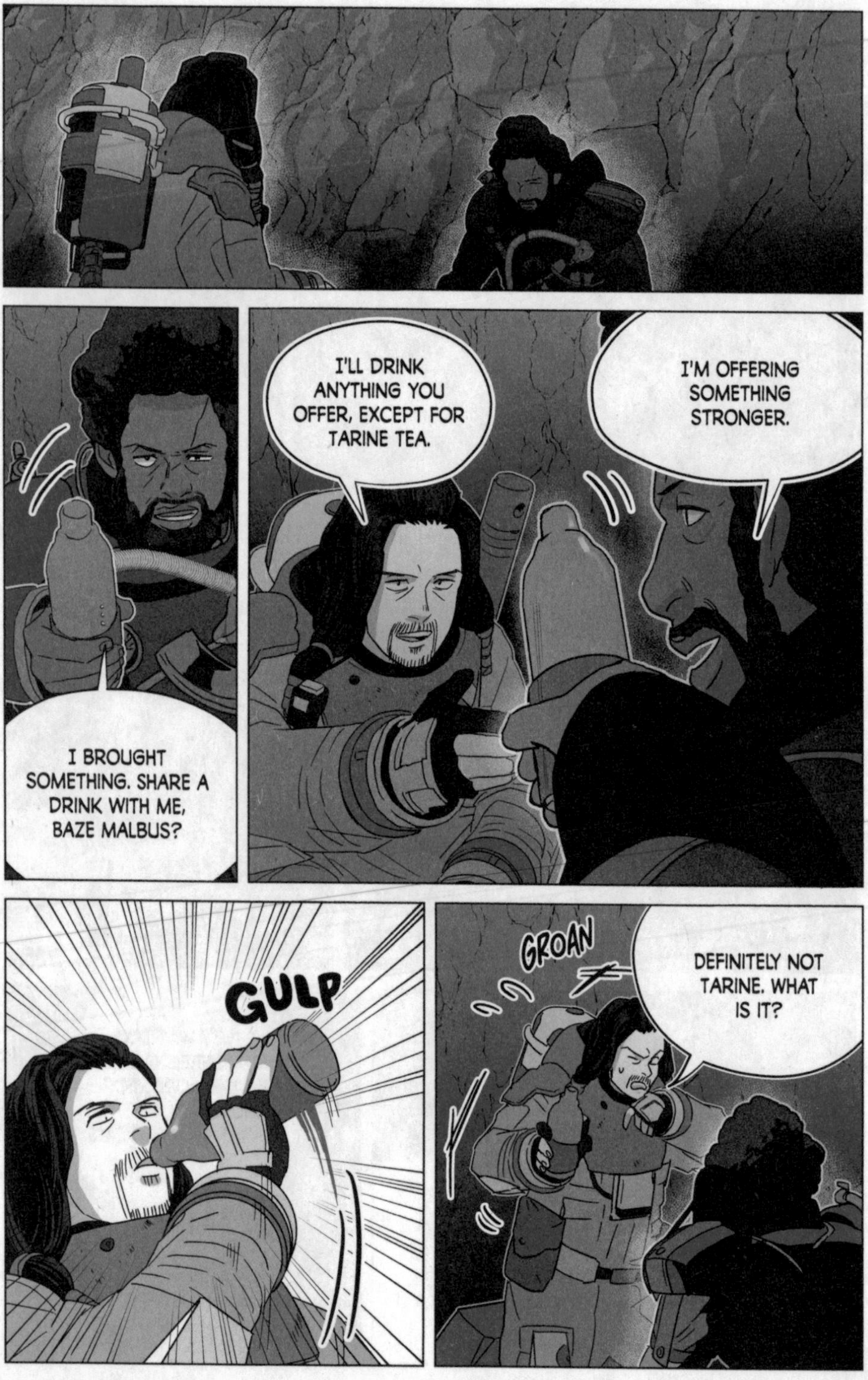
I BROUGHT SOMETHING. SHARE A DRINK WITH ME, BAZE MALBUS?
I'LL DRINK ANYTHING YOU OFFER, EXCEPT FOR TARINE TEA.
I'M OFFERING SOMETHING STRONGER.
GULP
GROAN
DEFINITELY NOT TARINE. WHAT IS IT?

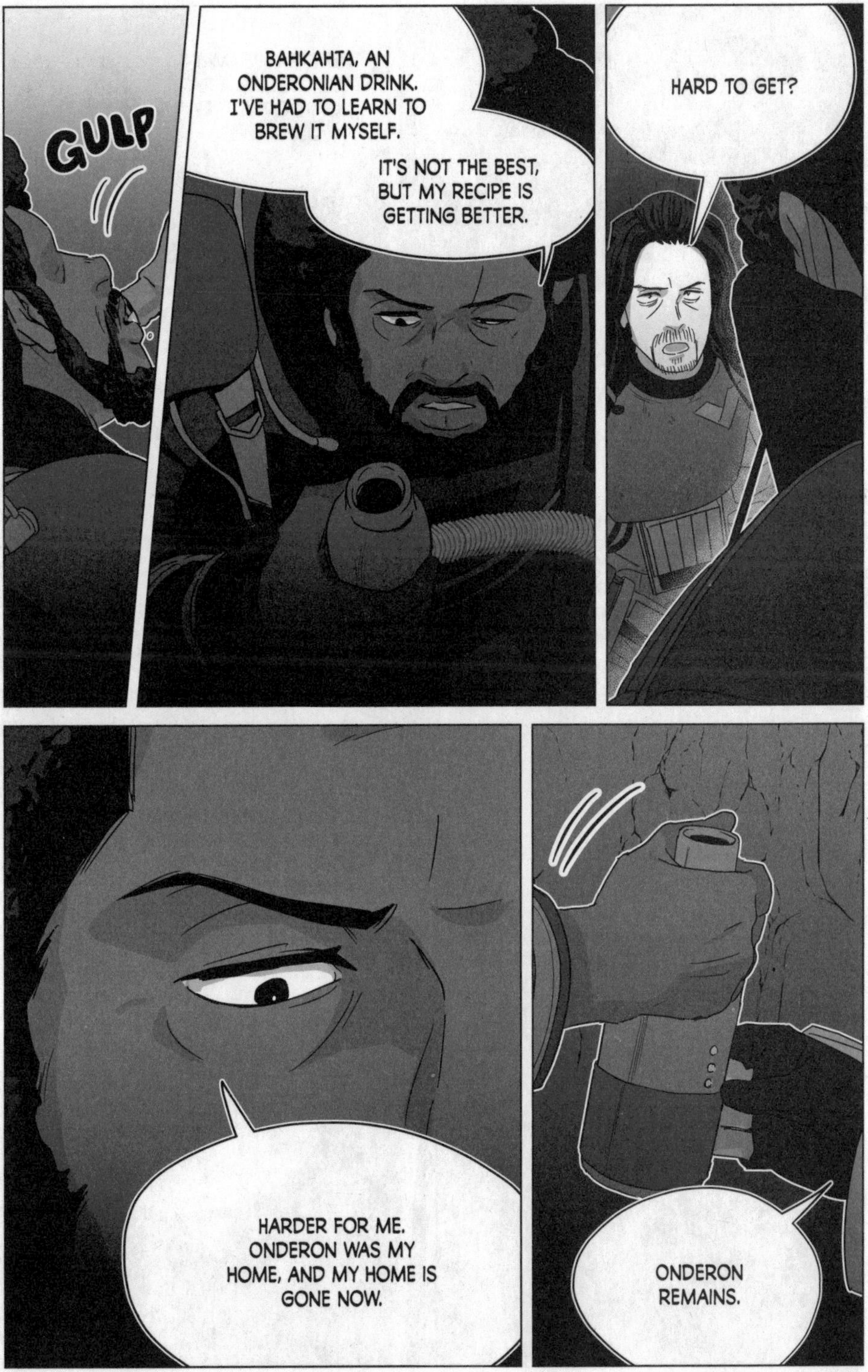
GULP
BAHKAHTA, AN ONDERONIAN DRINK. I'VE HAD TO LEARN TO BREW IT MYSELF.
IT'S NOT THE BEST, BUT MY RECIPE IS GETTING BETTER.
HARD TO GET?
HARDER FOR ME. ONDERON WAS MY HOME, AND MY HOME IS GONE NOW.
ONDERON REMAINS.

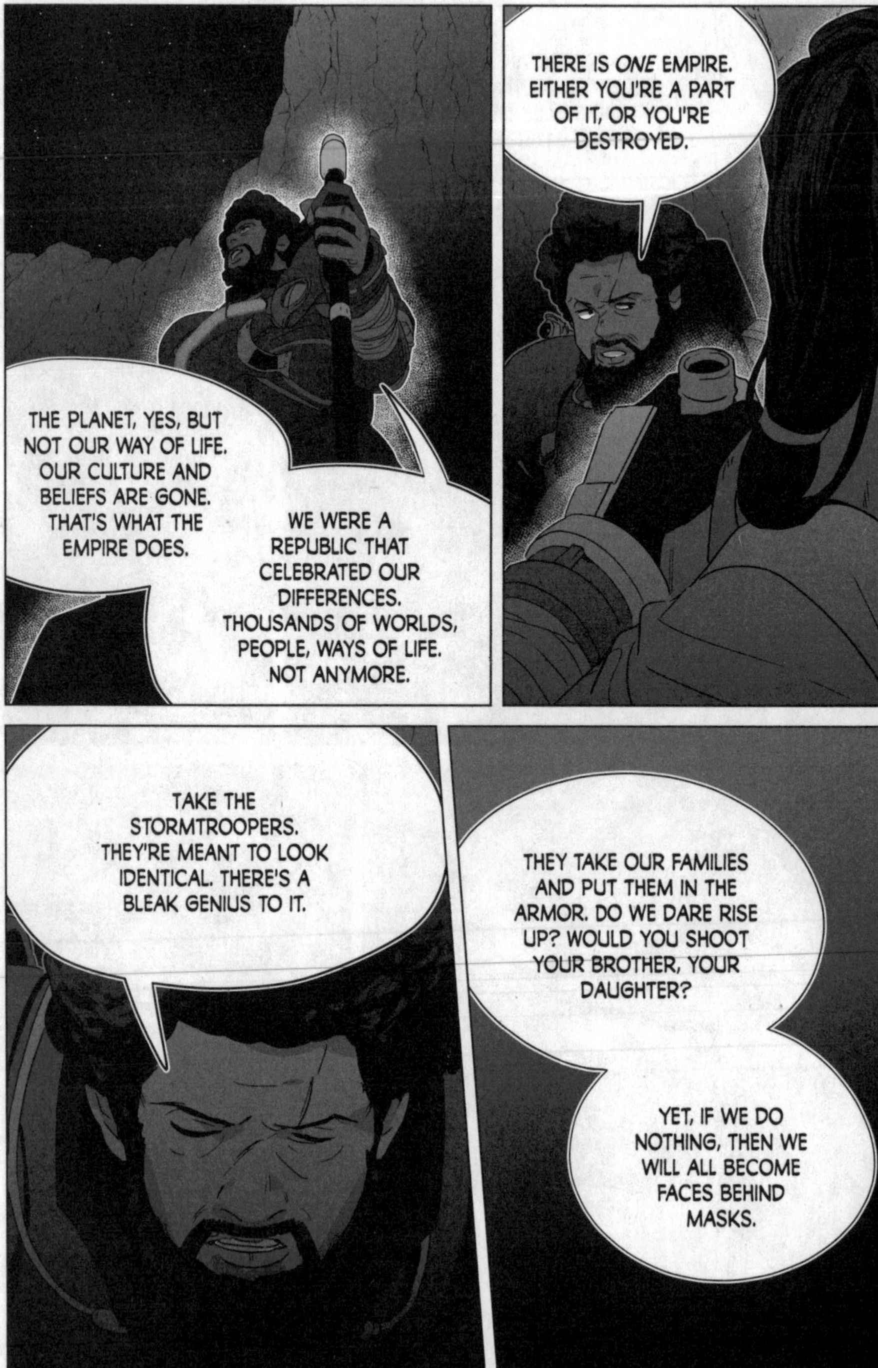
THE PLANET, YES, BUT NOT OUR WAY OF LIFE. OUR CULTURE AND BELIEFS ARE GONE. THAT'S WHAT THE EMPIRE DOES.
WE WERE A REPUBLIC THAT CELEBRATED OUR DIFFERENCES. THOUSANDS OF WORLDS, PEOPLE, WAYS OF LIFE. NOT ANYMORE.
THERE IS *ONE* EMPIRE. EITHER YOU'RE A PART OF IT, OR YOU'RE DESTROYED.
TAKE THE STORMTROOPERS. THEY'RE MEANT TO LOOK IDENTICAL. THERE'S A BLEAK GENIUS TO IT.
THEY TAKE OUR FAMILIES AND PUT THEM IN THE ARMOR. DO WE DARE RISE UP? WOULD YOU SHOOT YOUR BROTHER, YOUR DAUGHTER?
YET, IF WE DO NOTHING, THEN WE WILL ALL BECOME FACES BEHIND MASKS.

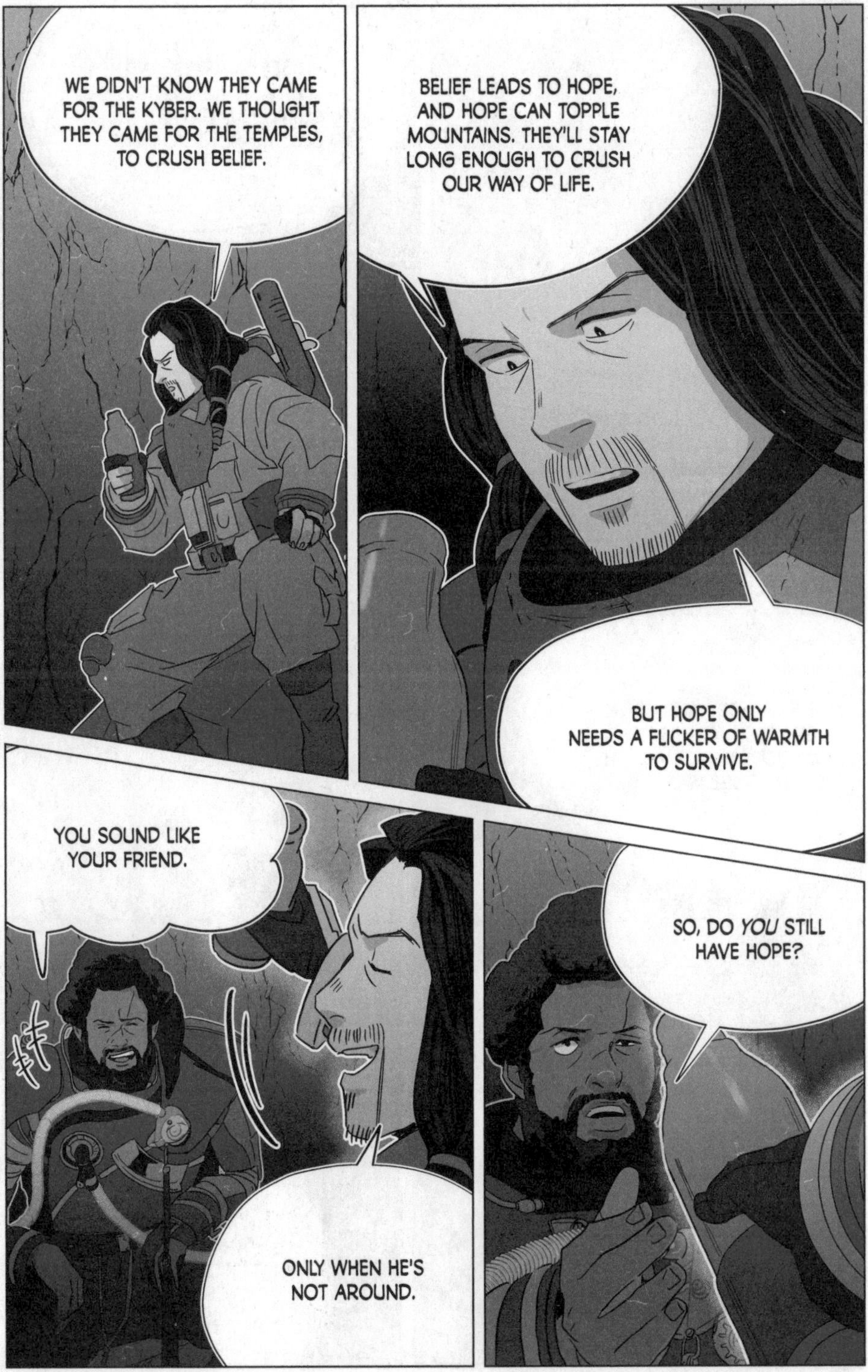
WE DIDN'T KNOW THEY CAME FOR THE KYBER. WE THOUGHT THEY CAME FOR THE TEMPLES, TO CRUSH BELIEF.
BELIEF LEADS TO HOPE, AND HOPE CAN TOPPLE MOUNTAINS. THEY'LL STAY LONG ENOUGH TO CRUSH OUR WAY OF LIFE.
BUT HOPE ONLY NEEDS A FLICKER OF WARMTH TO SURVIVE.
YOU SOUND LIKE YOUR FRIEND.
ONLY WHEN HE'S NOT AROUND.
SO, DO *YOU* STILL HAVE HOPE?

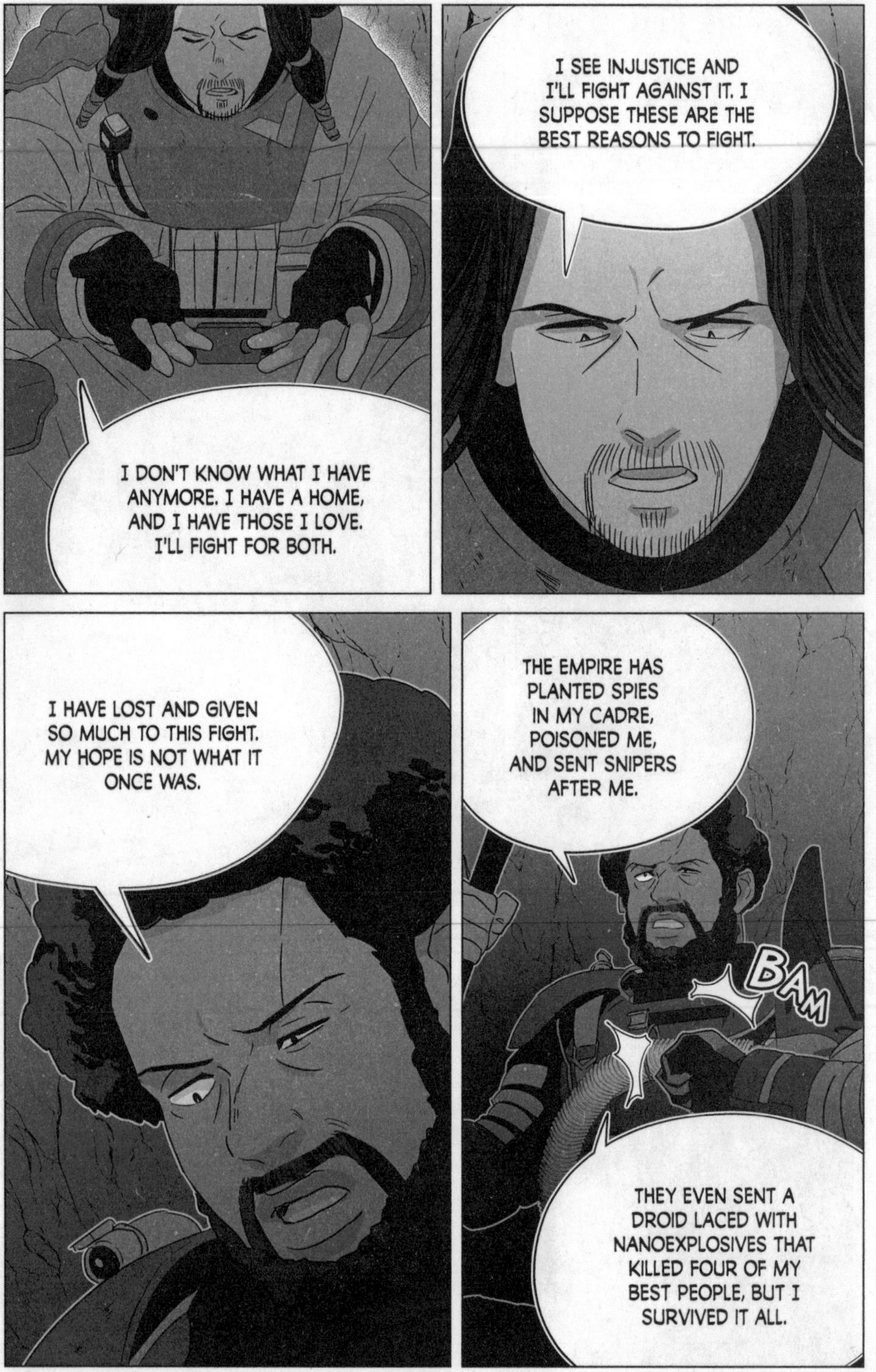
I DON'T KNOW WHAT I HAVE ANYMORE. I HAVE A HOME, AND I HAVE THOSE I LOVE. I'LL FIGHT FOR BOTH.
I SEE INJUSTICE AND I'LL FIGHT AGAINST IT. I SUPPOSE THESE ARE THE BEST REASONS TO FIGHT.
I HAVE LOST AND GIVEN SO MUCH TO THIS FIGHT. MY HOPE IS NOT WHAT IT ONCE WAS.
THE EMPIRE HAS PLANTED SPIES IN MY CADRE, POISONED ME, AND SENT SNIPERS AFTER ME.
BAM
THEY EVEN SENT A DROID LACED WITH NANOEXPLOSIVES THAT KILLED FOUR OF MY BEST PEOPLE, BUT I SURVIVED IT ALL.

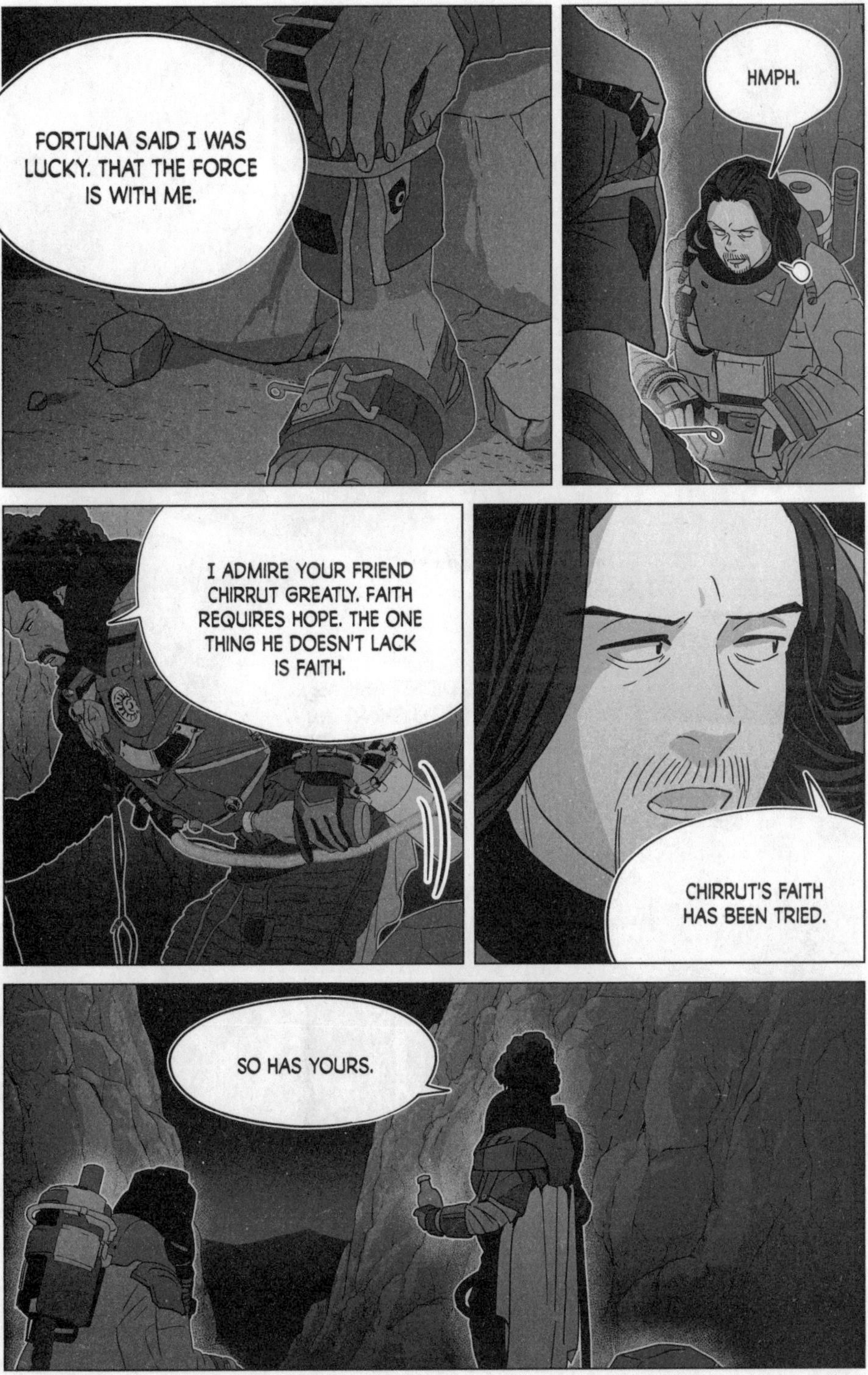
FORTUNA SAID I WAS LUCKY. THAT THE FORCE IS WITH ME.
HMPH.
I ADMIRE YOUR FRIEND CHIRRUT GREATLY. FAITH REQUIRES HOPE. THE ONE THING HE DOESN'T LACK IS FAITH.
CHIRRUT'S FAITH HAS BEEN TRIED.
SO HAS YOURS.

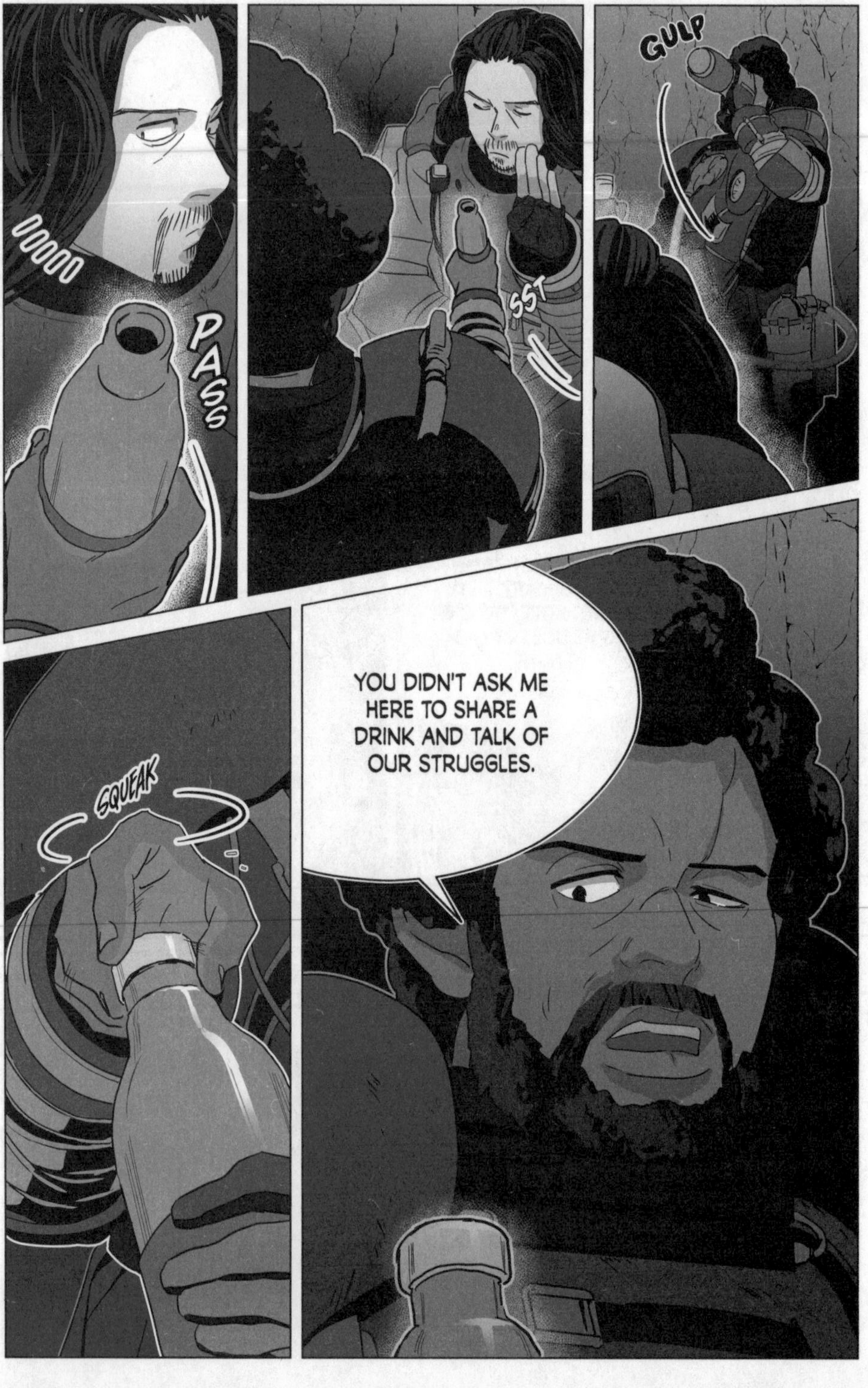
OOOOO
PASS
SST
GULP
SQUEAK
YOU DIDN'T ASK ME HERE TO SHARE A DRINK AND TALK OF OUR STRUGGLES.

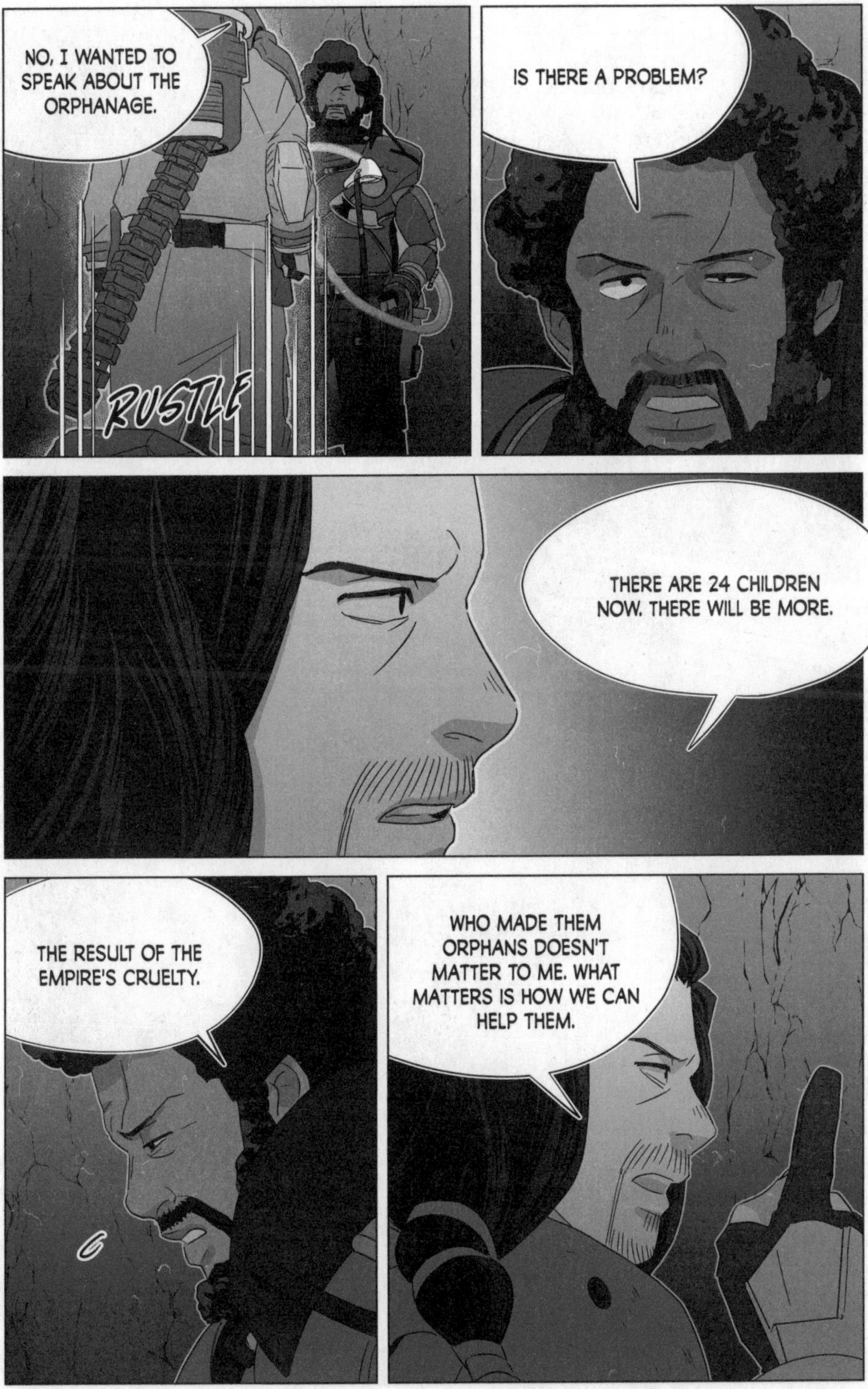
NO, I WANTED TO SPEAK ABOUT THE ORPHANAGE.
RUSTLE
IS THERE A PROBLEM?
THERE ARE 24 CHILDREN NOW. THERE WILL BE MORE.
THE RESULT OF THE EMPIRE'S CRUELTY.
G
WHO MADE THEM ORPHANS DOESN'T MATTER TO ME. WHAT MATTERS IS HOW WE CAN HELP THEM.

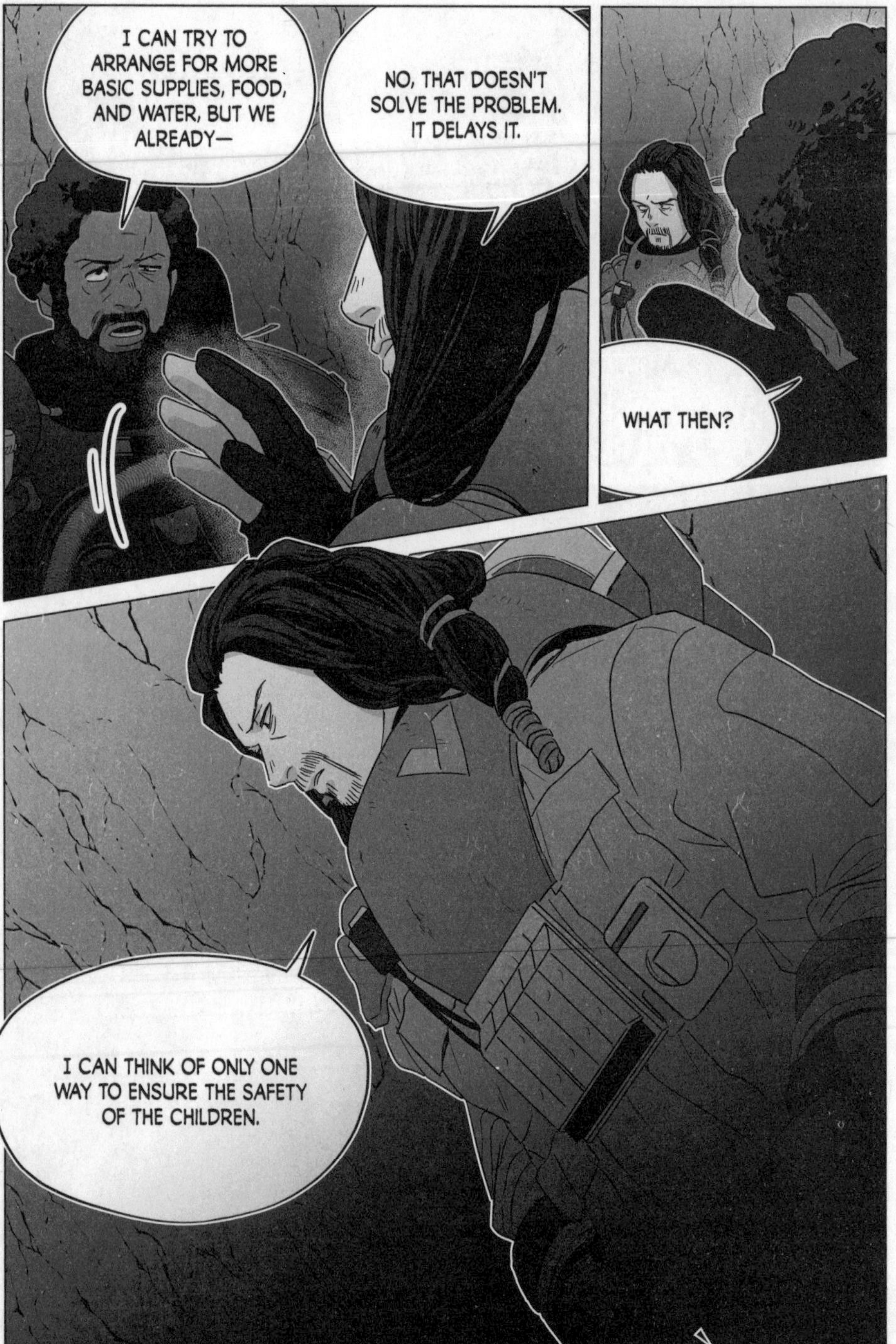
I CAN TRY TO ARRANGE FOR MORE BASIC SUPPLIES, FOOD, AND WATER, BUT WE ALREADY—
NO, THAT DOESN'T SOLVE THE PROBLEM. IT DELAYS IT.
WHAT THEN?
I CAN THINK OF ONLY ONE WAY TO ENSURE THE SAFETY OF THE CHILDREN.

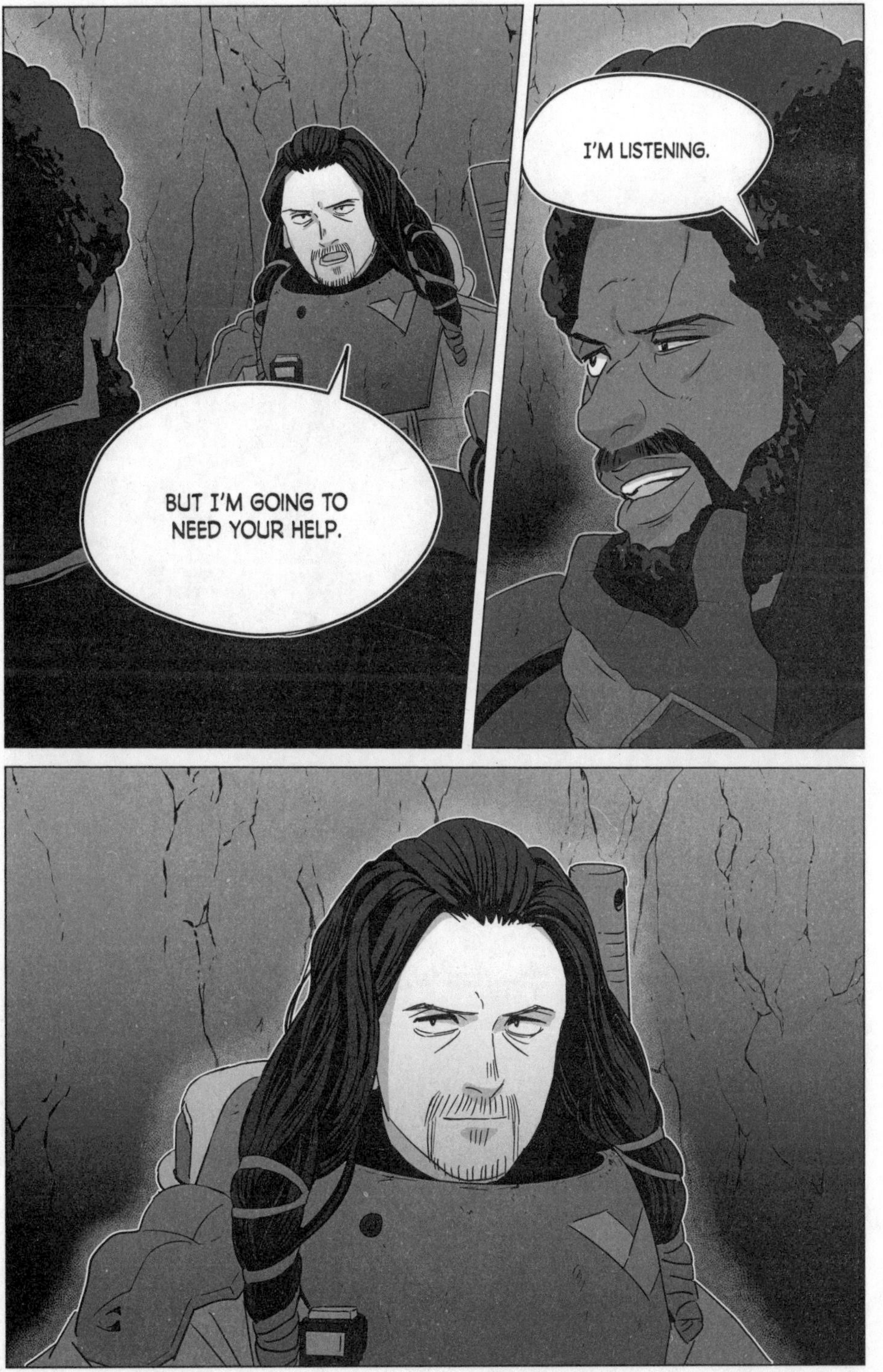
BUT I'M GOING TO NEED YOUR HELP.
I'M LISTENING.

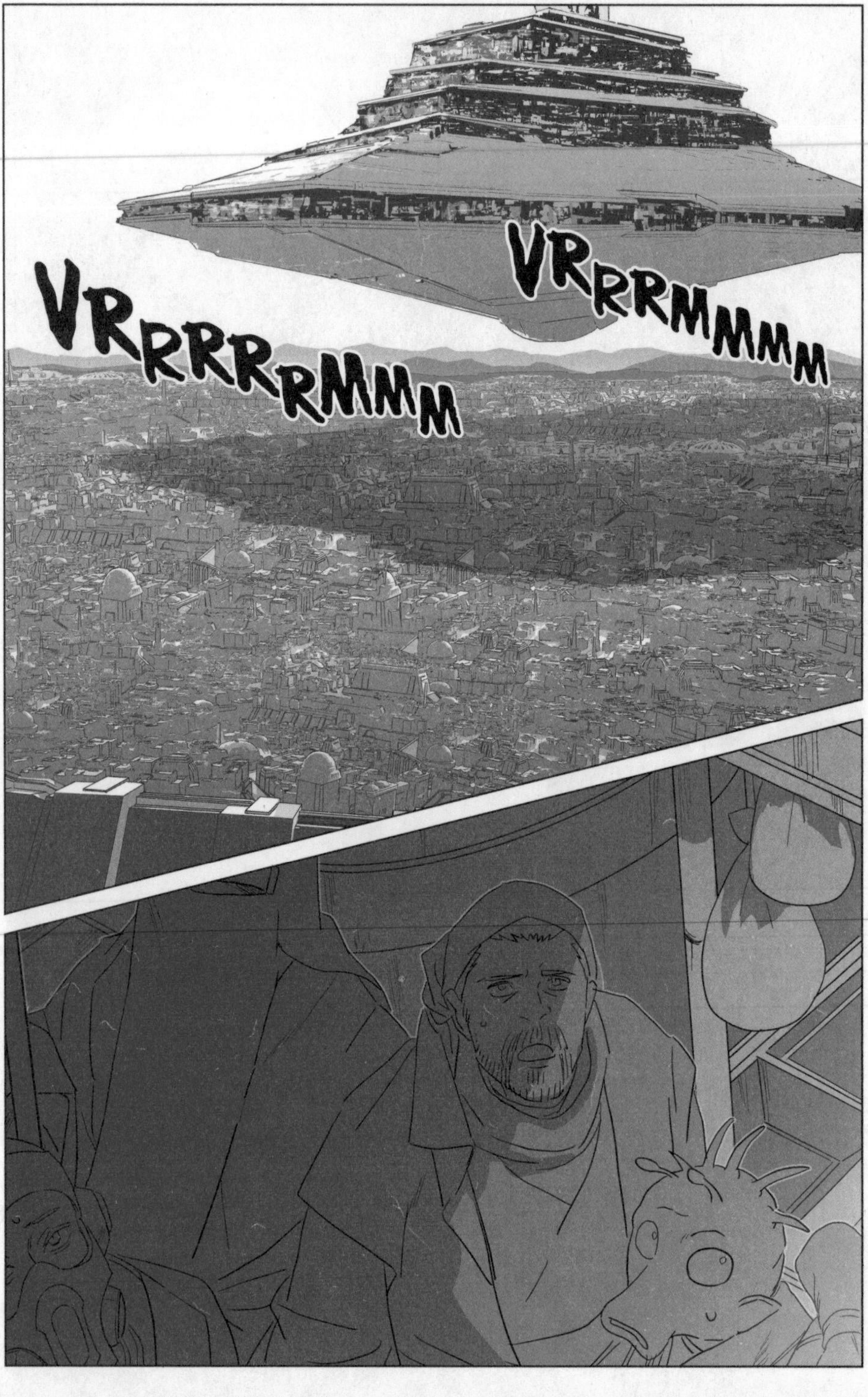
VRRRRRMMMM
VRRRMMMMM

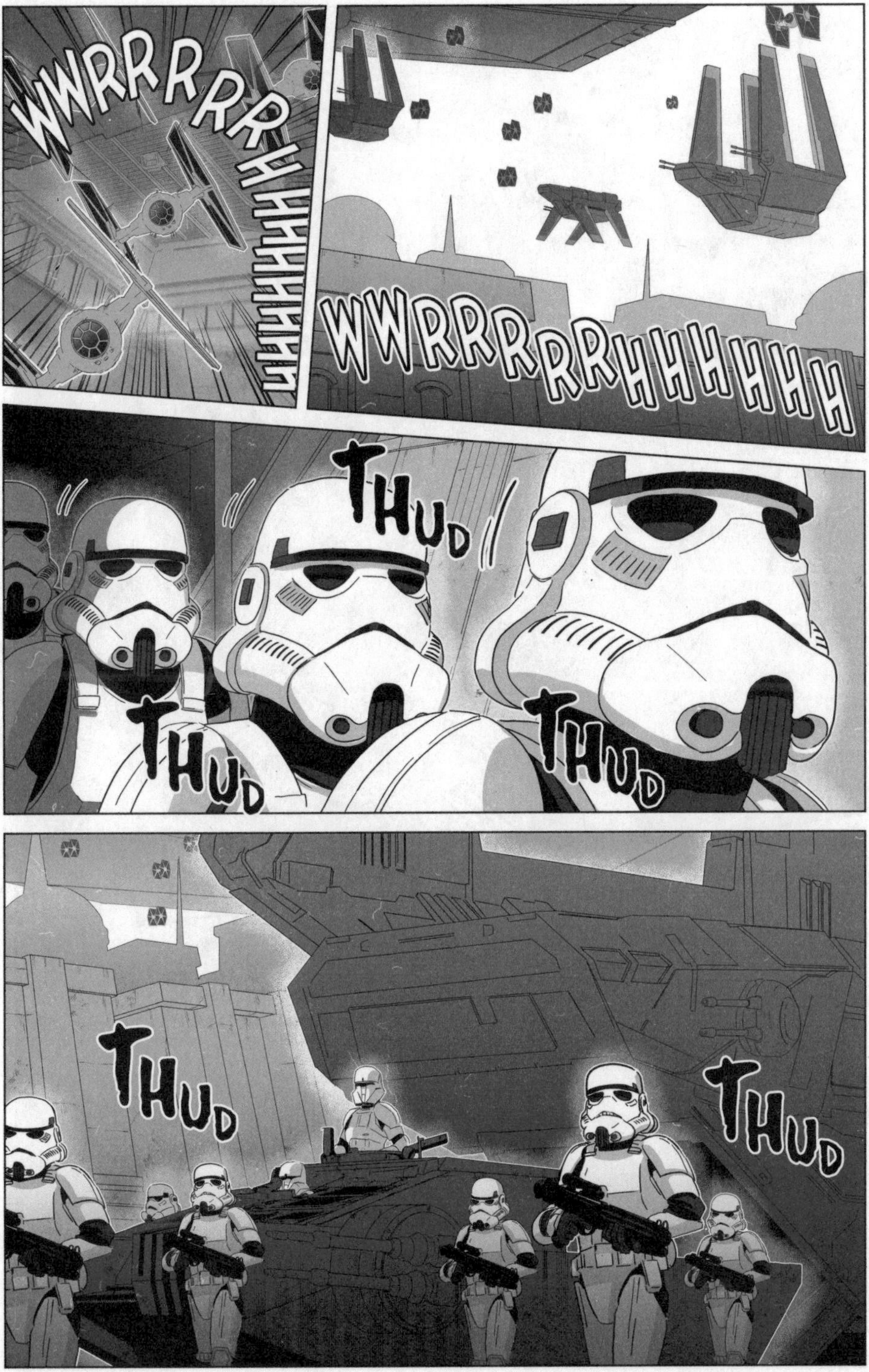
WWRRRRRHHHHHHHHH
WWRRRRRHHHHHHH
THUD
THUD
THUD
THUD
THUD

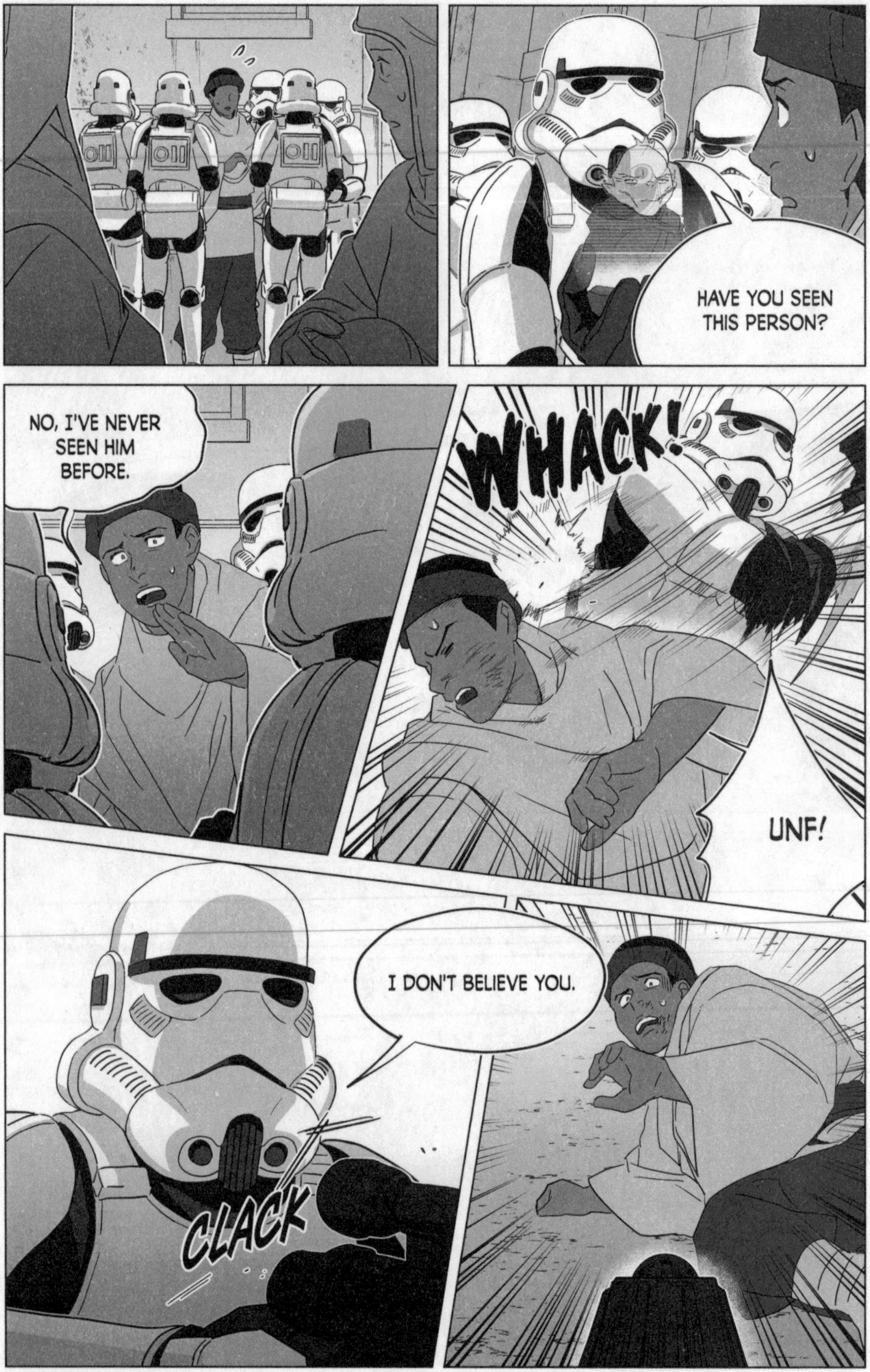
HAVE YOU SEEN THIS PERSON?
NO, I'VE NEVER SEEN HIM BEFORE.
WHACK!
UNF!
I DON'T BELIEVE YOU.
CLACK

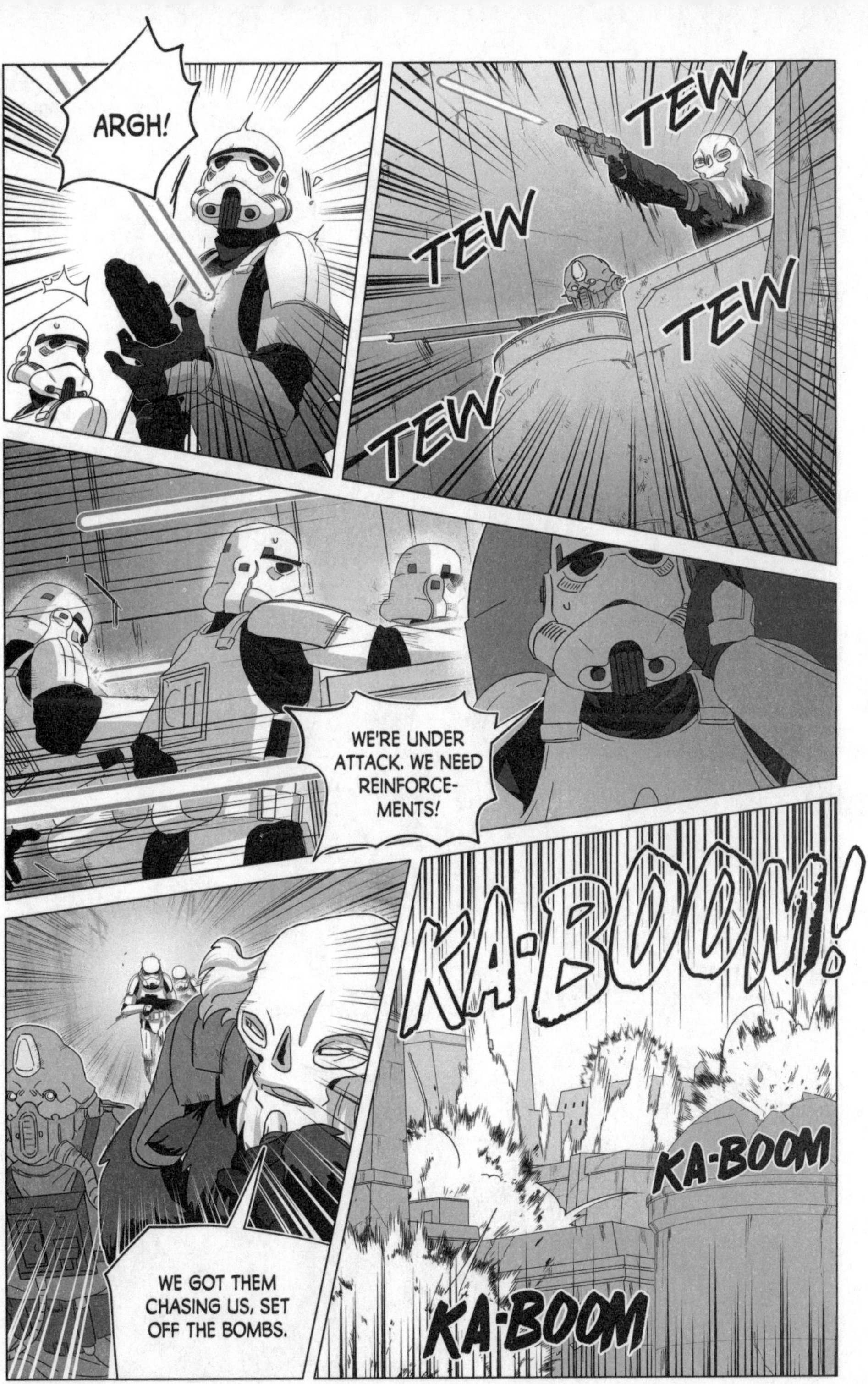
ARGH!
TEW
TEW
TEW
TEW
WE'RE UNDER ATTACK. WE NEED REINFORCE-MENTS!
WE GOT THEM CHASING US, SET OFF THE BOMBS.
KA-BOOM!
KA-BOOM
KA-BOOM

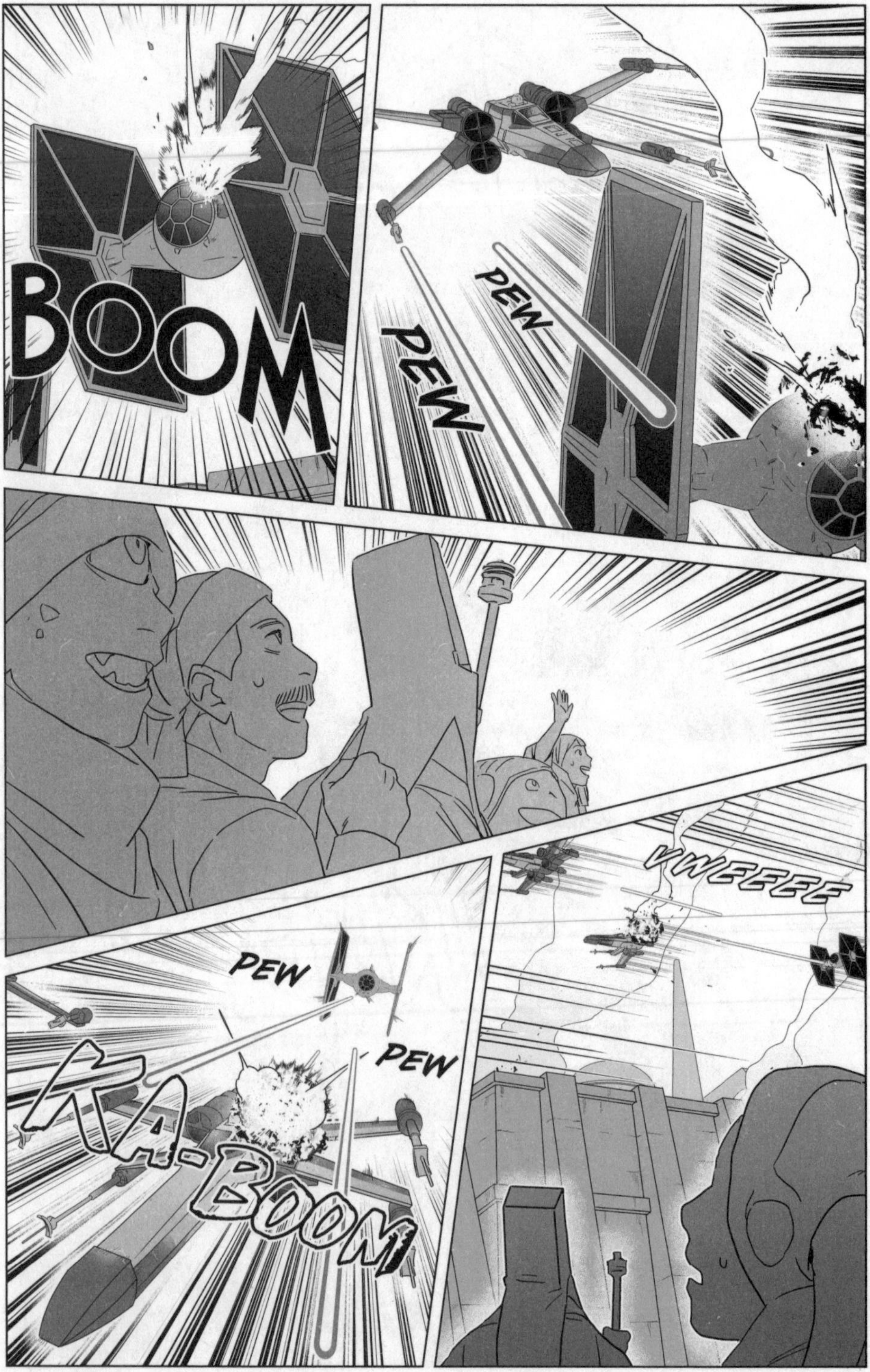
BOOM
PEW
PEW
VWEEEEE
PEW
PEW
KA-BOOM

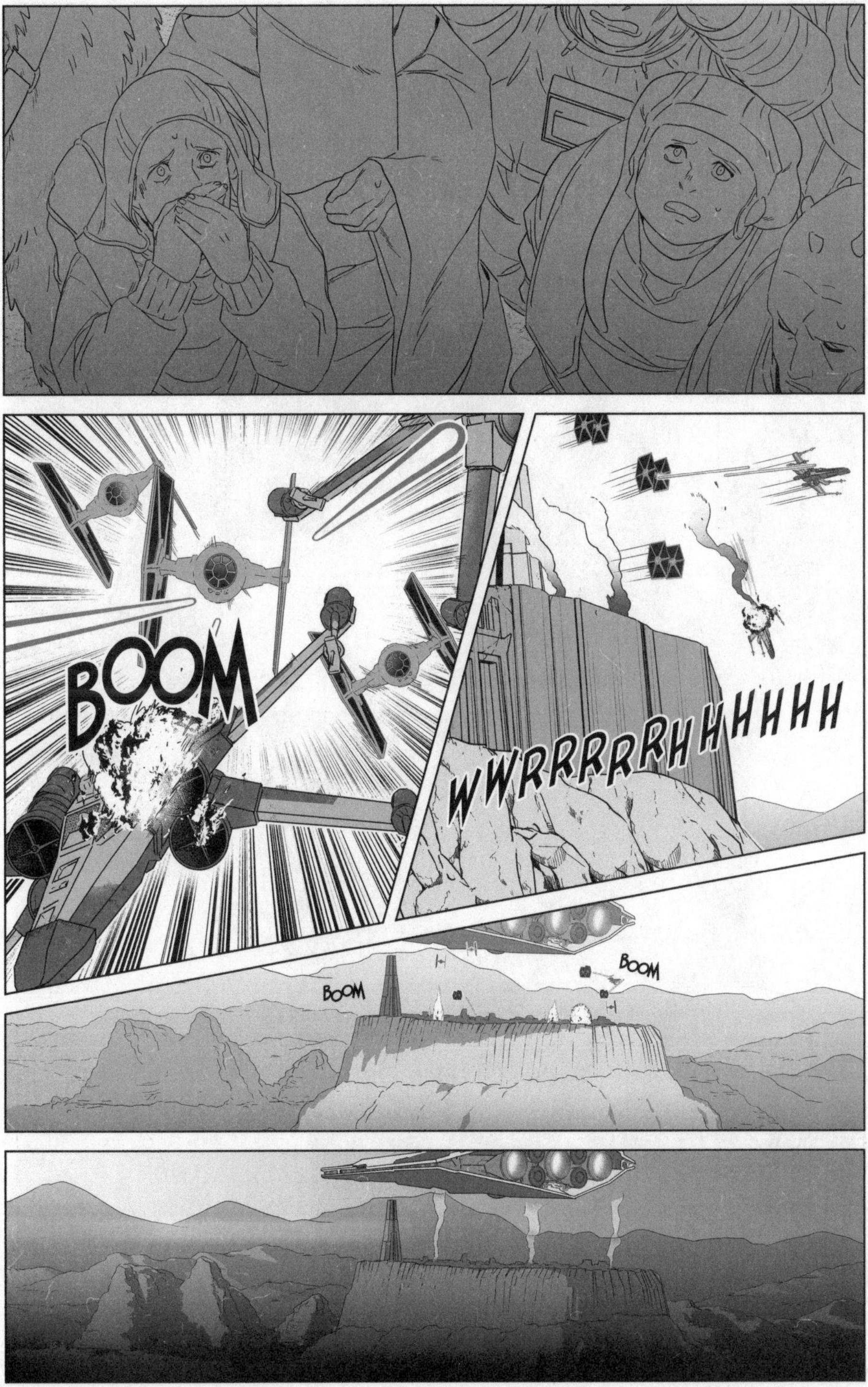
BOOM
WWRRRRRHHHHHH
BOOM
BOOM

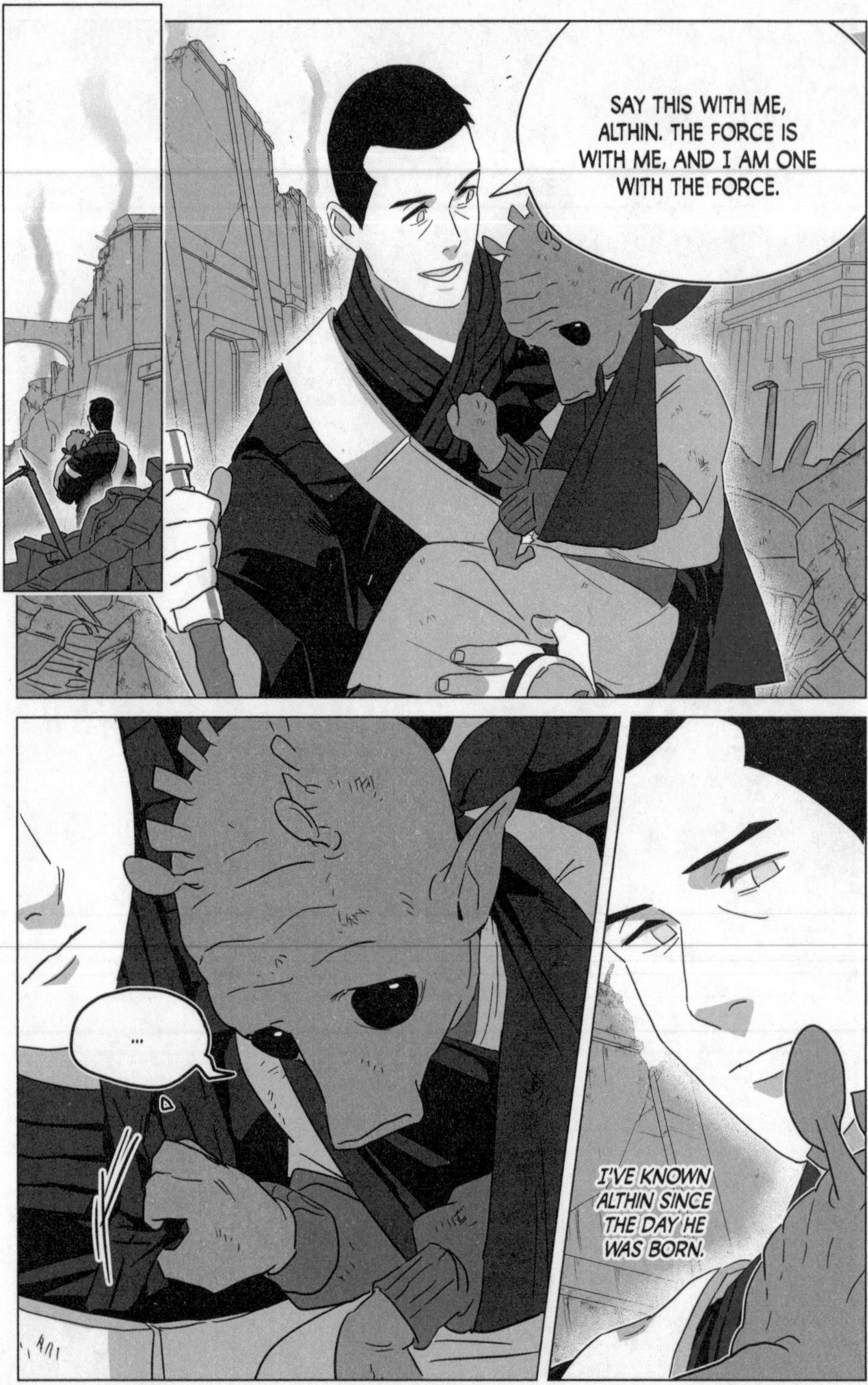
SAY THIS WITH ME, ALTHIN. THE FORCE IS WITH ME, AND I AM ONE WITH THE FORCE.
...
I'VE KNOWN ALTHIN SINCE THE DAY HE WAS BORN.

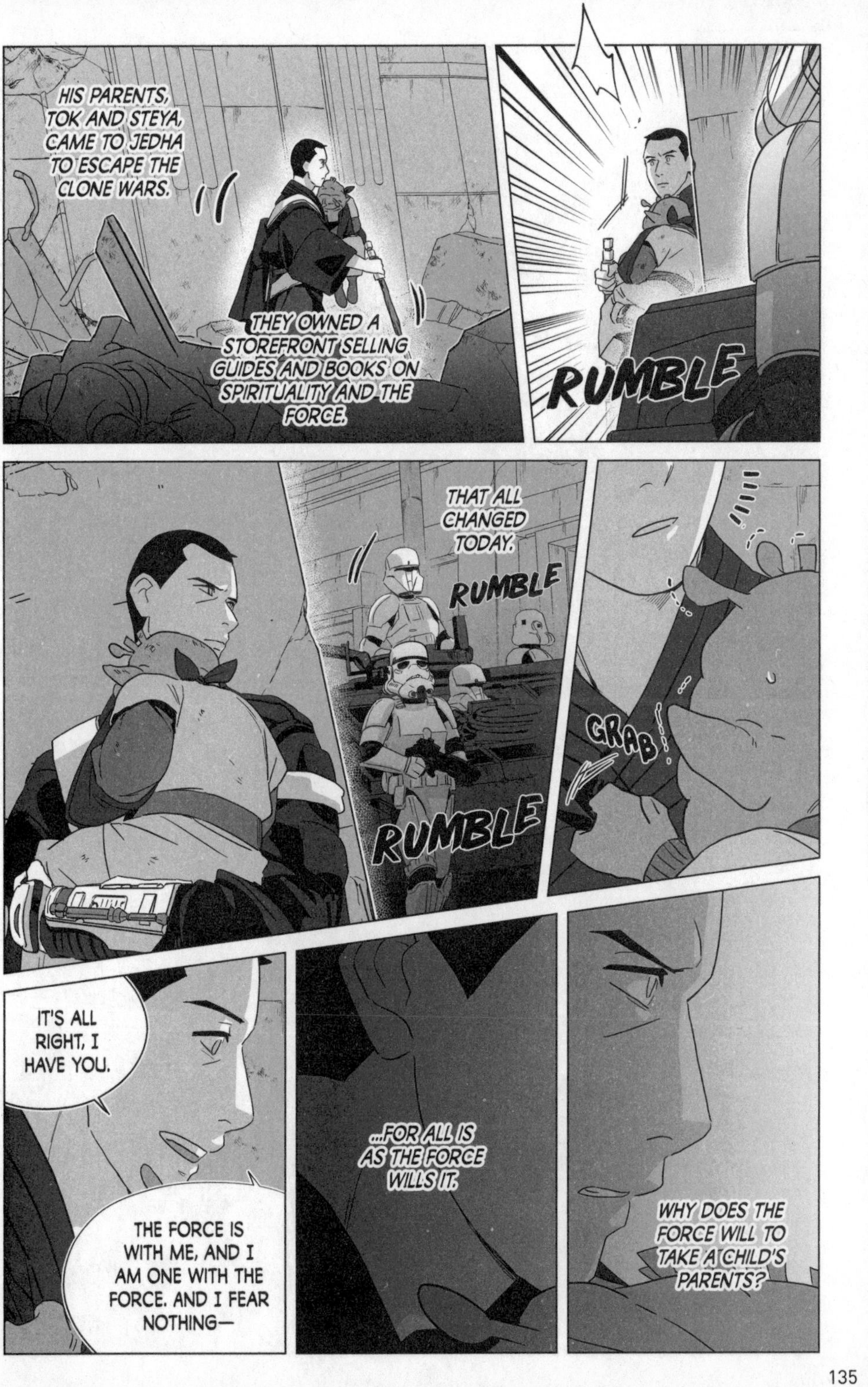
HIS PARENTS, TOK AND STEYA, CAME TO JEDHA TO ESCAPE THE CLONE WARS.
THEY OWNED A STOREFRONT SELLING GUIDES AND BOOKS ON SPIRITUALITY AND THE FORCE.
RUMBLE
THAT ALL CHANGED TODAY.
RUMBLE
RUMBLE
GRAB
IT'S ALL RIGHT, I HAVE YOU.
THE FORCE IS WITH ME, AND I AM ONE WITH THE FORCE. AND I FEAR NOTHING—
...FOR ALL IS AS THE FORCE WILLS IT.
WHY DOES THE FORCE WILL TO TAKE A CHILD'S PARENTS?

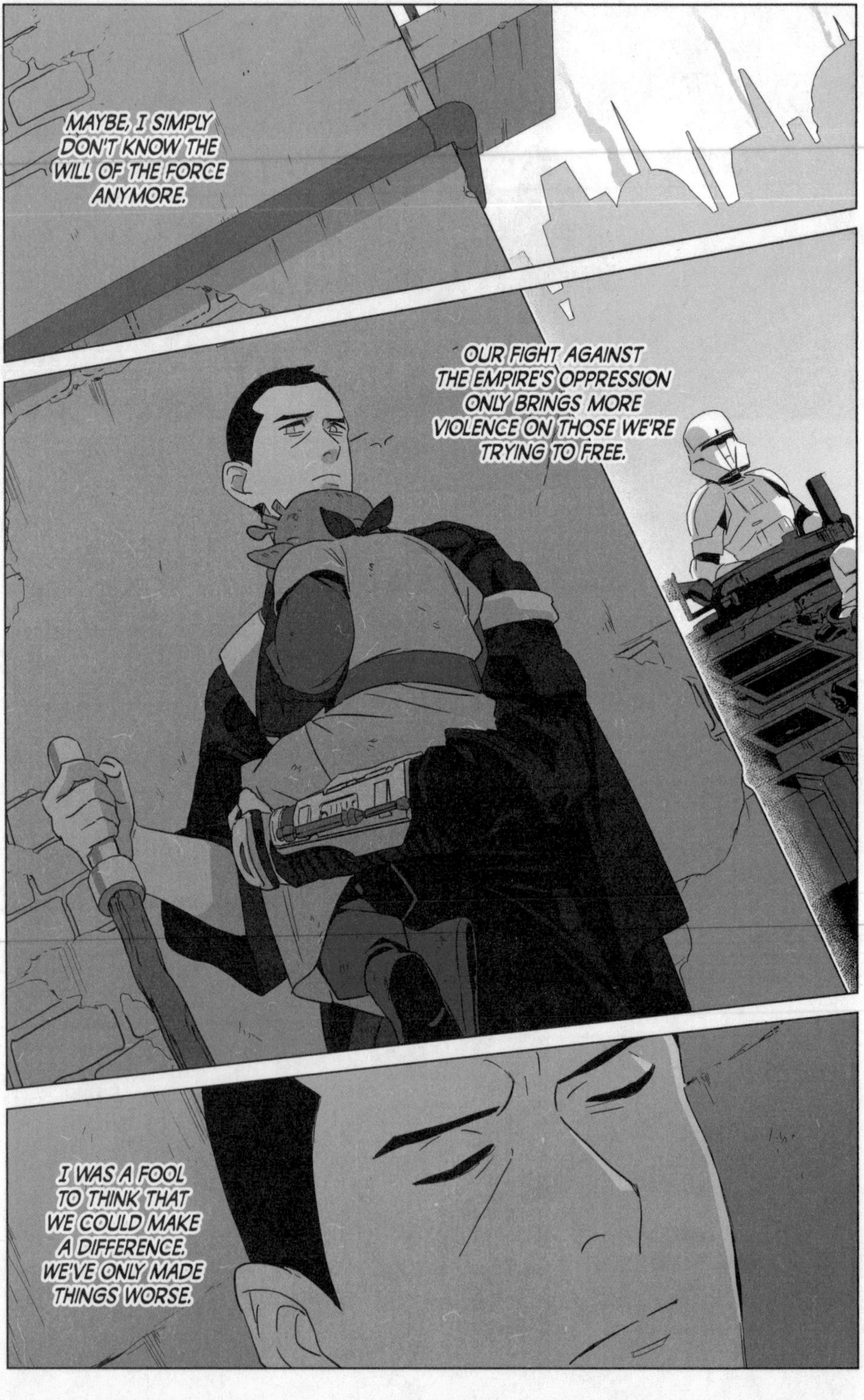
MAYBE, I SIMPLY DON'T KNOW THE WILL OF THE FORCE ANYMORE.
OUR FIGHT AGAINST THE EMPIRE'S OPPRESSION ONLY BRINGS MORE VIOLENCE ON THOSE WE'RE TRYING TO FREE.
I WAS A FOOL TO THINK THAT WE COULD MAKE A DIFFERENCE. WE'VE ONLY MADE THINGS WORSE.

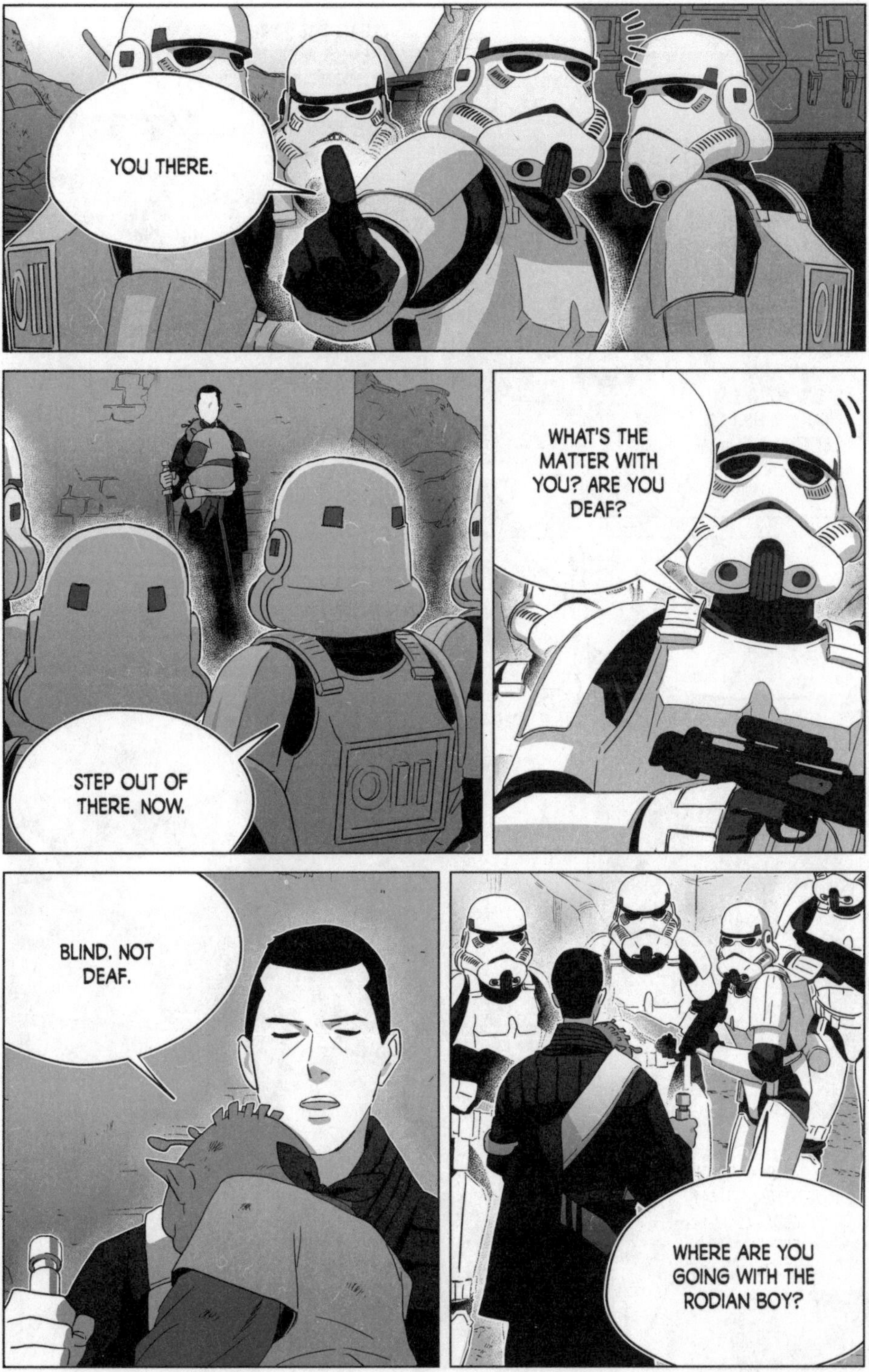
YOU THERE.
STEP OUT OF THERE. NOW.
WHAT'S THE MATTER WITH YOU? ARE YOU DEAF?
BLIND. NOT DEAF.
WHERE ARE YOU GOING WITH THE RODIAN BOY?

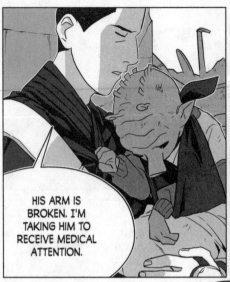

HIS ARM IS BROKEN. I'M TAKING HIM TO RECEIVE MEDICAL ATTENTION.

CLEAR THE STREET. THERE'S A CURFEW TONIGHT. ANYONE OUTSIDE WITHOUT AUTHORIZATION WILL BE SHOT.

THANK YOU FOR THE INFORMATION.

GRAB

THE FORCE IS WITH ME, AND I AM WITH THE FORCE.

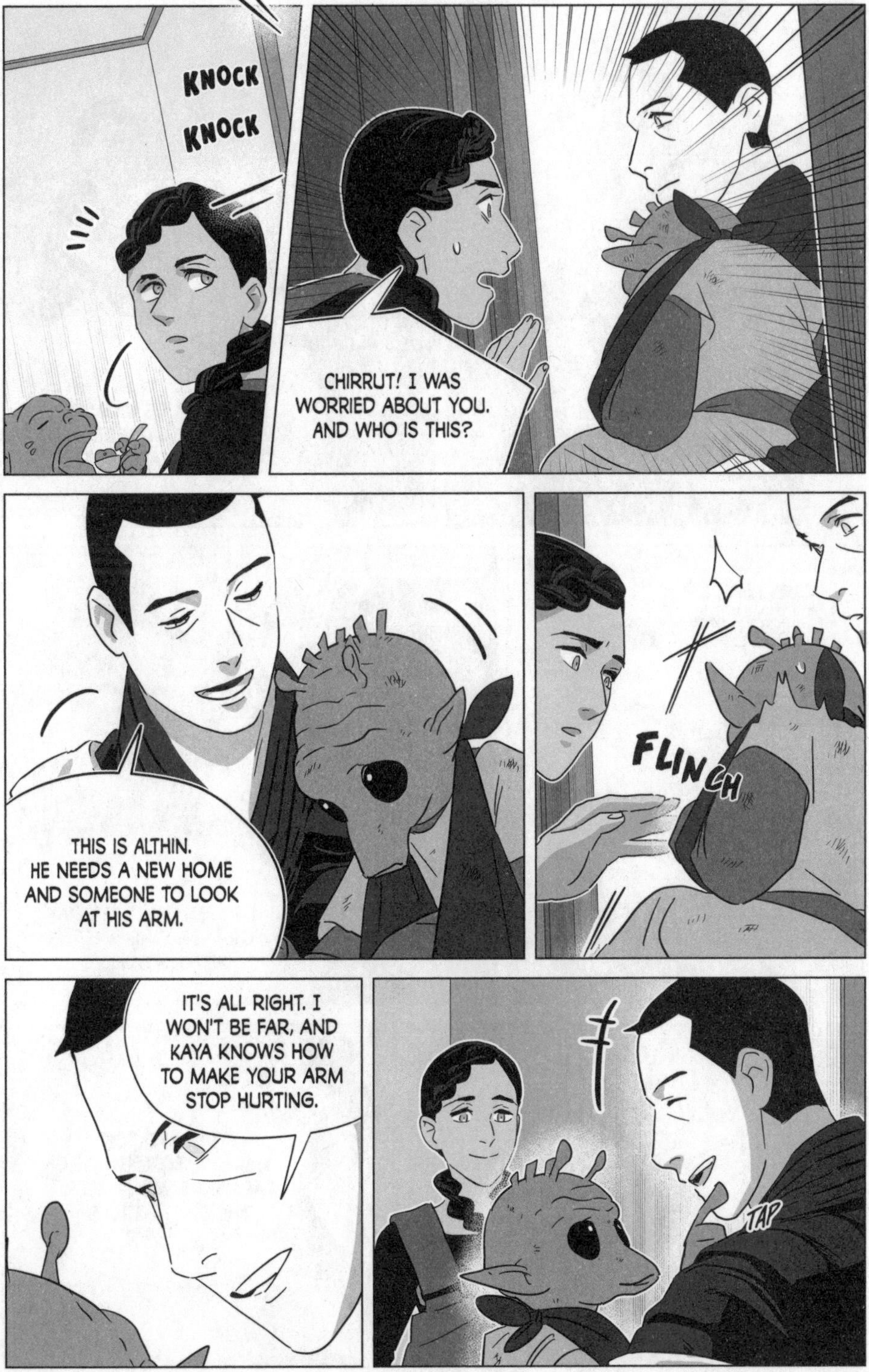
KNOCK
KNOCK
CHIRRUT! I WAS WORRIED ABOUT YOU. AND WHO IS THIS?
THIS IS ALTHIN. HE NEEDS A NEW HOME AND SOMEONE TO LOOK AT HIS ARM.
FLINCH
IT'S ALL RIGHT. I WON'T BE FAR, AND KAYA KNOWS HOW TO MAKE YOUR ARM STOP HURTING.
TAP

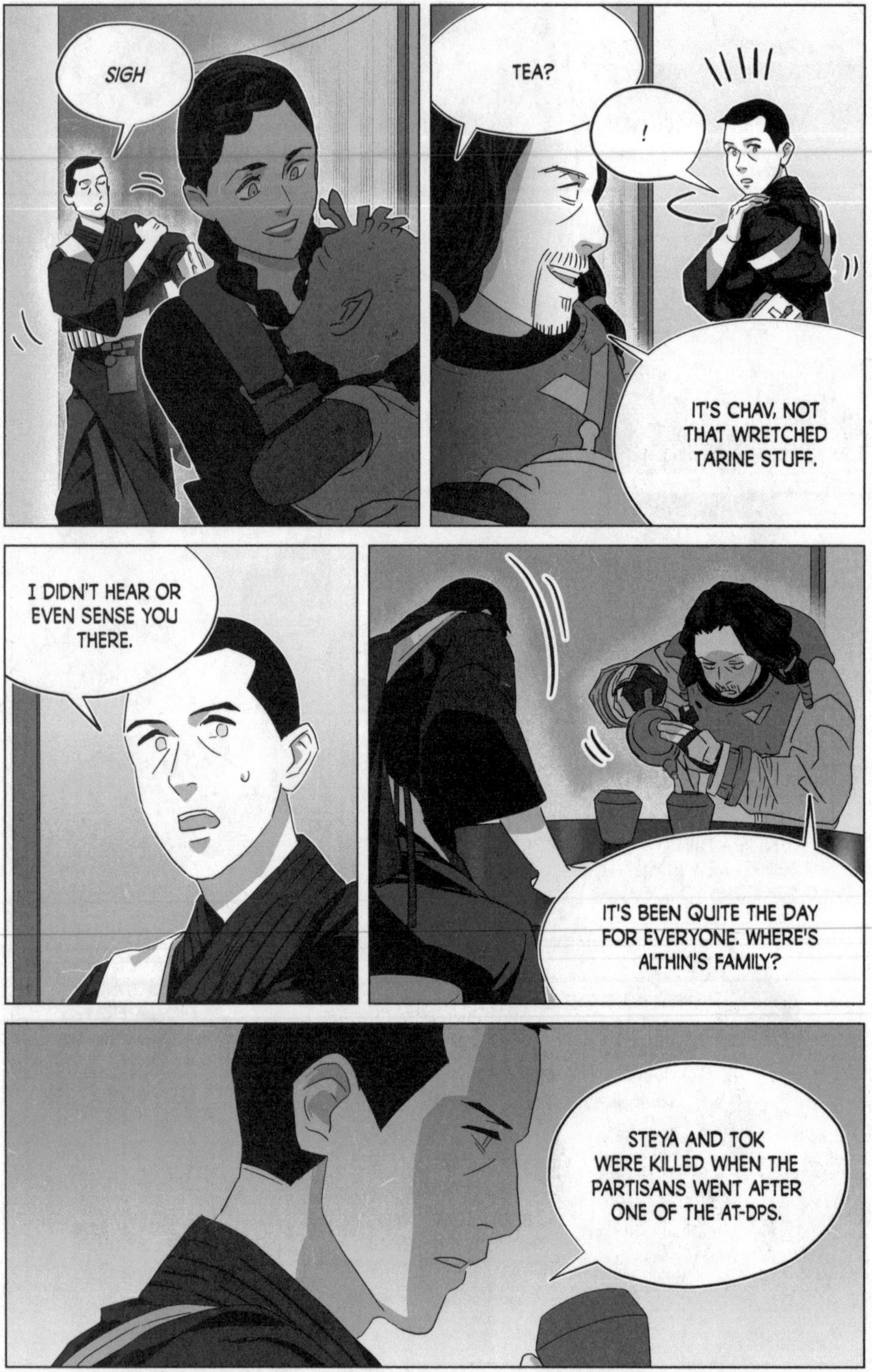
SIGH
TEA?
!
IT'S CHAV, NOT THAT WRETCHED TARINE STUFF.
I DIDN'T HEAR OR EVEN SENSE YOU THERE.
IT'S BEEN QUITE THE DAY FOR EVERYONE. WHERE'S ALTHIN'S FAMILY?
STEYA AND TOK WERE KILLED WHEN THE PARTISANS WENT AFTER ONE OF THE AT-DPS.

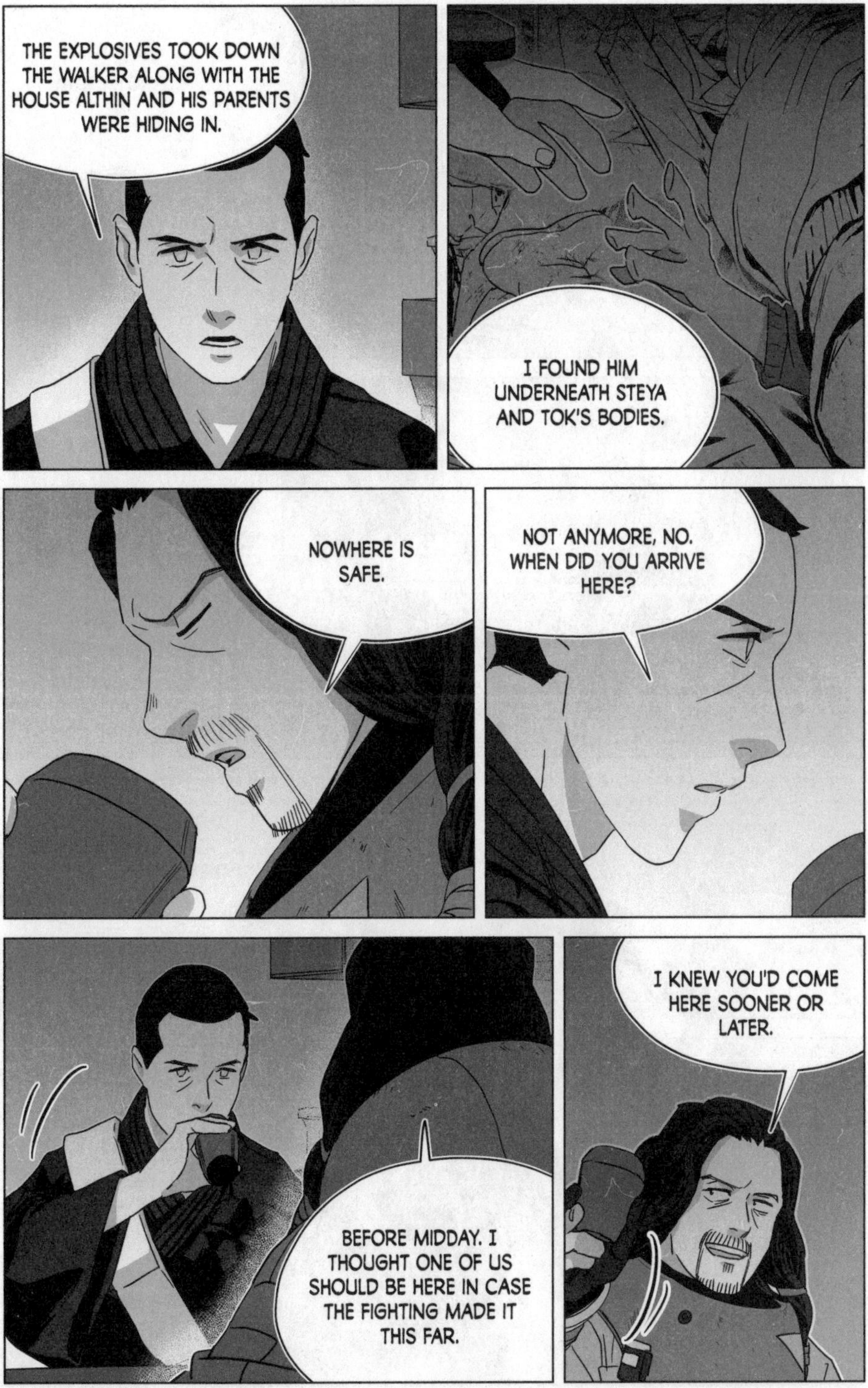
THE EXPLOSIVES TOOK DOWN THE WALKER ALONG WITH THE HOUSE ALTHIN AND HIS PARENTS WERE HIDING IN.
I FOUND HIM UNDERNEATH STEYA AND TOK'S BODIES.
NOWHERE IS SAFE.
NOT ANYMORE, NO. WHEN DID YOU ARRIVE HERE?
BEFORE MIDDAY. I THOUGHT ONE OF US SHOULD BE HERE IN CASE THE FIGHTING MADE IT THIS FAR.
I KNEW YOU'D COME HERE SOONER OR LATER.

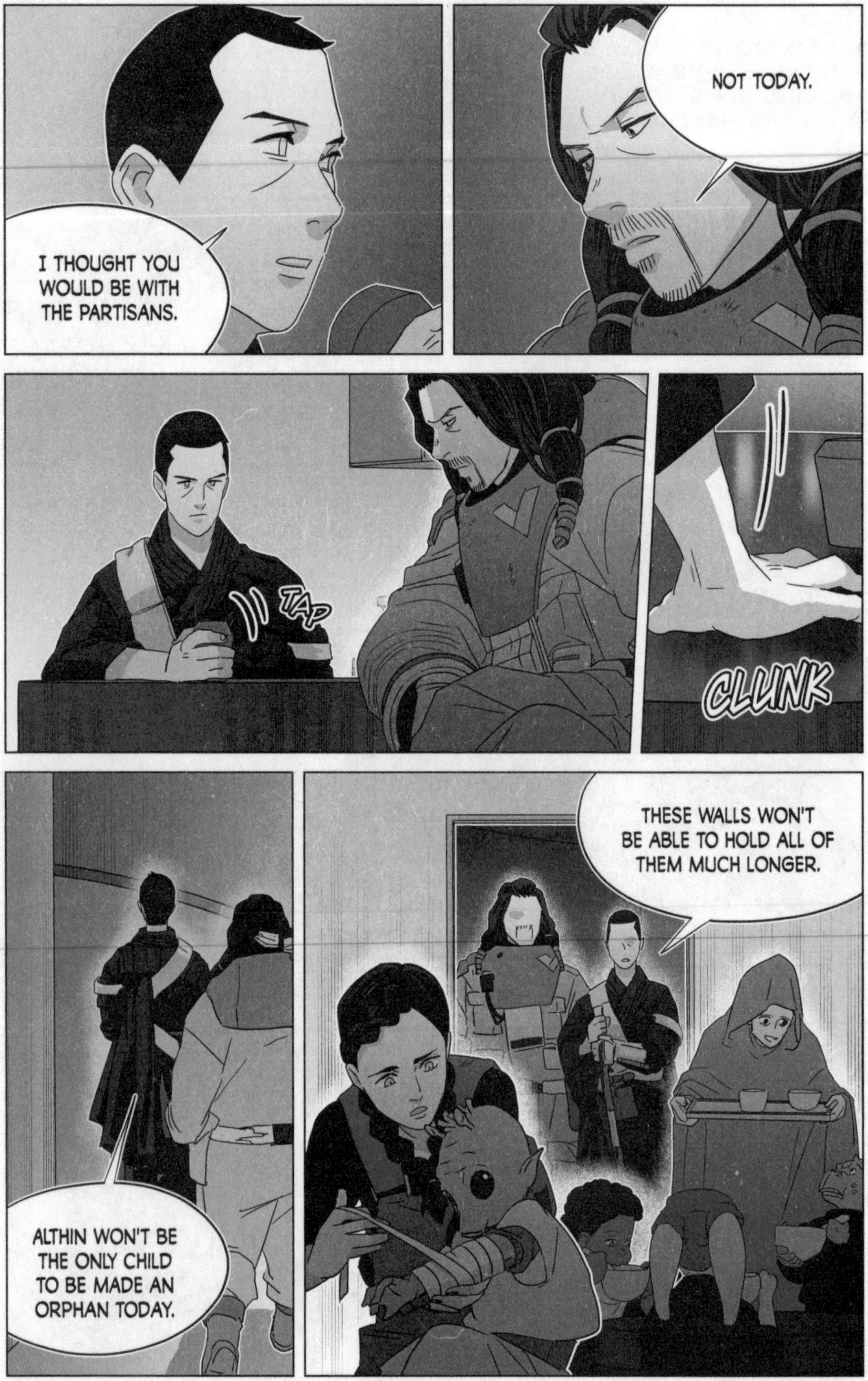
I THOUGHT YOU WOULD BE WITH THE PARTISANS.
NOT TODAY.
TAP
CLUNK
ALTHIN WON'T BE THE ONLY CHILD TO BE MADE AN ORPHAN TODAY.
THESE WALLS WON'T BE ABLE TO HOLD ALL OF THEM MUCH LONGER.

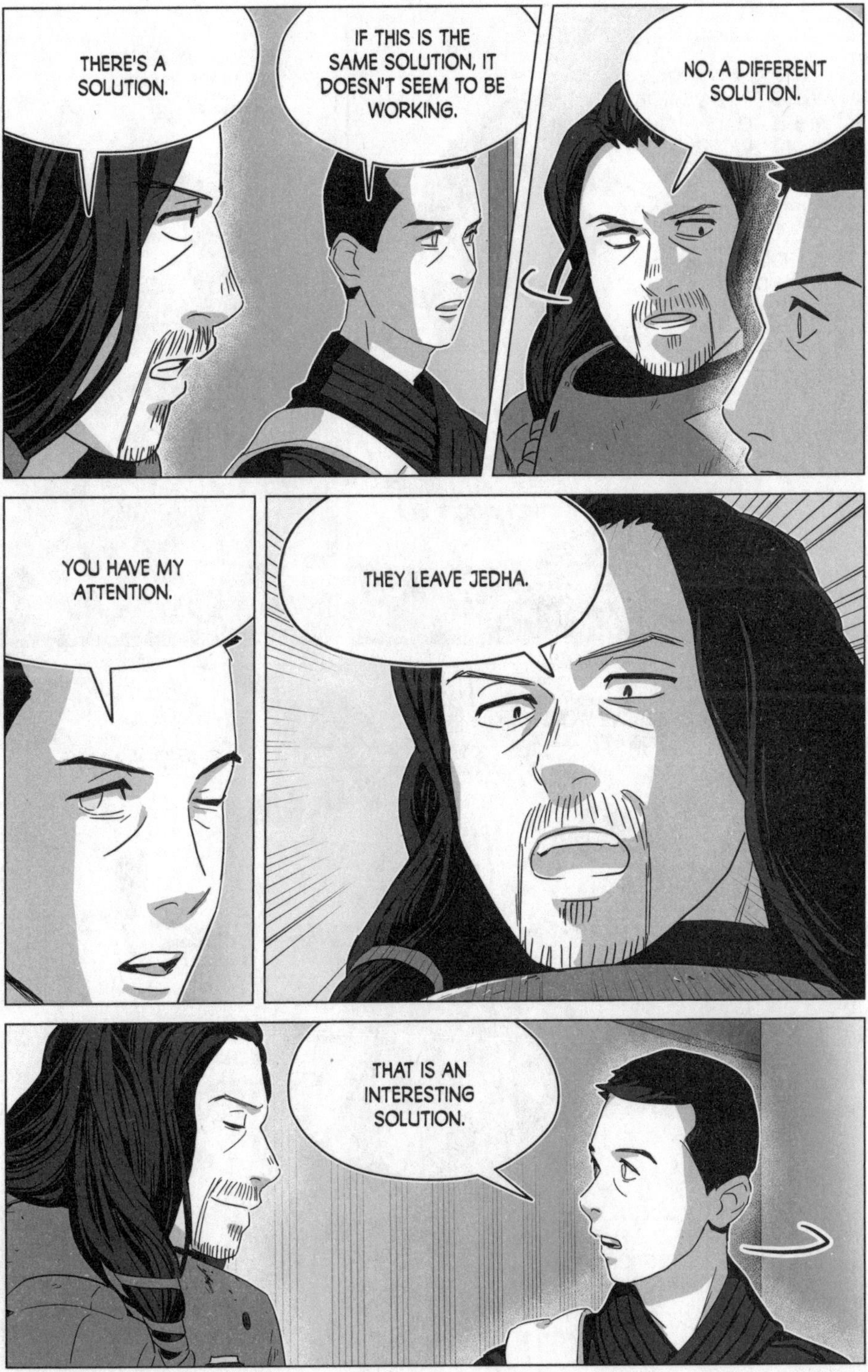
THERE'S A SOLUTION.
IF THIS IS THE SAME SOLUTION, IT DOESN'T SEEM TO BE WORKING.
NO, A DIFFERENT SOLUTION.
YOU HAVE MY ATTENTION.
THEY LEAVE JEDHA.
THAT IS AN INTERESTING SOLUTION.

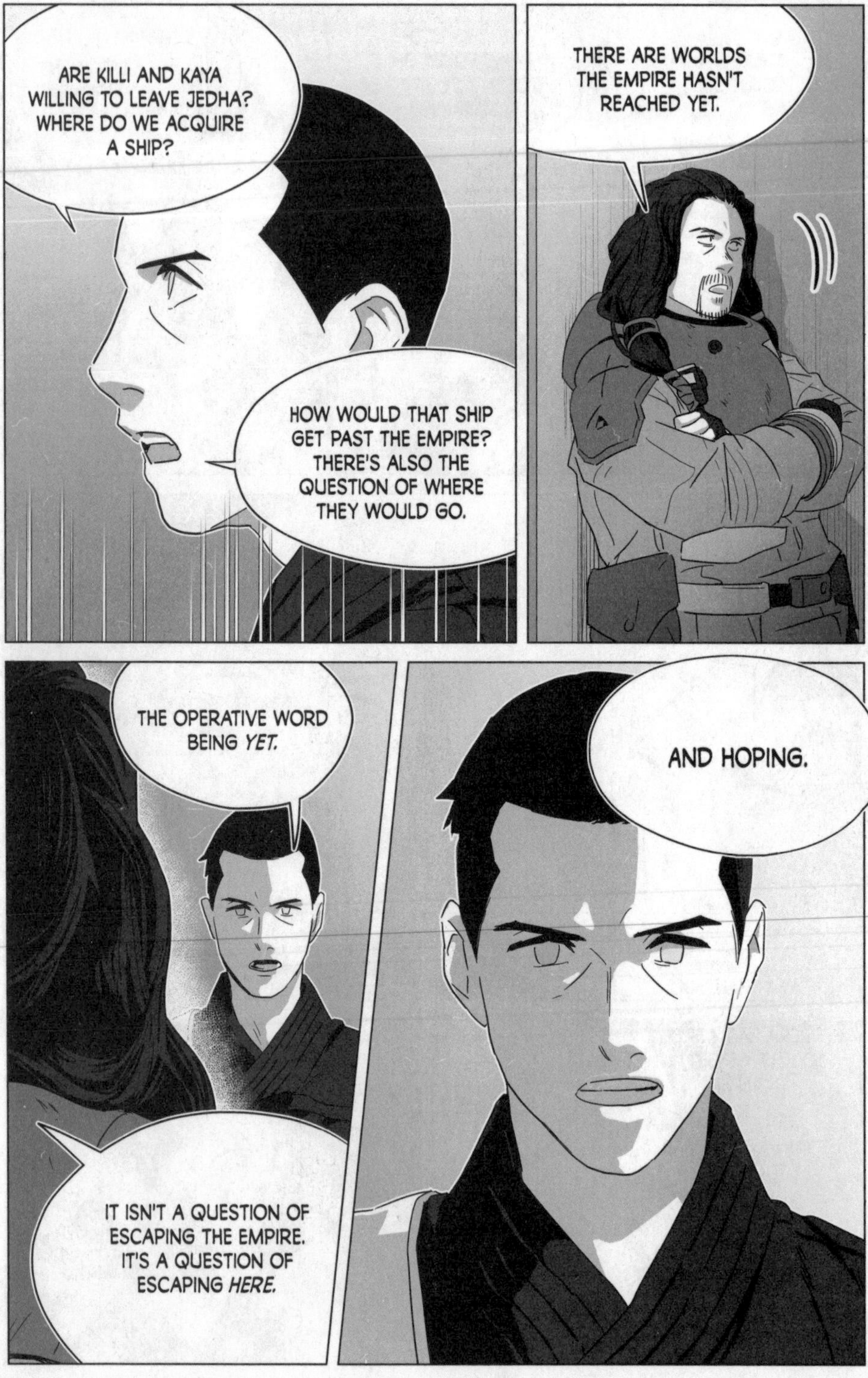
ARE KILLI AND KAYA WILLING TO LEAVE JEDHA? WHERE DO WE ACQUIRE A SHIP?
HOW WOULD THAT SHIP GET PAST THE EMPIRE? THERE'S ALSO THE QUESTION OF WHERE THEY WOULD GO.
THERE ARE WORLDS THE EMPIRE HASN'T REACHED YET.
THE OPERATIVE WORD BEING *YET.*
IT ISN'T A QUESTION OF ESCAPING THE EMPIRE. IT'S A QUESTION OF ESCAPING *HERE.*
AND HOPING.

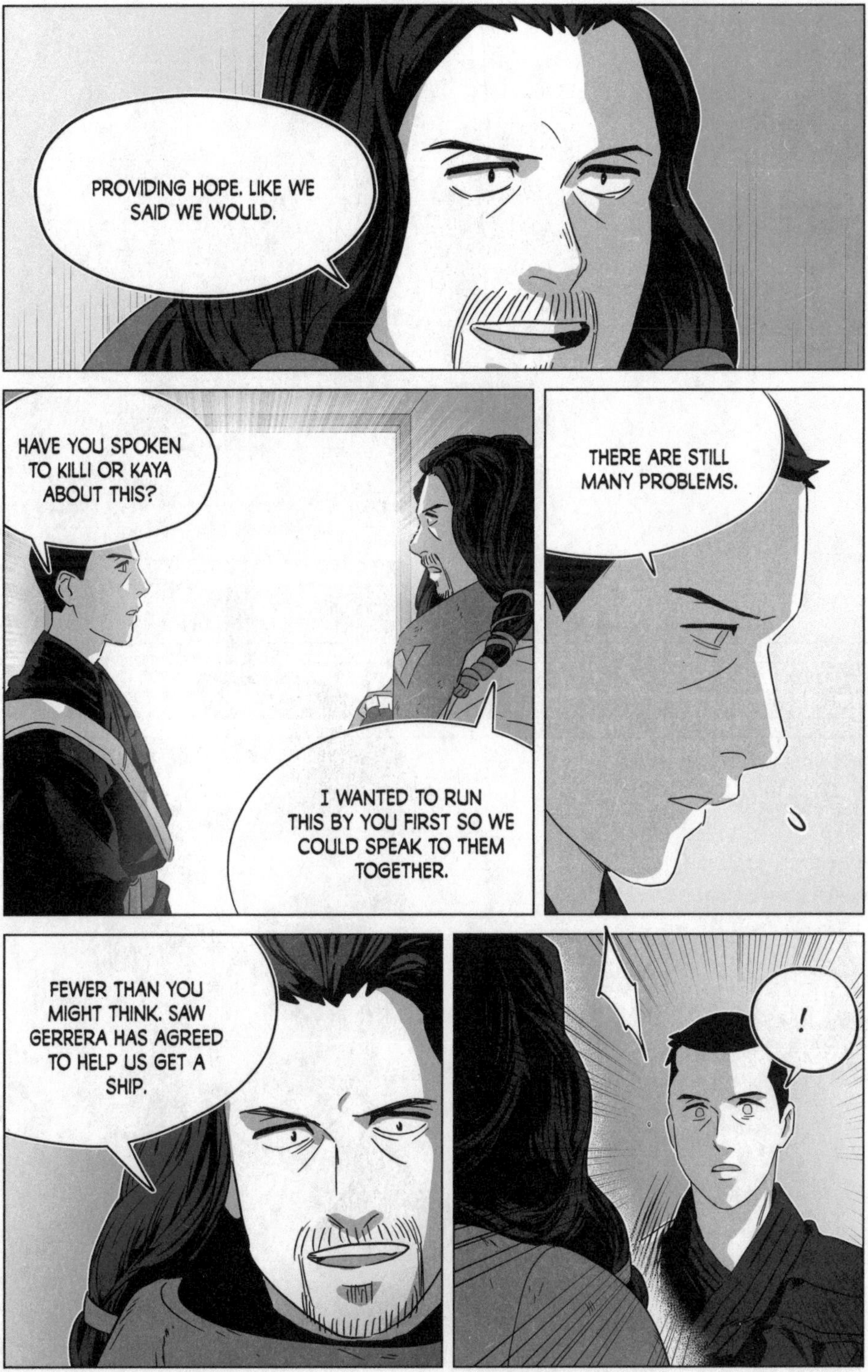
PROVIDING HOPE. LIKE WE SAID WE WOULD.
HAVE YOU SPOKEN TO KILLI OR KAYA ABOUT THIS?
I WANTED TO RUN THIS BY YOU FIRST SO WE COULD SPEAK TO THEM TOGETHER.
THERE ARE STILL MANY PROBLEMS.
FEWER THAN YOU MIGHT THINK. SAW GERRERA HAS AGREED TO HELP US GET A SHIP.
!

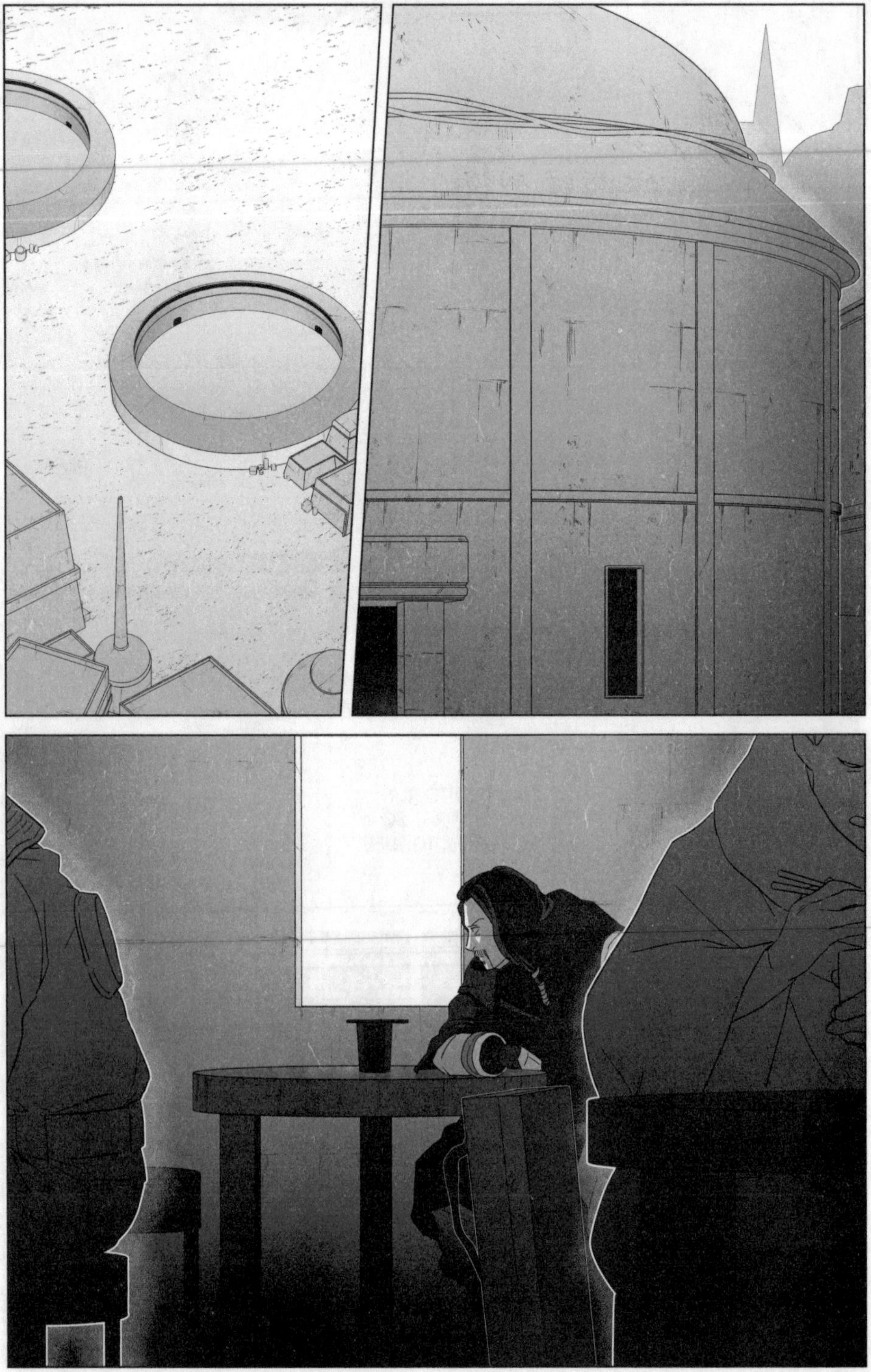

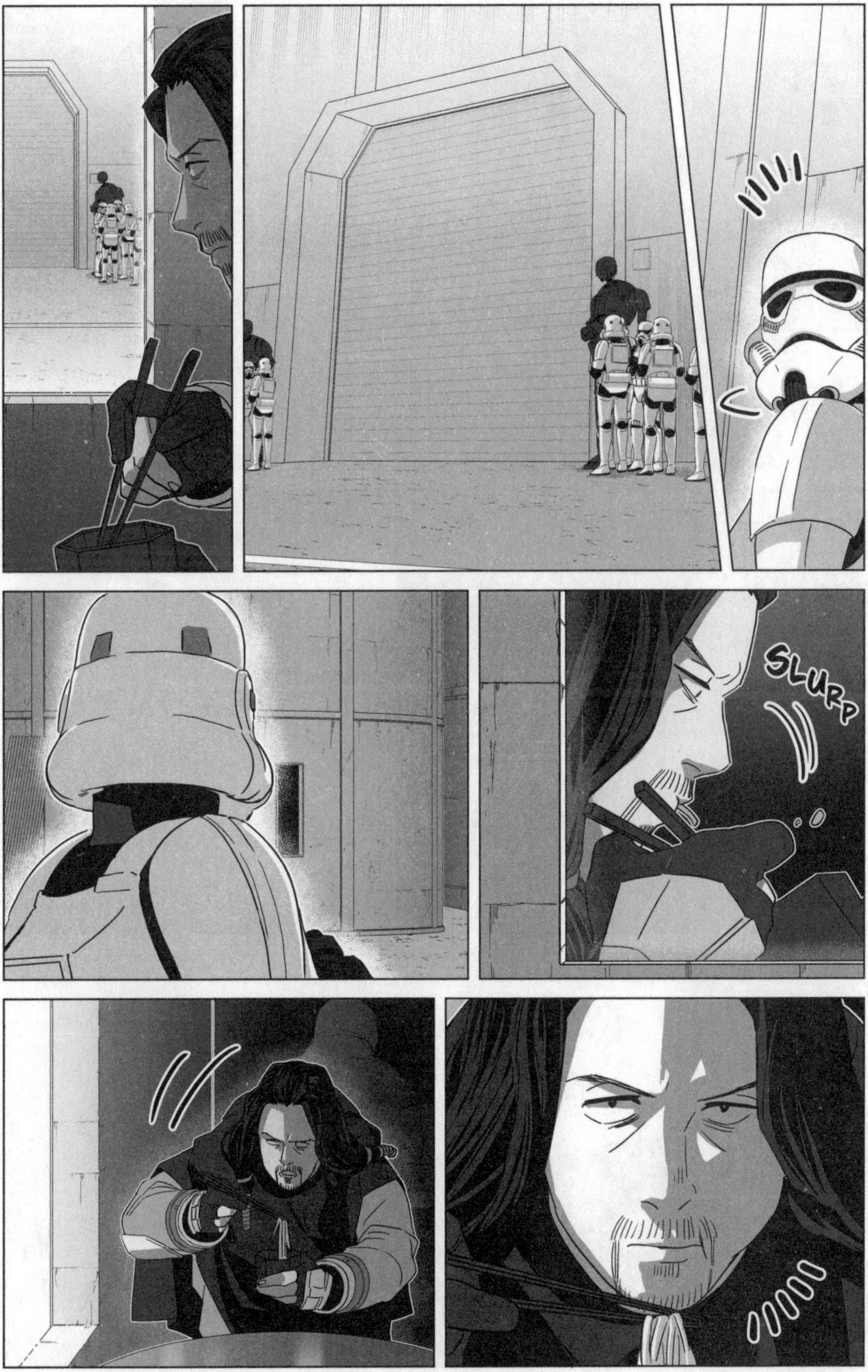
SLURP

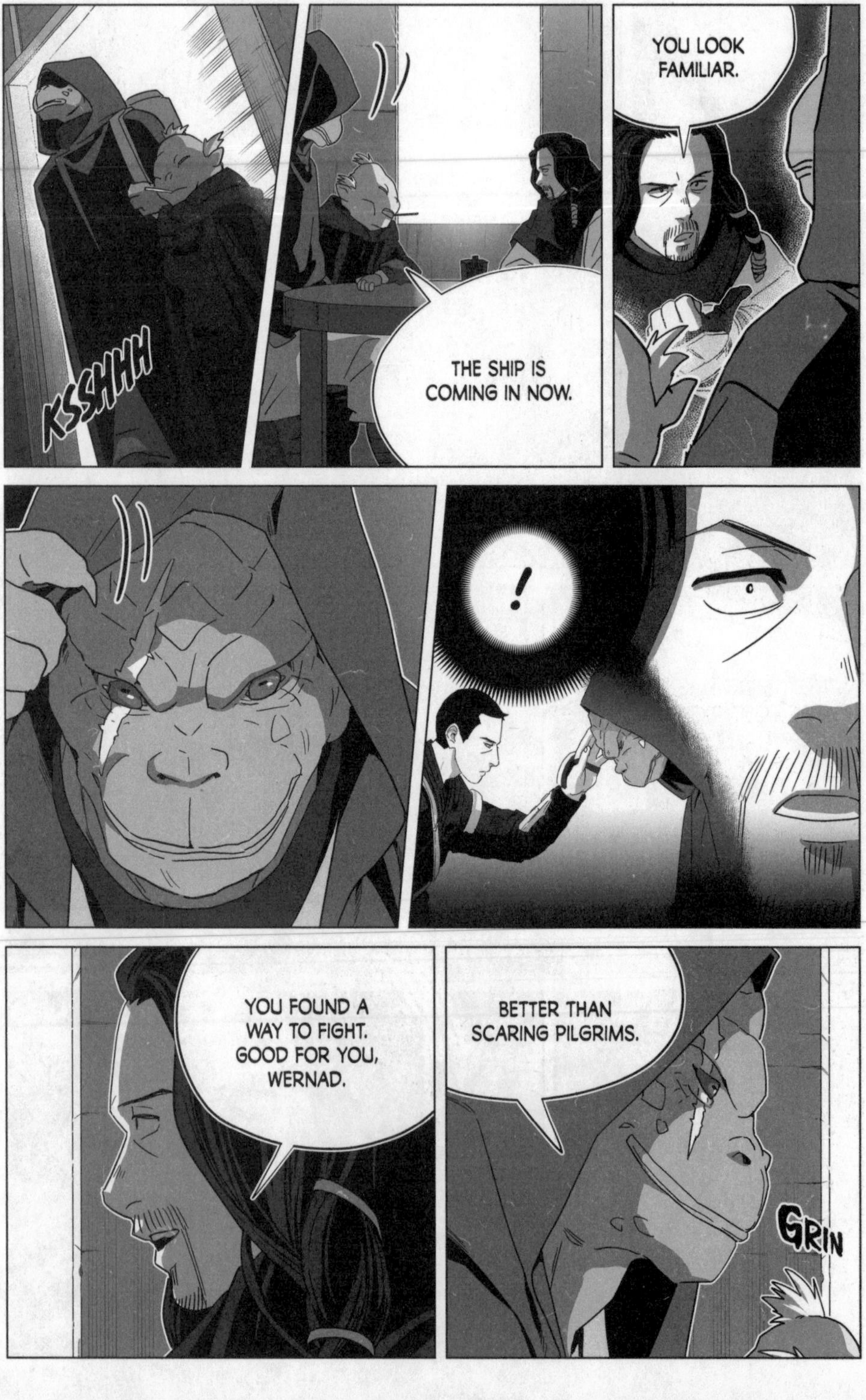
KSSHHH
THE SHIP IS COMING IN NOW.
YOU LOOK FAMILIAR.
!
YOU FOUND A WAY TO FIGHT. GOOD FOR YOU, WERNAD.
BETTER THAN SCARING PILGRIMS.
GRIN

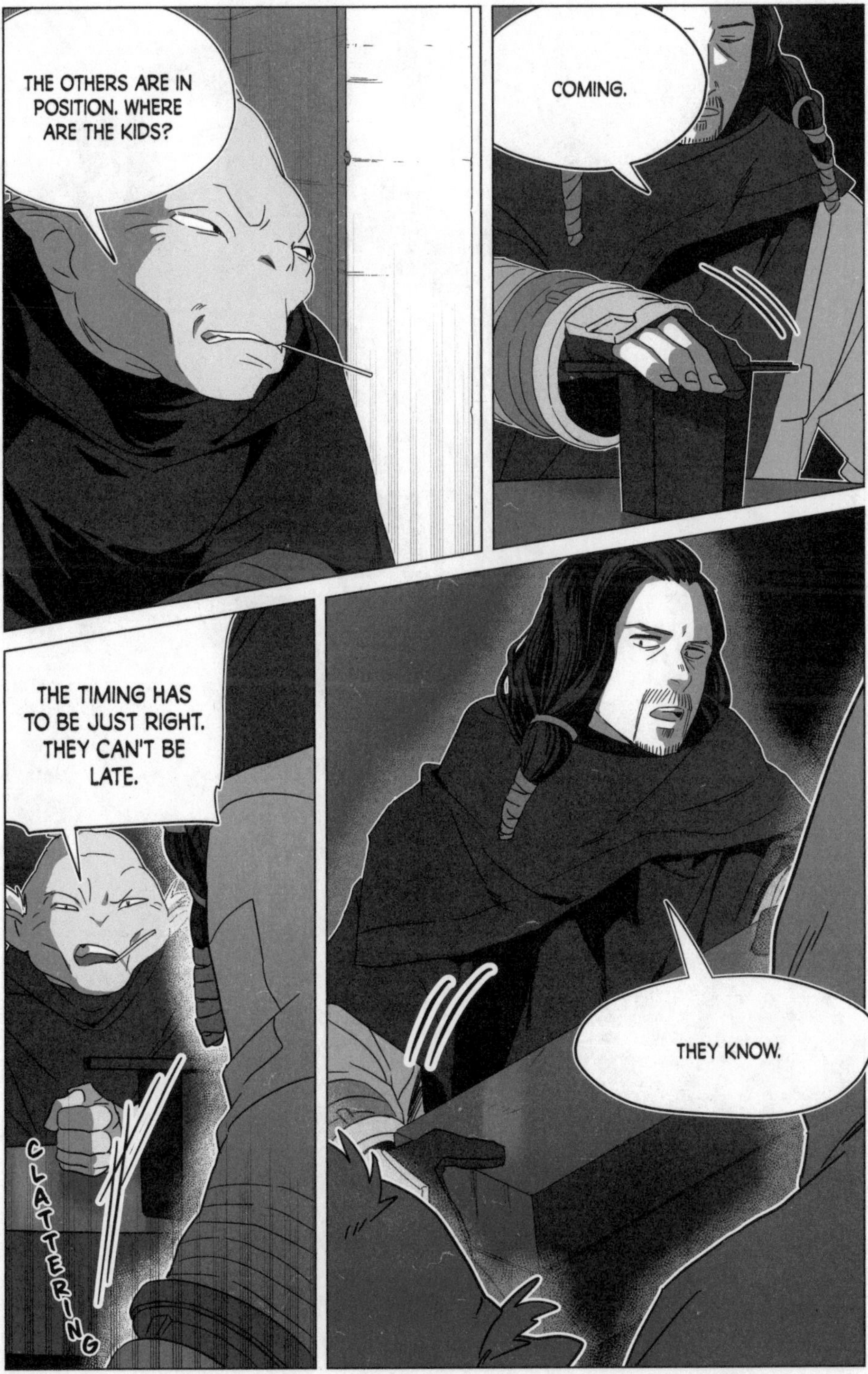
THE OTHERS ARE IN POSITION. WHERE ARE THE KIDS?
COMING.
THE TIMING HAS TO BE JUST RIGHT. THEY CAN'T BE LATE.
CLATTERING
THEY KNOW.

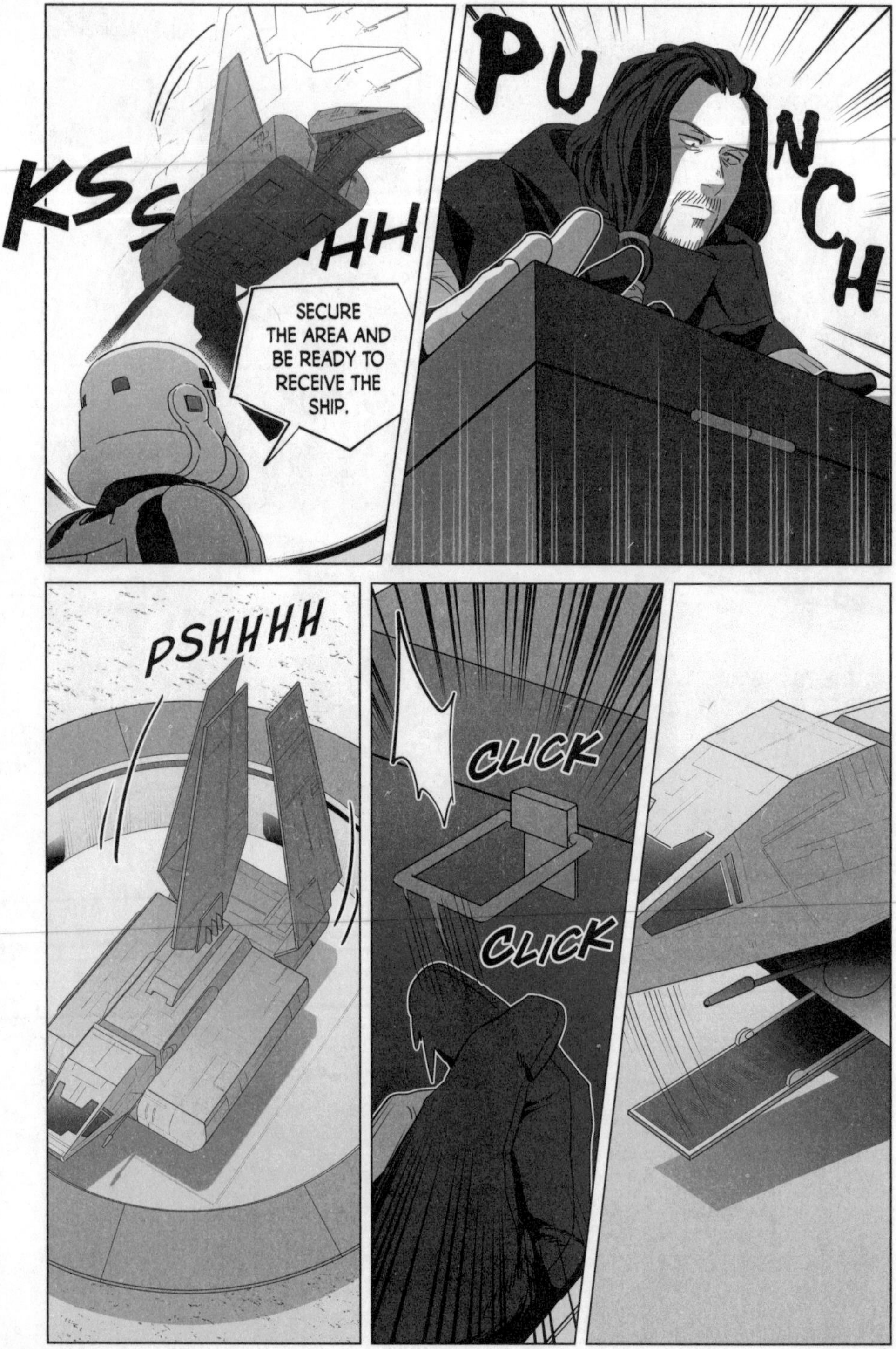
KSSHHH
SECURE THE AREA AND BE READY TO RECEIVE THE SHIP.
PUNCH
PSHHHH
CLICK
CLICK

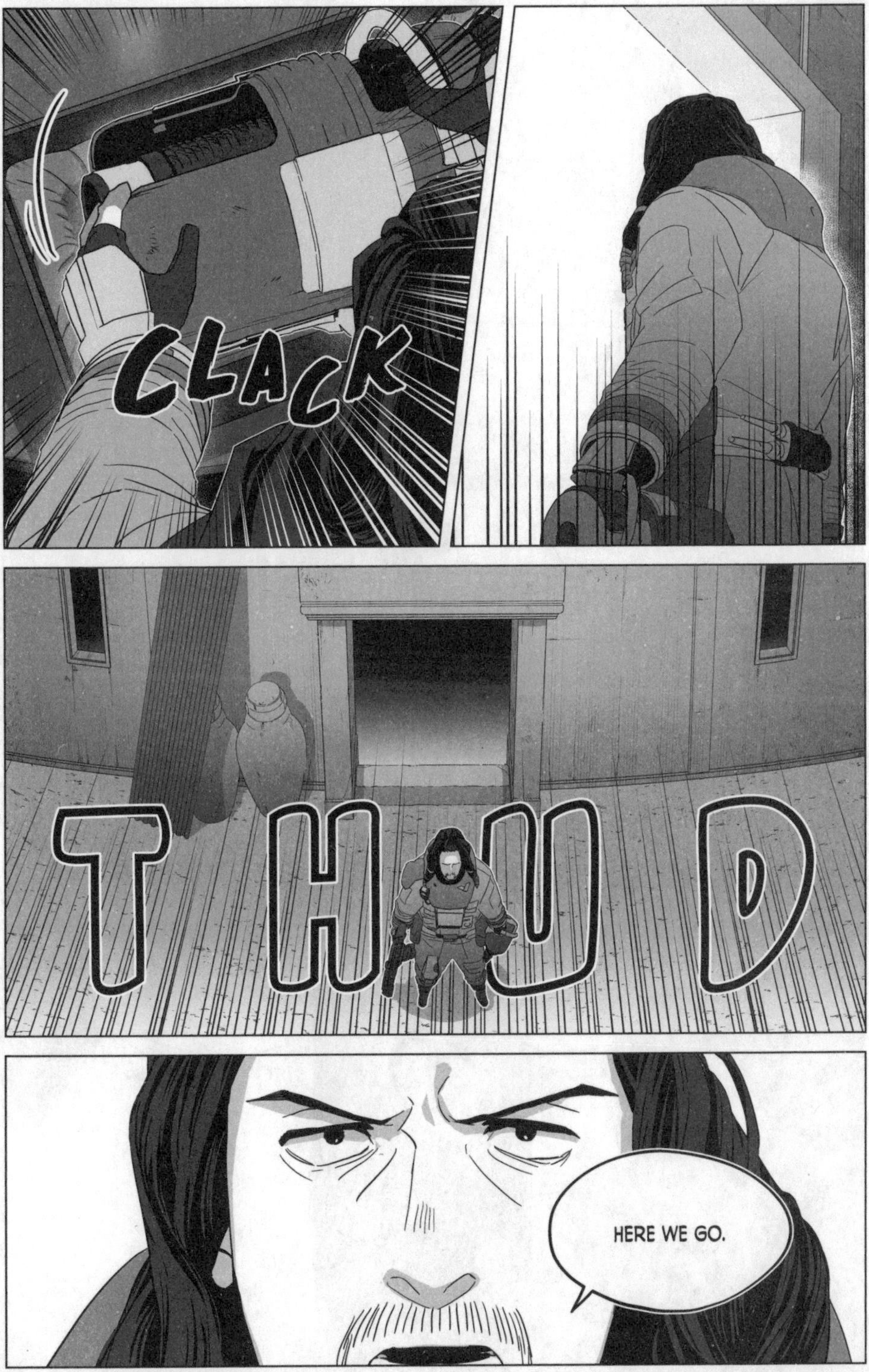
CLACK
THUD
HERE WE GO.

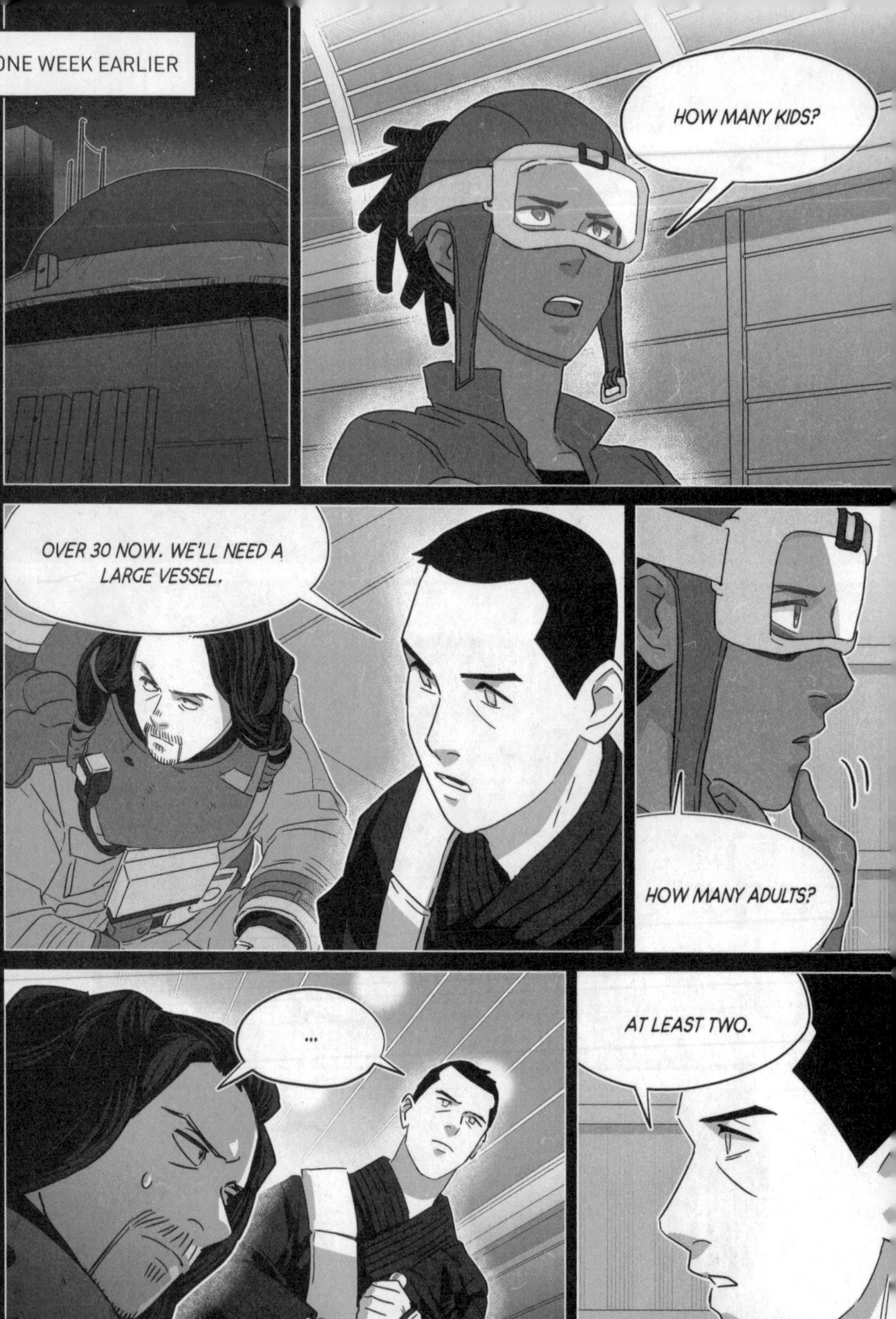
ONE WEEK EARLIER
HOW MANY KIDS?
OVER 30 NOW. WE'LL NEED A LARGE VESSEL.
HOW MANY ADULTS?
...
AT LEAST TWO.

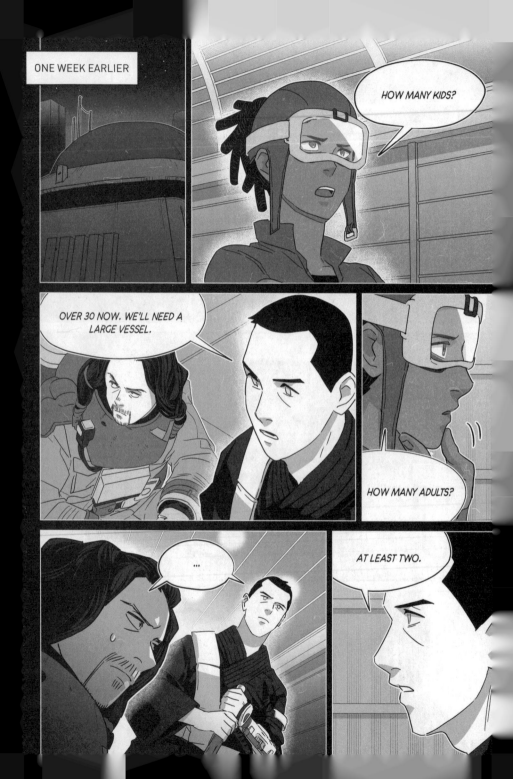

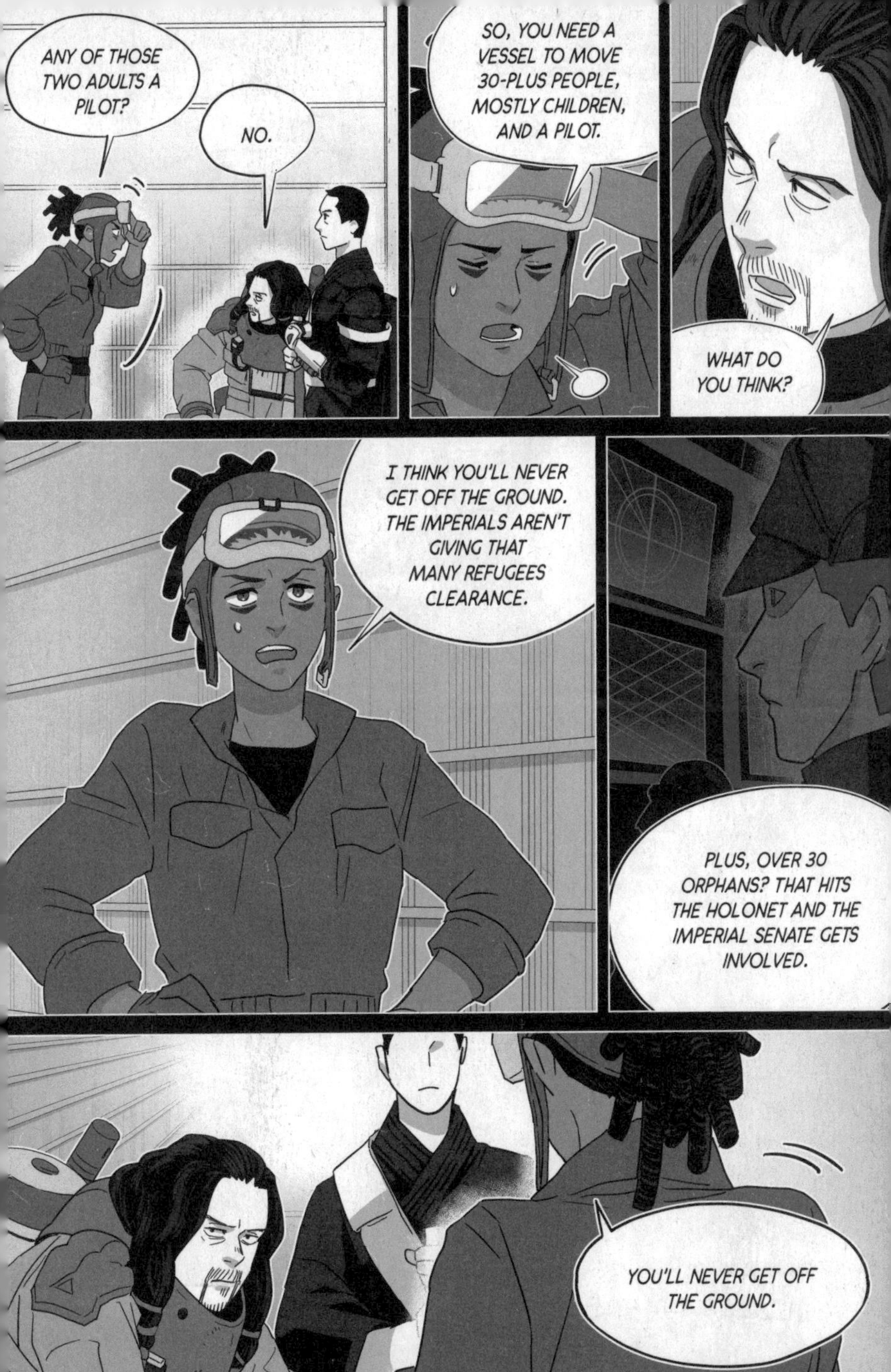
ANY OF THOSE TWO ADULTS A PILOT?
NO.
SO, YOU NEED A VESSEL TO MOVE 30-PLUS PEOPLE, MOSTLY CHILDREN, AND A PILOT.
WHAT DO YOU THINK?
I THINK YOU'LL NEVER GET OFF THE GROUND. THE IMPERIALS AREN'T GIVING THAT MANY REFUGEES CLEARANCE.
PLUS, OVER 30 ORPHANS? THAT HITS THE HOLONET AND THE IMPERIAL SENATE GETS INVOLVED.
YOU'LL NEVER GET OFF THE GROUND.

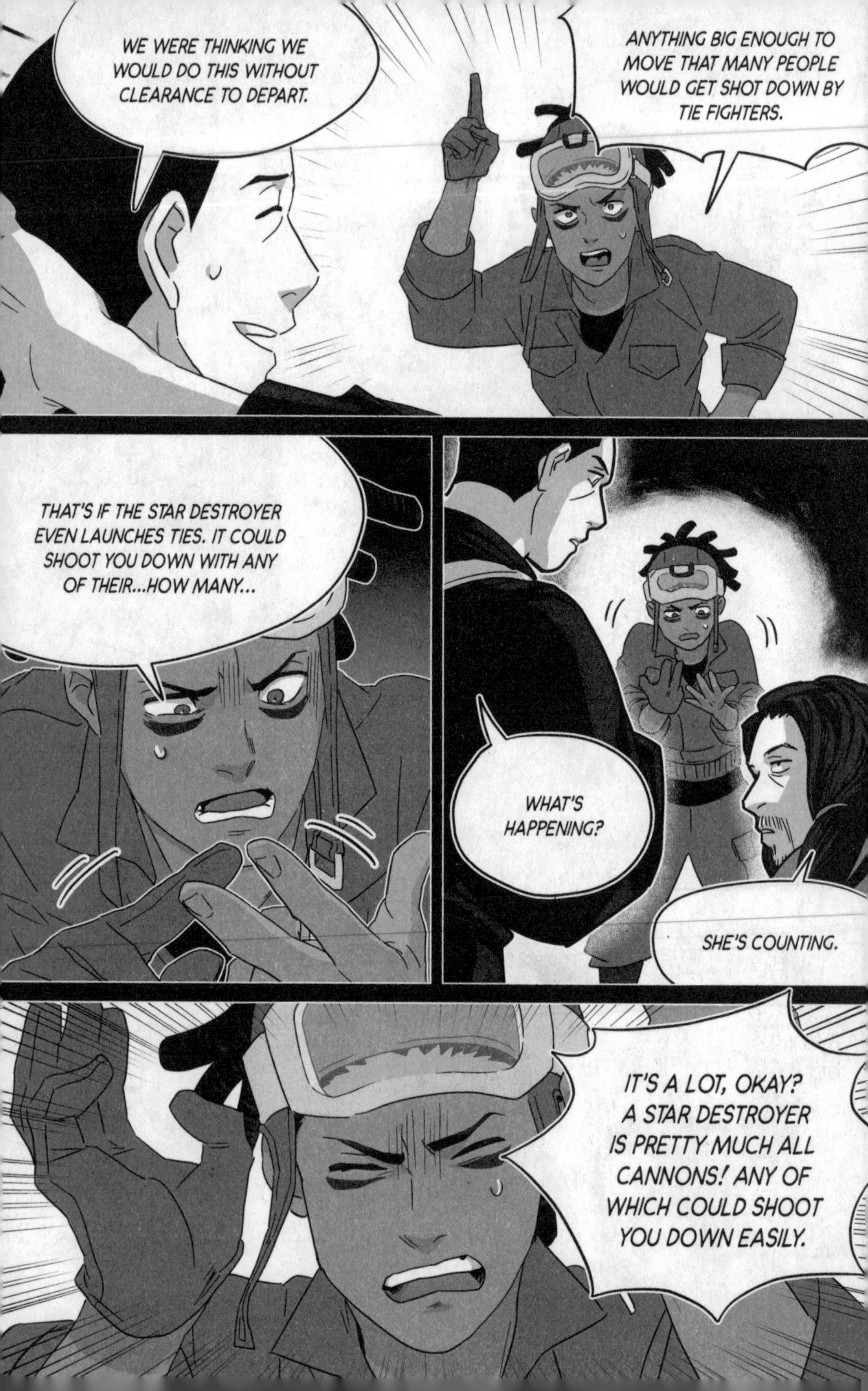
WE WERE THINKING WE WOULD DO THIS WITHOUT CLEARANCE TO DEPART.
ANYTHING BIG ENOUGH TO MOVE THAT MANY PEOPLE WOULD GET SHOT DOWN BY TIE FIGHTERS.
THAT'S IF THE STAR DESTROYER EVEN LAUNCHES TIES. IT COULD SHOOT YOU DOWN WITH ANY OF THEIR...HOW MANY...
WHAT'S HAPPENING?
SHE'S COUNTING.
IT'S A LOT, OKAY? A STAR DESTROYER IS PRETTY MUCH ALL CANNONS! ANY OF WHICH COULD SHOOT YOU DOWN EASILY.

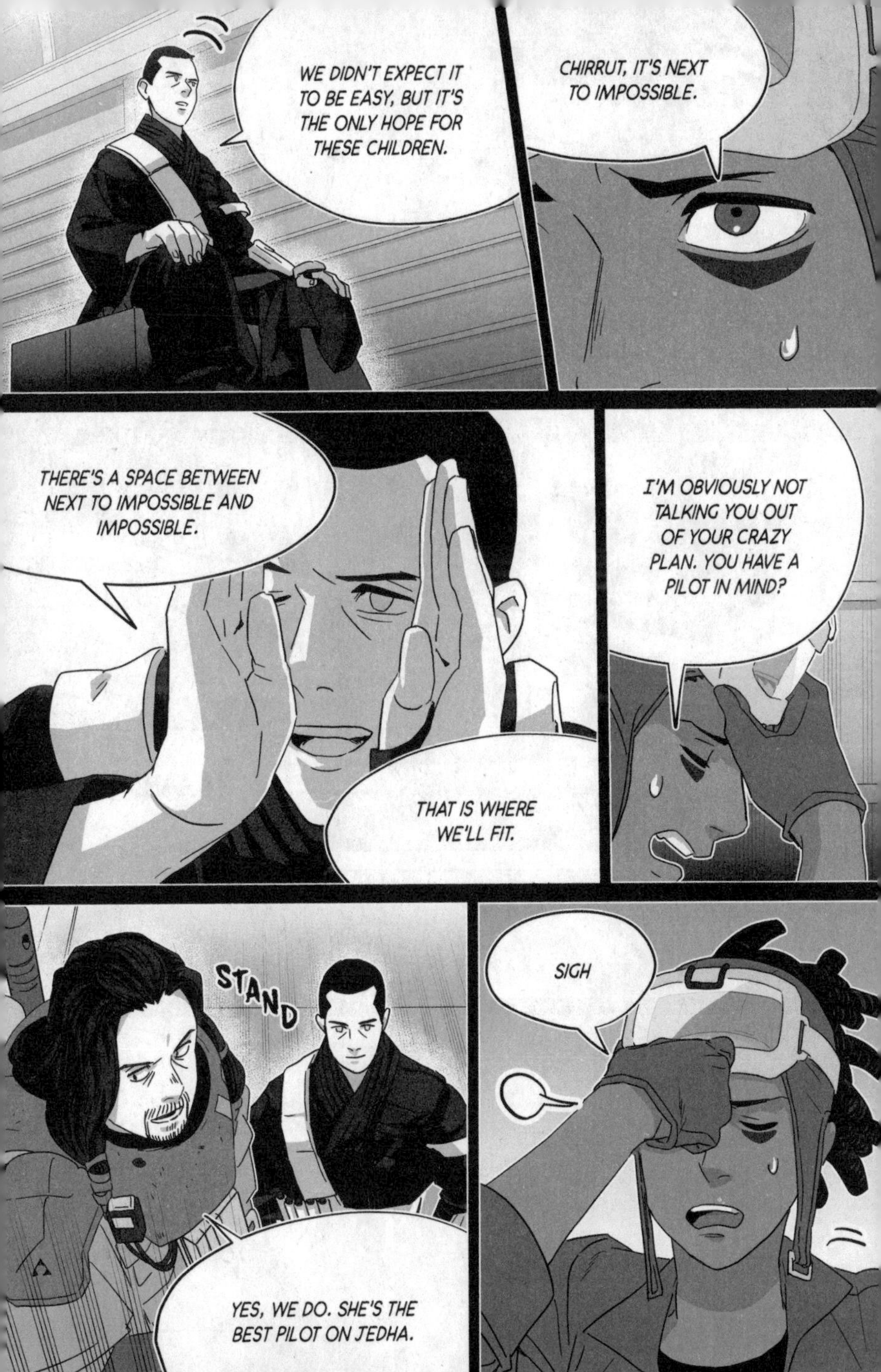
WE DIDN'T EXPECT IT TO BE EASY, BUT IT'S THE ONLY HOPE FOR THESE CHILDREN.
CHIRRUT, IT'S NEXT TO IMPOSSIBLE.
THERE'S A SPACE BETWEEN NEXT TO IMPOSSIBLE AND IMPOSSIBLE.
THAT IS WHERE WE'LL FIT.
I'M OBVIOUSLY NOT TALKING YOU OUT OF YOUR CRAZY PLAN. YOU HAVE A PILOT IN MIND?
STAND
YES, WE DO. SHE'S THE BEST PILOT ON JEDHA.
SIGH

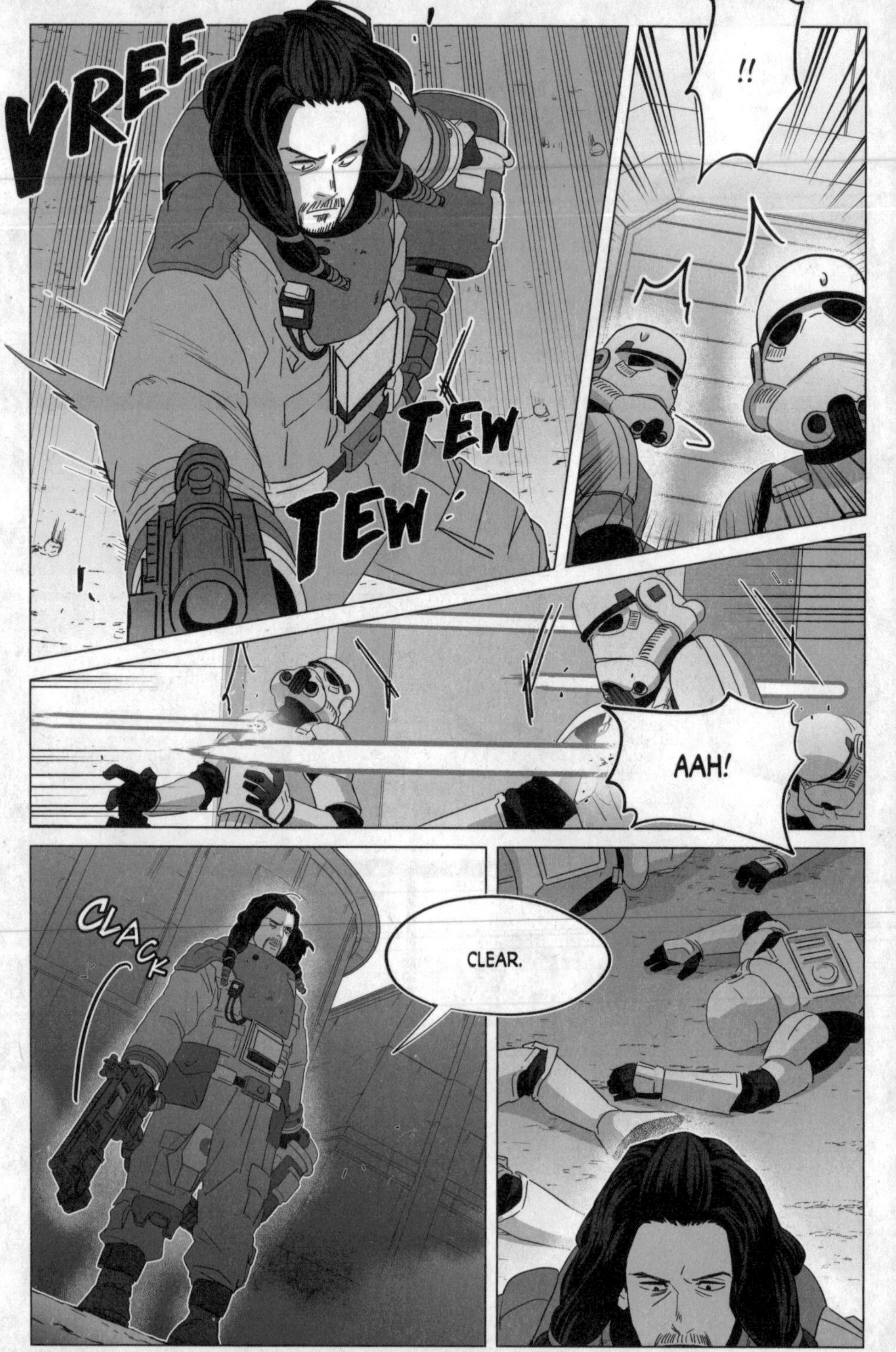
VREE
TEW
TEW
!!
AAH!
CLACK
CLEAR.

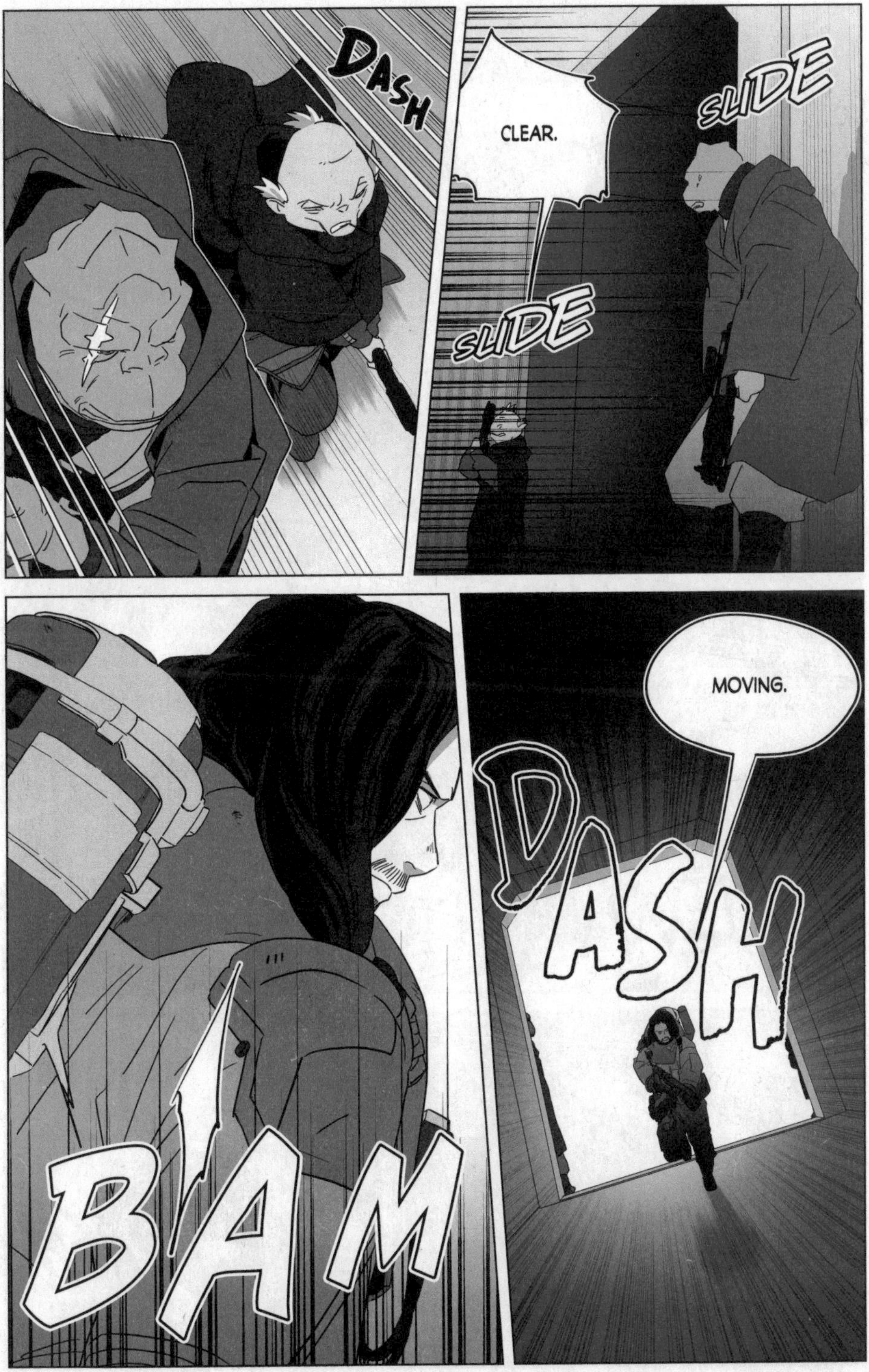
DASH
CLEAR.
SLIDE
SLIDE
BAM
MOVING.
DASH

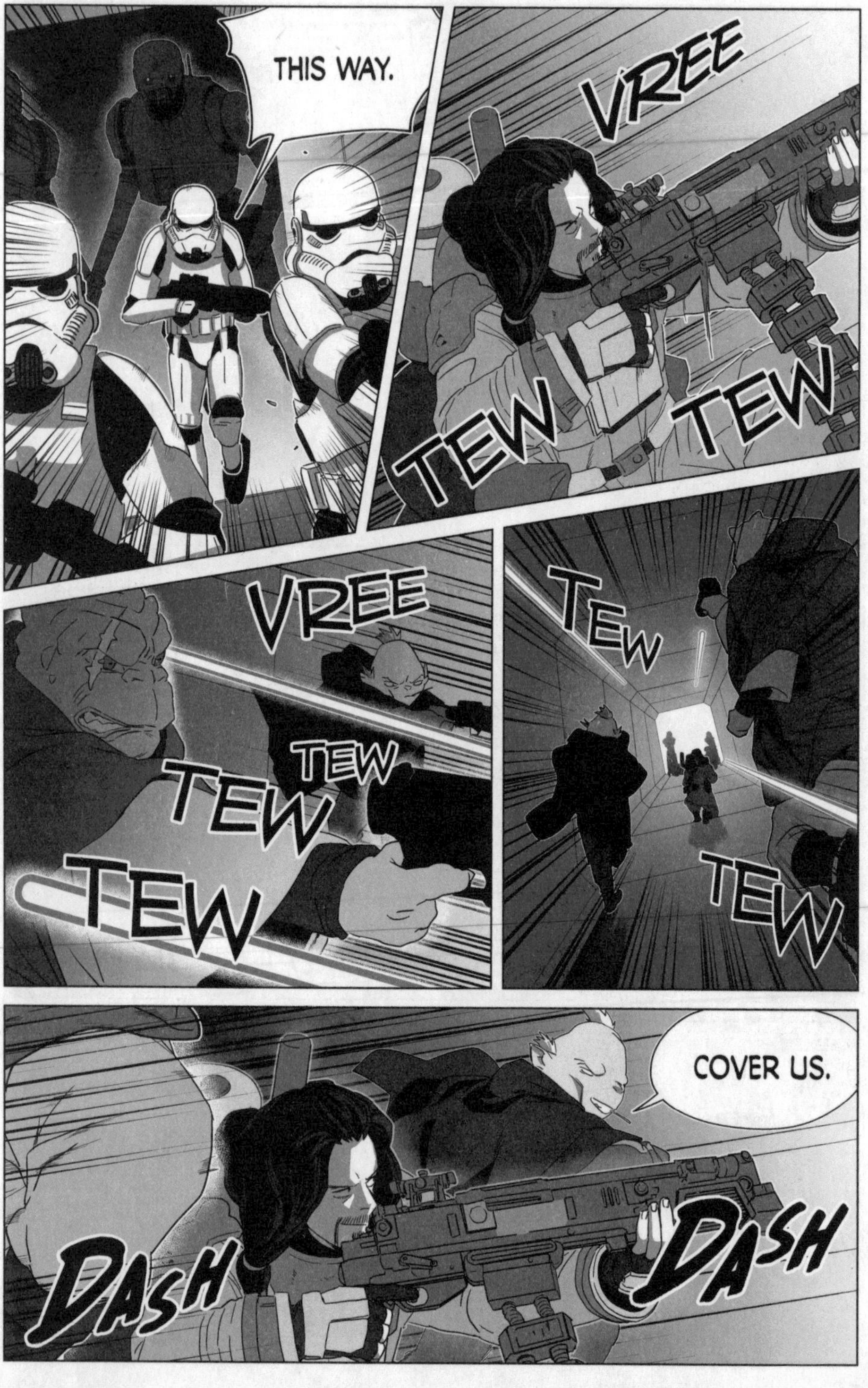
THIS WAY.
VREE
TEW
TEW
VREE
TEW
TEW
TEW
TEW
TEW
COVER US.
DASH
DASH

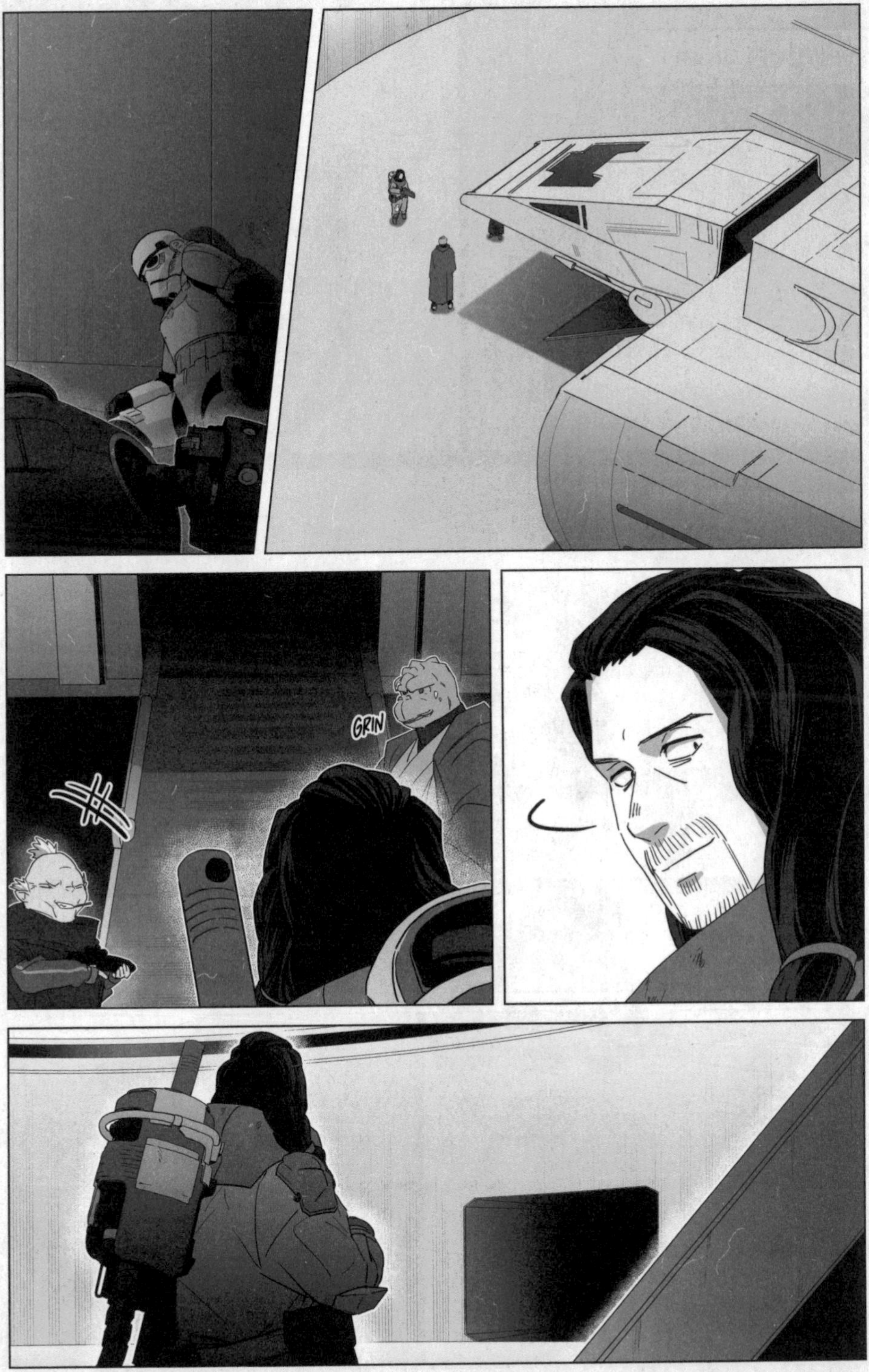
GRIN

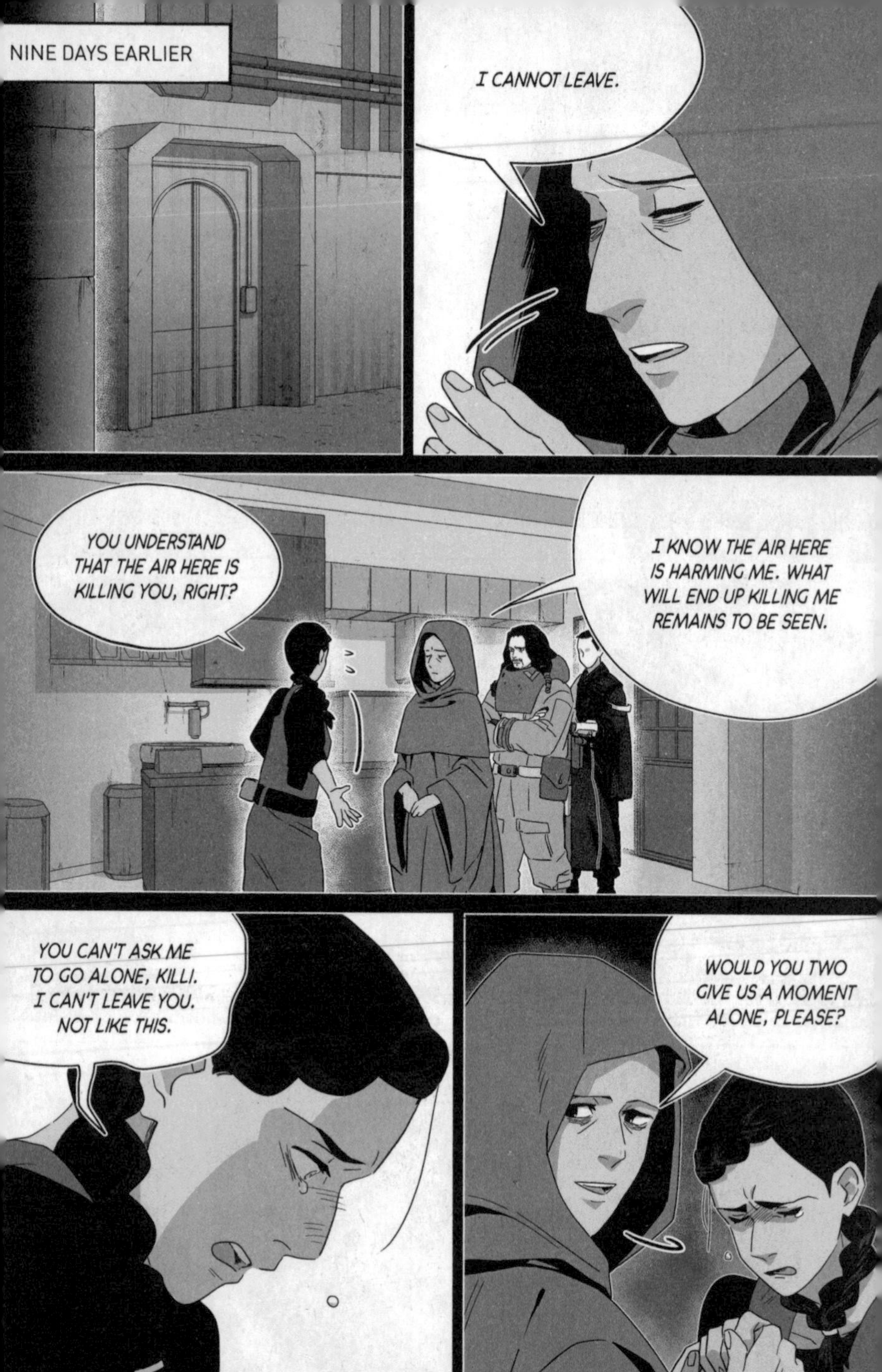
NINE DAYS EARLIER
I CANNOT LEAVE.
YOU UNDERSTAND THAT THE AIR HERE IS KILLING YOU, RIGHT?
I KNOW THE AIR HERE IS HARMING ME. WHAT WILL END UP KILLING ME REMAINS TO BE SEEN.
YOU CAN'T ASK ME TO GO ALONE, KILLI. I CAN'T LEAVE YOU. NOT LIKE THIS.
WOULD YOU TWO GIVE US A MOMENT ALONE, PLEASE?

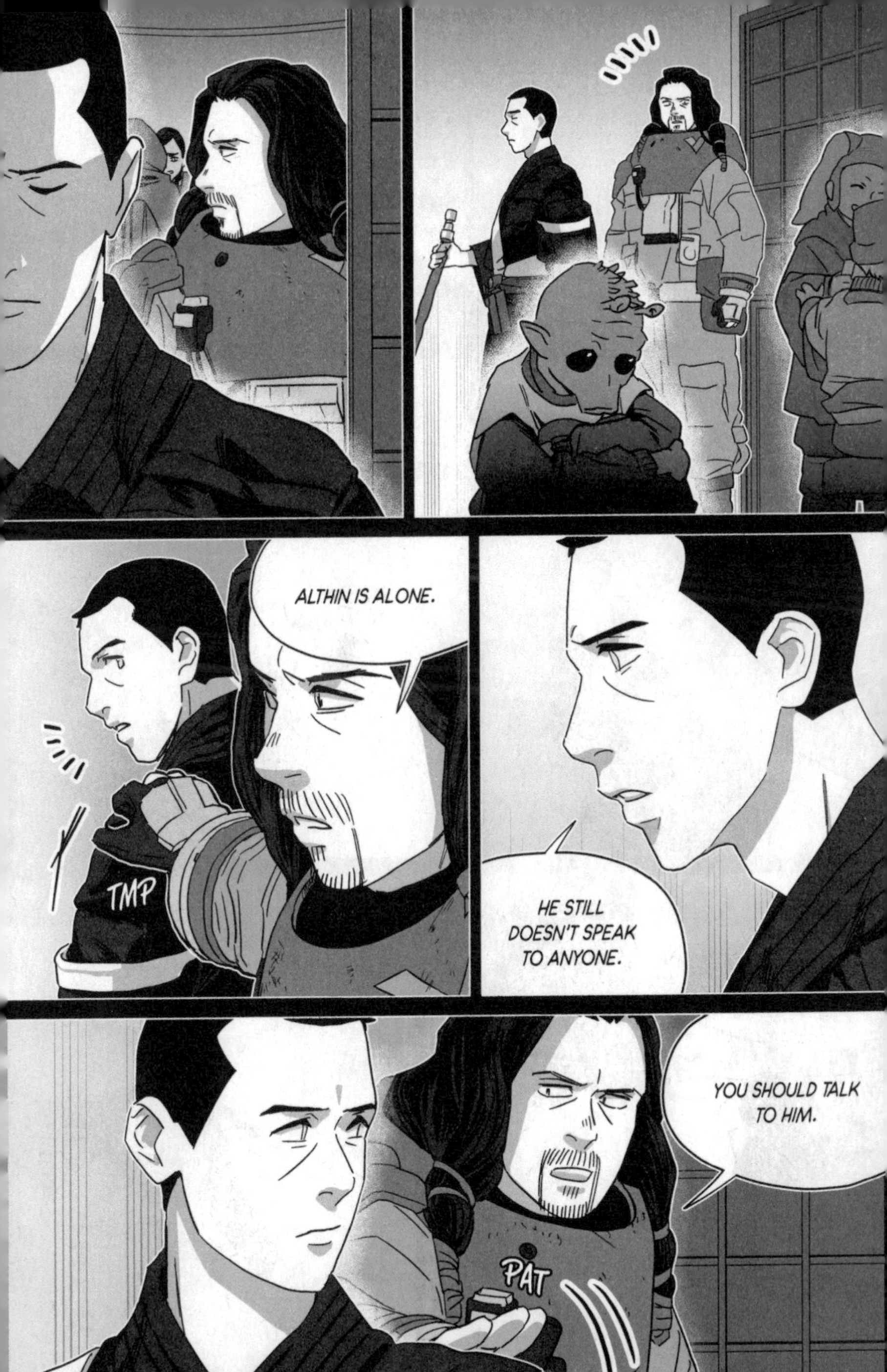
ALTHIN IS ALONE.
TMP
HE STILL DOESN'T SPEAK TO ANYONE.
YOU SHOULD TALK TO HIM.
PAT

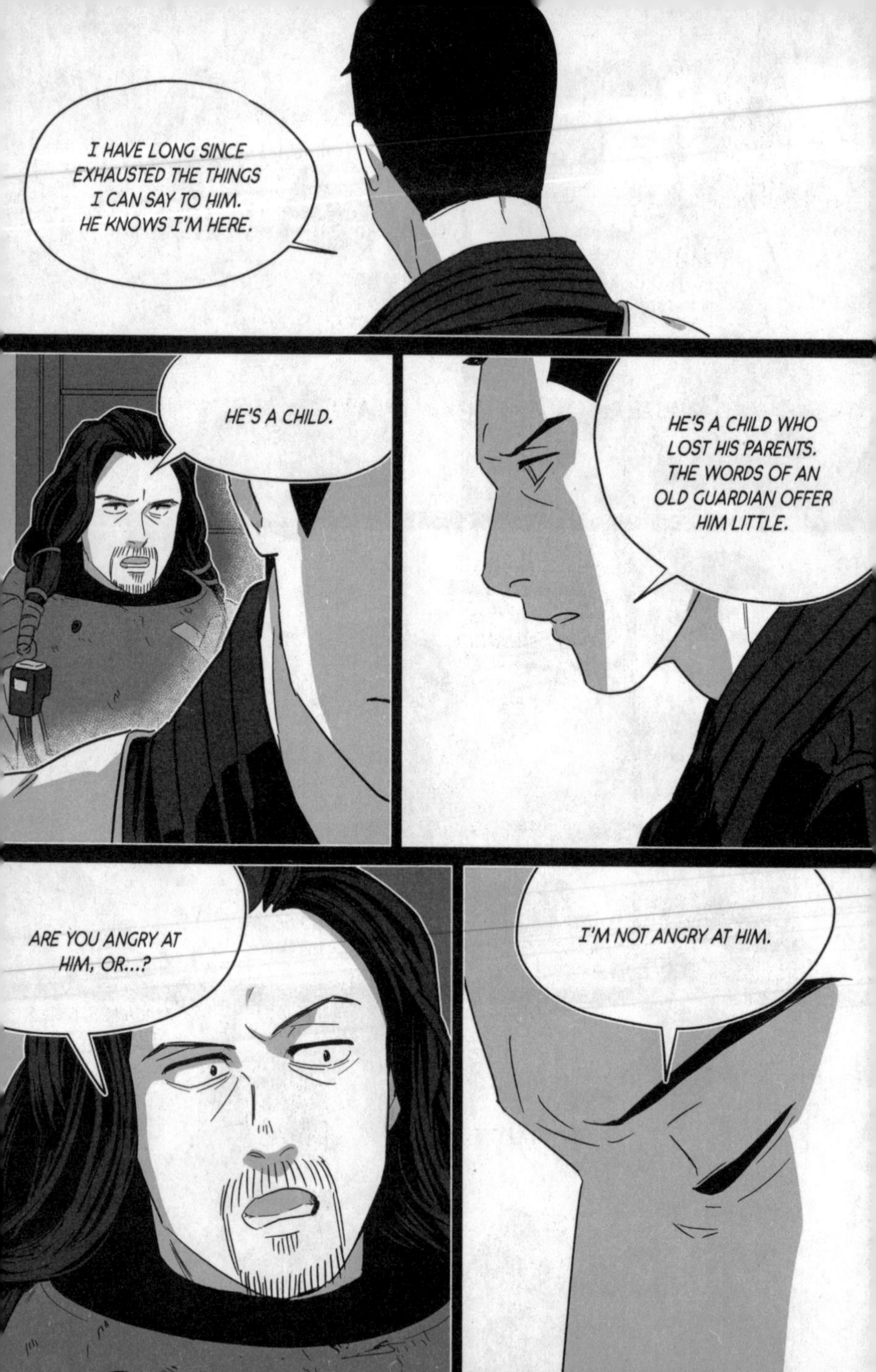
I HAVE LONG SINCE EXHAUSTED THE THINGS I CAN SAY TO HIM. HE KNOWS I'M HERE.
HE'S A CHILD.
HE'S A CHILD WHO LOST HIS PARENTS. THE WORDS OF AN OLD GUARDIAN OFFER HIM LITTLE.
ARE YOU ANGRY AT HIM, OR...?
I'M NOT ANGRY AT HIM.

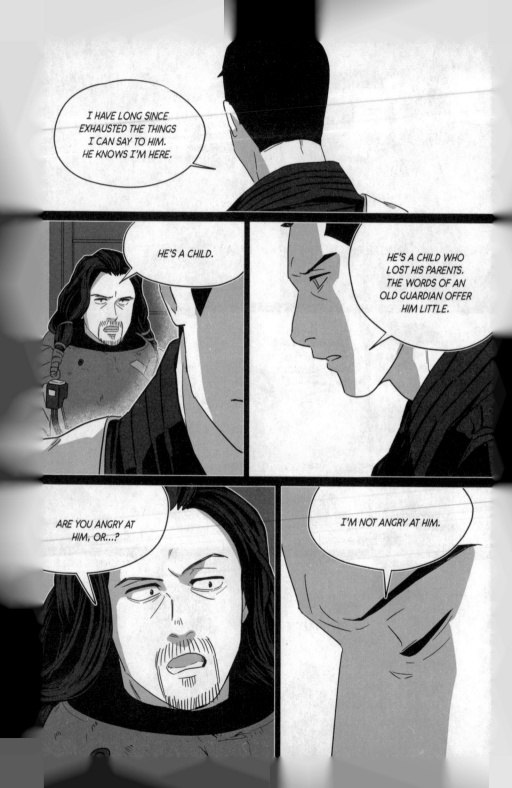

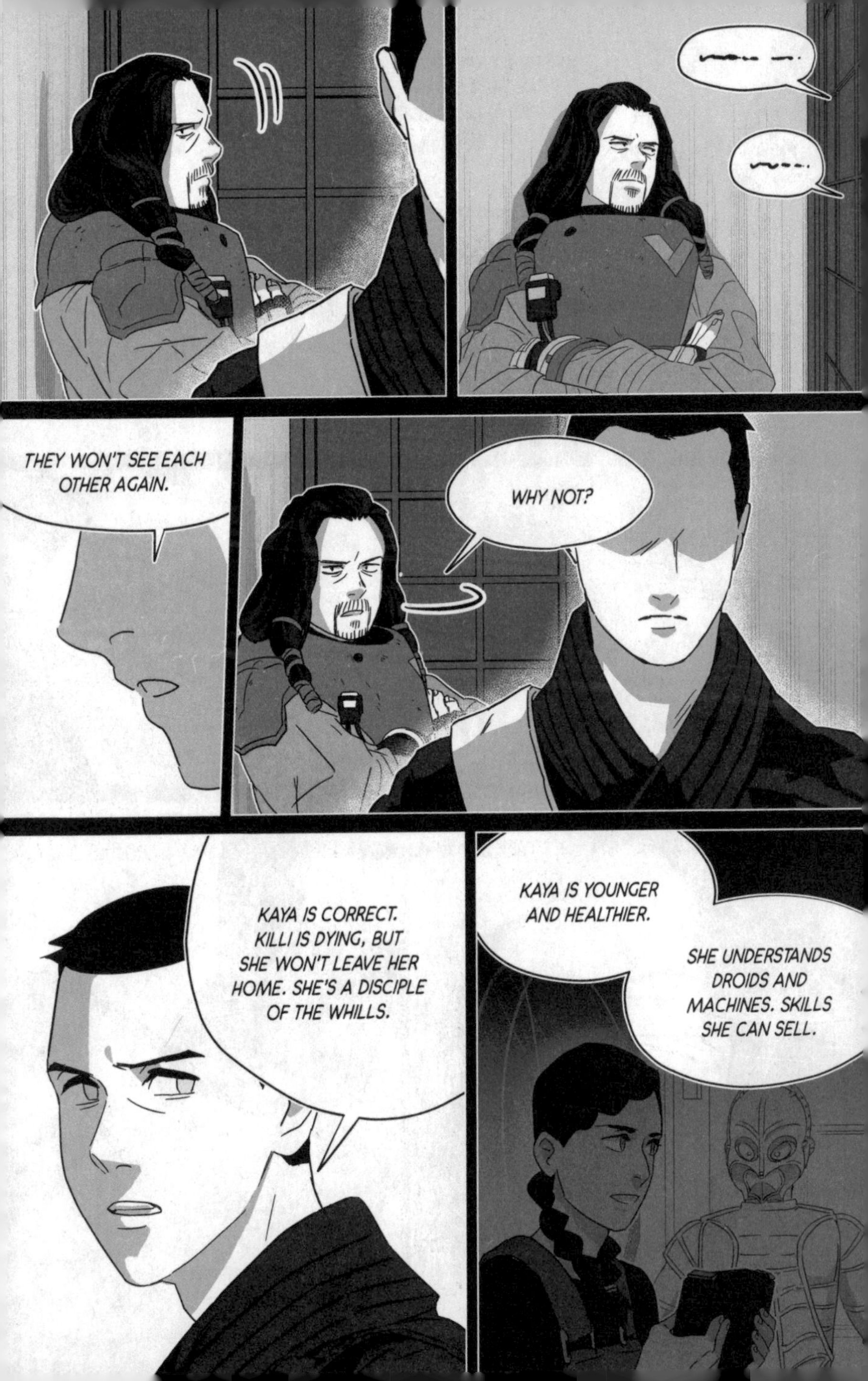
THEY WON'T SEE EACH OTHER AGAIN.
WHY NOT?
KAYA IS CORRECT. KILLI IS DYING, BUT SHE WON'T LEAVE HER HOME. SHE'S A DISCIPLE OF THE WHILLS.
KAYA IS YOUNGER AND HEALTHIER.
SHE UNDERSTANDS DROIDS AND MACHINES. SKILLS SHE CAN SELL.

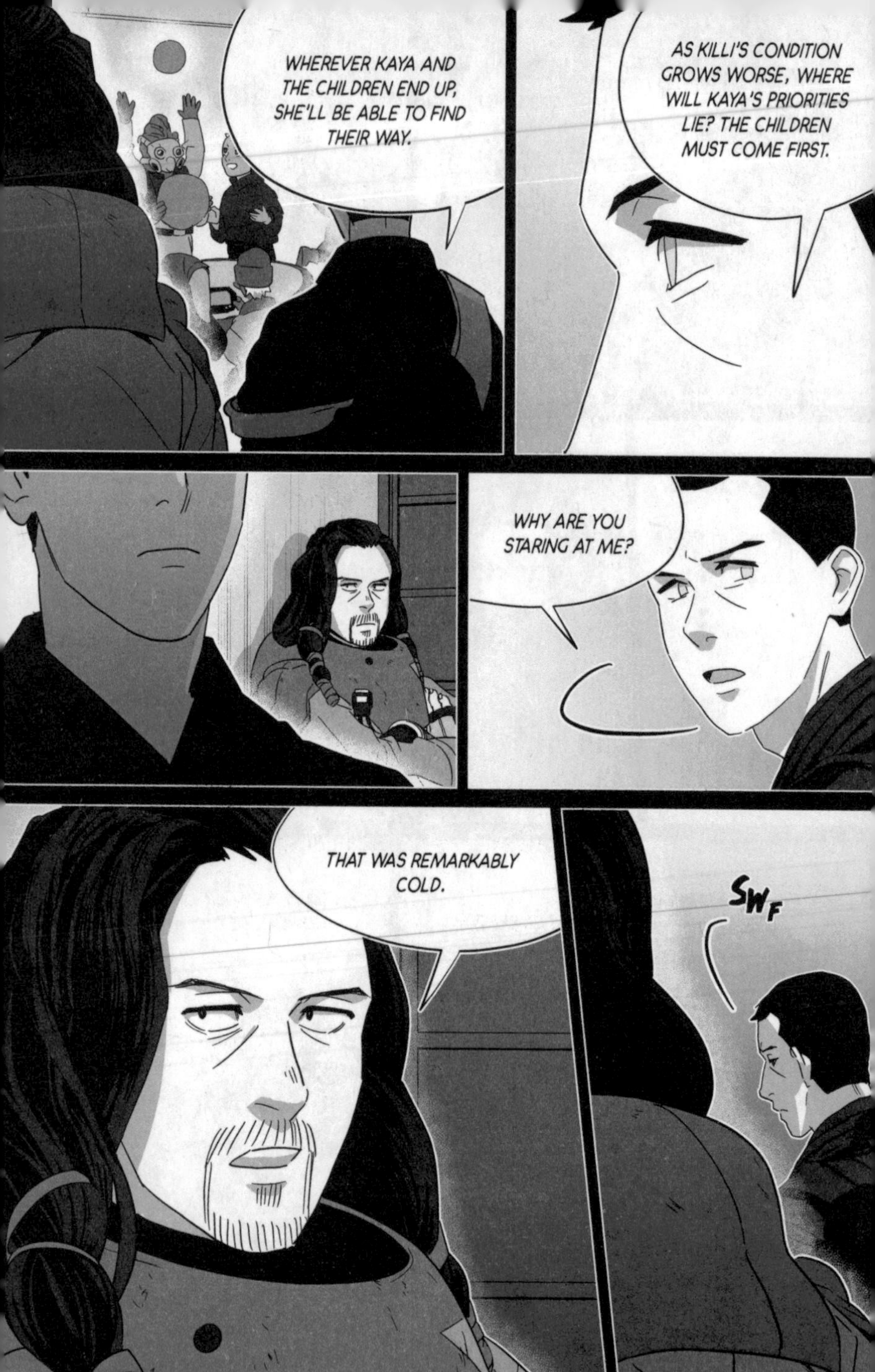
WHEREVER KAYA AND THE CHILDREN END UP, SHE'LL BE ABLE TO FIND THEIR WAY.
AS KILLI'S CONDITION GROWS WORSE, WHERE WILL KAYA'S PRIORITIES LIE? THE CHILDREN MUST COME FIRST.
WHY ARE YOU STARING AT ME?
THAT WAS REMARKABLY COLD.
SWF

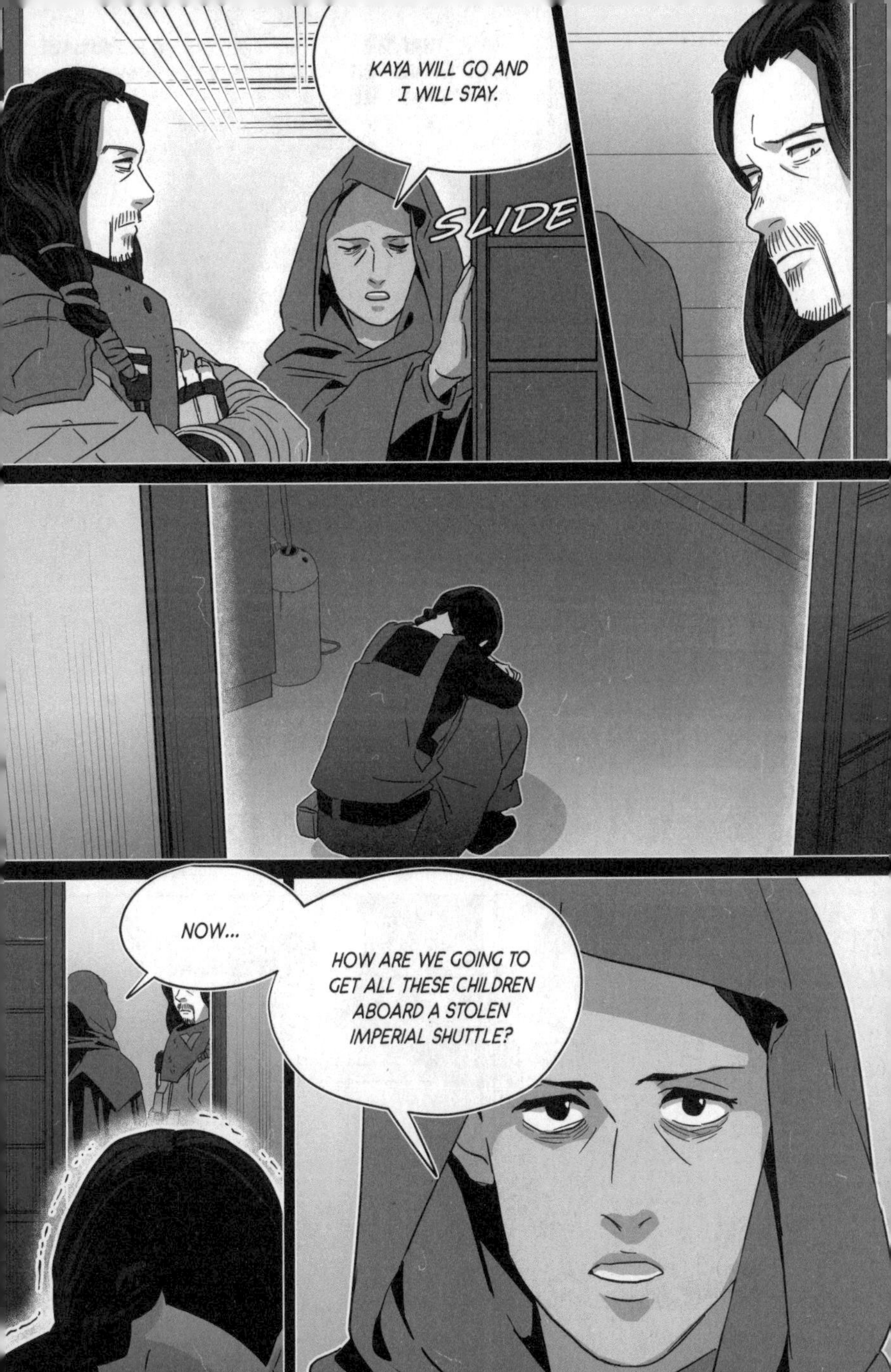
KAYA WILL GO AND I WILL STAY.
SLIDE
NOW...
HOW ARE WE GOING TO GET ALL THESE CHILDREN ABOARD A STOLEN IMPERIAL SHUTTLE?

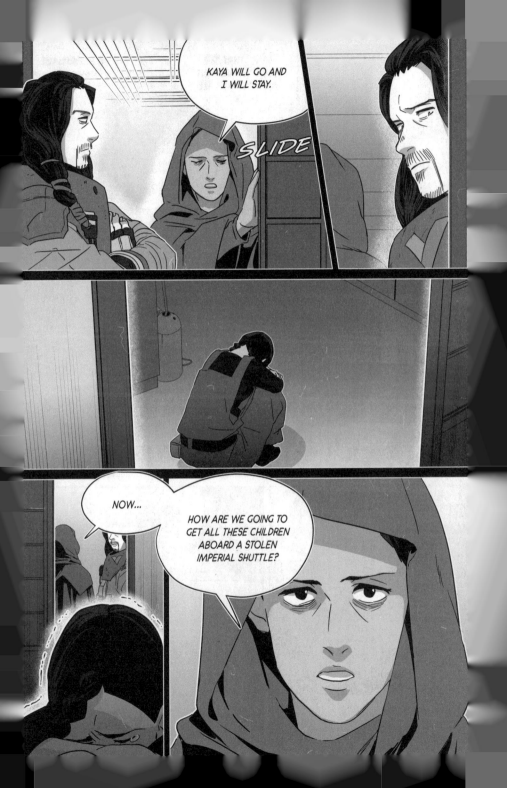

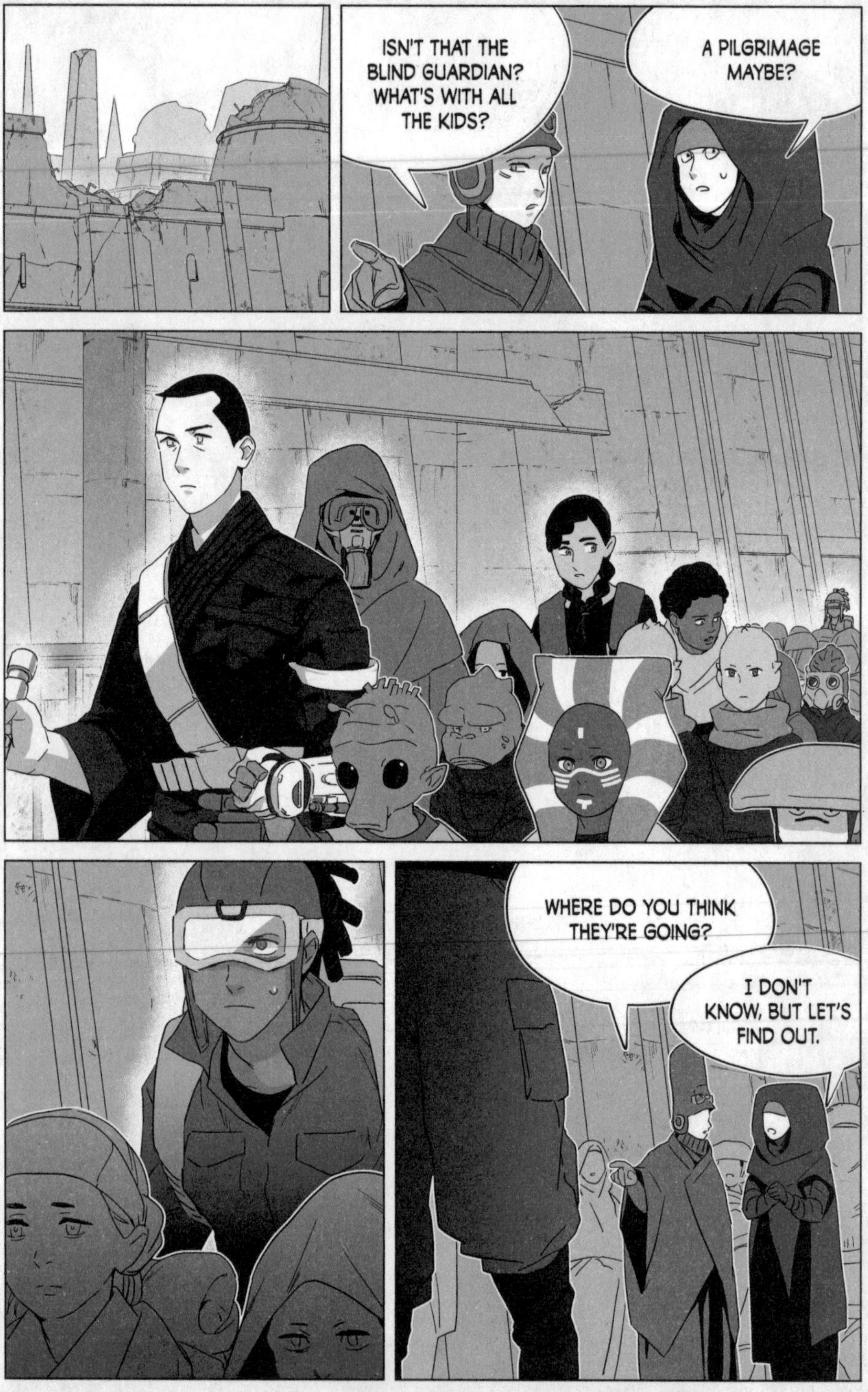

ISN'T THAT THE BLIND GUARDIAN? WHAT'S WITH ALL THE KIDS?
A PILGRIMAGE MAYBE?
WHERE DO YOU THINK THEY'RE GOING?
I DON'T KNOW, BUT LET'S FIND OUT.

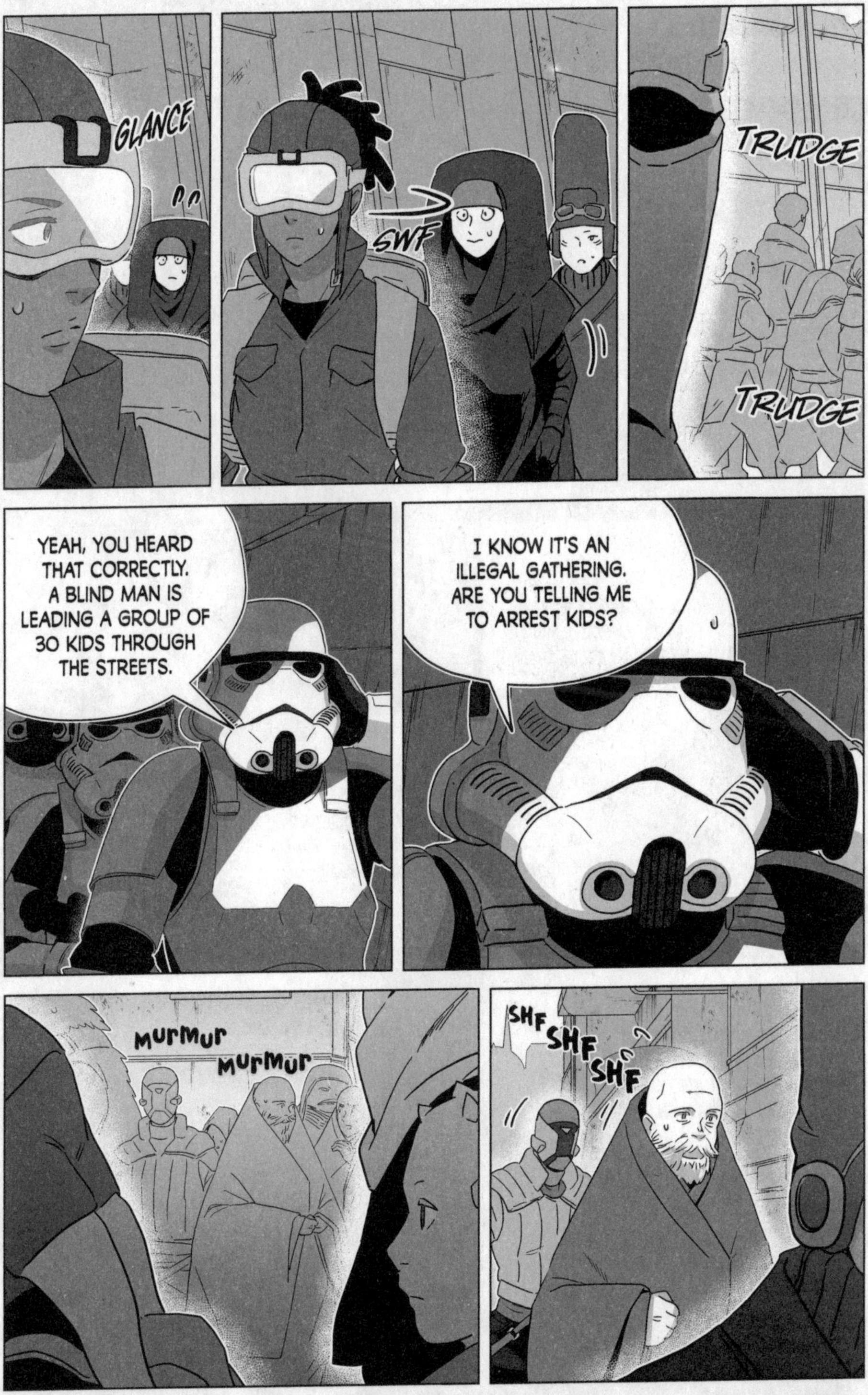
GLANCE
SWF
TRUDGE
TRUDGE
YEAH, YOU HEARD THAT CORRECTLY. A BLIND MAN IS LEADING A GROUP OF 30 KIDS THROUGH THE STREETS.
I KNOW IT'S AN ILLEGAL GATHERING. ARE YOU TELLING ME TO ARREST KIDS?
MURMUR
MURMUR
SHF
SHF
SHF

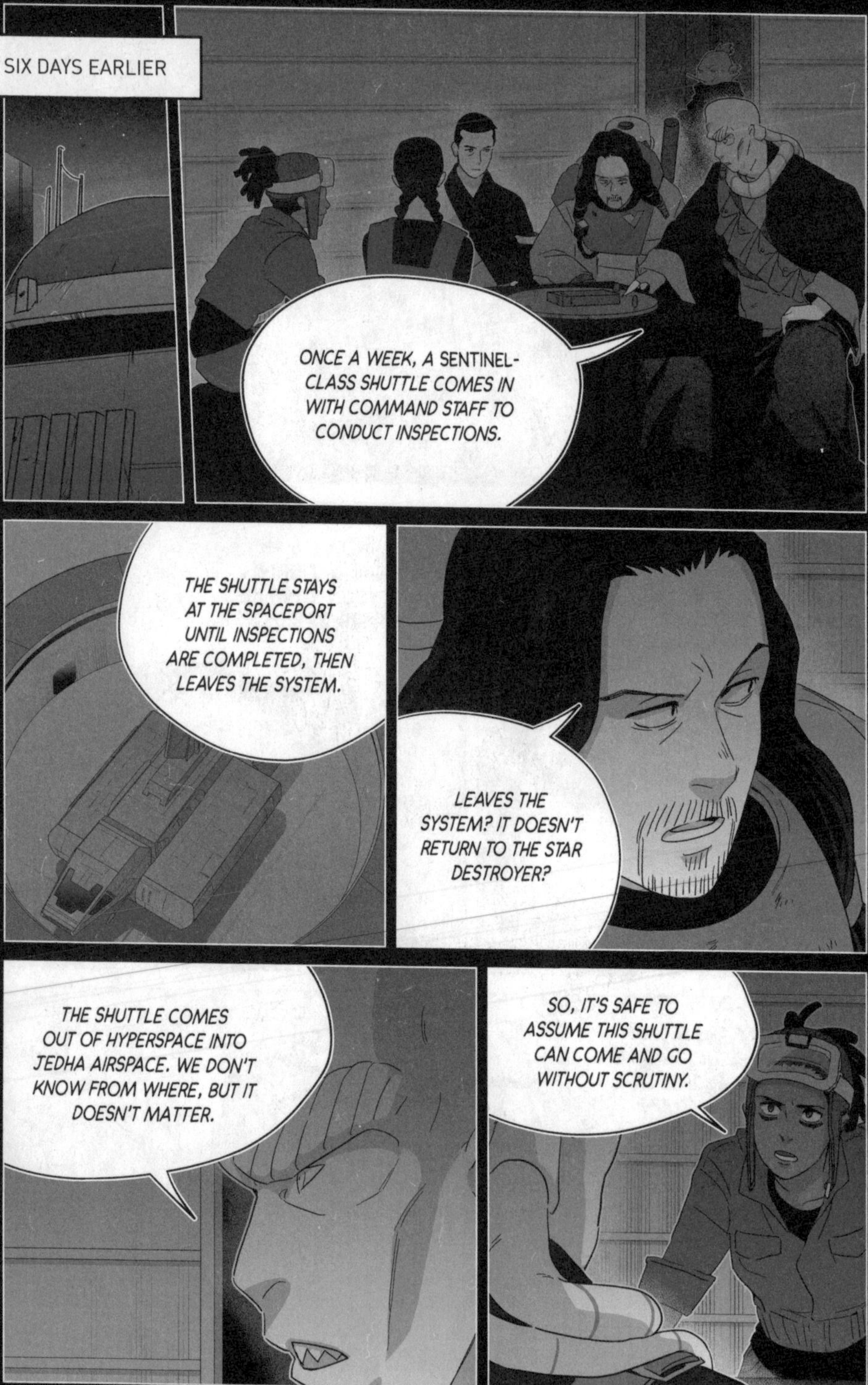
SIX DAYS EARLIER
ONCE A WEEK, A SENTINEL-CLASS SHUTTLE COMES IN WITH COMMAND STAFF TO CONDUCT INSPECTIONS.
THE SHUTTLE STAYS AT THE SPACEPORT UNTIL INSPECTIONS ARE COMPLETED, THEN LEAVES THE SYSTEM.
LEAVES THE SYSTEM? IT DOESN'T RETURN TO THE STAR DESTROYER?
THE SHUTTLE COMES OUT OF HYPERSPACE INTO JEDHA AIRSPACE. WE DON'T KNOW FROM WHERE, BUT IT DOESN'T MATTER.
SO, IT'S SAFE TO ASSUME THIS SHUTTLE CAN COME AND GO WITHOUT SCRUTINY.

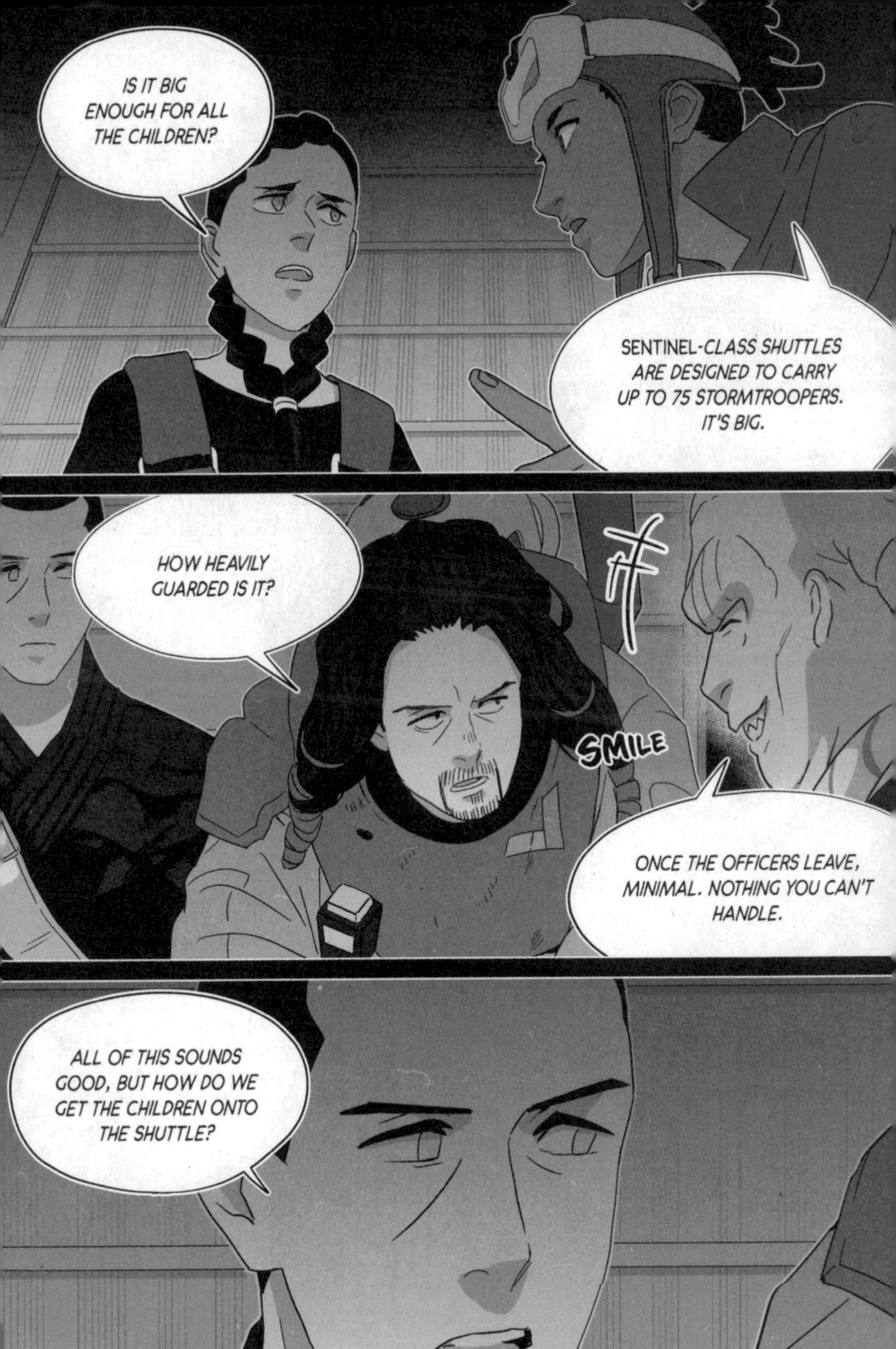
IS IT BIG ENOUGH FOR ALL THE CHILDREN?
SENTINEL-CLASS SHUTTLES ARE DESIGNED TO CARRY UP TO 75 STORMTROOPERS. IT'S BIG.
HOW HEAVILY GUARDED IS IT?
SMILE
ONCE THE OFFICERS LEAVE, MINIMAL. NOTHING YOU CAN'T HANDLE.
ALL OF THIS SOUNDS GOOD, BUT HOW DO WE GET THE CHILDREN ONTO THE SHUTTLE?

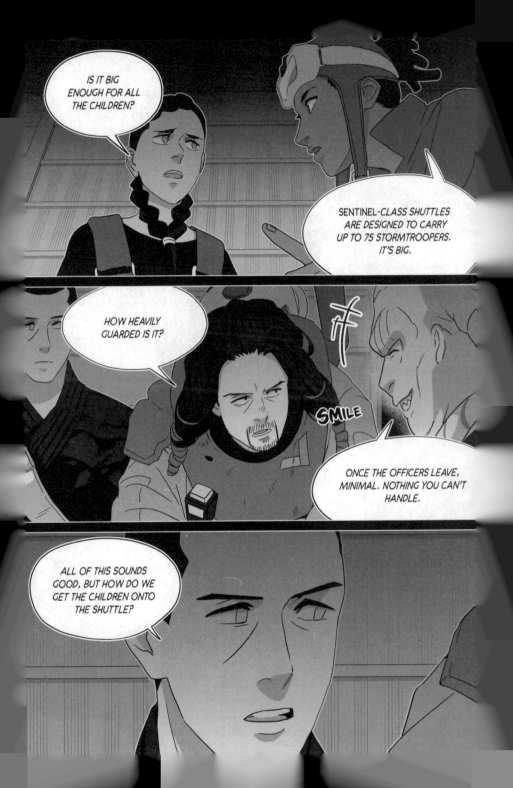

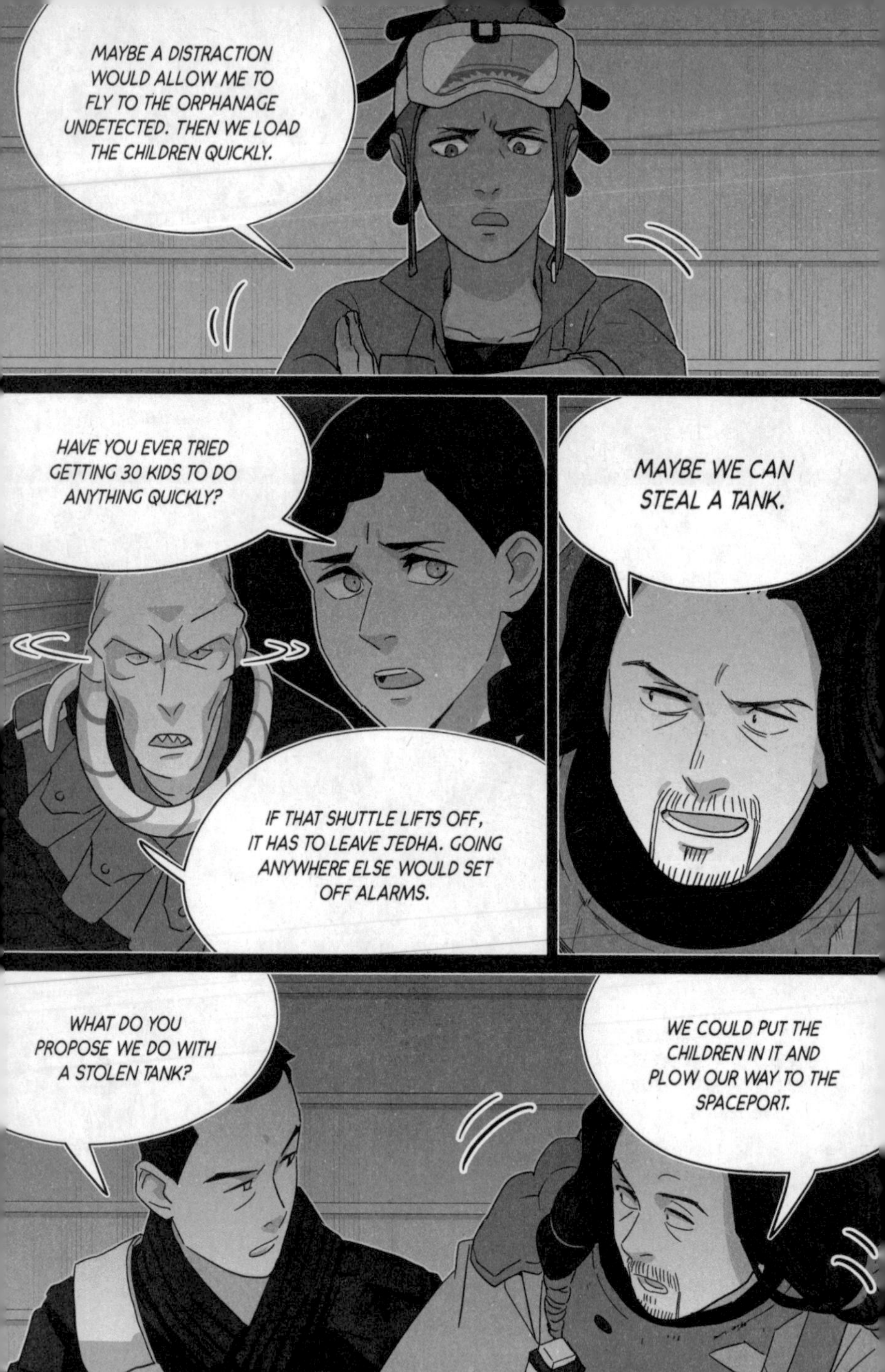
MAYBE A DISTRACTION WOULD ALLOW ME TO FLY TO THE ORPHANAGE UNDETECTED. THEN WE LOAD THE CHILDREN QUICKLY.
HAVE YOU EVER TRIED GETTING 30 KIDS TO DO ANYTHING QUICKLY?
IF THAT SHUTTLE LIFTS OFF, IT HAS TO LEAVE JEDHA. GOING ANYWHERE ELSE WOULD SET OFF ALARMS.
MAYBE WE CAN STEAL A TANK.
WHAT DO YOU PROPOSE WE DO WITH A STOLEN TANK?
WE COULD PUT THE CHILDREN IN IT AND PLOW OUR WAY TO THE SPACEPORT.

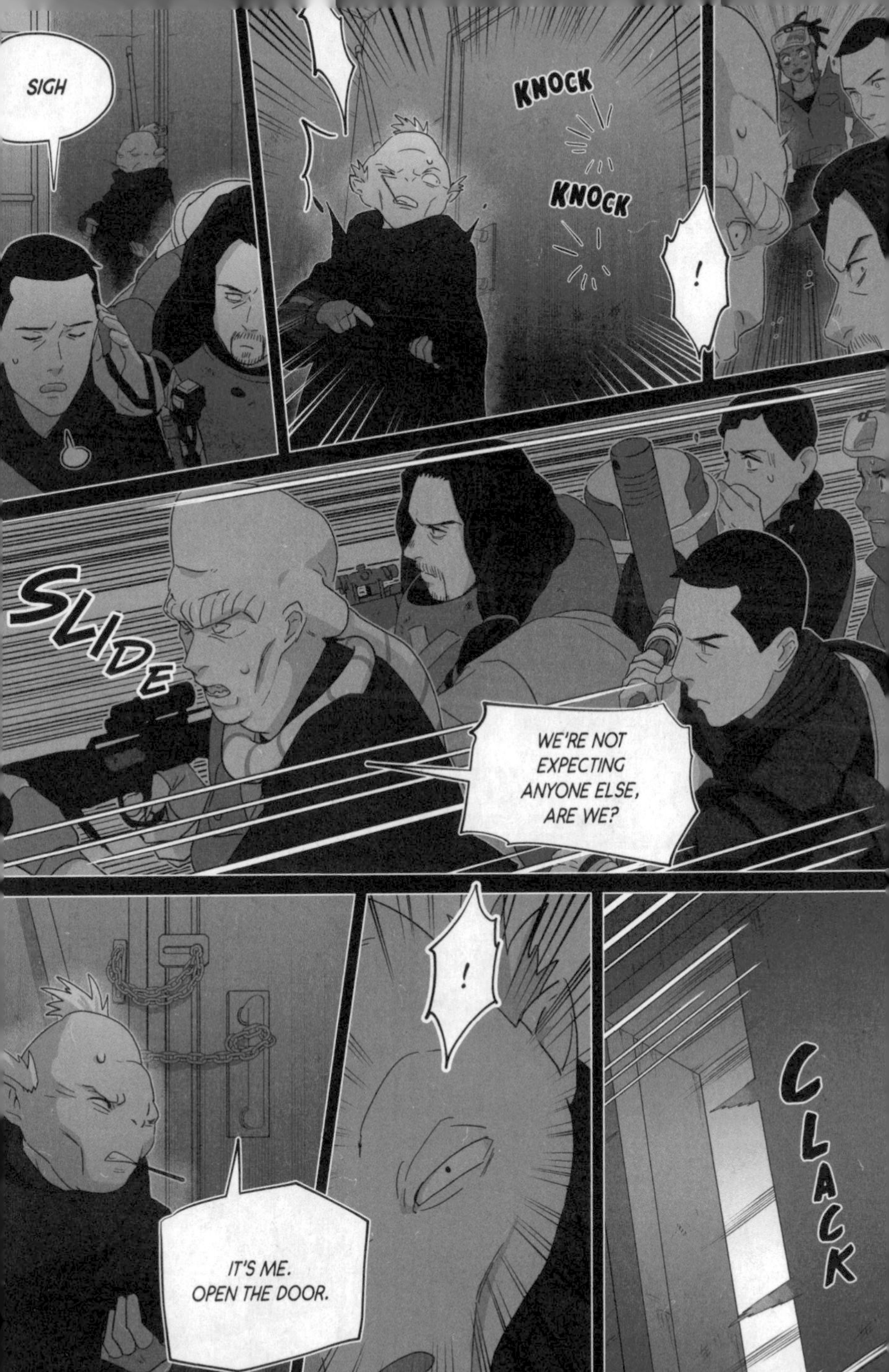
SIGH
KNOCK
KNOCK
!
SLIDE
WE'RE NOT EXPECTING ANYONE ELSE, ARE WE?
IT'S ME. OPEN THE DOOR.
!
CLACK

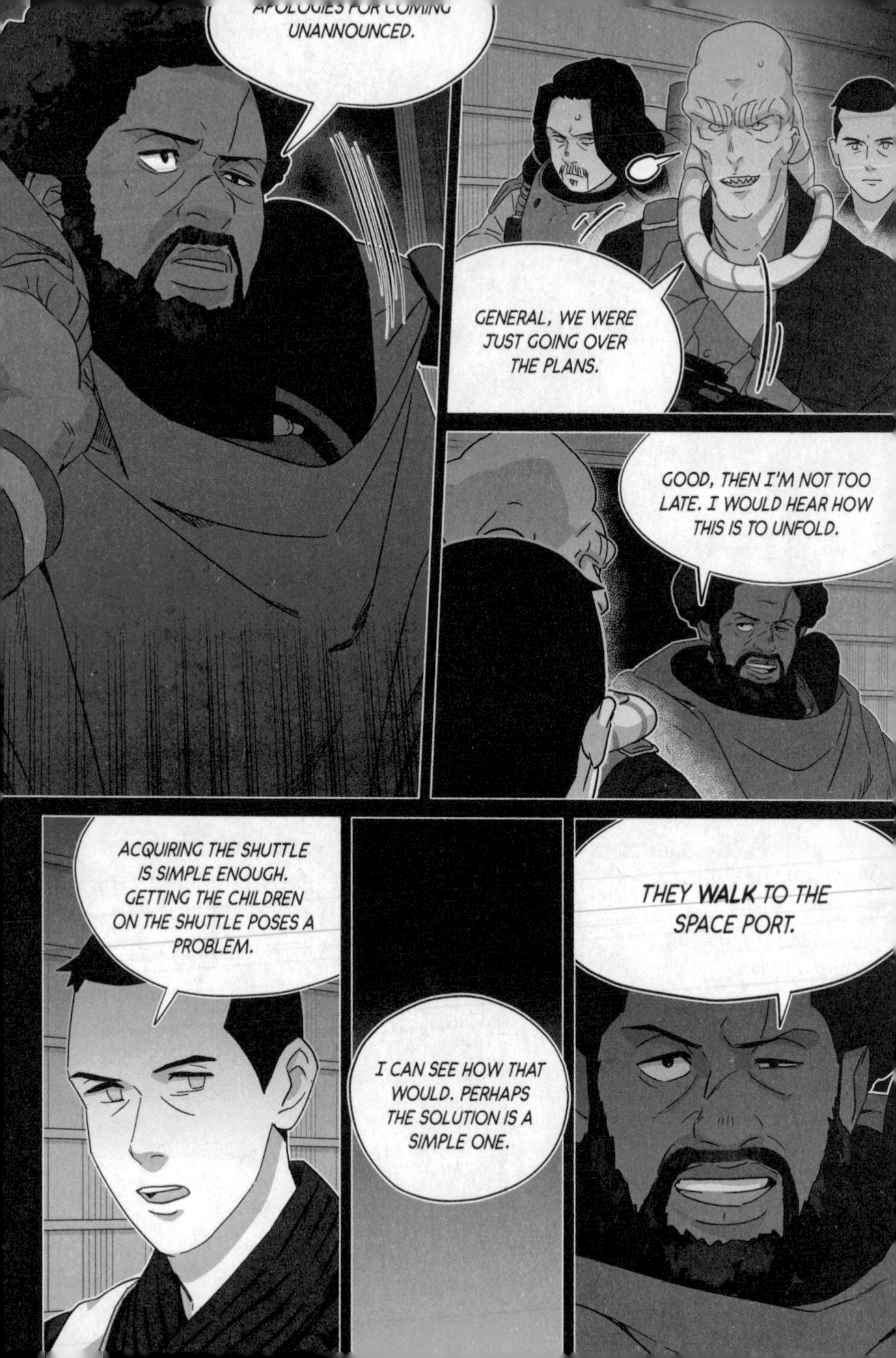
UNANNOUNCED.
GENERAL, WE WERE JUST GOING OVER THE PLANS.
GOOD, THEN I'M NOT TOO LATE. I WOULD HEAR HOW THIS IS TO UNFOLD.
ACQUIRING THE SHUTTLE IS SIMPLE ENOUGH. GETTING THE CHILDREN ON THE SHUTTLE POSES A PROBLEM.
I CAN SEE HOW THAT WOULD. PERHAPS THE SOLUTION IS A SIMPLE ONE.
THEY **WALK** TO THE SPACE PORT.

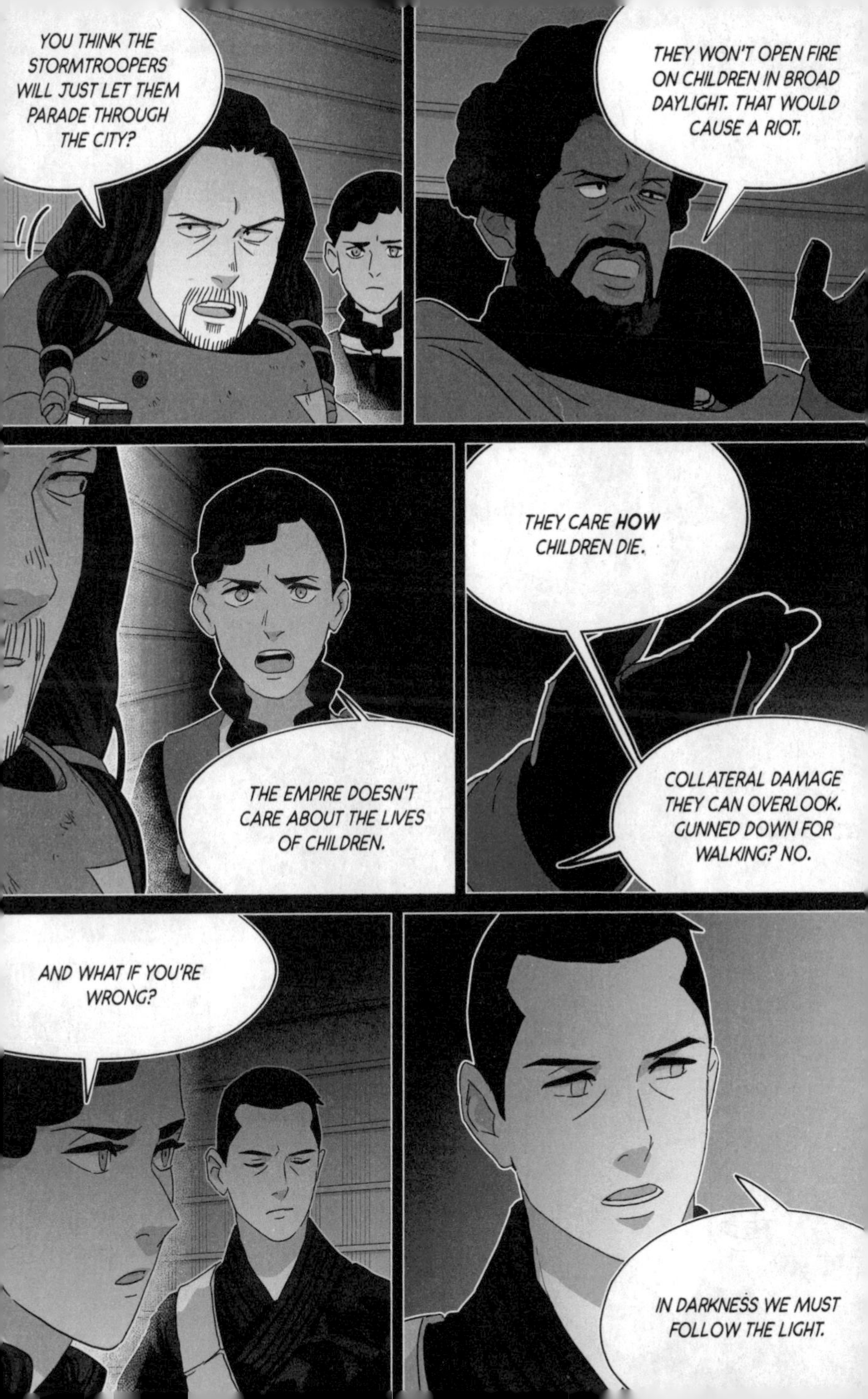
YOU THINK THE STORMTROOPERS WILL JUST LET THEM PARADE THROUGH THE CITY?
THEY WON'T OPEN FIRE ON CHILDREN IN BROAD DAYLIGHT. THAT WOULD CAUSE A RIOT.
THE EMPIRE DOESN'T CARE ABOUT THE LIVES OF CHILDREN.
THEY CARE HOW CHILDREN DIE.
COLLATERAL DAMAGE THEY CAN OVERLOOK. GUNNED DOWN FOR WALKING? NO.
AND WHAT IF YOU'RE WRONG?
IN DARKNESS WE MUST FOLLOW THE LIGHT.

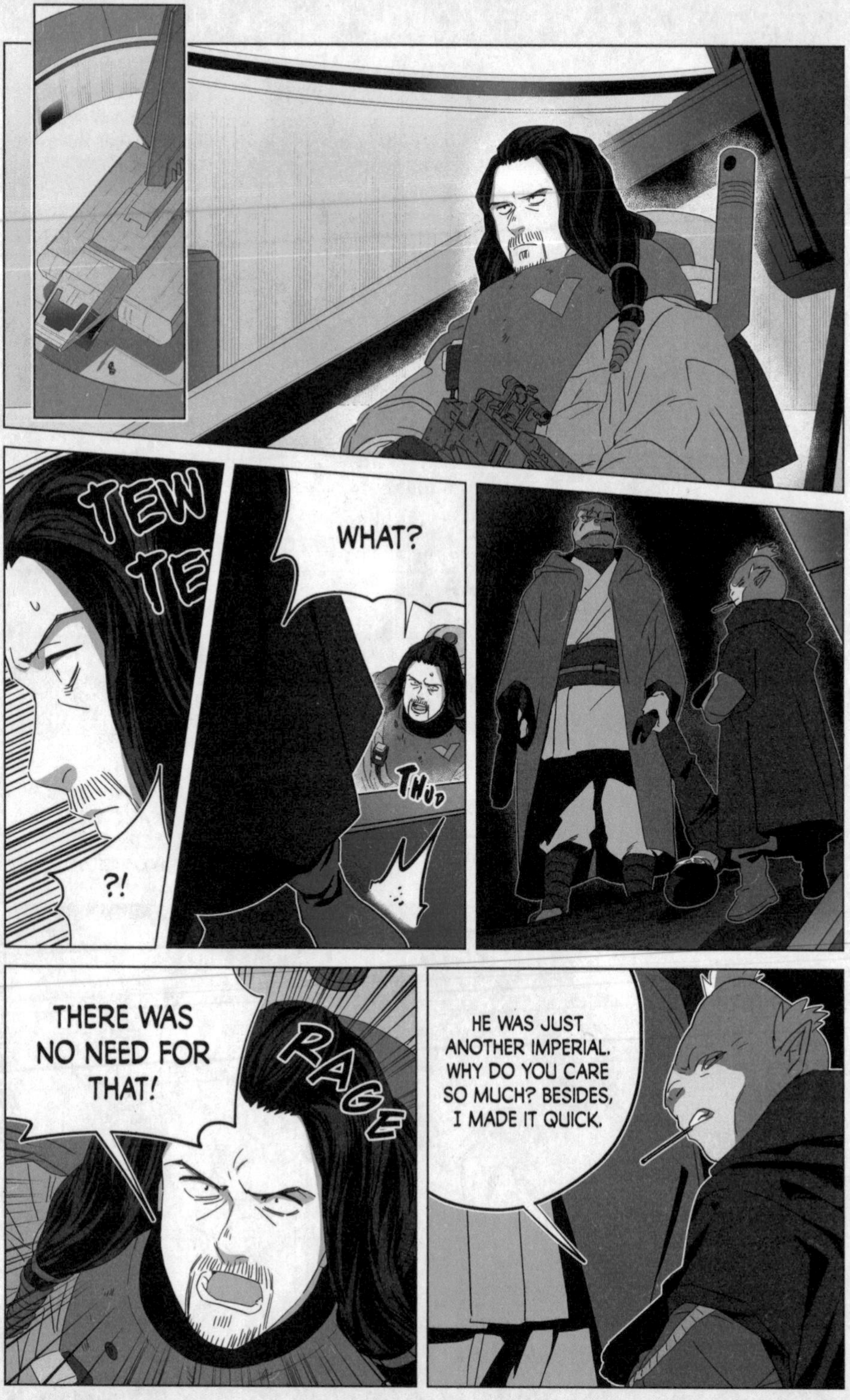
TEW TEW
?!
WHAT?
THUD
THERE WAS NO NEED FOR THAT!
RAGE
HE WAS JUST ANOTHER IMPERIAL. WHY DO YOU CARE SO MUCH? BESIDES, I MADE IT QUICK.

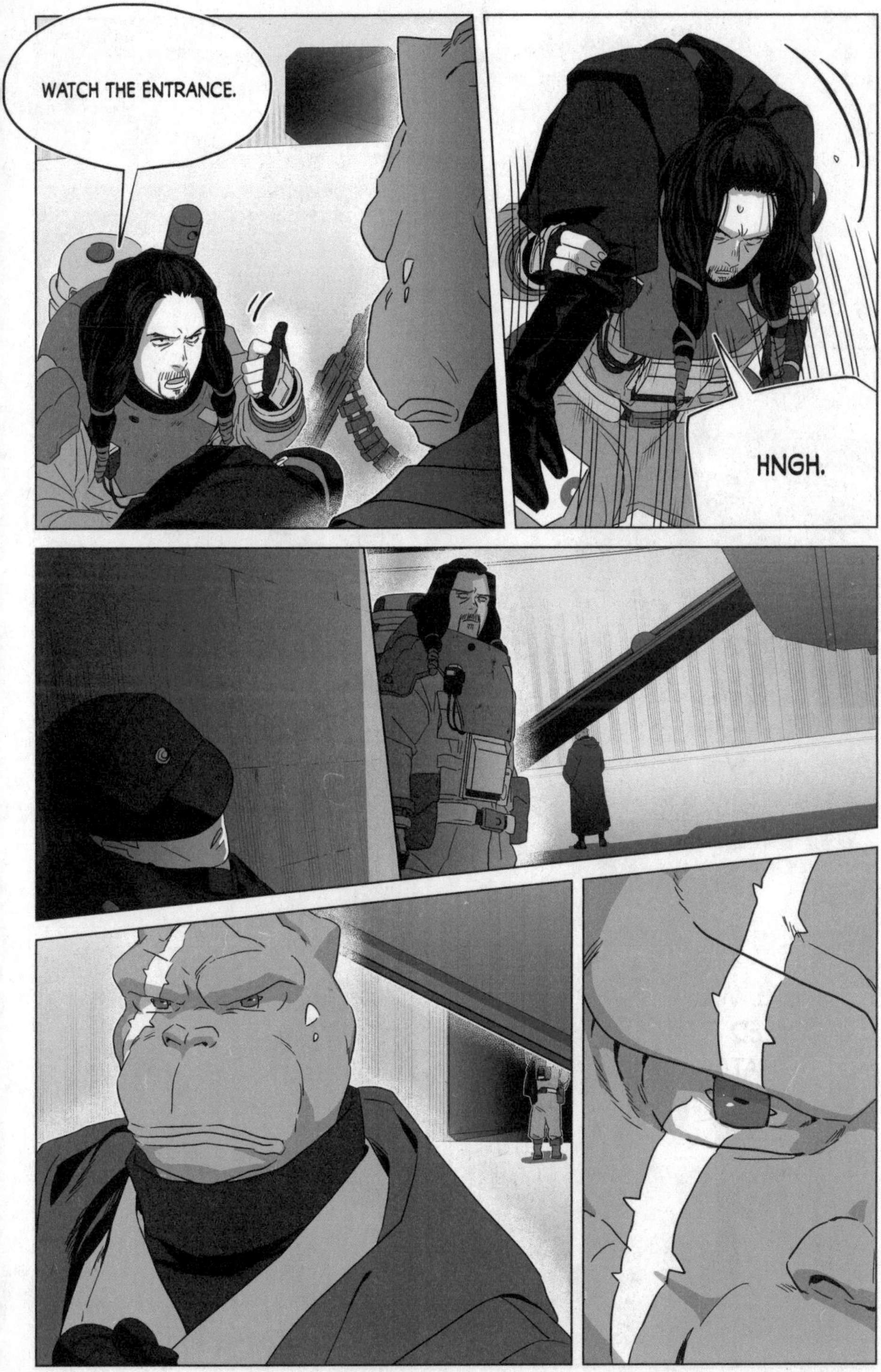
WATCH THE ENTRANCE.
HNGH.

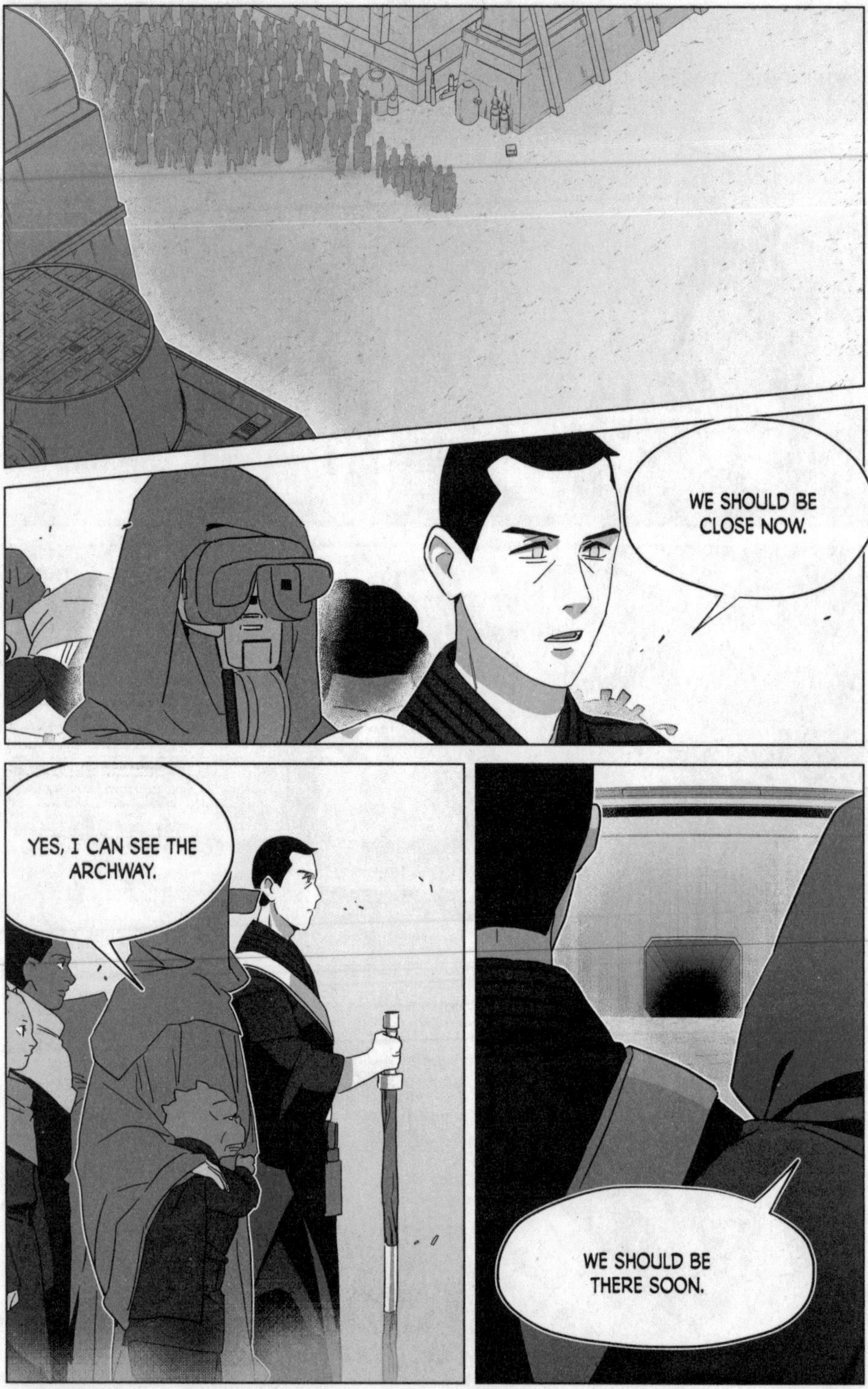
WE SHOULD BE CLOSE NOW.
YES, I CAN SEE THE ARCHWAY.
WE SHOULD BE THERE SOON.

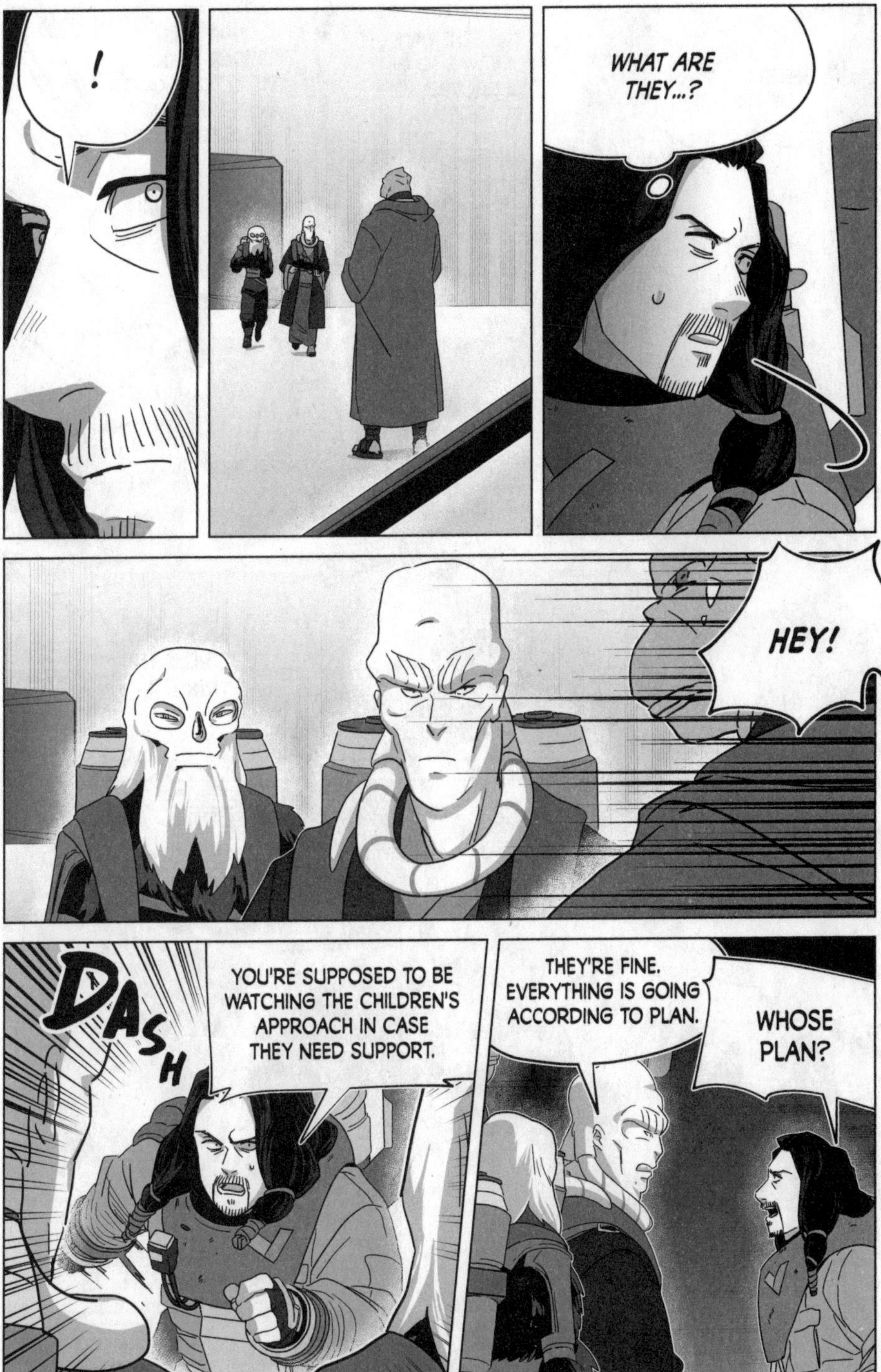
!
WHAT ARE THEY...?
HEY!
DASH
YOU'RE SUPPOSED TO BE WATCHING THE CHILDREN'S APPROACH IN CASE THEY NEED SUPPORT.
THEY'RE FINE. EVERYTHING IS GOING ACCORDING TO PLAN.
WHOSE PLAN?

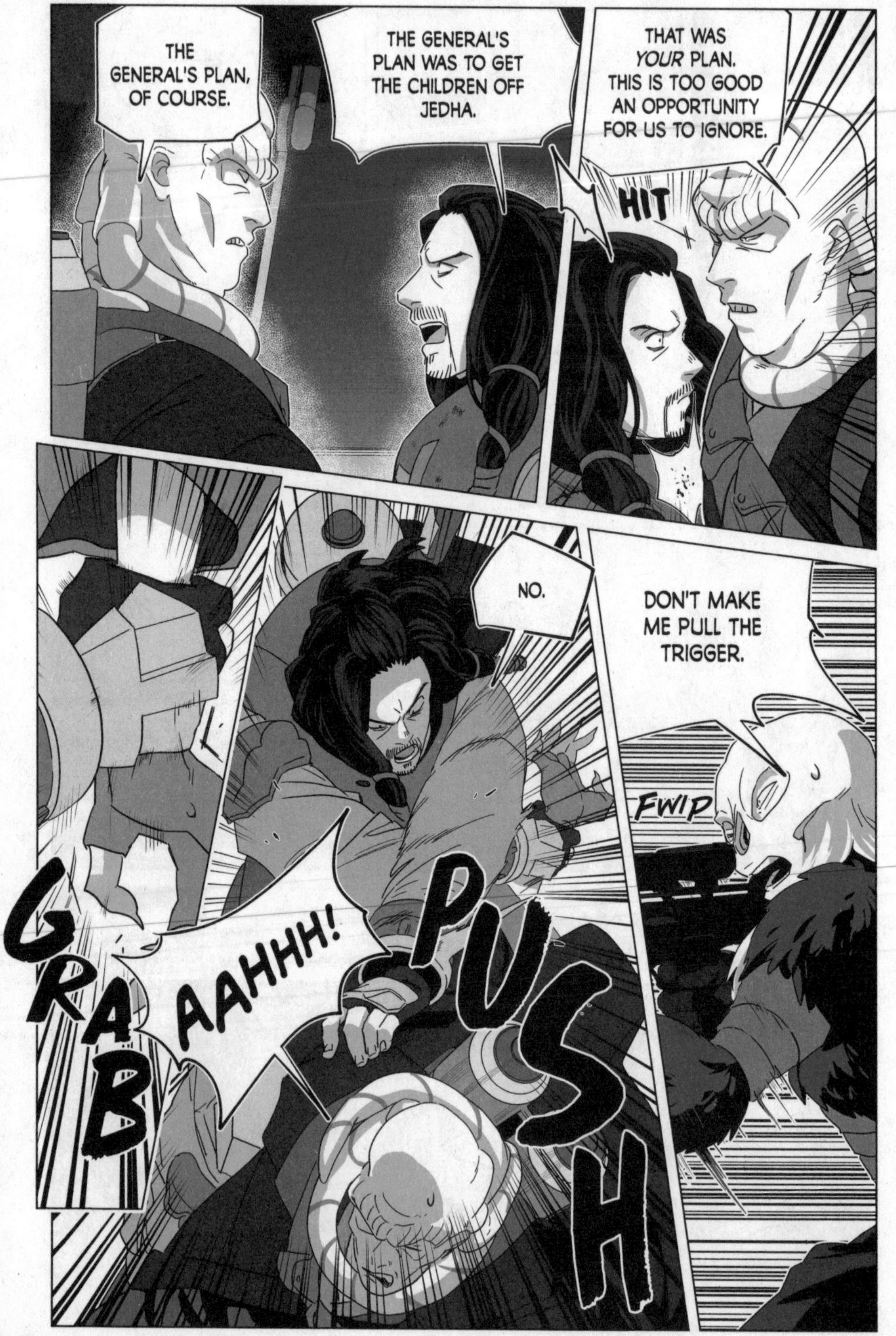
THE GENERAL'S PLAN, OF COURSE.
THE GENERAL'S PLAN WAS TO GET THE CHILDREN OFF JEDHA.
THAT WAS *YOUR* PLAN. THIS IS TOO GOOD AN OPPORTUNITY FOR US TO IGNORE.
HIT
NO.
GRAB
AAHHH!
PUSH
DON'T MAKE ME PULL THE TRIGGER.
FWIP

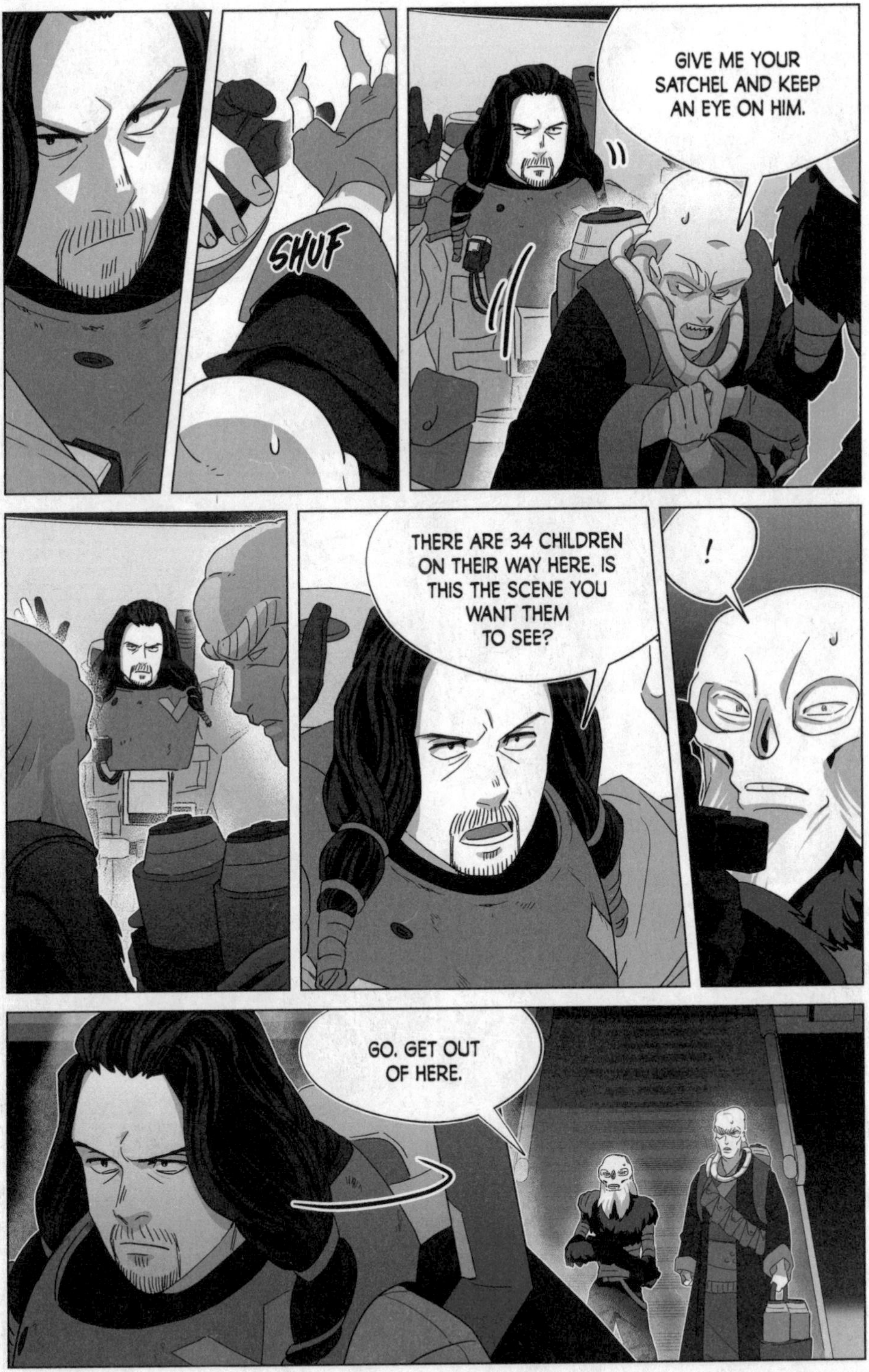
SHUF
GIVE ME YOUR SATCHEL AND KEEP AN EYE ON HIM.
THERE ARE 34 CHILDREN ON THEIR WAY HERE. IS THIS THE SCENE YOU WANT THEM TO SEE?
!
GO. GET OUT OF HERE.

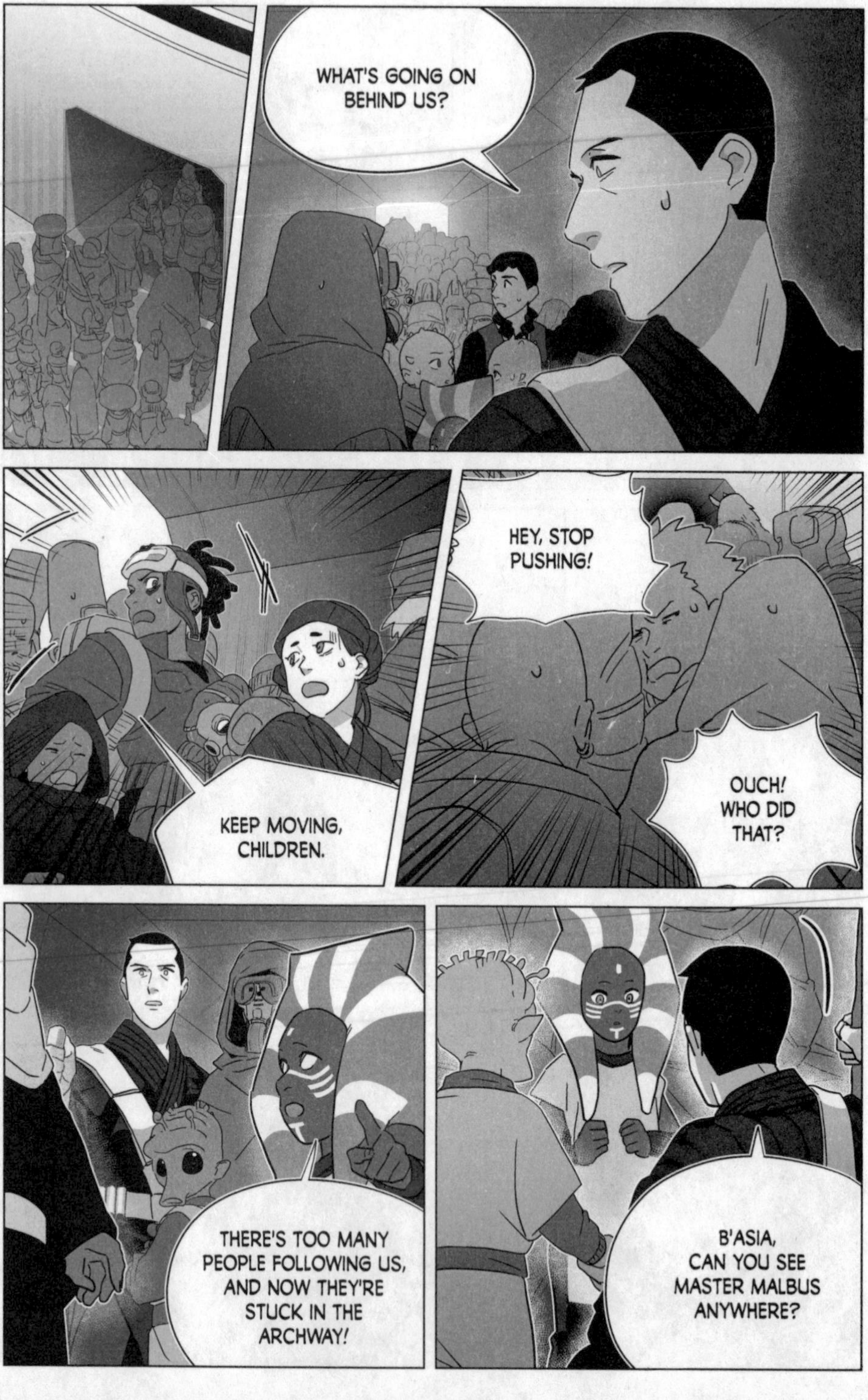
WHAT'S GOING ON BEHIND US?
KEEP MOVING, CHILDREN.
HEY, STOP PUSHING!
OUCH! WHO DID THAT?
THERE'S TOO MANY PEOPLE FOLLOWING US, AND NOW THEY'RE STUCK IN THE ARCHWAY!
B'ASIA, CAN YOU SEE MASTER MALBUS ANYWHERE?

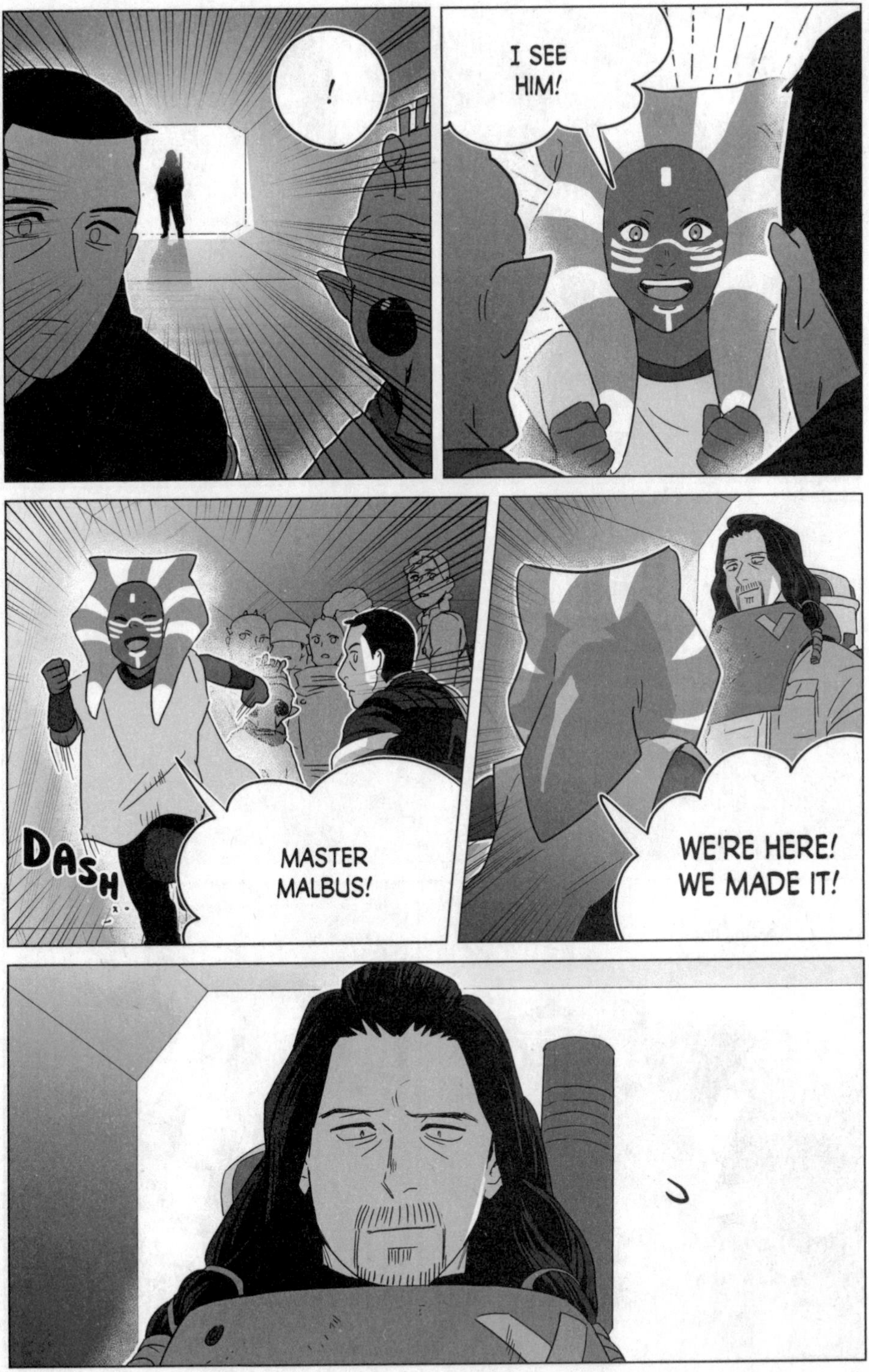
!
I SEE HIM!
DASH
MASTER MALBUS!
WE'RE HERE! WE MADE IT!

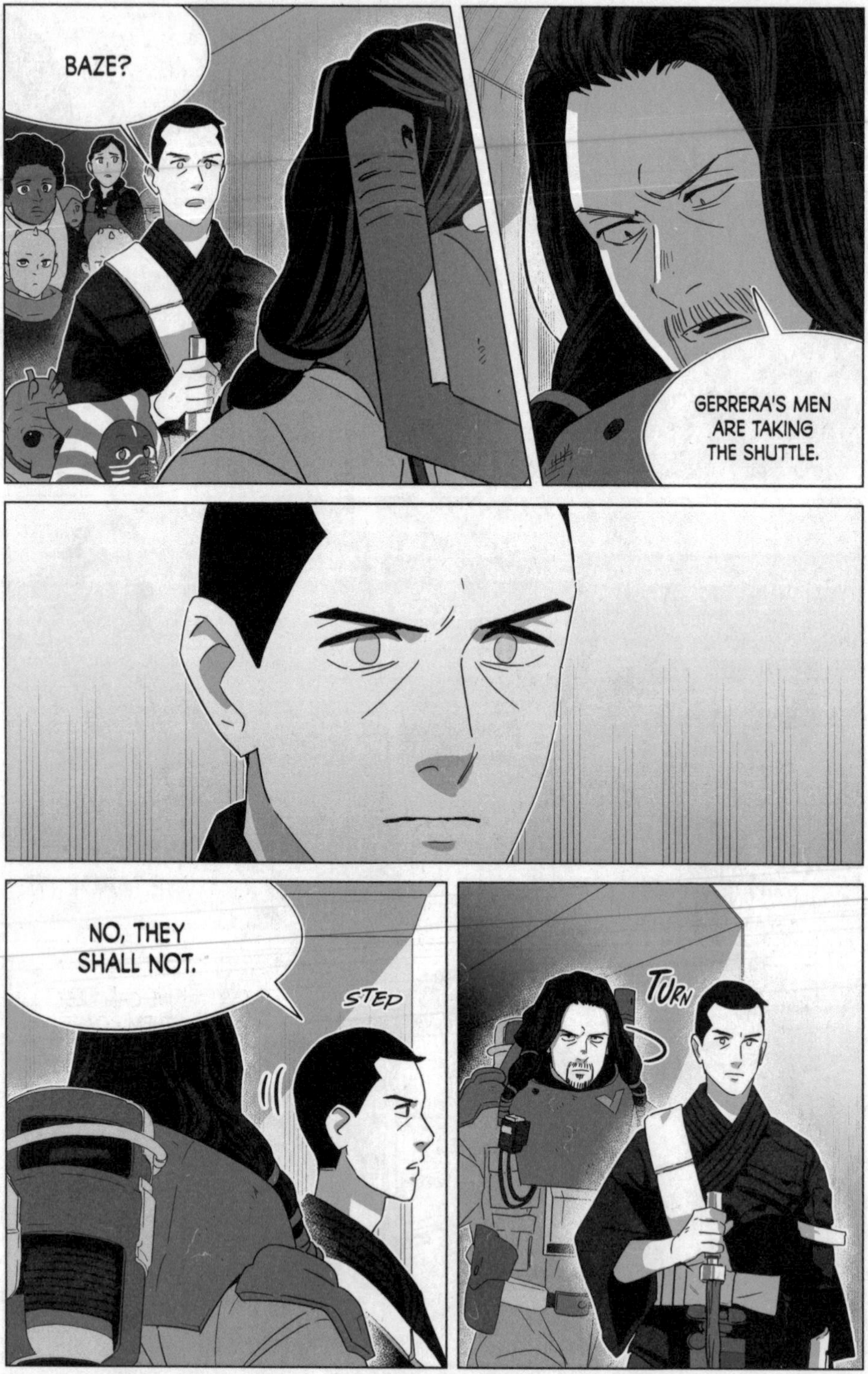
BAZE?
GERRERA'S MEN ARE TAKING THE SHUTTLE.
NO, THEY SHALL NOT.
STEP
TURN

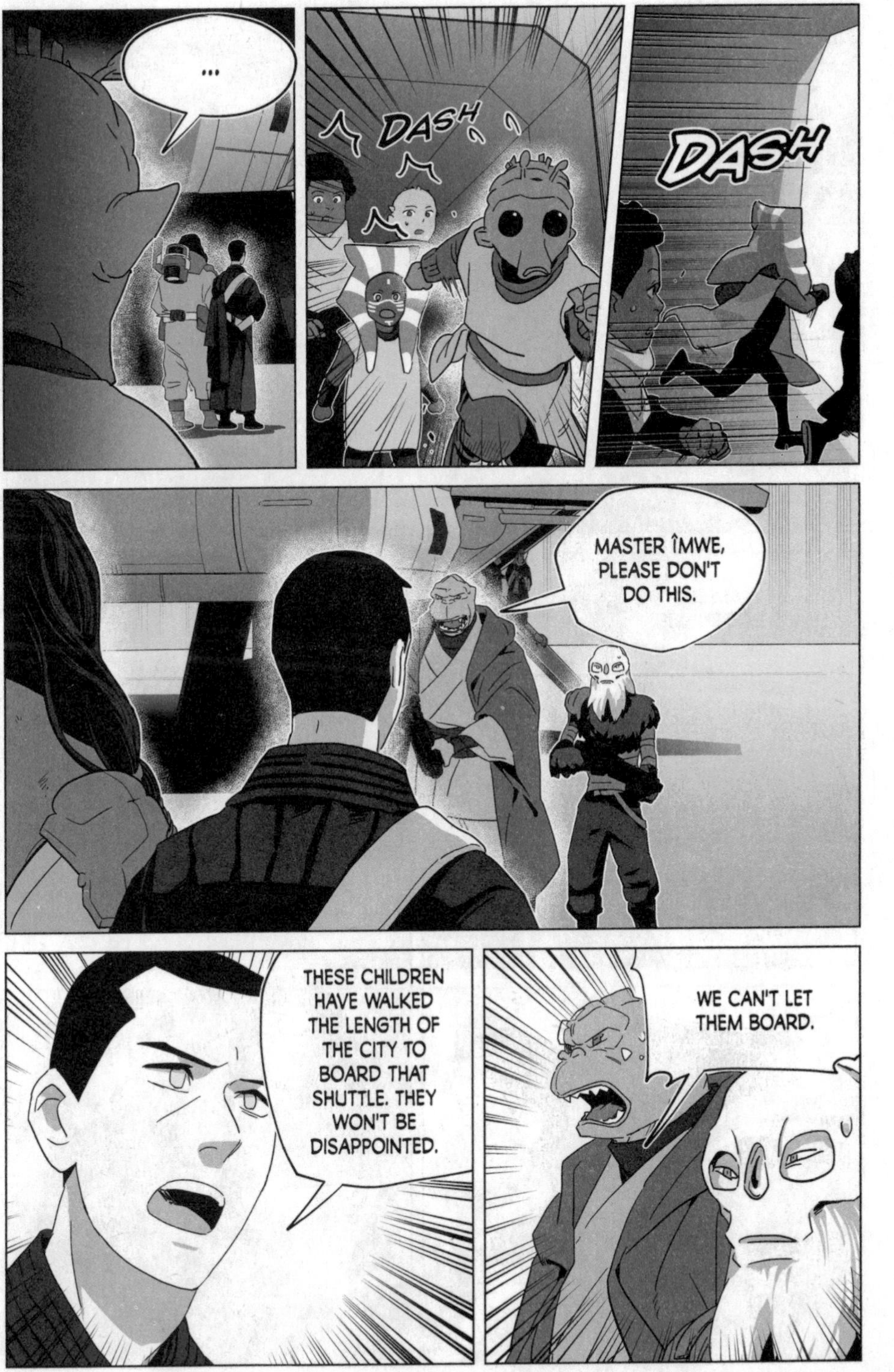
...
DASH
DASH
MASTER ÎMWE, PLEASE DON'T DO THIS.
THESE CHILDREN HAVE WALKED THE LENGTH OF THE CITY TO BOARD THAT SHUTTLE. THEY WON'T BE DISAPPOINTED.
WE CAN'T LET THEM BOARD.

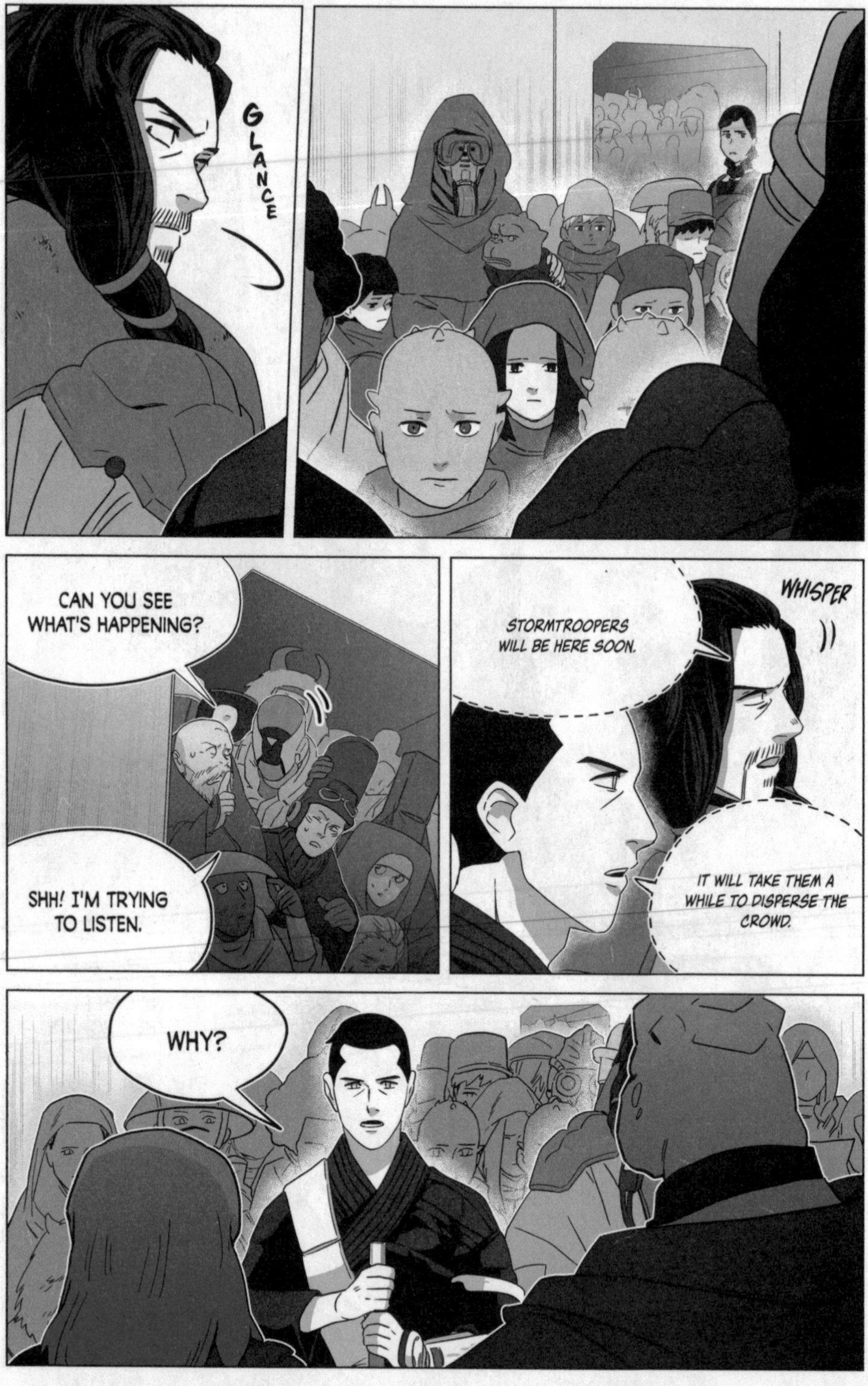
GLANCE
CAN YOU SEE WHAT'S HAPPENING?
SHH! I'M TRYING TO LISTEN.
WHISPER
STORMTROOPERS WILL BE HERE SOON.
IT WILL TAKE THEM A WHILE TO DISPERSE THE CROWD.
WHY?

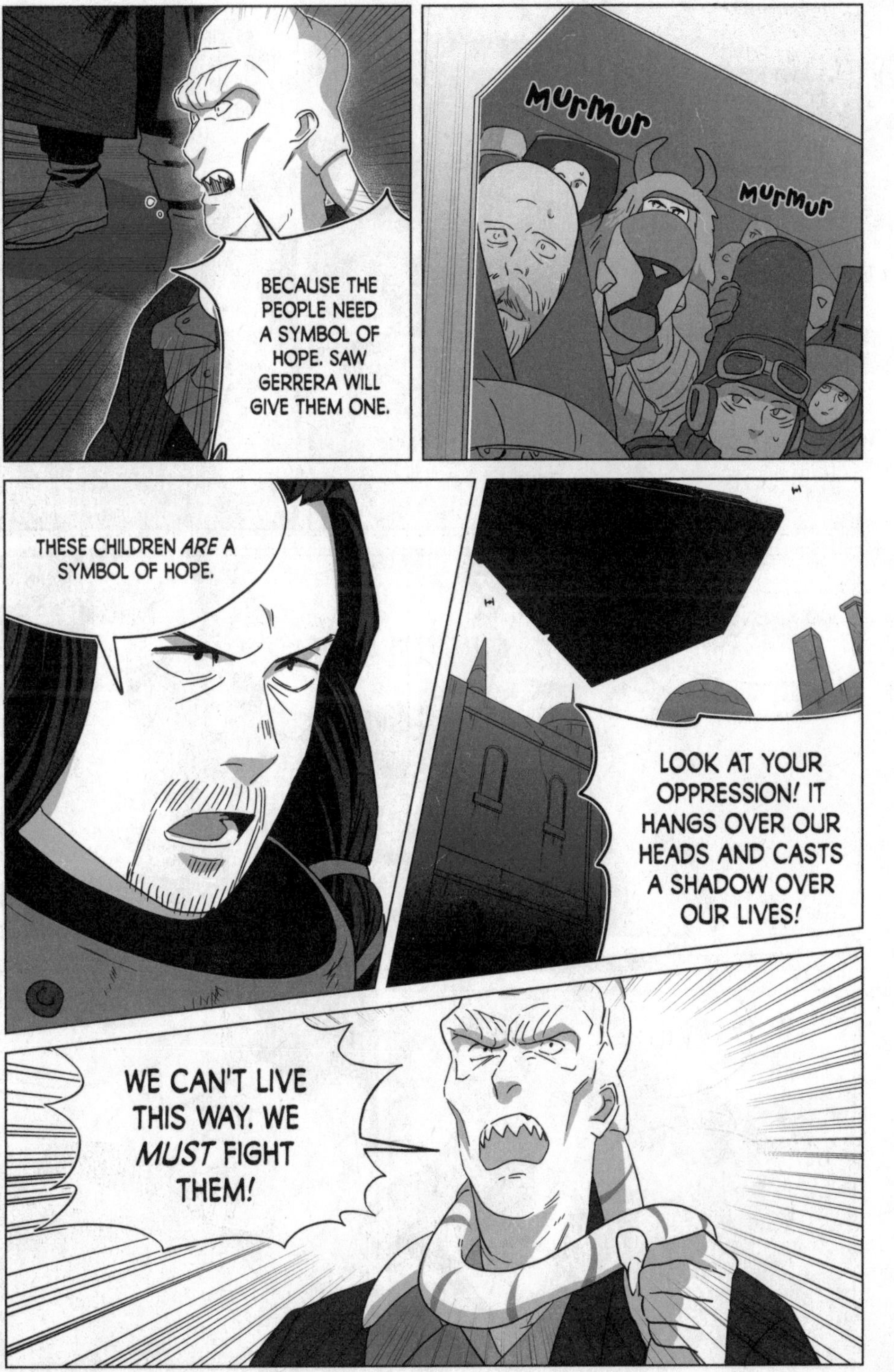
BECAUSE THE PEOPLE NEED A SYMBOL OF HOPE. SAW GERRERA WILL GIVE THEM ONE.
MURMUR
MURMUR
THESE CHILDREN *ARE* A SYMBOL OF HOPE.
LOOK AT YOUR OPPRESSION! IT HANGS OVER OUR HEADS AND CASTS A SHADOW OVER OUR LIVES!
WE CAN'T LIVE THIS WAY. WE *MUST* FIGHT THEM!

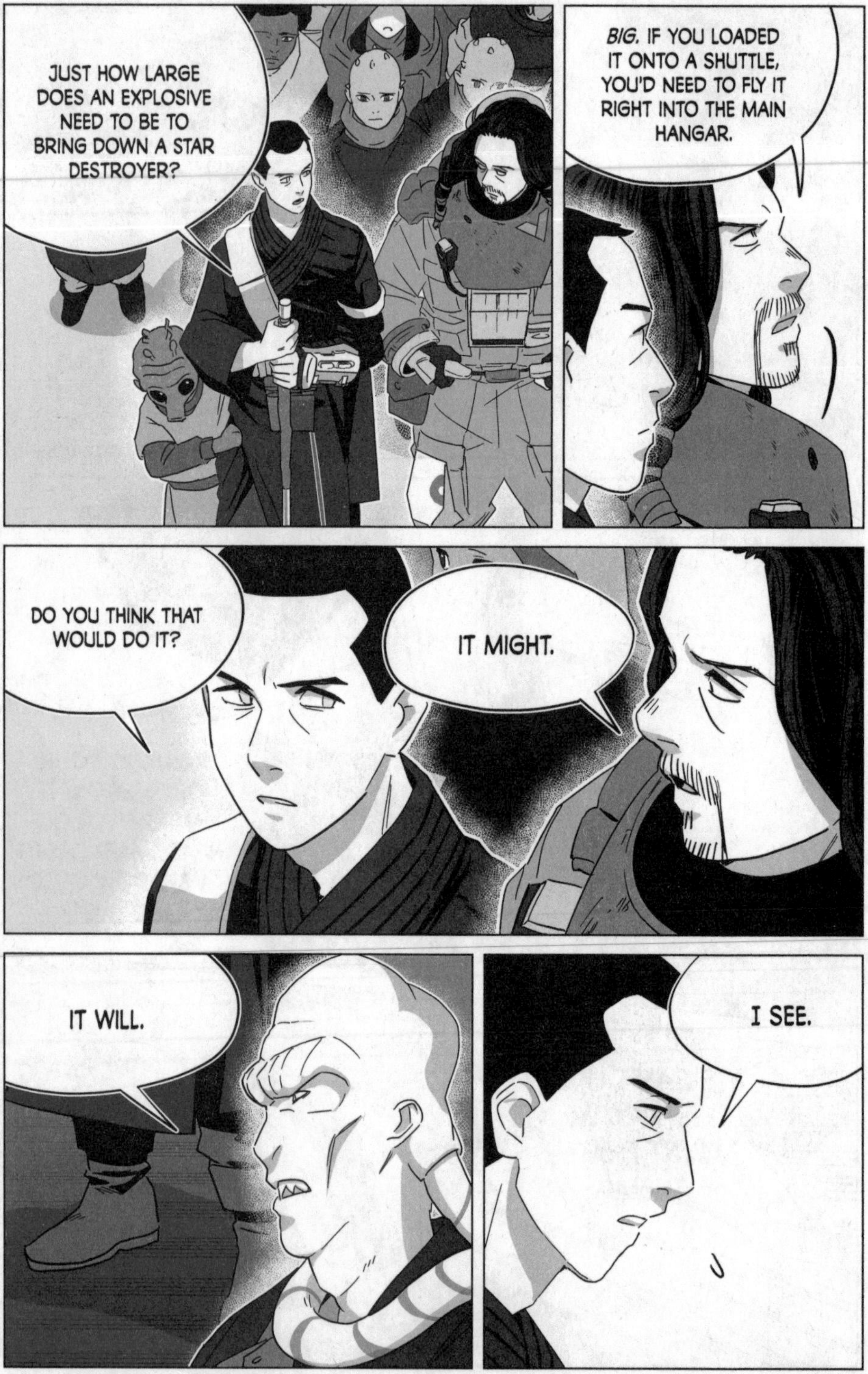
JUST HOW LARGE DOES AN EXPLOSIVE NEED TO BE TO BRING DOWN A STAR DESTROYER?
BIG. IF YOU LOADED IT ONTO A SHUTTLE, YOU'D NEED TO FLY IT RIGHT INTO THE MAIN HANGAR.
DO YOU THINK THAT WOULD DO IT?
IT MIGHT.
IT WILL.
I SEE.

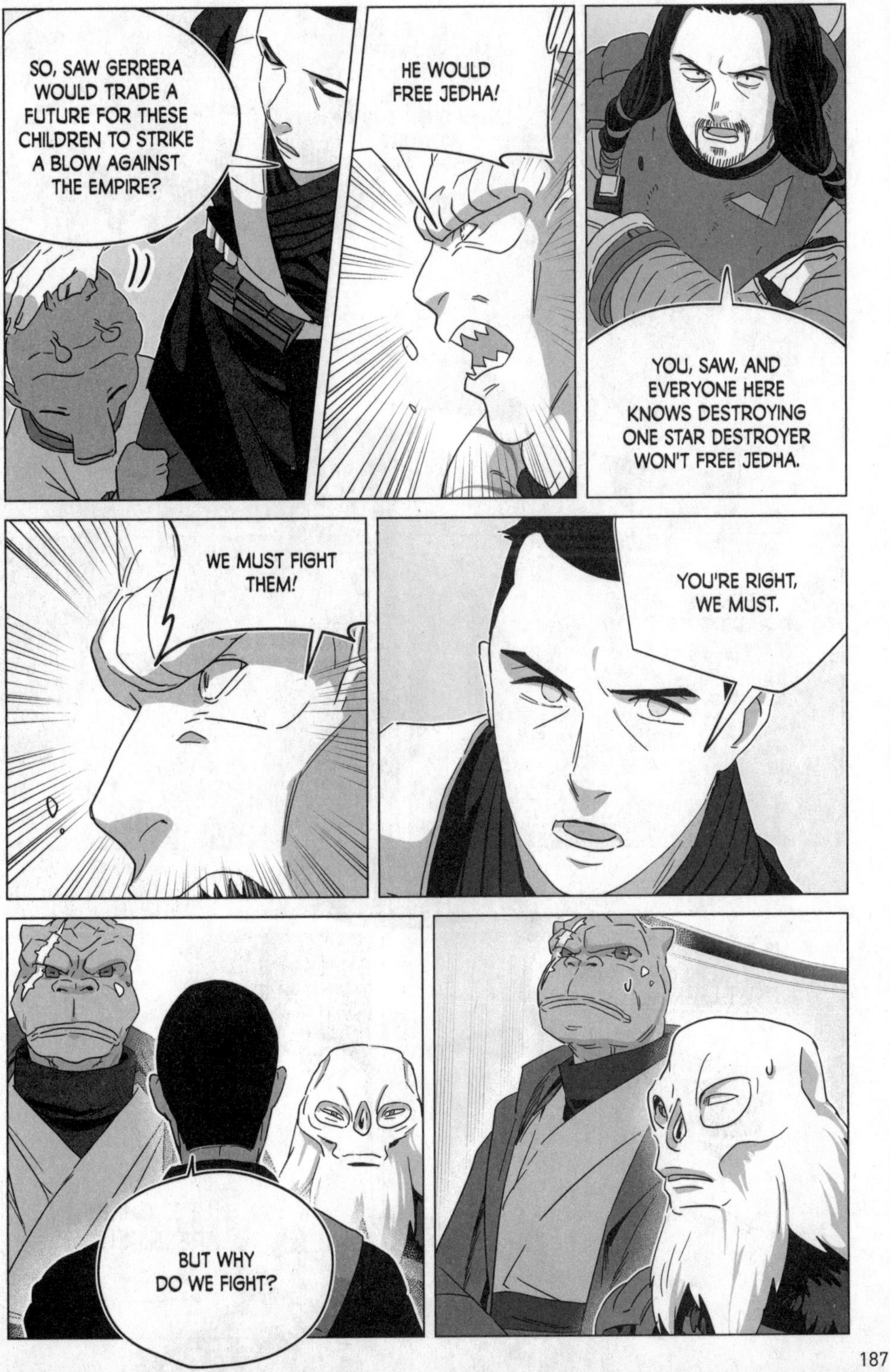
SO, SAW GERRERA WOULD TRADE A FUTURE FOR THESE CHILDREN TO STRIKE A BLOW AGAINST THE EMPIRE?
HE WOULD FREE JEDHA!
YOU, SAW, AND EVERYONE HERE KNOWS DESTROYING ONE STAR DESTROYER WON'T FREE JEDHA.
WE MUST FIGHT THEM!
YOU'RE RIGHT, WE MUST.
BUT WHY DO WE FIGHT?

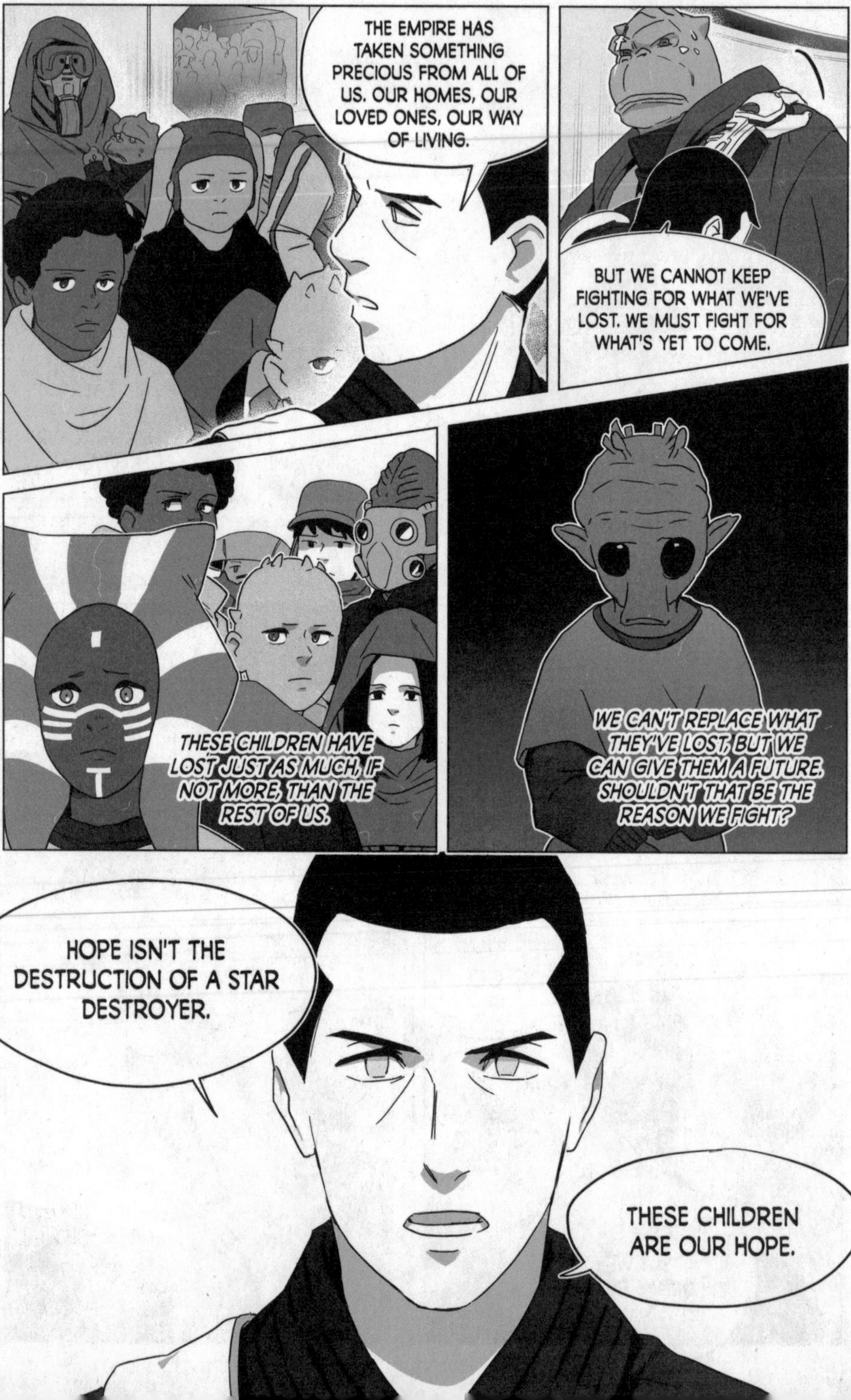
THE EMPIRE HAS TAKEN SOMETHING PRECIOUS FROM ALL OF US. OUR HOMES, OUR LOVED ONES, OUR WAY OF LIVING.
BUT WE CANNOT KEEP FIGHTING FOR WHAT WE'VE LOST. WE MUST FIGHT FOR WHAT'S YET TO COME.
THESE CHILDREN HAVE LOST JUST AS MUCH, IF NOT MORE, THAN THE REST OF US.
WE CAN'T REPLACE WHAT THEY'VE LOST, BUT WE CAN GIVE THEM A FUTURE. SHOULDN'T THAT BE THE REASON WE FIGHT?
HOPE ISN'T THE DESTRUCTION OF A STAR DESTROYER.
THESE CHILDREN ARE OUR HOPE.

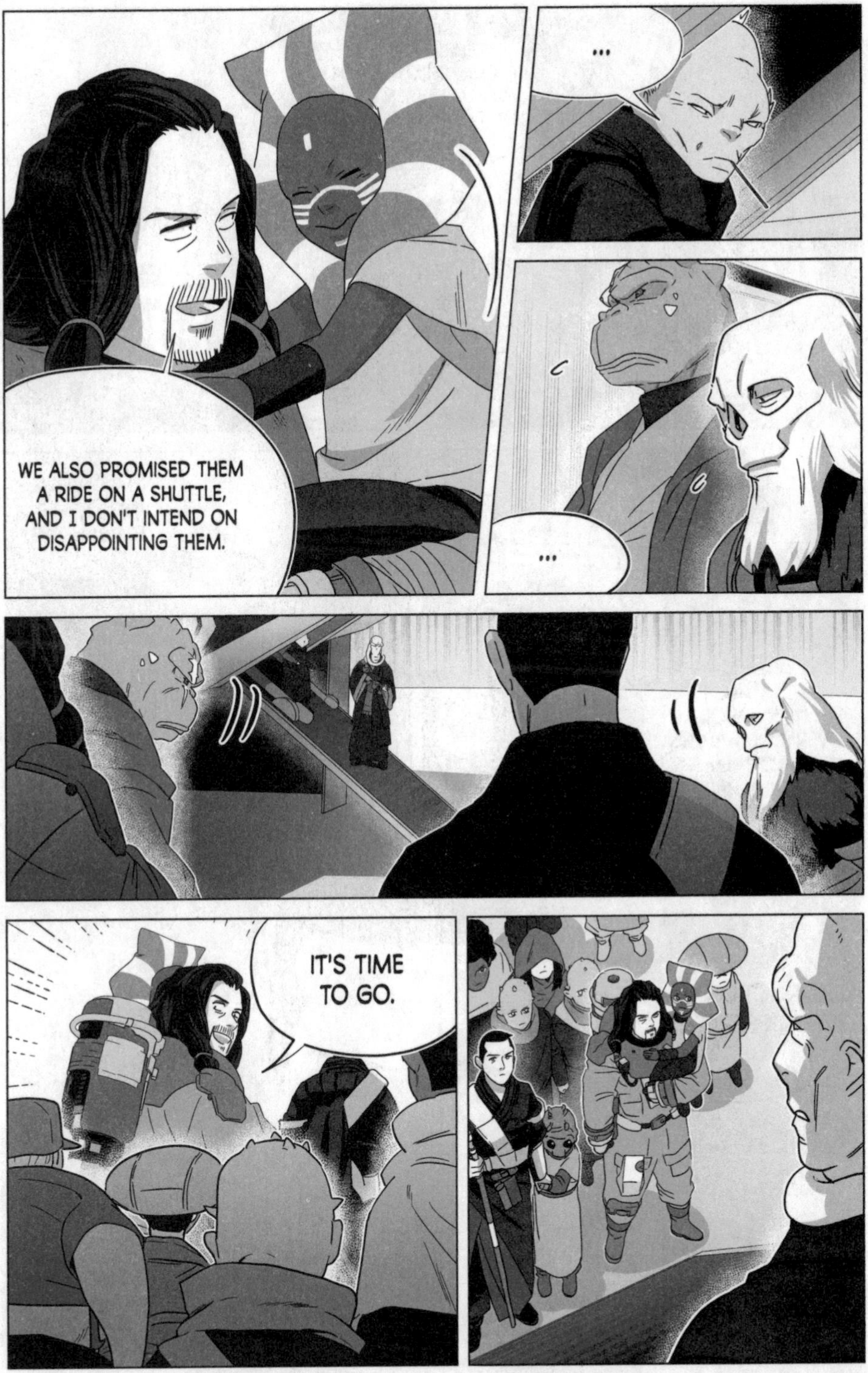
WE ALSO PROMISED THEM A RIDE ON A SHUTTLE, AND I DON'T INTEND ON DISAPPOINTING THEM.
...
...
IT'S TIME TO GO.

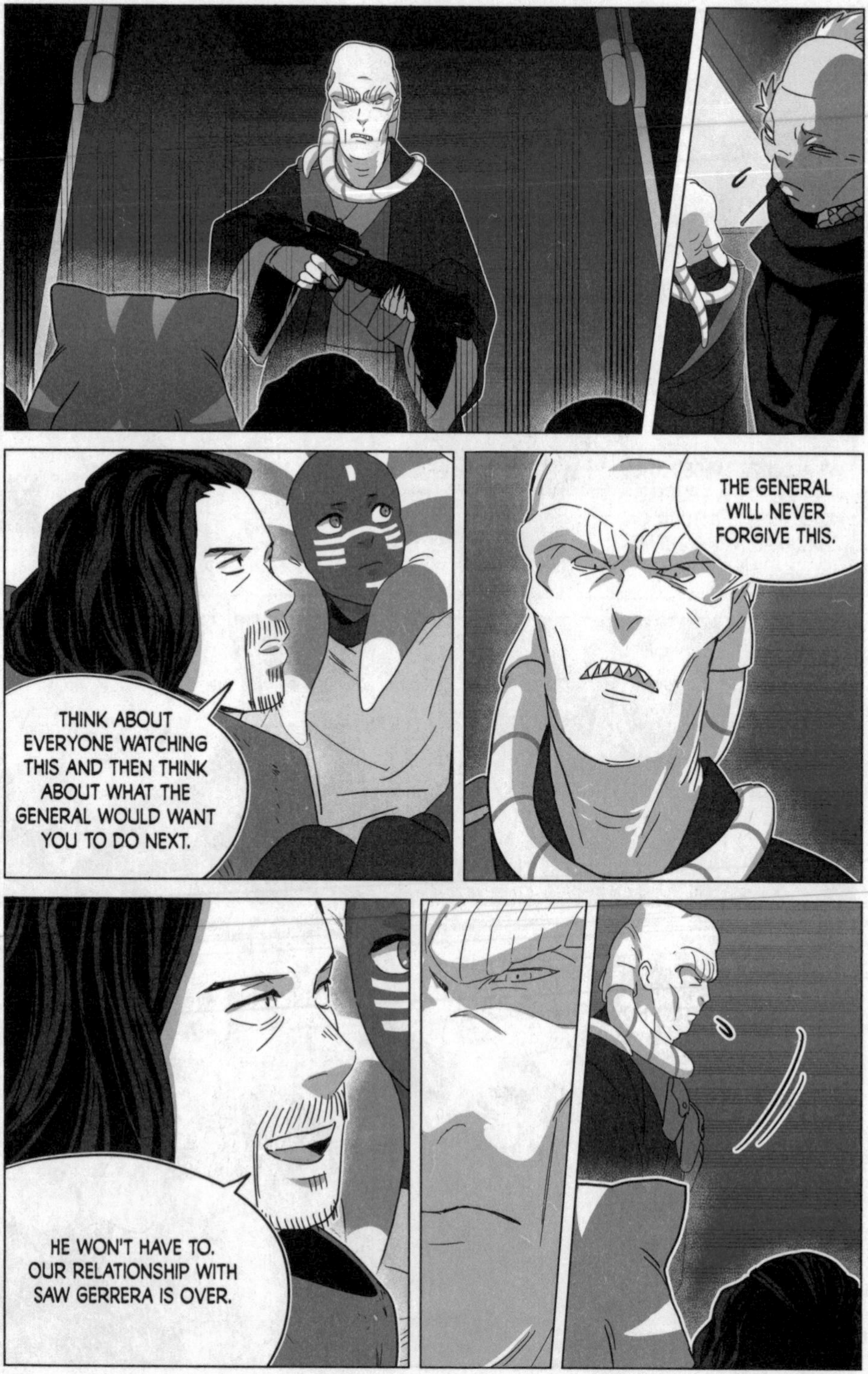
THINK ABOUT EVERYONE WATCHING THIS AND THEN THINK ABOUT WHAT THE GENERAL WOULD WANT YOU TO DO NEXT.
THE GENERAL WILL NEVER FORGIVE THIS.
HE WON'T HAVE TO. OUR RELATIONSHIP WITH SAW GERRERA IS OVER.

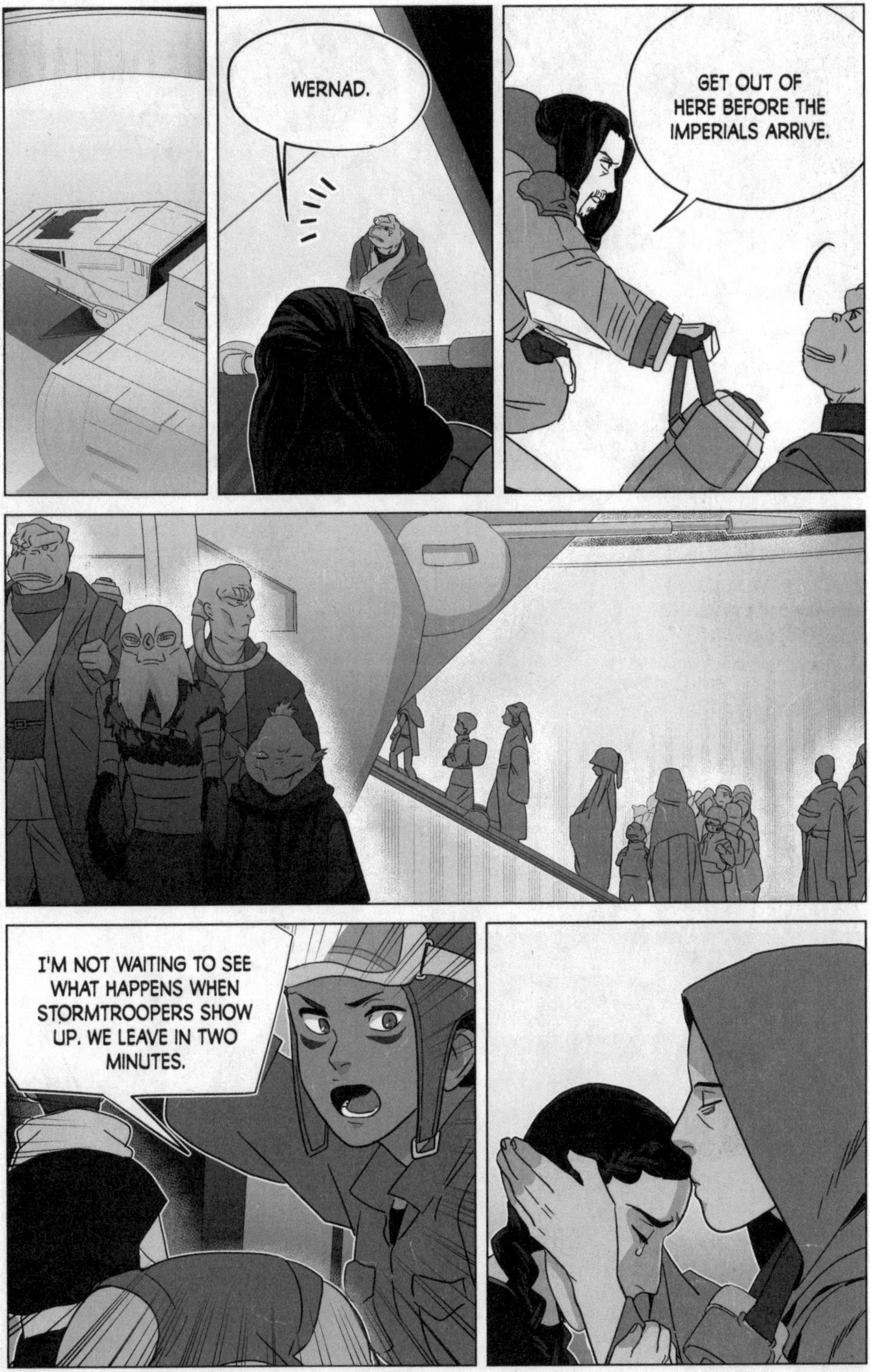
WERNAD.
GET OUT OF HERE BEFORE THE IMPERIALS ARRIVE.
I'M NOT WAITING TO SEE WHAT HAPPENS WHEN STORMTROOPERS SHOW UP. WE LEAVE IN TWO MINUTES.

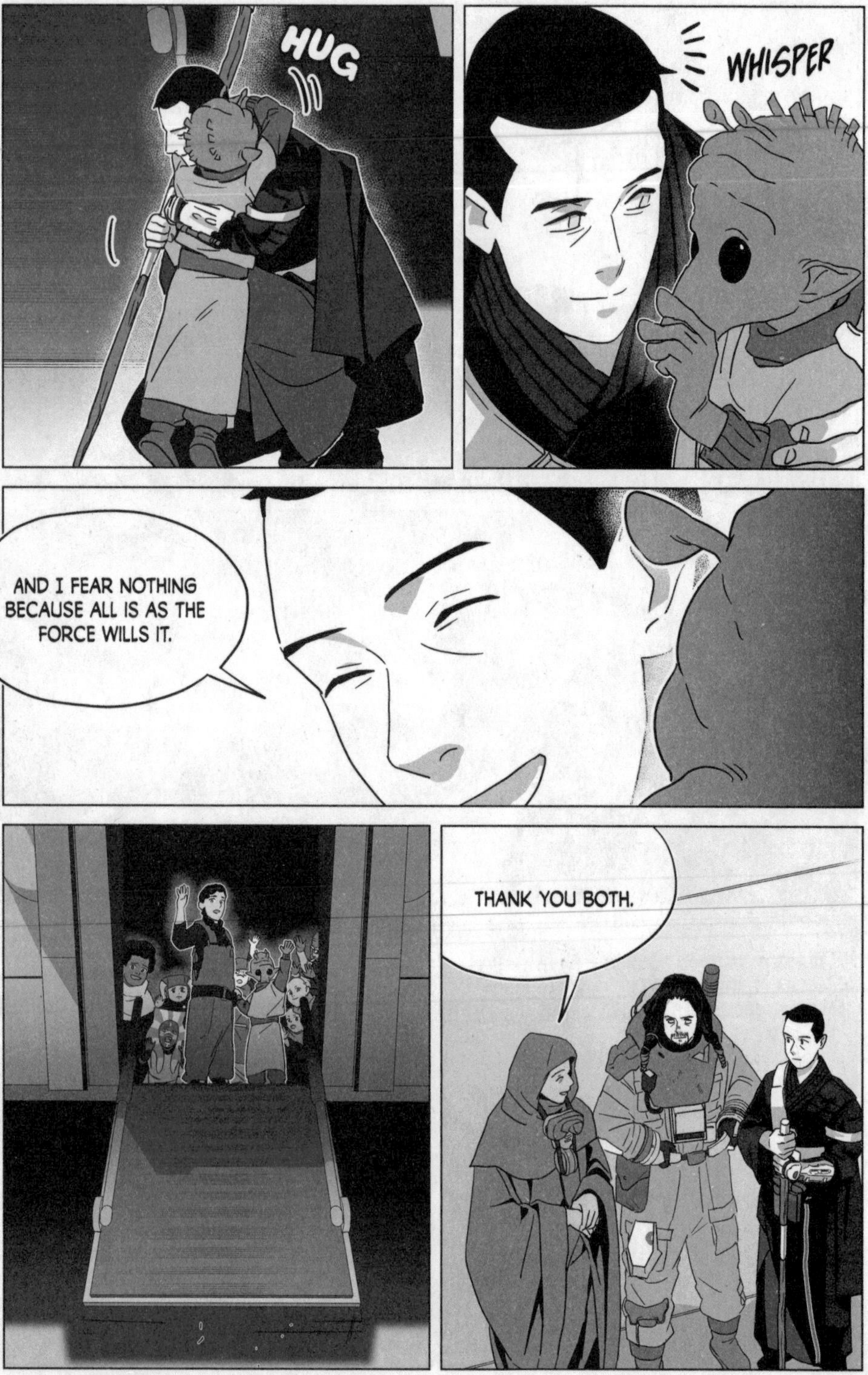
HUG
WHISPER
AND I FEAR NOTHING BECAUSE ALL IS AS THE FORCE WILLS IT.
THANK YOU BOTH.

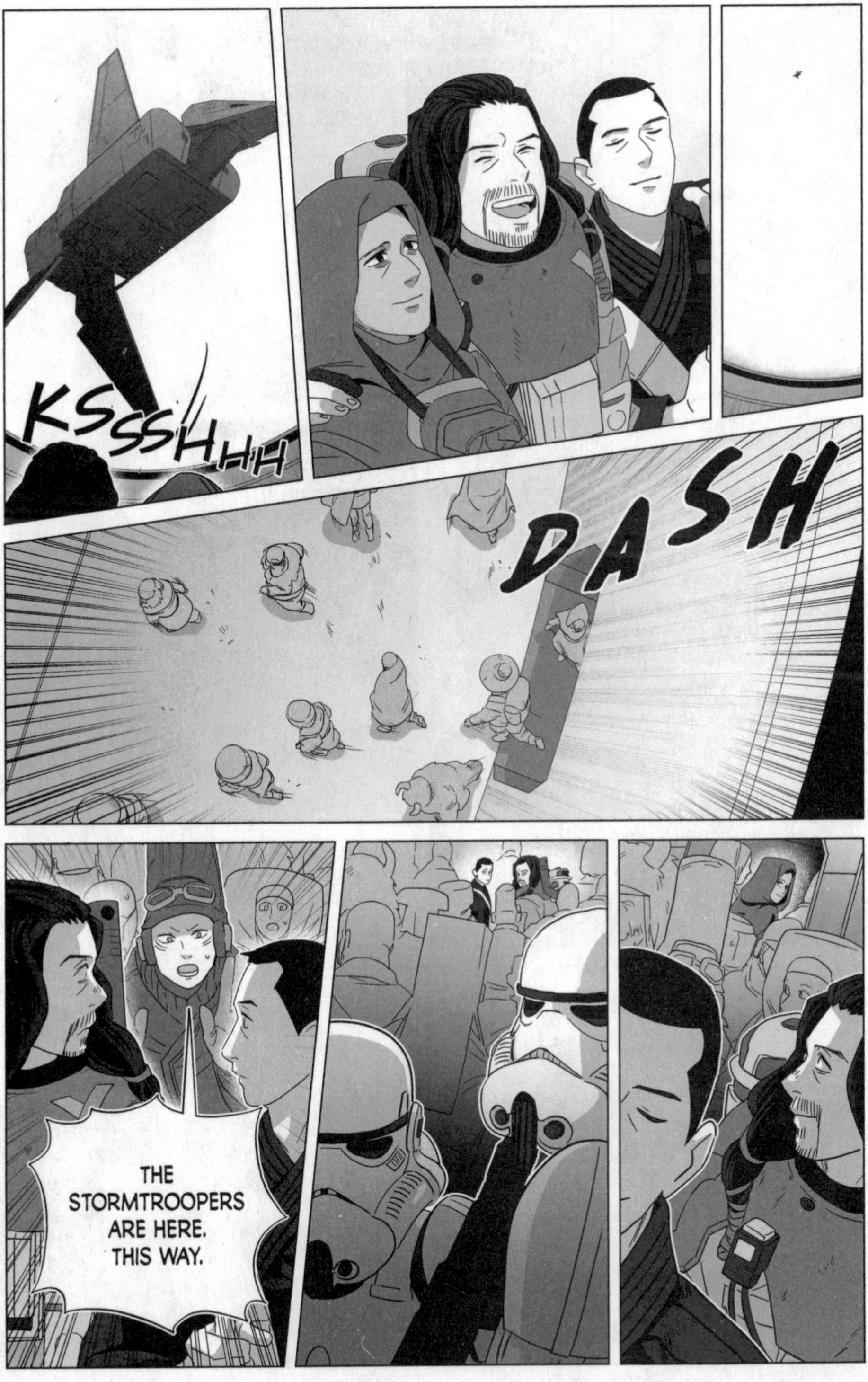
KSSSHHHH
DASH
THE STORMTROOPERS ARE HERE. THIS WAY.

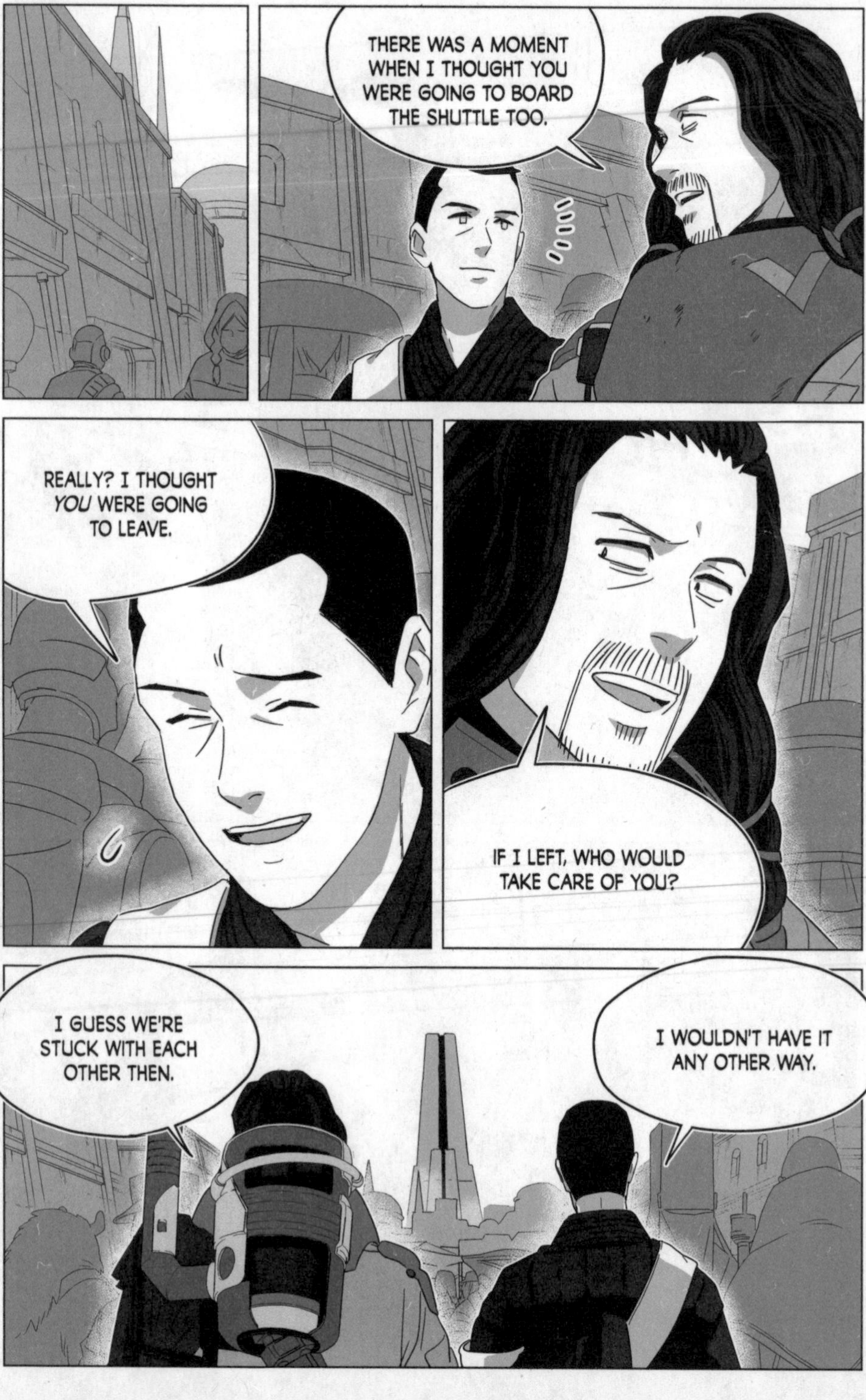
THERE WAS A MOMENT WHEN I THOUGHT YOU WERE GOING TO BOARD THE SHUTTLE TOO.
REALLY? I THOUGHT *YOU* WERE GOING TO LEAVE.
IF I LEFT, WHO WOULD TAKE CARE OF YOU?
I GUESS WE'RE STUCK WITH EACH OTHER THEN.
I WOULDN'T HAVE IT ANY OTHER WAY.

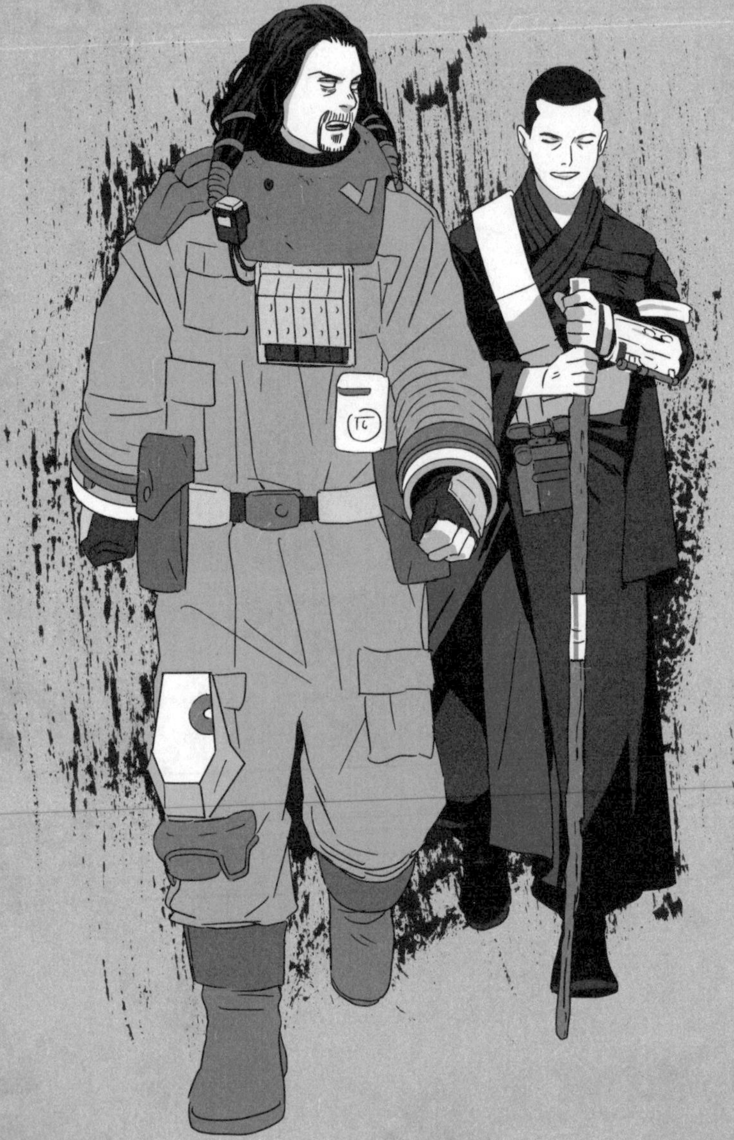

JON TSUEI

JON TSUEI is best known for writing and co-creating the high-fantasy comic book series *Sera and the Royal Stars* and science fiction series *RUNLOVEKILL*. He has also contributed to various comic book anthologies, including *Bitch Planet: Triple Feature*.

SUBARU

SUBARU debuted in the *Star Wars: The Legends of Luke Skywalker, The Manga* anthology with the adaptation of the short story "The Tale of Lugubrious Mote" and currently lives in Tokyo, Japan, working in the animation industry.

STAR WARS
GUARDIANS OF THE WHILLS
· THE MANGA ·

VIZ MEDIA EDITION

Original Story by GREG RUCKA
Adapted by JON TSUEI
Illustrated by SUBARU

Special thanks to EUGENE PARASZCZUK,
KEVIN PEARL, CHRISTOPHER G. TROISE

Translation and Communications SATSUKI YAMASHITA
Cover & Interior Design JIMMY PRESLER
Editor FAWN LAU, MAYUKO HIRAO, JULIA PATRICK

For Lucasfilm
Senior Editor ROBERT SIMPSON
Creative Director MICHAEL SIGLAIN
Lucasfilm Story Group MATT MARTIN, PABLO HIDALGO,
LELAND CHEE, & EMILY SHKOUKANI
Lucasfilm Art Department PHIL SZOSTAK

Printed in Canada

Published by VIZ Media, LLC
P.O. Box 77010
San Francisco, CA 94107

10 9 8 7 6 5 4 3 2 1
First printing, August 2021

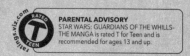

viz.com

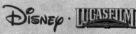

starwars.com

STAR WARS
THE HIGH REPUBLIC

Centuries before the Skywalker saga,
a new adventure begins....

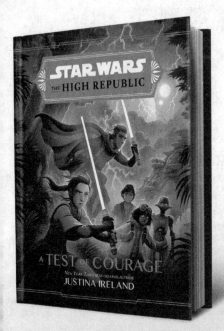

9781368057301 $14.99

9781368057288 $17.99

"LUKE SKYWALKER? I THOUGHT HE WAS A MYTH." – REY

STAR WARS

THE LEGENDS OF
LUKE SKYWALKER
THE MANGA

ADAPTED BY AKIRA HIMEKAWA, HARUICHI, SUBARU,
AKIRA FUKAYA, AND TAKASHI KISAKI

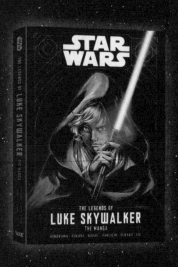

WHO IS LUKE SKYWALKER?

Across the galaxies many have heard his
name, but few have met the legendary
Jedi. There are those who call him a
merciless war criminal—others say he's
not even a human, but a droid! Whether
he is myth or man, those who claim
they've encountered the elusive Luke
Skywalker all have an unforgettable
adventure to share.

The manga anthology inspired by Ken Liu's hit *Star Wars* novel,
*JOURNEY TO STAR WARS: THE LAST JEDI—
THE LEGENDS OF LUKE SKYWALKER*